An Introduction to
Market Risk Measurement

An Introduction to
Market Risk Measurement

Kevin Dowd

JOHN WILEY & SONS, LTD

Published 2002   John Wiley & Sons Ltd, The Atrium, Southern Gate, Chichester,
West Sussex PO19 8SQ, England

Telephone (+44) 1243 779777

Email (for orders and customer service enquiries): cs-books@wiley.co.uk
Visit our Home Page on www.wileyeurope.com or www.wiley.com

Reprinted June 2008

Other Wiley Editorial Offices

John Wiley & Sons Inc., 111 River Street, Hoboken, NJ 07030, USA

Jossey-Bass, 989 Market Street, San Francisco, CA 94103-1741, USA

Wiley-VCH Verlag GmbH, Boschstr. 12, D-69469 Weinheim, Germany

John Wiley & Sons Australia Ltd, 33 Park Road, Milton, Queensland 4064, Australia

John Wiley & Sons (Asia) Pte Ltd, 2 Clementi Loop #02-01, Jin Xing Distripark, Singapore
129809

John Wiley & Sons Canada Ltd, 22 Worcester Road, Etobicoke, Ontario, Canada M9W 1L1

Library of Congress Cataloging-in-Publication Data

British Library Cataloguing in Publication Data

A catalogue record for this book is available from the British Library

ISBN-13 978-0-470-84748-0 (P/B)

Typeset in 10/12pt Times by TechBooks, New Delhi, India

Contents

NOTE TO READER:

Please note the CD has been converted to URL. Go to the following website

www.wiley.com/go/dowdintro

Preface

> You are responsible for managing your company's foreign exchange positions. Your boss, or your boss's boss, has been reading about derivatives losses suffered by other companies, and wants to know if the same thing could happen to his company. That is, he wants to know just how much market risk the company is taking. What do you say?
>
> You could start by listing and describing the company's positions, but this isn't likely to be helpful unless there are only a handful. Even then, it helps only if your superiors understand all of the positions and instruments, and the risks inherent in each. Or you could talk about the portfolio's sensitivities, i.e., how much the value of the portfolio changes when various underlying market rates or prices change, and perhaps option delta's and gamma's. However, you are unlikely to win favor with your superiors by putting them to sleep. Even if you are confident in your ability to explain these in English, you still have no natural way to net the risk in your short position in Deutsche marks against the long position in Dutch guilders.... You could simply assure your superiors that you never speculate but rather use derivatives only to hedge, but they understand that this statement is vacuous. They know that the word 'hedge' is so ill-defined and flexible that virtually any transaction can be characterized as a hedge. So what do you say? (Linsmeier and Pearson (1996, p. 1))

The obvious answer, 'The most we can lose is...' is also clearly unsatisfactory, because the most we can possibly lose is everything, and we would hope that the board already knows that. Consequently, Linsmeier and Pearson continue, "Perhaps the best answer starts: 'The value at risk is...'".

So what is value at risk? Value at risk (VaR) is our maximum likely loss over some target period — the most we expect to lose over that period, at a specified probability level. It says that on 95 days out of 100, say, the most we can expect to lose is $10 million or whatever. This is a good answer to the problem posed by Linsmeier and Pearson. The board or other recipients specify their probability level — 95%, 99% and so on — and the risk manager can tell them the maximum they can lose at that probability level. The recipients can also specify the horizon period — the next day, the next week, month, quarter, etc. — and again the risk manager can tell them the maximum amount they stand to lose over that horizon period. Indeed, the recipients can specify any combination of probability and horizon period, and the risk manager can give them the VaR applicable to that probability and horizon period.

We then have to face the problem of how to measure the VaR. This is a tricky question, and the answer is very involved and takes up much of this book. The short answer is, therefore, to read this book or others like it.

However, before we get too involved with VaR, we also have to face another issue. Is a VaR measure the best we can do? The answer is no. There are alternatives to VaR, and at least one of these — the so-called expected tail loss (ETL) or expected shortfall — is demonstrably superior. The ETL is the loss we can expect to make if we get a loss in excess of VaR. Consequently, I would take issue with Linsmeier and Pearson's answer. 'The VaR is . . .' is generally a reasonable answer, but it is not the best one. A better answer would be to tell the board the ETL — or better still, show them curves or surfaces plotting the ETL against probability and horizon period. Risk managers who use VaR as their preferred risk measure should really be using ETL instead. VaR is already passé.

But if ETL is superior to VaR, why both with VaR measurement? This is a good question, and also a controversial one. Part of the answer is that there will be a need to measure VaR for as long as there is a demand for VaR itself: if someone wants the number, then someone has to measure it, and whether they should want the number in the first place is another matter. In this respect VaR is a lot like the infamous beta. People still want beta numbers, regardless of the well-documented problems of the Capital Asset Pricing Model on whose validity the beta risk measure depends. A purist might say they shouldn't, but the fact is that they do. So the business of estimating betas goes on, even though the CAPM is now widely discredited. The same goes for VaR: a purist would say that VaR is inferior to ETL, but people still want VaR numbers and so the business of VaR estimation goes on. However, there is also a second, more satisfying, reason to continue to estimate VaR: we often need VaR estimates to be able to estimate ETL. We don't have many formulas for ETL and, as a result, we would often be unable to estimate ETL if we had to rely on ETL formulas alone. Fortunately, it turns out that we can always estimate the ETL if we can estimate VaR. The reason is that the VaR is a quantile and, if we can estimate the quantile, we can easily estimate the ETL — because the ETL itself is just a quantile average.

INTENDED READERSHIP

This book provides an introduction to VaR and ETL estimation, and is a more basic, student-oriented version of *Measuring Market Risk*, also published by John Wiley. The present book differs from *Measuring Market Risk* in cutting out some of the more difficult material — quasi-Monte Carlo methods, lattice methods, analytical and algorithmic approaches to options VaR, non-parametric density estimation, copulas, and other either advanced or exotic material. The reader who wants the more advanced material is therefore advised to go for the other book. However, most students should find *An Introduction to Market Risk Measurement* is better suited to their needs.

To get the most out of the book requires a basic knowledge of computing and spreadsheets, statistics (including some familiarity with moments and density/distribution functions), mathematics (including basic matrix algebra), and some prior knowledge of finance, most especially derivatives and fixed-income theory. Most practitioners and academics should have relatively little difficulty with it, but for students this material is best taught after they have already done their quantitative methods, derivatives, fixed-income and other 'building block' courses.

USING THIS BOOK

This book is divided into two parts — the chapters that discuss risk measurement, presupposing that the reader has the technical tools (i.e., the statistical, programming and other skills) to follow the discussion; and the toolkit at the end, which explains the main tools needed to measure market risk. This division separates the material dealing with risk measurement *per se* from the material dealing with the technical tools needed to carry out risk measurement. This helps to simplify the discussion and should make the book much easier to read: instead of going back and forth between technique and risk measurement, as many books do, we can read the technical material first; once we have the tools under our belt, we can then focus on the risk measurement without having to pause occasionally to re-tool.

I would suggest that the reader begin with the technical material — the tools at the end — and make sure that this material is adequately digested. Once that is done, the reader will be equipped to follow the risk measurement material without needing to take any technical breaks. My advice to those who might use the book for teaching purposes is the same: first cover the tools, and then do the risk measurement. However, much of the chapter material can, I hope, be followed without too much difficulty by readers who don't cover the tools first; but some of those who read the book in this way will occasionally find themselves having to pause to tool up.

In teaching market risk material over the last few years, it has also become clear to me that one cannot teach this material effectively — and students cannot really absorb it — if one teaches only at an abstract level. Of course, it is important to have lectures to convey the conceptual material, but risk measurement is not a purely abstract subject, and in my experience students only really grasp the material when they start playing with it — when they start working out VaR figures for themselves on a spreadsheet, when they have exercises and assignments to do, and so on. When teaching, it is therefore important to balance lecture-style delivery with practical sessions in which the students use computers to solve illustrative risk measurement problems.

If the book is to be read and used practically, readers also need to use appropriate spreadsheets or other software to carry out estimations for themselves. Again, my teaching and supervision experience is that the use of software is critical in learning this material, and we can only ever claim to understand something when we have actually measured it. The software and risk material are also intimately related, and the good risk measurer knows that risk measurement always boils down to some spreadsheet or other computer function. In fact, much of the action in this area boils down to software issues — comparing alternative software routines, finding errors, improving accuracy and speed, and so forth. Any risk measurement book should come with at least some indication of how risk measurement routines can be implemented on a computer.

It is better still for such books to come with their own software, and this book comes with a CD that contains two different sets of useful risk measurement software:

- A set of Excel workbooks showing how to carry out some basic risk measurement tasks using Excel: estimation of different types of VaR, and so forth.
- A set of risk measurement and related functions in the form of *An Introduction to Market Risk Measurement* Toolbox in MATLAB and a manual explaining their use.[1] My advice to users is to print out the manual and go through the functions on a computer, and then keep the manual to hand for later reference.[2] The examples and figures in the book are produced using this software, and readers should be able to reproduce them for themselves.

Readers are welcome to contact me with any feedback; however, I would ask that they bear in mind that because of time pressures I cannot provide a query answer service — and this is probably

---

[1] MATLAB is a registered trademark of The MathWorks, Inc. For more information on MATLAB, please visit their website, www.mathworks.com. or contact The MathWorks, Inc., 3 Apple Hill Drive, Natick, MA 01760–2098, USA.

[2] The user should copy the *An Introduction to Market Risk Measurement* (IMRM) folder into his or her MATLAB works folder and activate the path to the IMRM folder thus created (so MATLAB knows the folder is there). The functions were written in MATLAB 6.0 and most of the IMRM functions should work if the user has the Statistics Toolbox as well as the basic MATLAB 6.0 or later software installed on their machine. However, a small number of IMRM functions draw on functions in other MATLAB toolboxes (e.g., such as the Garch Toolbox), so users with only the Statistics Toolbox will find that the occasional IMRM function does not work on their machine.

educationally best in any case, because the only way to really learn this material is to strug-
gle through it. Nonetheless, I will keep the software and the manual up-to-date on my website
(www.nottingham.ac.uk/~lizkd) and readers are welcome to download updates from there.

In writing this software, I should explain that I focused on MATLAB mainly because it is both
powerful and user-friendly, unlike its obvious alternatives (VBA, which is neither powerful nor
particularly user-friendly, or the C or S languages, which are certainly not user-friendly). I also
chose MATLAB in part because it produces very nice graphics, and a good graph or chart is often
an essential tool for risk measurement. Unfortunately, the downside of MATLAB is that many users
of the book will not be familiar with it or will not have ready access to it, and I can only advise such
readers to think seriously about going through the expense and/or effort to get it.[3]

In explaining risk measurement throughout this book, I have tried to focus on the underlying ideas
rather than on programming code: understanding the ideas is much more important, and the coding
itself is mere implementation. My advice to risk measurers is that they should aim to get to the level
where they can easily write their own code once they know what they are trying to do. However, for
those who want it, the code I use is easily accessible — one simply opens up MATLAB, goes into
the IMRM Toolbox, and opens the relevant function. The reader who wants the code should refer
directly to the program coding rather than searching around in the text: I have tried to keep the text
itself free of such detail to focus on more important conceptual issues.

The IMRM Toolbox also has many other functions besides those used to produce the examples or
figures in the text. I have tried to produce a fairly extensive set of software functions that would cover
all the obvious VaR or ETL measurement problems, as well as some of the more advanced ones.
Users — such as students doing their dissertations, academics doing their research, and practitioners
working on practical applications — might find some of these functions useful, and they are welcome
to make whatever use of these functions they wish. However, before anyone takes these functions too
seriously, they should appreciate that I am not a programmer and anyone who uses these functions
must do so at his or her own risk. As always in risk measurement, we should keep our wits about us
and not be too trusting of the software we use or the results we get.

OUTLINE OF THE BOOK

As mentioned earlier, the book is divided into the chapters proper and the toolkit at the end that deals
with the technical issues underlying (or the tools needed for) market risk measurement. It might be
helpful to give a brief overview of these so readers know what to expect.

The Chapters

The first chapter provides a brief overview of recent developments in risk measurement — market
risk measurement especially — to put VaR and ETL in their proper context. Chapter 2 then looks at
different measures of financial risk. We begin here with the traditional mean–variance framework.
This framework is very convenient and provides the underpinning for modern portfolio theory, but it
is also limited in its applicability because it has difficulty handling skewness (or asymmetry) and 'fat

---

[3] When I first started working on this book, I initially tried writing the software functions in VBA to take advantage of the
fact that almost everyone has access to Excel; unfortunately, I ran into too many problems and eventually had to give up. Had
I not done so, I would still be struggling with VBA code even now, and this book would never have seen the light of day. So,
whilst I sympathise with those who might feel pressured to learn MATLAB or some other advanced language and obtain the
relevant software, I don't see any practical alternative: if you want software, Excel/VBA is just not up to the job — although
it can be useful for many simpler tasks and for teaching at a basic level.

tails' (or fatter than normal tails) in our P/L or return probability density functions. We then consider VaR and ETL as risk measures, and compare them to traditional risk measures and to each other.

Having established what our basic risk measures actually are, Chapter 3 has a first run through the issues involved in estimating them. We cover three main sets of issues here:

- Preliminary data issues — how to handle data in profit/loss (or P/L) form, rate of return form, etc.
- How to estimate VaR based on alternative sets of assumptions about the distribution of our data and how our VaR estimation procedure depends on the assumptions we make.
- How to estimate ETL — and, in particular, how we can always approximate ETL by taking it as an average of 'tail VaRs' or losses exceeding VaR.

Chapter 3 ends with an appendix dealing with the important subject of mapping — the process of describing the positions we hold in terms of combinations of standard building blocks. We would use mapping to cut down on the dimensionality of our portfolio, or deal with possible problems caused by having closely correlated risk factors or missing data. Mapping enables us to estimate market risk in situations that would otherwise be very demanding or even impossible.

Chapter 4 then takes a closer look at non-parametric VaR and ETL estimation. Non-parametric approaches are those in which we estimate VaR or ETL making minimal assumptions about the distribution of P/L or returns: we let the P/L data speak for themselves as much as possible. There are various non-parametric approaches, and the most popular is historical simulation (HS), which is conceptually simple, easy to implement, widely used and has a fairly good track record. We can also carry out non-parametric estimation using principal components methods (see Tool No. 4), and the latter methods are sometimes useful when dealing with high-dimensionality problems (i.e., when dealing with portfolios with very large numbers of risk factors). As a general rule, non-parametric methods work fairly well if market conditions remain reasonably stable, and they are capable of considerable refinement and improvement. However, they can be unreliable if market conditions change, their results are totally dependent on the data set, and their estimates of VaR and ETL are subject to distortions from one-off events and ghost effects.

Chapter 5 looks more closely at parametric approaches, the essence of which is that we fit probability curves to the data and then infer the VaR or ETL from the fitted curve. Parametric approaches are more powerful than non-parametric ones, because they make use of additional information contained in the assumed probability density function. They are also easy to use, because they give rise to straightforward formulas for VaR and sometimes ETL, but are vulnerable to error if the assumed density function does not adequately fit the data. The chapter discusses parametric VaR and ETL at two different levels — at the portfolio level, where we are dealing with portfolio P/L or returns, and assume that the underlying distribution is normal, Student t, extreme value or whatever; and at the sub-portfolio or individual-position level, where we deal with the P/L or returns to individual positions and assume that these are multivariate normal. This chapter ends with an appendix dealing with the use of delta–gamma and related approximations to deal with non-linear risks (e.g., such as those arising from options).

Chapter 6 examines how we can estimate VaR and ETL using simulation (or random number) methods. These methods are very powerful and flexible, and can be applied to many different types of VaR or ETL estimation problem. Simulation methods can be highly effective for many problems that are too complicated or too messy for analytical or algorithmic approaches, and they are particularly good at handling complications like path-dependency, non-linearity and optionality. Amongst the many possible applications of simulation methods are to estimate the VaR or ETL of options positions and fixed-income positions, including those in interest-rate derivatives, as well as the VaR or ETL of credit-related positions (e.g., in default-risky bonds, credit derivatives, etc.), and of insurance and pension-fund portfolios. We can also use simulation methods for other purposes — for example, to estimate VaR or ETL in the context of dynamic portfolio management strategies. However, simulation methods are less easy to use than some alternatives, usually require a lot of calculations, and can have difficulty dealing with early-exercise features.

Chapter 7 considers risk addition and decomposition — how changing our portfolio alters our risk, and how we can decompose our portfolio risk into constituent or component risks. We are concerned here with:

• *Incremental risks*. These are the changes in risk when a factor changes — for example, how VaR changes when we add a new position to our portfolio.
• *Component risks*. These are the component or constituent risks that make up a certain total risk — if we have a portfolio made up of particular positions, the portfolio VaR can be broken down into components that tell us how much each position contributes to the overall portfolio VaR.

Both these (and their ETL equivalents) are extremely useful measures in portfolio risk management: amongst other uses, they give us new methods of identifying sources of risk, finding natural hedges, defining risk limits, reporting risks and improving portfolio allocations.

Chapter 8 examines liquidity issues and how they affect market risk measurement. Liquidity issues affect market risk measurement not just through their impact on our standard measures of market risk, VaR and ETL, but also because effective market risk management involves an ability to measure and manage liquidity risk itself. The chapter considers the nature of market liquidity and illiquidity, and their associated costs and risks, and then considers how we might take account of these factors to estimate VaR and ETL in illiquid or partially liquid markets. Furthermore, since liquidity is important in itself and because liquidity problems are particularly prominent in market crises, we also need to consider two other aspects of liquidity risk measurement — the estimation of liquidity at risk (i.e., the liquidity equivalent to value at risk), and the estimation of crisis-related liquidity risks.

Chapter 9 deals with backtesting — the application of quantitative, typically statistical, methods to determine whether a model's risk estimates are consistent with the assumptions on which the model is based or to rank models against each other. To backtest a model, we first assemble a suitable data set — we have to 'clean' accounting data, etc. — and it is good practice to produce a backtest chart showing how P/L compares to measured risk over time. After this preliminary data analysis, we can proceed to a formal backtest. The main classes of backtest procedure are:

• Statistical approaches based on the frequency of losses exceeding VaR.
• Statistical approaches based on the sizes of losses exceeding VaR.
• Forecast evaluation methods, in which we score a model's forecasting performance in terms of a forecast error loss function.

Each of these classes of backtest comes in alternative forms, and it is generally advisable to run a number of them to get a broad feel for the performance of the model. We can also backtest models at the position level as well as the portfolio level, and using simulation or bootstrap data as well as 'real' data. Ideally, 'good' models should backtest well and 'bad' models should backtest poorly, but in practice results are often much less clear: in this game, separating the sheep from the goats is often much harder than many imagine.

Chapter 10 examines stress testing — 'what if' procedures that attempt to gauge the vulnerability of our portfolio to hypothetical events. Stress testing is particularly good for quantifying what we might lose in crisis situations where 'normal' market relationships break down and VaR or ETL risk measures can be very misleading. VaR and ETL are good on the probability side, but poor on the 'what if' side, whereas stress tests are good for 'what if' questions and poor on probability questions. Stress testing is therefore good where VaR and ETL are weak, and vice versa. As well as helping to quantify our exposure to bad states, the results of stress testing can be a useful guide to management decision-making and help highlight weaknesses (e.g., questionable assumptions, etc.) in our risk management procedures.

The final chapter considers the subject of model risk — the risk of error in our risk estimates due to inadequacies in our risk measurement models. The use of any model always entails exposure to model risk of some form or another, and practitioners often overlook this exposure because it is out of sight and because most of those who use models have a tendency to end up 'believing' them. We therefore need to understand what model risk is, where and how it arises, how to measure it, and what its possible consequences might be. Interested parties, such as risk practitioners and their managers also also need to understand what they can do to combat it. The problem of model risk never goes away, but we can learn to live with it.

The Toolkit

The toolkit at the end consists of seven different 'tools', each of which is useful for risk measurement purposes. Tool No. 1 deals with the use of the theory of order statistics for estimating VaR and ETL. Order statistics are ordered observations — the biggest observation, the second biggest observation, etc. — and the theory of order statistics enables us to predict the distribution of each ordered observation. This is very useful because the VaR itself is an order statistic — for example, with 100 P/L observations, we might take the VaR at the 95% confidence level as the sixth largest loss observation. Hence, the theory of order statistics enables us to estimate the whole of the VaR probability density function — and this enables us to estimate confidence intervals for our VaR. Estimating confidence intervals for ETLs is also easy, because there is a one-to-one mapping from the VaR observations to the ETL ones: we can convert the P/L observations into average loss observations, and apply the order statistics approach to the latter to obtain ETL confidence intervals.

Tool No. 2 deals with the Cornish–Fisher expansion, which is useful for estimating VaR and ETL when the underlying distribution is near normal. If our portfolio P/L or return distribution is not normal, we cannot take the VaR to be given by the percentiles of an inverse normal distribution function; however, if the non-normality is not too severe, the Cornish–Fisher expansion gives us an adjustment factor that we can use to correct the normal VaR estimate for non-normality. The Cornish–Fisher adjustment is easy to apply and enables us to retain the easiness of the normal approach to VaR in at least some circumstances where the normality assumption itself does not hold.

Tool No. 3 deals with bootstrap procedures. These methods enable us to sample repeatedly from a given set of data, and they are very useful because they give a reliable and easy way of estimating confidence intervals for any parameters of interest, including VaRs and ETLs.

Tool No. 4 covers principal components analysis, which is an alternative method of gaining insight into the properties of a data set. It is helpful in risk measurement because it can provide a simpler representation of the processes that generate a given data set, which then enables us to reduce the dimensionality of our data and so reduce the number of variance-covariance parameters that we need to estimate. Such methods can be very useful when we have large dimension problems (e.g., variance-covariance matrices with hundreds of different instruments), but they can also be useful for cleaning data and developing data mapping systems.

Tool No. 5 deals with extreme value theory (EVT) and its applications in financial risk management. EVT is a branch of statistics tailor-made to deal with problems posed by extreme or rare events — and in particular, the problems posed by estimating extreme quantiles and associated probabilities that go well beyond our sample range. The key to EVT is a theorem — the extreme value theorem — that tells us what the distribution of extreme values should look like, at least asymptotically. This theorem and various associated results tell us what we should be estimating, and also give us some guidance on estimation and inference issues.

Tool No. 6 then deals with Monte Carlo simulation methods. These methods can be used to price derivatives, estimate their hedge ratios, and solve risk measurement problems of almost any degree of complexity. The idea is to simulate repeatedly the random processes governing the prices or returns of the financial instruments we are interested in. If we take enough simulations, the simulated distribution of portfolio values will converge to the portfolio's unknown 'true' distribution, and we can use the simulated distribution of end-period portfolio values to infer the VaR or ETL.

Tool No. 7 discusses the forecasting of volatilities, covariances and correlations. This is one of the most important subjects in modern risk measurement, and is critical to derivatives pricing, hedging, and VaR and ETL estimation. The focus of our discussion is the estimation of volatilities, in which we go through each of four main approaches to this problem: historical estimation, exponentially weighted moving average (EWMA) estimation, GARCH estimation, and implied volatility estimation. The treatment of covariances and correlations parallels that of volatilities, and we end with a brief discussion of the issues involved with estimating variance–covariance and correlation matrices.

Acknowledgements

It is a real pleasure to acknowledge those who have contributed in one way or another to this book. To begin with, I should like to thank Barry Schachter for his excellent website, www.gloriamundi.org, which was my primary source of research material. I thank Naomi Fernandes and the The MathWorks, Inc., for making MATLAB available to me through their authors' program. I thank Christian Bauer, David Blake, Carlos Blanco, Andrew Cairns, Marc de Ceuster, Jon Danielsson, Kostas Giannopoulos, Paul Glasserman, Glyn Holton, Imad Moosa, and Paul Stefiszyn for their valuable comments on parts of the draft manuscript and/or other contributions, I thank Mark Garman for permission to include Figures 7.2 and 7.3, and Peter Urbani for allowing me to include some of his Excel software with the CD. I also thank the Wiley team — Sam Hartley, Sarah Lewis, Carole Millett, and, especially, Sam Whittaker — for many helpful inputs. I should also like to thank participants in the Dutch National Bank's Capital Markets Program and seminar participants at the Office of the Superintendent of Financial Institutions in Canada for allowing me to test out many of these ideas on them, and for their feedback.

In addition, I would like to thank my colleagues and students at the Centre for Risk and Insurance Studies (CRIS) and also in the rest of Nottingham University Business School, for their support and feedback. I also thank many friends for their encouragement and support over the years: particularly Mark Billings, Dave Campbell, David and Yabing Fisher, Ian Gow, Duncan Kitchin, Anneliese Osterspey, Dave and Frances Owen, Sheila Richardson, Stan and Dorothy Syznkaruk, and Basil and Margaret Zafiriou. Finally, as always, my greatest debts are to my family — to my mother, Maureen, my brothers Brian and Victor, and most of all, to my wife Mahjabeen and my daughters Raadhiyah and Safiah — for their love and unfailing support, and their patience. I would therefore like to dedicate this book to Mahjabeen and the girls. I realise of course that other authors' families get readable books dedicated to them, and all I have to offer is another soporific statistical tome. But maybe next time I will take their suggestion and write a novel instead. On second thoughts, perhaps not.

1
The Risk Measurement Revolution

Financial risk is the prospect of financial loss — or gain — due to unforeseen changes in underlying risk factors. In this book we are concerned with the measurement of one particular form of financial risk — namely, market risk, or the risk of loss (or gain) arising from unexpected changes in market prices (e.g., such as security prices) or market rates (e.g., such as interest or exchange rates). Market risks, in turn, can be classified into interest-rate risks, equity risks, exchange rate risks, commodity price risks, and so on, depending on whether the risk factor is an interest rate, a stock price, or whatever. Market risks can also be distinguished from other forms of financial risk, most especially credit risk (or the risk of loss arising from the failure of a counterparty to make a promised payment) and operational risk (or the risk of loss arising from the failures of internal systems or the people who operate in them).

The theory and the practice of risk management — and, included within that, risk measurement — have developed enormously since the pioneering work of Harry Markowitz in the 1950s. The theory has developed to the point where risk management/measurement is now regarded as a distinct sub-field of the theory of finance, and one that is increasingly taught as a separate subject in the more advanced master's and MBA programmes in finance. The subject has attracted a huge amount of intellectual energy, not just from finance specialists but also from specialists in other disciplines who are attracted to it — as is illustrated by the large number of ivy league theoretical physics PhDs who now go into finance research, attracted not just by high salaries but also by the challenging intellectual problems it poses.

1.1 CONTRIBUTORY FACTORS

1.1.1 A Volatile Environment

One factor behind the rapid development of risk management was the high level of instability in the economic environment within which firms operated. A volatile environment exposes firms to greater financial risk, and therefore provides an incentive for firms to find new and better ways of managing this risk. The volatility of the economic environment is reflected in various factors:

- *Stock market volatility.* Stock markets have always been volatile, but sometimes extremely so: for example, on October 19, 1987, the Dow Jones fell 23% and in the process knocked off over $1 trillion in equity capital; and from July 21 through August 31, 1998, the Dow Jones lost 18% of its value. Other western stock markets have experienced similar falls, and some Asian ones have experienced much worse ones (e.g., the South Korean stock market lost over half of its value during 1997).
- *Exchange rate volatility.* Exchange rates have been volatile ever since the breakdown of the Bretton Woods system of fixed exchange rates in the early 1970s. Occasional exchange rate crises have also led to sudden and significant exchange rate changes, including — among many others — the ERM devaluations of September 1992, the problems of the peso in 1994, the East Asian currency problems of 1997–98, the rouble crisis of 1998, and Brazil in 1999.

- *Interest rate volatility.* There have been major fluctuations in interest rates, with their attendant effects on funding costs, corporate cash flows and asset values. For example, the Fed Funds rate, a good indicator of short-term market rates in the US, approximately doubled over 1994.
- *Commodity market volatility.* Commodity markets are notoriously volatile, and commodity prices often go through long periods of apparent stability and then suddenly jump by enormous amounts: for instance, in 1990, the price of West Texas Intermediate crude oil rose from a little over $15 a barrel to around $40 a barrel. Some commodity prices (e.g., electricity prices) also show extremely pronounced day-to-day and even hour-to-hour volatility.

1.1.2   Growth in Trading Activity

Another factor contributing to the transformation of risk management is the huge increase in trading activity since the late 1960s. The average number of shares traded per day in the New York Stock Exchange has grown from about 3.5m in 1970 to around 100m in 2000; and turnover in foreign exchange markets has grown from about a billion dollars a day in 1965 to $1,210 billion in April 2001.[1] There have been massive increases in the range of instruments traded over the past two or three decades, and trading volumes in these new instruments have also grown very rapidly. New instruments have been developed in offshore markets and, more recently, in the newly emerging financial markets of Eastern Europe, China, Latin America, Russia, and elsewhere. New instruments have also arisen for assets that were previously illiquid, such as consumer loans, commercial and industrial bank loans, mortgages, mortgage-based securities, and similar assets, and these markets have grown very considerably since the early 1980s.

There has also been a phenomenal growth of derivatives activity. Until 1972 the only derivatives traded were certain commodity futures and various forwards and over-the-counter (OTC) options. The Chicago Mercantile Exchange then started trading foreign currency futures contracts in 1972, and in 1973 the Chicago Board Options Exchange started trading equity call options. Interest-rate futures were introduced in 1975, and a large number of other financial derivatives contracts were introduced in the following years: swaps and exotics (e.g., swaptions, futures on interest rate swaps, etc.) then took off in the 1980s, and catastrophe, credit, electricity and weather derivatives in the 1990s. From negligible amounts in the early 1970s, the daily notional amounts turned over in derivatives contracts grew to nearly $2,800 billion by April 2001.[2] However, this figure is misleading, because notional values give relatively little indication of what derivatives contracts are really worth. The true size of derivatives trading is better represented by the replacement cost of outstanding derivatives contracts, and these are probably no more than 4% or 5% of the notional amounts involved. If we measure size by replacement cost rather than notional principals, the size of the daily turnover in the derivatives market in 2001 was therefore around $126 billion — which is still not an inconsiderable amount.

1.1.3   Advances in Information Technology

A third contributing factor to the development of risk management was the rapid advance in the state of information technology. Improvements in IT have made possible huge increases in both computational power and the speed with which calculations can be carried out. Improvements in computing power mean that new techniques can be used (e.g., such as computer-intensive simulation

---

[1] The latter figure is from Bank for International Settlements (2001, p. 1).
[2] Bank for International Settlements (2001, p. 9).

techniques) to enable us to tackle more difficult calculation problems. Improvements in calculation speed then help make these techniques useful in real time, where it is often essential to get answers quickly.

This technological progress has led to IT costs falling by about 25–30% a year over the past 30 years or so. To quote Guldimann:

> Most people know that technology costs have dropped rapidly over the years but few realise how steep and continuous the fall has been, particularly in hardware and data transmission. In 1965, for example, the cost of storing one megabyte of data (approximately the equivalent of the content of a typical edition of the *Wall Street Journal*) in random access memory was about $100,000. Today it is about $20. By 2005, it will probably be less than $1.
>
> The cost of transmitting electronic data has come down even more dramatically. In 1975, it cost about $10,000 to send a megabyte of data from New York to Tokyo. Today, it is about $5. By 2005, it is expected to be about $0.01. And the cost of the processor needed to handle 1 million instructions a second has declined from about $1 million in 1965 to $1.50 today. By 2005, it is expected to drop to a few cents. (All figures have been adjusted for inflation.)
>
> (Guldimann (1996, p. 17))

Improvements in computing power, increases in computing speed, and reductions in computing costs have thus come together to transform the technology available for risk management. Decision makers are no longer tied down to the simple 'back of the envelope' techniques that they had to use earlier when they lacked the means to carry out more complex calculations. They can now use sophisticated algorithms programmed into computers to carry out real-time calculations that were not possible before. The ability to carry out such calculations then creates a whole new range of risk measurement and risk management possibilities.

1.2 RISK MEASUREMENT BEFORE VAR

To understand recent developments in risk measurement, we need first to appreciate the more traditional risk measurement tools.

1.2.1 Gap Analysis

One common approach was (and, in fact, still is) gap analysis, which was initially developed by financial institutions to give a simple, albeit crude, idea of interest-rate risk exposure.[3] Gap analysis starts with the choice of an appropriate horizon period — 1 year, or whatever. We then determine how much of our asset or liability portfolio will re-price within this period, and the amounts involved give us our rate-sensitive assets and rate-sensitive liabilities. The gap is the difference between these, and our interest-rate exposure is taken to be the change in net interest income that occurs in response to a change in interest rates. This in turn is assumed to be equal to the gap times the interest-rate change:

$$\Delta NII = (GAP)\Delta r \tag{1.1}$$

where ΔNII is the change in net interest income and Δr is the change in interest rates.

Gap analysis is fairly simple to carry out, but has its limitations: it only applies to on-balance sheet interest-rate risk, and even then only crudely; it looks at the impact of interest rates on income, rather than on asset or liability values; and results can be sensitive to the choice of horizon period.

---

[3]For more on gap analysis, see, e.g., Sinkey (1992, ch. 12).

1.2.2 Duration Analysis

Another method traditionally used by financial institutions for measuring interest-rate risk is duration analysis.[4] The (Macaulay) duration D of a bond (or any other fixed-income security) can be defined as the weighted average term to maturity of the bond's cash flows, where the weights are the present values of each cash flow relative to the present value of all cash flows:

$$D = \sum_{i=1}^{n} [i \times PVCF_i] \bigg/ \sum_{i=1}^{n} PVCF_i \tag{1.2}$$

where $PVCF_i$ is the present value of the period i cash flow, discounted at the appropriate spot period yield. The duration measure is useful because it gives an approximate indication of the sensitivity of a bond price to a change in yield:

$$\% \text{ Change in bond price} \approx -D \times \Delta y / (1 + y) \tag{1.3}$$

where y is the yield and Δy the change in yield. The bigger the duration, the more the bond price changes in response to a change in yield. The duration approach is very convenient because duration measures are easy to calculate and the duration of a bond portfolio is a simple weighted average of the durations of the individual bonds in that portfolio. It is also better than gap analysis because it looks at changes in asset (or liability) values, rather than just changes in net income.

However, duration approaches have similar limitations to gap analysis: they ignore risks other than interest-rate risk; they are crude,[5] and even with various refinements to improve accuracy,[6] duration-based approaches are still inaccurate relative to more recent approaches to fixed-income analysis (e.g., such as HJM models). Moreover, the main reason for using duration approaches in the past — their (comparative) ease of calculation — is no longer of much significance, since more sophisticated models can now be programmed into micro-computers to give their users more accurate answers rapidly.

1.2.3 Scenario Analysis

A third approach is scenario analysis (or 'what if' analysis), in which we set out different scenarios and investigate what we stand to gain or lose under them. To carry out scenario analysis, we select a set of scenarios — or paths describing how relevant variables (e.g., stock prices, interest rates, exchange rates, etc.) might evolve over a horizon period. We then postulate the cash flows and/or accounting values of assets and liabilities as they would develop under each scenario, and use the results to come to a view about our exposure.

---

[4]For more on duration approaches, see, e.g., Fabozzi (1993, ch. 11 and 12) or Tuckman (1995, ch. 11–13).

[5]They are crude because they only take a first-order approximation to the change in the bond price, and because they implicitly presuppose that any changes in the yield curve are parallel ones (i.e., all yields across the maturity spectrum change by the same amount). Duration-based hedges are therefore inaccurate against yield changes that involve shifts in the slope of the yield curve.

[6]There are two standard refinements. (1) We can take a second-order rather than a first-order approximation to the bond price change. The second-order term — known as convexity — is related to the change in duration as yield changes, and this duration–convexity approach gives us a better approximation to the bond price change as the yield changes. (For more on this approach, see, e.g., Fabozzi (1993, ch. 12) or Tuckman (1995, ch. 11).) However, the duration–convexity approach generally only gives modest improvements in accuracy. (2) An alternative refinement is to use key rate durations: if we are concerned about shifts in the yield curve, we can construct separate duration measures for yields of specified maturities (e.g., short-term and long-term yields); these would give us estimates of our exposure to changes in these specific yields and allow us to accommodate non-parallel shifts in the yield curve. For more on this key rate duration approach, see Ho (1992) or Tuckman (1995, ch. 13).

Scenario analysis is not easy to carry out. A lot hinges on our ability to identify the 'right' scenarios, and there are relatively few rules to guide us when selecting them. We need to ensure that the scenarios we examine are reasonable and do not involve contradictory or excessively implausible assumptions, and we need to think through the interrelationships between the variables involved.[7] We also want to make sure, as best we can, that we have all the main scenarios covered. Scenario analysis also tells us nothing about the likelihood of different scenarios, so we need to use our judgement when assessing the practical significance of different scenarios. In the final analysis, the results of scenario analyses are highly subjective and depend to a very large extent on the skill or otherwise of the analyst.

1.2.4 Portfolio Theory

A somewhat different approach to risk measurement is provided by portfolio theory.[8] Portfolio theory starts from the premise that investors choose between portfolios on the basis of their expected return, on the one hand, and the standard deviation (or variance) of their return, on the other.[9] The standard deviation of the portfolio return can be regarded as a measure of the portfolio's risk. Other things being equal, an investor wants a portfolio whose return has a high expected value and a low standard deviation. These objectives imply that the investor should choose a portfolio that maximises expected return for any given portfolio standard deviation or, alternatively, minimises standard deviation for any given expected return. A portfolio that meets these conditions is efficient, and a rational investor will always choose an efficient portfolio. When faced with an investment decision, the investor must therefore determine the set of efficient portfolios and rule out the rest. Some efficient portfolios will have more risk than others, but the more risky ones will also have higher expected returns. Faced with the set of efficient portfolios, the investor then chooses one particular portfolio on the basis of his or her own preferred trade-off between risk and expected return. An investor who is very averse to risk will choose a safe portfolio with a low standard deviation and a low expected return, and an investor who is less risk averse will choose a more risky portfolio with a higher expected return.

One of the key insights of portfolio theory is that the risk of any individual asset is not the standard deviation of the return to that asset, but rather the extent to which that asset contributes to overall portfolio risk. An asset might be very risky (i.e., have a high standard deviation) when considered on its own, and yet have a return that correlates with the returns to other assets in our portfolio in such a way that acquiring the new asset adds nothing to the overall portfolio standard deviation. Acquiring the new asset would then be riskless, even though the asset held on its own would still be risky. The moral of the story is that the extent to which a new asset contributes to portfolio risk depends on

---

[7] We will often want to examine scenarios that take correlations into account as well (e.g., correlations between interest-rate and exchange-rate risks), but in doing so, we need to bear in mind that correlations often change, and sometimes do so at the most awkward times (e.g., during a market crash). Hence, it is often good practice to base scenarios on relatively conservative assumptions that allow for correlations to move against us.

[8] The origin of portfolio theory is usually traced to the work of Markowitz (1952, 1959). Later scholars then developed the Capital Asset Pricing Model (CAPM) from the basic Markowitz framework. However, I believe the CAPM — which I interpret to be portfolio theory combined with the assumptions that everyone is identical and that the market is in equilibrium — was an unhelpful digression and the current discredit into which it has fallen is justified. (For the reasons behind this view, I strongly recommend Frankfurter's withering assessment of the rise and fall of the CAPM empire (Frankfurter (1995)).) That said, in going over the wreckage of the CAPM, it is also important not to lose sight of the tremendous insights provided by portfolio theory (i.e., à la Markowitz). I therefore see the way forward as building on portfolio theory (and, indeed, I believe that much of what is good in the VaR literature does exactly that) whilst throwing out the CAPM.

[9] This framework is often known as the mean–variance framework, because it implicitly presupposes that the mean and variance (or standard deviation) of the return are sufficient to guide investors' decisions. In other words, investors are assumed not to need information about higher order moments of the return probability density function, such as the skewness or kurtosis coefficients.

the correlation or covariance of its return with the returns to the other assets in our portfolio — or, if one prefers, the beta, which is equal to the covariance between the return to asset i and the return to the portfolio, r_p, divided by the variance of the portfolio return. The lower the correlation, other things being equal, the less the asset contributes to overall risk. Indeed, if the correlation is sufficiently negative, it will offset existing risks and lower the portfolio standard deviation.

Portfolio theory provides a useful framework for handling multiple risks and taking account of how those risks interact with each other. It is therefore of obvious use to — and is in fact widely used by — portfolio managers, mutual fund managers and other investors. However, it tends to run into problems over data. The risk-free return and the expected market return are not too difficult to estimate, but estimating the betas is often more problematic. Each beta is specific not only to the individual asset to which it belongs, but also to our current portfolio. To estimate a beta coefficient properly, we need data on the returns to the new asset and the returns to all our existing assets, and we need a sufficiently long data set to make our statistical estimation techniques reliable. The beta also depends on our existing portfolio and we should, in theory, re-estimate all our betas every time our portfolio changes. Using the portfolio approach can require a considerable amount of data and a substantial amount of ongoing work.

In practice users often wish to avoid this burden, and in any case they sometimes lack the data to estimate the betas accurately in the first place. Practitioners are then tempted to seek a short-cut, and work with betas estimated against some hypothetical market portfolio. This leads them to talk about *the* beta for an asset, as if the asset had only a single beta. However, this short-cut only gives us good answers if the beta estimated against the hypothetical market portfolio is close to the beta estimated against the portfolio we actually hold, and in practice we seldom know whether it is.[10] If the two portfolios are sufficiently different, the 'true' beta (i.e., the beta measured against our actual portfolio) might be very different from the hypothetical beta we are using.[11]

1.2.5 Derivatives Risk Measures

When dealing with derivatives positions, we can also estimate their risks by their Greek parameters: the delta, which gives us the change in the derivatives price in response to a small change in the underlying price; the gamma, which gives us the change in the delta in response to a small change in the underlying price (or, if we prefer, the second derivative of the derivatives price with respect to a change in the underlying price); the rho, which gives us the change in derivatives price for a small change in the interest rate; the vega, which gives us the change in derivatives price with respect to

---

[10]There are also other problems. (1) If we wish to use this short-cut, we have relatively little firm guidance on what the hypothetical portfolio should be. In practice, investors usually use some 'obvious' portfolio such as the basket of shares behind a stock index, but we never really know whether this is a good proxy for the CAPM market portfolio or not. It is probably not. (2) Even if we pick a good proxy for the CAPM market portfolio, it is still very doubtful that *any* such portfolio will give us good results (see, e.g., Markowitz (1992, p. 684)). If we wish to use proxy risk estimates, there is a good argument that we should abandon single-factor models in favour of multi-factor models that can mop up more systematic risks. This leads us to the arbitrage pricing theory (APT) of Ross (1976). However, the APT has its own problems: we can't easily identify the risk factors, and even if we did identify them, we still don't know whether the APT will give us a good proxy for the systematic risk we are trying to proxy.

[11]We can also measure risk using statistical approaches applied to equity, FX, commodity and other risks, as well as interest-rate risks. The idea is that we postulate a measurable relationship between the exposure variable we are interested in (e.g., the loss/gain on our bond or FX portfolio or whatever) and the factors that we think influence that loss or gain. We then estimate the parameters of this relationship by an appropriate econometric technique, and the parameter estimates give us an idea of our risk exposures. This approach is limited by the availability of data (i.e., we need enough data to estimate the relevant parameters) and by linearity assumptions, and there can also be problems caused by misspecification and instability in estimated statistical relationships.

a change in volatility; the theta, which gives us the change in derivatives price with respect to time; and so forth. A seasoned derivatives practitioner can make good use of estimates of these parameters to assess and manage the risks of a derivatives position — Taleb (1997c) has a very good discussion of the issues involved — but doing so requires considerable skill. The practitioner needs to be able to deal with a number of different risk 'signals' at the same time, under real-time constraints, and the Greeks themselves can be very volatile: for instance, it is well known that the gamma of an at-the-money vanilla option goes to infinity as the option approaches expiry, and the volatility of vega is legendary.

In using these measures, we should also keep in mind that they make sense only within the confines of a dynamic hedging strategy: the measures, and resulting hedge positions, only work against small changes in risk factors, and only then if they are revised sufficiently frequently. There is always a worry that these measures and their associated hedging strategies might fail to cover us against major market moves such as stock market or bond market crashes, or a major devaluation. We may have hedged against a small price change, but a large adverse price move in the wrong direction could still be very damaging: our underlying position might take a large loss that is not adequately compensated for by the gain on our hedge instrument.[12] Moreover, there is also the danger that we may be dealing with a market whose liquidity dries up just as we most need to sell. When the stock market crashed in October 1987, the wave of sell orders prompted by the stock market fall meant that such orders could take hours to execute, and sellers got even lower prices than they had anticipated. The combination of large market moves and the sudden drying up of market liquidity can mean that positions take large losses even though they are supposedly protected by dynamic hedging strategies. It was this sort of problem that undid portfolio insurance and other dynamic hedging strategies in the stock market crash, when many people suffered large losses on positions that they thought they had hedged. As one experienced observer later ruefully admitted:

> When O'Connor set up in London at Big Bang, I built an option risk control system incorporating all the Greek letters — deltas, gammas, vegas, thetas and even some higher order ones as well.... And I'll tell you that during the crash it was about as useful as a US theme park on the outskirts of Paris.
>
> (Robert Gumerlock (1994))[13]

1.3   VALUE AT RISK

1.3.1   The Origin and Development of VaR

In the late 1970s and 1980s, a number of major financial institutions started work on internal models to measure and aggregate risks across the institution as a whole. They started work on these models in the first instance for their own internal risk management purposes — as firms became more complex,

---

[12]This problem is especially acute for gamma risk. As one risk manager noted:

> On most option desks, gamma is a local measure designed for very small moves up and down [in the underlying price]. You can have zero gamma but have the firm blow up if you have a 10% move in the market.
>
> (Richard Bookstaber, quoted in Chew (1994, p. 65))

The solution, in part, is to adopt a wider perspective. To quote Bookstaber again:

> The key for looking at gamma risks on a global basis is to have a wide angle lens to look for the potential risks. One, two or three standard deviation stress tests are just not enough. The crash of 1987 was a 20 standard deviation event — if you had used a three standard deviation move [to assess vulnerability] you would have completely missed it.
>
> (Bookstaber, quoted in Chew (1994, pp. 65–66))

[13]Quoted in Chew (1994, p. 66).

it was becoming increasingly difficult, but also increasingly important, to be able to aggregate their risks, taking account of how they interact with each other, and firms lacked the methodology to do so.

The best known of these systems is the RiskMetrics system developed by JP Morgan. According to industry legend, this system is said to have originated when the chairman of JP Morgan, Dennis Weatherstone, asked his staff to give him a daily one-page report indicating risk and potential losses over the next 24 hours, across the bank's entire trading portfolio. This report — the famous '4:15 report' — was to be given to him at 4:15 each day, after the close of trading. In order to meet this demand, the Morgan staff had to develop a system to measure risks across different trading positions, across the whole institution, and also aggregate these risks into a single risk measure. The measure used was value at risk (or VaR), or the maximum likely loss over the next trading day,[14] and the VaR was estimated from a system based on standard portfolio theory, using estimates of the standard deviations and correlations between the returns to different traded instruments. While the theory was straightforward, making this system operational involved a huge amount of work: measurement conventions had to be chosen, data sets constructed, statistical assumptions agreed, procedures determined to estimate volatilities and correlations, computing systems established to carry out estimations, and many other practical problems resolved. Developing this methodology took a long time, but by around 1990, the main elements — the data systems, the risk measurement methodology, and the basic mechanics — were all in place and working reasonably well. At that point it was decided to start using the '4:15 report', and it was soon found that the new risk management system had a major positive effect. In particular, it 'sensitised senior management to risk–return trade-offs and led over time to a much more efficient allocation of risks across the trading businesses' (Guldimann (2000, p. 57)). The new risk system was highlighted in JP Morgan's 1993 research conference and aroused a great deal of interest from potential clients who wished to buy or lease it for their own purposes.

Meanwhile, other financial institutions had been working on their own internal models, and VaR software systems were also being developed by specialist companies that concentrated on software but were not in a position to provide data. The resulting systems differed quite considerably from each other. Even where they were based on broadly similar theoretical ideas, there were still considerable differences in terms of subsidiary assumptions, use of data, procedures to estimate volatility and correlation, and many other 'details'. Besides, not all VaR systems were based on portfolio theory: some systems were built using historical simulation approaches that estimate VaR from histograms of past profit and loss data, and other systems were developed using Monte Carlo simulation techniques.

These firms were keen to encourage their management consultancy businesses, but at the same time they were conscious of the limitations of their own models and wary about giving too many secrets away. Whilst most firms kept their models secret, JP Morgan decided to make its data and basic methodology available so that outside parties could use them to write their own risk management software. Early in 1994, Morgan set up the RiskMetrics unit to do this and the RiskMetrics model — a simplified version of the firm's own internal model — was completed in eight months. In October that year, Morgan then made its RiskMetrics system and the necessary data freely available on the internet: outside users could now access the RiskMetrics model and plug their own position data into it.

---

[14]One should however note a possible source of confusion. The literature put out by JP Morgan (e.g., such as the *RiskMetrics Technical Document*) uses the term 'value at risk' somewhat idiosyncratically to refer to the maximum likely loss over the next 20 days, and uses the term 'daily earnings at risk' (DeaR) to refer to the maximum likely loss over the next day. However, outside Morgan, the term 'value at risk' is used as a generic term for the maximum likely loss over the chosen horizon period.

This bold move attracted a lot of attention, and the resulting public debate about the merits of RiskMetrics was useful in raising awareness of VaR and of the issues involved in establishing and operating VaR systems.[15] In addition, making the RiskMetrics data available gave a major boost to the spread of VaR systems by giving software providers and their clients access to data sets that they were often unable to construct themselves.[16] It also encouraged many of the smaller software providers to adopt the RiskMetrics approach or make their own systems compatible with it.

The subsequent adoption of VaR systems was very rapid, first among securities houses and investment banks, and then among commercial banks, pension funds and other financial institutions, and non-financial corporates. Needless to say, the state of the art also improved rapidly. Developers and users became more experienced; the combination of plummeting IT costs and continuing software development meant that systems became more powerful and much faster, and able to perform tasks that were previously not feasible; VaR systems were extended to cover more types of instruments; and the VaR methodology itself was extended to deal with other types of risk besides the market risks for which VaR systems were first developed, including credit risks, liquidity risks and cash-flow risks.

Box 1.1   Portfolio Theory and VaR

In some respects VaR is a natural progression from earlier portfolio theory (PT). Yet there are also important differences between them:

- PT interprets risk in terms of the standard deviation of the return, while VaR approaches interpret it in terms of the maximum likely loss. The VaR notion of risk — the VAR itself — is more intuitive and easier for laypeople to grasp.
- PT presupposes that P/L or returns are normally (or, at best, elliptically) distributed, whereas VaR approaches can accommodate a very wide range of possible distributions. VaR approaches are therefore more general.
- VaR approaches can be applied to a much broader range of risk problems: PT theory is limited to market risks, while VaR approaches can be applied to credit, liquidity and other risks, as well as to market risks.
- The variance–covariance approach to VaR has the same theoretical basis as PT — in fact, its theoretical basis *is* portfolio theory — but other two approaches to VaR (e.g., the historical simulation and simulation approaches) do not. It would therefore be a mistake to regard all VaR approaches as applications (or developments) of portfolio theory.

---

[15] A notable example is the exchange between Longerstaey and Zangari (1995) and Lawrence and Robinson (1995a) on the safety or otherwise of RiskMetrics. The various issues covered in this debate — the validity of underlying statistical assumptions, the estimation of volatilities and correlations, and similar issues — go right to the heart of risk measurement, and will be dealt with in more detail in later chapters.

[16] Morgan continued to develop the RiskMetrics system after its public launch in October 1994. By and large, these developments consisted of expanding data coverage, improving data handling, broadening the instruments covered, and various methodological refinements (see, e.g., the fourth edition of the *RiskMetrics Technical Document*). In June 1996, Morgan teamed up with Reuters in a partnership to enable Morgan to focus on the risk management system while Reuters handled the data, and in April 1997, Morgan and five other leading banks launched their new CreditMetrics system, which is essentially a variance–covariance approach tailored to credit risk. The RiskMetrics Group was later spun off as a separate company, and the later RiskMetrics work has focused on applying the methodology to corporate risk management, long-run risk management, and other similar areas. For more on these, see the relevant technical documents, e.g., the *CorporateMetrics Technical Document* (1999), etc.

1.3.2 Attractions of VaR

So what is VaR, and why is it important? The basic concept was nicely described by Linsmeier and Pearson (1996):

> Value at risk is a single, summary, statistical measure of possible portfolio losses. Specifically, value at risk is a measure of losses due to 'normal' market movements. Losses greater than the value at risk are suffered only with a specified small probability. Subject to the simplifying assumptions used in its calculation, value at risk aggregates all of the risks in a portfolio into a single number suitable for use in the boardroom, reporting to regulators, or disclosure in an annual report. Once one crosses the hurdle of using a statistical measure, the concept of value at risk is straightforward to understand. It is simply a way to describe the magnitude of the likely losses on the portfolio.
>
> (Linsmeier and Pearson (1996, p. 3))

The VaR figure has two important characteristics. The first is that it provides a *common* consistent measure of risk across different positions and risk factors. It enables us to measure the risk associated with a fixed-income position, say, in a way that is comparable to and consistent with a measure of the risk associated with equity positions. VaR provides us with a common risk yardstick, and this yardstick makes it possible for institutions to manage their risks in new ways that were not possible before. The other characteristic of VaR is that it takes account of the correlations between different risk factors. If two risks offset each other, the VaR allows for this offset and tells us that the overall risk is fairly low. If the same two risks don't offset each other, the VaR takes this into account as well and gives us a higher risk estimate. Clearly, a risk measure that accounts for correlations is essential if we are to be able to handle portfolio risks in a statistically meaningful way.

VaR information can be used in many ways. (1) Senior management can use it to set their overall risk target, and from that determine risk targets and position limits down the line. If they want the firm to increase its risks, they would increase the overall VaR target, and vice versa. (2) Since VaR tells us the maximum amount we are likely to lose, we can use it to determine capital allocation. We can use it to determine capital requirements at the level of the firm, but also right down the line, to the level of the individual investment decision: the riskier the activity, the higher the VaR and the greater the capital requirement. (3) VaR can be very useful for reporting and disclosing purposes, and firms increasingly make a point of reporting VaR information in their annual reports.[17] (4) We can use VaR information to assess the risks of different investment opportunities before decisions are made. VaR-based decision rules can guide investment, hedging and trading decisions, and do so taking account of the implications of alternative choices for the portfolio risk as a whole.[18] (5) VaR information can be used to implement portfolio-wide hedging strategies that are otherwise rarely possible.[19] (6) VaR information can be used to provide new remuneration rules for traders, managers and other employees that take account of the risks they take, and so discourage the excessive risk-taking that occurs when employees are rewarded on the basis of profits alone, without any reference to the risks they took to get those profits. In short, VaR can help provide for a more consistent and integrated approach to the management of different risks, leading also to greater risk transparency and disclosure, and better strategic management.

---

[17]For more on the use of VaR for reporting and disclosure purposes, see Dowd (2000b), Jorion (2001) or Moosa and Knight (2001).

[18]For further information on VaR-based decision rules, see Dowd (1999).

[19]Such strategies are explained in more detail in, e.g., Kuruc and Lee (1998) and Dowd (1999).

Box 1.2   What Exactly is VaR?

The term VaR can be used in one of four different ways, depending on the particular context:

1. In its most literal sense, VaR refers to a particular *amount of money*, the maximum amount we are likely to lose over some period, at a specific confidence level.
2. There is a VaR estimation *procedure*, a numerical, statistical or mathematical procedure to produce VaR figures. A VaR procedure is what produces VaR numbers.
3. We can also talk of a VaR *methodology*, a procedure or set of procedures that can be used to produce VaR figures, but can also be used to estimate other risks as well. VaR methodologies can be used to estimate other amounts at risk — such as credit at risk and cash flow at risk — as well as values at risk.
4. Looking beyond measurement issues, we can also talk of a distinctive *VaR approach to risk management*. This refers to how we use VaR figures, how we restructure the company to produce them, and how we deal with various associated risk management issues (e.g., how we adjust remuneration for risks taken, etc.).

1.3.3   Criticisms of VaR

Most risk practitioners embraced VaR with varying degrees of enthusiasm, and most of the debate over VaR dealt with the relative merits of different VaR systems — the pros and cons of RiskMetrics, of parametric approaches relative to historical simulation approaches, and so on. However, there were also those who warned that VaR had deeper problems and could be dangerous.

A key issue was the validity or otherwise of the statistical and other assumptions underlying VaR, and both Nassim Taleb[20] (1997a,b) and Richard Hoppe (1998, 1999) were very critical of the naïve transfer of mathematical and statistical models from the physical sciences, where they were well suited, to social systems where they were often invalid. Such applications often ignore important features of social systems — the ways in which intelligent agents learn and react to their environment, the non-stationarity and dynamic interdependence of many market processes, and so forth — features that undermine the plausibility of many models and leave VaR estimates wide open to major errors. A good example of this problem is suggested by Hoppe (1999, p. 1): Long Term Capital Management (LTCM) had a risk model that suggested the loss it suffered in the summer and autumn of 1998 was 14 times the standard deviation of its P/L, and a 14-sigma event shouldn't occur once in the entire history of the universe. So either LTCM was *incredibly* unlucky or it had a very poor risk measurement model: take your pick.

A related argument was that VaR estimates are too imprecise to be of much use, and empirical evidence presented by Tanya Beder (1995a) and others in this regard is very worrying, as it suggests that different VaR models can give very different VaR estimates. To make matters worse, work by Marshall and Siegel (1997) showed that VaR models are exposed to considerable implementation risk as well — so even theoretically similar models could give quite different VaR estimates because

---

[20]Taleb was also critical of the tendency of some VaR proponents to overstate the usefulness of VaR. He was particularly dismissive of Philippe Jorion's (1997) claim that VaR might have prevented disasters such as Orange County. Taleb's response was that these disasters had other causes — especially, excessive leverage. As he put it, a Wall Street clerk would have picked up these excesses with an abacus, and VaR defenders overlook the point that there are simpler and more reliable risk measures than VaR (Taleb (1997b)). Taleb is clearly right: any simple duration analysis should have revealed the rough magnitude of Orange County's interest-rate exposure. So the problem was not the absence of VaR, as such, but the absence of any basic risk measurement at all. Similar criticisms of VaR were also made by Culp *et al.* (1997): they (correctly) point out that the key issue is not how VaR is measured, but how it is used; they also point out that VaR measures would have been of limited use in averting these disasters, and might actually have been misleading in some cases.

of the differences in the ways in which the models are implemented. It is therefore difficult for VaR advocates to deny that VaR estimates can be very imprecise.

The danger here is obvious: if VaR estimates are too inaccurate and users take them seriously, they could take on much bigger risks and lose much more than they had bargained for. As Hoppe put it, 'believing a spuriously precise estimate of risk is worse than admitting the irreducible unreliability of one's estimate. False certainty is more dangerous than acknowledged ignorance' (Hoppe (1998, p. 50)). Taleb put the same point a different way: 'You're worse off relying on misleading information than on not having any information at all. If you give a pilot an altimeter that is sometimes defective he will crash the plane. Give him nothing and he will look out the window' (Taleb (1997a, p. 37)). These are serious criticisms, and they are not easy to counter.

Another problem was pointed out by Ju and Pearson (1999): if VaR measures are used to control or remunerate risk taking, traders will have an incentive to seek out positions where risk is over- or underestimated and trade them. They will therefore take on more risk than suggested by VaR estimates — so our VaR estimates will be biased downwards — and their empirical evidence suggests that the magnitude of these underestimates can be very substantial.

Others suggested that the use of VaR might destabilise the financial system. Thus, Taleb (1997a) pointed out that VaR players are dynamic hedgers, and need to revise their positions in the face of changes in market prices. If everyone uses VaR, there is then a danger that this hedging behaviour will make uncorrelated risks become very correlated — and firms will bear much greater risk than their VaR models might suggest. Taleb's argument is all the more convincing because he wrote this *before* the summer 1998 financial crisis, where this sort of problem was widely observed. Similarly, Danielsson (2001), Danielsson and Zigrand (2001), Danielsson *et al.* (2001) and Basak and Shapiro (2001) suggested good reasons to believe that poorly thought through regulatory VaR constraints could destabilise the financial system by inducing banks to increase their risk taking: for example, a VaR cap can give risk managers an incentive to protect themselves against mild losses, but not against larger ones.

VaR risk measures are also open to criticism from a very different direction. Even if one grants the usefulness of risk measures based on the lower tail of a probability density function, there is still the question of whether VaR is the best tail-based risk measure, and it is now clear that it is not. In some important theoretical work in the mid to late 1990s, Artzner, Delbaen, Eber and Heath examined this issue by setting out the axioms that a 'good' (or, in their terms, coherent) risk measure should satisfy. They then looked for risk measures that satisfied these coherence properties, and found that VaR did not satisfy them. It turns out that the VaR measure has various problems, but perhaps the most striking of these is its failure to satisfy the property of sub-additivity — namely, we cannot guarantee that the VaR of a combined position will not be greater than the VaR of the constituent positions individually considered. The risk of the sum, as measured by VaR, might be greater than the sum of the risks. We will have more to say on these issues in the next chapter, but suffice it for the moment to say that this is a serious drawback. Fortunately there are other tail-based risk measures that satisfy the coherence properties — most notably the expected tail loss (ETL), the expected value of losses exceeding VaR. The ETL is thus demonstrably superior to the VaR, but many of the other criticisms made of VaR also apply to the ETL as well — so risk measurers must still proceed with great caution.

1.4 RECOMMENDED READING

Culp *et al.* (1997); Danielsson (2001); Holton (1997, 2002); Hoppe (1998); Linsmeier and Pearson (1996); Moosa and Knight (2001); Schachter (1997); Taleb (1997a,b).

2

Measures of Financial Risk

This chapter deals with alternative measures of financial risk. To elaborate, suppose we are working to a daily holding or horizon period. At the end of day $t - 1$, we observe that the value of our portfolio is P_{t-1}. However, looking forward, the value of our portfolio at the end of tomorrow, P_t, is uncertain. Ignoring any intra-day returns or intra-day interest, if P_t turns out to exceed P_{t-1}, we will make a profit equal to the difference, $P_t - P_{t-1}$; and if P_t turns out to be less than P_{t-1}, we will make a loss equal to $P_{t-1} - P_t$. Since P_t is uncertain, as viewed from the end of $t - 1$, then so too is the profit or loss (P/L). Our next-period P/L is risky, and we want a framework to measure this risk.

2.1 THE MEAN–VARIANCE FRAMEWORK FOR MEASURING FINANCIAL RISK

2.1.1 The Normality Assumption

The traditional solution to this problem is to assume a mean–variance framework: we model financial risk in terms of the mean and variance (or standard deviation, the square root of the variance) of P/L (or returns). As a convenient (although oversimplified) starting point, we can regard this framework as underpinned by the assumption that daily P/L (or returns) obeys a normal distribution.[1] A random variable X is normally distributed with mean μ and variance σ^2 (or standard deviation σ) if the probability that X takes the value x, $f(x)$, obeys the following probability density function (pdf):

$$f(x) = \frac{1}{\sigma\sqrt{2\pi}} \exp\left[-\frac{1}{2}((x - \mu)/\sigma)^2\right] \tag{2.1}$$

where X is defined over $-\infty < x < \infty$. A normal pdf with mean 0 and standard deviation 1, known as a standard normal, is illustrated in Figure 2.1.

This pdf tells us that outcomes are more likely to occur close to the mean μ. The spread of the probability mass around the mean depends on the standard deviation σ: the greater the standard deviation, the more dispersed the probability mass. The pdf is also symmetric around the mean: X is as likely to take a particular value $x - \mu$ as to take the corresponding negative value $-(x - \mu)$. Outcomes well away from the mean are very unlikely, and the pdf tails away on both sides: the left-hand tail corresponds to extremely low realisations of the random variable, and the right-hand tail to extremely high realisations of it. In risk management, we are particularly concerned about the left-hand tail, which corresponds to high negative values of P/L — or big losses, in plain English.

---

[1] Strictly speaking, the mean–variance framework does not require normality, and many accounts of it make little or no mention of normality. Nonetheless, the statistics of the mean–variance framework are easiest understood in terms of an underlying normality assumption, and viable alternatives (e.g., such as assumptions of elliptical distributions) are usually harder to understand and less tractable to use.

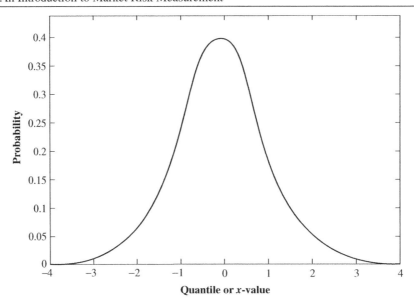

Figure 2.1   The normal probability density function.

A pdf gives a complete representation of possible random outcomes: it tells us what outcomes are possible, and how likely these outcomes are. Such a representation enables us to answer questions about possible outcomes and, hence, about the risks we face. These questions come in two basic forms:

- The first are questions about likelihood or probability. We specify the quantity (or quantile), and then ask about the associated probability. For example, how likely is it that profit (or loss) will be greater than, or less than, a certain amount?
- The others are questions about quantiles. We specify the probability, and then ask about the associated amount. For example, what is the maximum likely profit (or loss) at a particular level of probability?

These questions and their answers are illustrated in Figure 2.2. This figure shows the same normal pdf, but with a particular X-value, equal to -1.645. We can regard this value as a profit of -1.645 or a loss of 1.645. The probability of a P/L value less than -1.645 is given by the left-hand tail — the area under the curve to the left of the vertical line marking off $X = -1.645$. This area turns out to be 0.05, or 5%, so there is a 5% probability that we will get a P/L value less than -1.645, or a loss greater than 1.645. Conversely, we can say that the maximum likely loss at a 95% probability level is 1.645. This is often put another way: we can be 95% confident of making a profit or making a loss no greater than 1.645. This value of 1.645 can then be described as the value at risk (or VaR) of our portfolio at the 95% level of confidence, and we will have more to say about this presently.

The assumption that P/L is normally distributed is attractive for three reasons. The first is that it often has some, albeit limited, plausibility in circumstances where we can appeal to the central limit theorem.

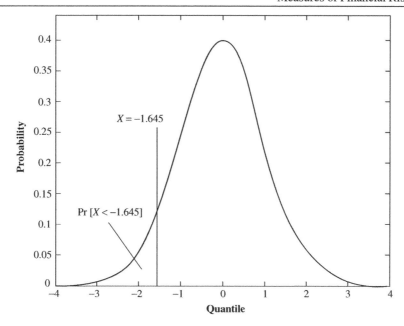

Figure 2.2   Normal quantiles and probabilities.

The second is that it provides us with straightforward formulas for both cumulative probabilities and quantiles, namely:

$$\Pr[x \leq X] = \int_{-\infty}^{X} \frac{1}{\sigma\sqrt{2\pi}} \exp\left[-\frac{1}{2}((x-\mu)/\sigma)^2\right]dx \tag{2.2a}$$

$$X_{cl} = \mu + \alpha_{cl}\sigma \tag{2.2b}$$

where *cl* is the chosen confidence level (e.g., 95%), and α_{cl} is the standard normal variate for that confidence level (e.g., $\alpha_{0.95} = -1.645$). α_{cl} can be obtained from standard statistical tables or from spreadsheet functions (e.g., the 'normsinv' function in Excel or the 'norminv' function in MATLAB). Equation (2.2a) is the normal distribution (or cumulative density) function: it gives the normal probability of *x* being less than or equal to *X*, and enables us to answer probability questions. Equation (2.2b) is the normal quantile corresponding to the confidence level *cl* (i.e., the lowest value we can expect at the stated confidence level) and enables us to answer quantity questions. The normal distribution is thus very easy to apply in practice.

The third advantage of the normal distribution is that it only requires estimates of two parameters — the mean and the standard deviation (or variance) — because it is completely described by these two parameters alone.

2.1.2   Limitations of the Normality Assumption

Nonetheless, the assumption of normality also has its limitations. Ironically, the key ones stem from the last point — that the normal distribution requires only two parameters. Generally speaking, any statistical distribution can be described in terms of its moments. The first moment is the mean, and

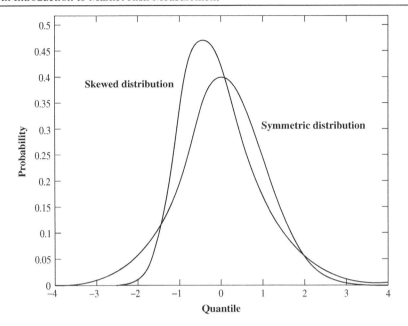

Figure 2.3   A skewed distribution.

the second moment corresponds to the variance. However, there are also higher moments, and the third and fourth moments can be of great importance.

The third moment gives an indication of the asymmetry or skewness of the distribution. This leads to the skewness:

$$Skew = E(x - \mu)^3/\sigma^3 \tag{2.3}$$

The skewness coefficient will be zero for a symmetric distribution, and non-zero for an asymmetric one. The sign of the coefficient indicates the direction of the skew: a positive skew indicates a short tail on the left and a long tail on the right, and a negative skew indicates the opposite.

An example of a positively skewed distribution is shown in Figure 2.3, along with the earlier symmetric normal distribution for comparison. The skew alters the whole distribution, and tends to pull one tail in whilst pushing the other tail out. If a distribution is skewed, we must therefore take account of its skewness if we are to be able to estimate its probabilities and quantiles correctly.

The fourth moment, the kurtosis, gives an indication of the flatness of the distribution. In risk measurement practice, this is usually taken to be an indication of the fatness of the tails of the distribution. The kurtosis parameter is:

$$Kurtosis = E(x - \mu)^4/\sigma^4 \tag{2.4}$$

If we ignore any skewness for convenience, there are three cases to consider:

- If the kurtosis parameter is 3, the tails of our P/L distribution are the same as those we would get under normality.
- If the kurtosis parameter is greater than 3, our tail is fatter than under normality. Such fat tails are common in financial returns, and indicate that extreme events are more likely, and more likely to be large, than under normality.

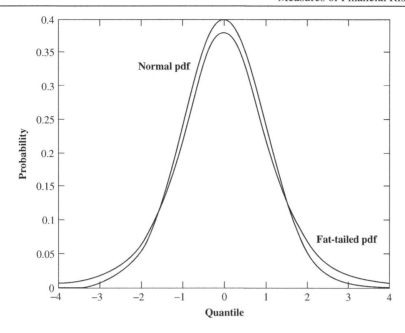

Figure 2.4   A fat-tailed distribution.

- If the kurtosis parameter is less than 3, our tail is thinner than under normality. Thin tails indicate that extreme events are less likely, and less likely to be large, than under normality.

The effect of kurtosis is illustrated in Figure 2.4, which shows how a symmetric fat-tailed distribution — in this case, a Student t-distribution with five degrees of freedom — compares to a normal one. Because the area under the pdf curve must always be 1, the distribution with the fatter tails also has less probability mass in the centre. Tail-fatness — kurtosis in excess of 3 — means that we are more likely to gain a lot or lose a lot, and the gains or losses will tend to be larger, relative to normality.

The moral of the story is that the normality assumption is only strictly appropriate if we are dealing with a symmetric (i.e., zero-skew) distribution with a kurtosis of 3. If these conditions are not met — if our distribution is skewed, or (in particular) has fat tails — then the normality assumption is inappropriate and can lead to major errors in risk analysis.

Box 2.1   Other Risk Measures

The most widely used measure of risk (or dispersion) is the standard deviation (or its square, the variance), but the standard deviation has been criticised for the arbitrary way in which deviations from the mean are squared and for giving equal treatment to upside and downside outcomes. If we are concerned about these, we can use the mean absolute deviation or the downside semi-variance instead: the former replaces the squared deviations in the standard deviation formula with absolute deviations and gets rid of the square root operation; the latter can be obtained from the variance formula by replacing upside values (i.e., observations above the mean) with zeros. We can also replace the standard deviation with other simple dispersion measures such as the entropy measure or the Gini coefficient (see, e.g., Kroll and Kaplanski (2001, pp. 13–14)).

A more general approach to dispersion is provided by Fishburn $\alpha - t$ measures, defined as $\int_{-\infty}^{t} (t - x)^{\alpha} f(x)\, dx$ (Fishburn (1977)). This measure is defined on two parameters: α, which describes our attitude to risk, and t, which specifies the cut-off between the downside that we worry about and other outcomes that we don't worry about. Many risk measures are special cases of the Fishburn measure or are closely related to it. These includes the downside semi-variance, which is very closely related to the Fishburn measure with $\alpha = 2$ and t equal to the mean; Roy's safety-first criterion, where $\alpha \to 0$; and the expected tail loss (ETL), which is closely related to the Fishburn measure with $\alpha = 1$. In addition, the Fishburn measure encompasses the stochastic dominance rules that are sometimes used for ranking risky alternatives:[2] the Fishburn measure with $\alpha = n + 1$ is proportional to the nth-order distribution function, so ranking risks by this Fishburn measure is equivalent to ranking by nth-order stochastic dominance.[3]

2.1.3 Traditional Approaches to Financial Risk Measurement

2.1.3.1 Portfolio Theory

It is also important to check for normality because of its close connection with some of the most popular traditional approaches to financial risk measurement. A good example is portfolio theory, whose starting point is the assumption that the behaviour of the returns to any set of assets can be described in terms of a vector of expected returns and a variance–covariance matrix that captures the relationships between individual returns. Any portfolio formed from this set of assets will then have a return whose mean and standard deviation are determined by these factors. If the specification of the behaviour of portfolio returns is to be complete, and if we leave aside various exceptions and disguises (e.g., such as elliptical distributions or lognormality), we then require either that individual asset returns be multivariate normally distributed, or (less restrictively) that our portfolio has a normally distributed return. Either way, we end up with a portfolio whose returns are normally distributed. If we are to use portfolio theory, we have to make assumptions somewhere along the line that lead us to normality or something closely related to it.

Unfortunately, once we are signed up to normality, we are stuck with it: we have a framework that cannot (again, honourable exceptions aside) be relied upon to give us good answers in the presence of major departures from normality, such as skewness or fat tails.

2.1.3.2 Duration Approaches to Fixed-income Risk Measurement

Another traditional method is the duration approach to fixed-income risk measurement. This method gives us approximation rules that help us to determine how bond prices will change in the face of specified changes in bond yields or interest rates. For example, suppose we start with a bond's price–yield

---

[2] An nth-order distribution function is defined as $F^{(n)}(x) = \frac{1}{(n-1)!} \int_{-\infty}^{x} (x - u)^{n-1} f(u) du$, and X_1 is said to be nth-order stochastically dominant over X_2 if $F_1^{(n)}(x) \leq F_2^{(n)}(x)$, where $F_1^{(n)}(x)$ and $F_2^{(n)}(x)$ are the nth-degree distribution functions of X_1 and X_2 (Yoshiba and Yamai (2001, p. 8)). First-order stochastic dominance therefore implies that the distribution function for X_1 is never above the distribution function for X_2, second-order stochastic dominance implies that their second-degree distribution functions do not cross, and so on. Since a risk measure with nth-degree stochastic dominance is also consistent with higher degrees of stochastic dominance, we can say that first-order stochastic dominance implies second and higher orders of stochastic dominance, but not the reverse. First-order stochastic dominance is a fairly strict condition, second-order stochastic dominance is less restrictive, and so forth: higher orders of stochastic dominance are less strict than lower orders of stochastic dominance.

[3] See Ingersoll (1987, p. 139) or Yoshiba and Yamai (2001, p. 8).

relationship, $P(y)$, and take a linear first-order approximation around the current combination of price (P) and yield (y):

$$P(y + \Delta y) \approx P(y) + (dP/dy)\Delta y \tag{2.5}$$

where Δy is some small change in yield. Fixed-income theory tells us that:

$$dP/P \approx -D^m dy \tag{2.6}$$

where D^m is the bond's modified duration (see, e.g., Fabozzi (2000, p. 66)). Expressions such as Equation (2.6) are usually used to provide approximate answers to 'what if' questions (e.g., what if yields rise by 10 basis points?) and, as such, they are useful, though limited, tools in the risk measurer's armoury.

However, risk analysis in the proper sense of the term requires that we link events (i.e., changes in bond price) to probabilities. If we are to use duration measures for risk measurement purposes in this sense, our best option is to derive the standard deviation of holding-period return and then feed that into a normal risk framework. Thus, the percentage change in bond price is:

$$\Delta P/P \approx -D^m \Delta y = -D^m y(\Delta y/y) \tag{2.7}$$

and the volatility of the bond price is approximately:

$$\sigma_P \approx D^m y \sigma_y \tag{2.8}$$

If we want a risk measure, the easiest step is to assume that bond prices are approximately normal and we can then work out the probabilities of specified gains or losses, and so forth. We could also assume alternative distributions if we wished to, but the normal distribution is certainly the most convenient, and makes duration-based measures of risk more tractable than they would otherwise be.

2.2 VALUE AT RISK

2.2.1 VaR Basics

A much better approach is to allow the P/L or return distribution to be less restricted, but focus on the tail of that distribution — the worst p percent of outcomes. This brings us back again to the notion of the VaR, and the reader will recall that the VaR on a portfolio is the maximum loss we might expect over a given holding or horizon period, at a given level of confidence.[4] Hence, the VaR is defined contingent on two arbitrarily chosen parameters — a holding or horizon period, which is the period of time over which we measure our portfolio profit or loss, and which might be daily, weekly, monthly, or whatever; and a confidence level, which indicates the likelihood that we will get an outcome no worse than our VaR, and which might be 50%, 90%, 95%, 99%, or indeed any fraction between 0 and 1.

The VaR is illustrated in Figure 2.5, which shows a common pdf of profit/loss (P/L) over a chosen holding period.[5] Positive P/L values correspond to profits, and negative observations to losses, and

---

[4]The roots of the VaR risk measure go back to Baumol (1963, p. 174), who suggested a risk measure equal to $\mu - k\sigma$, where μ and σ are the mean and standard deviation of the distribution concerned, and k is a subjective confidence-level parameter that reflects the user's attitude to risk. As we shall see, this risk measure is the same as the VaR under the assumption that P/L is elliptical, and the class of elliptical distributions includes the normal and the Student t, among others. Of course, Baumol did not use the term 'value at risk', which only came into use later.

[5]The figure is constructed on the assumption that P/L is normally distributed with mean 0 and standard deviation 1 over a holding period of 1 day.

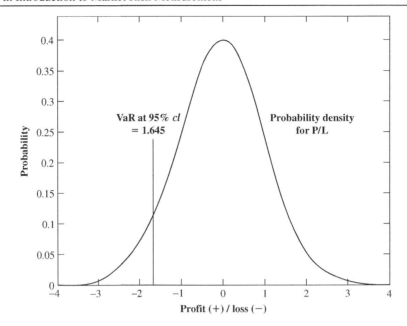

Figure 2.5   Value at risk.

Note: Produced using the 'normalvarfigure' function.

positive values will typically be more common than negative ones. To get the VaR, we must choose a confidence level (*cl*). If this is 95%, say, then the VaR is given by the negative of the point on the *x*-axis that cuts off the top 95% of P/L observations from the bottom 5% of tail observations. In this case, the relevant *x*-axis value is –1.645, so the VaR is 1.645. The negative P/L value corresponds to a positive VaR, indicating that the worst outcome at this level of confidence is a loss of 1.645.

In practice, the point on the *x*-axis corresponding to our VaR will usually be negative and, where it is, will correspond to a (positive) loss and a positive VaR. However, this *x*-point can sometimes be positive, in which case it indicates a profit rather than a loss, and in this case the VaR will be negative. This also makes sense: if the worst outcome at this confidence level is a particular profit rather than a loss, then the VaR, the likely loss, must be negative.

As mentioned already, the VaR is contingent on the choice of confidence level, and will generally change when the confidence level changes. This is illustrated in Figure 2.6, which shows the corresponding VaR at the 99% level of confidence. In this case, the VaR is determined by the cut-off between the top 99% and the bottom 1% of observations, so we are dealing with a 1% tail rather than the earlier 5% tail. In this case, the cut-off point is −2.326, so the VaR is 2.326. The higher confidence level means a smaller tail, a cut-off point further to the left and, therefore, a higher VaR.

This suggests the more general point that, other things being equal, the VaR tends to rise as the confidence level rises.[6] This point is further illustrated in the next figure (Figure 2.7), which shows

---

[6] Strictly speaking, the VaR is non-decreasing with the confidence level, which means that the VaR can remain the same as *cl* rises. However, the VaR will never fall as the confidence level rises, and cases where the VaR remains flat are not too common.

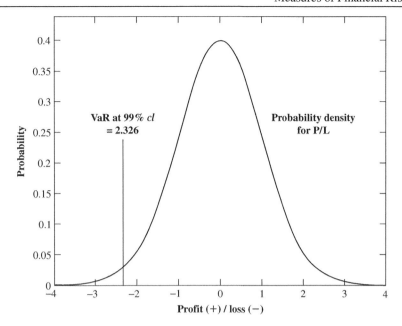

Figure 2.6   VaR at the 99% confidence level.

Note: Produced using the 'normalvarfigure' function.

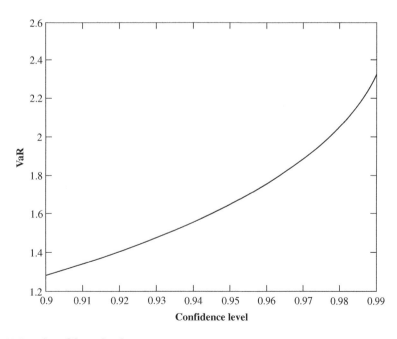

Figure 2.7   VaR and confidence level.

Note: Produced using the 'normalvarplot2D_cl' function.

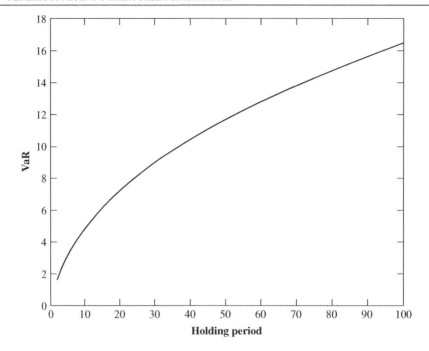

Figure 2.8   VaR and holding period.

Note: Produced using the 'normalvarplot2D_hp' function.

how the same VaR varies as we change the confidence level and keep other parameters constant. In this particular case, the VaR not only rises with the confidence level, but also rises at an increasing rate — a point that risk managers might care to note.

We should also remember that the VaR is contingent on the choice of holding period as well, and so we should consider how the VaR varies with the holding period. This behaviour is illustrated in Figure 2.8, which plots the VaR at the 95% confidence level against a holding period that varies from 1 day to 100 days. In this case, the VaR rises with the square root of the holding period, from a value of 1.645 at the start to 16.449 at the end. This 'square root' case is commonly cited in the literature, but we should recognise that VaR might rise in a different way, or even fall, as the holding period rises.

Of course, each of the last two figures only gives a partial view of the relationship between the VaR and the confidence level/holding period: the first takes the holding period as given and varies the confidence level, and the second varies the holding period whilst taking the confidence level as given. To form a more complete picture, we need to see how VaR changes as we allow both parameters to change. The result is a VaR surface — illustrated in Figure 2.9 — that enables us to read off the value of the VaR for any given combination of these two parameters. The shape of the VaR surface shows how VaR changes as the underlying parameters change, and conveys a great deal of risk information. In this particular case, which is also typical of many, the surface rises with both confidence level and holding period to culminate in a spike — indicating where our portfolio is most vulnerable — as both parameters approach their maximum values.

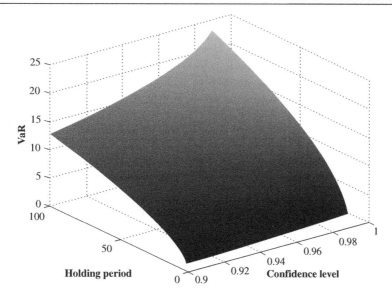

Figure 2.9 A VaR surface.

Note: Produced using the 'normalvarplot3D' function.

Box 2.2   Value at Risk as a Regulatory Risk Measure

Value at risk is also used by bank regulators to determine bank capital requirements against market risk.[7] Under the 1996 Amendment to the Basle Accord, institutions judged to have sound risk management practices are allowed the option of having their capital requirements determined by their own VaR estimates. This is known as the 'internal models' approach to regulatory capital requirements. The effective daily capital requirement is the maximum of the previous day's VaR and k times the average of the daily VaR over the last 60 days, where k is a multiplier in the range between 3 and 4. This multiplier is set by the bank's supervisors, conditional on the results of a set of standardised backtests (see Box 9.1: Regulatory Backtesting Requirements), with better backtesting results leading to a lower value of k. The application of this multiplier is sometimes justified as providing insurance against model risk, non-normal market moves, and similar factors. The Amendment also requires that VaR be derived at the 99% confidence level using a 10-day holding period.[8] However, in the initial implementation of this approach, banks are allowed to proxy the 10-day VaR by multiplying the 1-day VaR by the square root of 10. Banks are allowed to calculate the VaR using their own preferred models, subject to certain minimum criteria (e.g., that the model covers non-linear Greek factors, and so forth). Finally, there are also certain additional

---

[7]For good accounts of the current regulatory capital requirements, see Crouhy *et al.* (1998; 2001, ch. 4).

[8]These parameters imply that the VaR will be exceeded in only about one 10-day period in every four years. This should lead to a very low probability of failure, because the capital requirement itself is at least three times the VaR. Our estimated failure probability will then depend on what we assume about the P/L distribution. If we assume that the P/L is normal — which, strictly speaking, we shouldn't, because of extreme value theory — my calculations lead to a probability of failure indistinguishable from zero; but if we assume a Gumbel distribution, which *is* consistent with extreme value theory, then the probability of failure is no more than 0.25% per year, and less if we have a multiplier of greater than 3. This means that our institutions should be pretty safe — unless, like Barings or LTCM, they have a poor risk measurement model.

capital charges for 'specific risk' or credit-related risks on market instruments (e.g., counter-party default risk on OTC positions), and these too can be determined using an internal models approach.

Even if we grant that there is any need for regulatory capital requirements in the first place — and I would suggest there isn't — then perhaps the best thing we can say about the internal models approach is that it does at least make some effort to tie capital requirements to a rea-sonably respectable measure of market risk. Unfortunately, it does so in a very arbitrary and indefensible way. The multiplier is essentially pulled out of thin air, give or take a certain amount of adjustment for the results of a primitive backtest. The confidence level enshrined in the regulation — 99% — is also of no real relevance to bank solvency, and the regulations give con-siderable scope for manipulation and regulatory avoidance (i.e., they encourage institutions to seek ways to minimise the impact of capital regulations whilst technically complying with them). In some respects the regulations also tend to discourage the development of good market prac-tice and there are good reasons to believe that they might make the financial system less rather than more stable (see, e.g., Danielsson (2001) and Danielsson et al. (2001)). If regulators wished to determine market risk capital requirements in an intellectually coherent fashion, they would be better advised to work from some target probability of financial distress and use extreme value theory to work out the capital charges — but it would be much better if governments ab-stained from capital regulation and other forms of intervention altogether (e.g., such as deposit insurance) and allowed banks to determine their own capital requirements under free-market conditions.

2.2.2 Choice of VaR Parameters

The use of VaR involves two arbitrarily chosen parameters — the holding period and the confidence level. How do we choose these parameters?

The usual holding periods are one day or one month, but institutions can also operate on other holding periods (e.g., one quarter) and BIS capital adequacy rules stipulate that banks should operate with a holding period of two weeks (or 10 business days). One factor that determines the length of the holding period is the liquidity of the markets in which the institution operates: other things being equal, the holding period appropriate in any given market is, ideally, the length of time it takes to ensure orderly liquidation of positions in that market. However, other factors favour a short holding period:

- The assumption that the portfolio does not change over the holding period is more easily defended if we have a shorter holding period.
- A short holding period is preferable for model validation or backtesting purposes: reliable valida-tion requires a large data set, and a large data set requires a short holding period.

And the confidence level? For backtesting, we would usually want relatively low confidence levels to get a reasonable proportion of excess-loss observations. The choice of confidence level also depends on theoretical considerations (e.g., we would need to work with a high confidence level if we were using extreme value theory), and the purposes to which our risk measures were being put. For example, we might want a high confidence level if we were using our risk measures to set capital requirements. However, if we wished to estimate VaRs for reporting or comparison purposes, we would probably wish to use confidence levels (and, indeed, holding periods) that were comparable to those used by other institutions, and these are typically in the range from 95–99%.

We should keep in mind that the 'best' choice of these parameters often depends on the context and, where appropriate, we should work with ranges of parameter values rather than particular point values: a VaR surface is much more informative than a single VaR number.

Box 2.3   Using VaR Systems for Firm-wide Risk Management

In addition to the various specific uses explained already in section 1.3.2, VaR also has more far-reaching uses and leads to a radically new approach to firm-wide risk management. This new approach requires a major transformation in the way that firms currently structure and govern themselves, and has many attractions:

- It gives senior management a better handle on risks than they could otherwise have, thus leading to more informed and better risk management.
- It leads to robust new control systems that make it harder for fraud and human error to go undetected. Such systems can go a long way towards preventing repeats of some of the major risk management disasters of recent years.
- It provides a consistent, integrated treatment of risks across the institution, leading to greater risk transparency and a more consistent treatment of risks across the firm.
- It provides new operational decision rules to guide investment, hedging and trading decisions, and substantially improve the quality of decision-making.
- Systems based on VaR methodologies can be used to measure other risks such as credit, liquidity and operational risks. This leads to a more integrated approach to the management of different kinds of risks, and to improved budget planning and better strategic management.
- This new approach enables firms to respond appropriately to regulations, particularly the capital adequacy regulations that financial institutions face. In particular, they can be used to tell institutions how to comply with such regulations whilst rearranging their portfolios to minimise the burden that such regulations impose on them.

2.2.3   Limitations of VaR as a Risk Measure

VaR also has its drawbacks as a risk measure. Some of these are fairly obvious — that VaR estimates can be subject to error, that VaR systems can be subject to model risk (i.e., the risk of errors arising from inappropriate assumptions on which models are based) or implementation risk (i.e., the risk of errors arising from the way in which systems are implemented). However, such problems are common to all risk measurement systems, and are not unique to VaR.

2.2.3.1   *VaR Uninformative of Tail Losses*

Yet VaR does have its own distinctive limitations. One of these is that VaR only tells us the most we can lose if a tail event does not occur — it tells us the most we can lose 95% of the time, or whatever — but tells us nothing about what we can lose in the remaining 5% of occasions. If a tail event (i.e., a loss in excess of VaR) does occur, we can expect to lose more than the VaR, but the VaR figure itself gives us no indication of how much that might be.

This can lead to some awkward consequences. A trader or asset manager might 'spike' his firm by entering into deals that produce small gains under most circumstances and the occasional very large loss. If the probability of loss is low enough, then this position would have a low VaR and so appear to have little risk, and yet the firm would now be exposed to the danger of a very large loss. A single VaR figure can also give a misleading impression of relative riskiness: we might have two positions with equal VaRs at some given confidence level and holding period, and yet one position might involve much heavier tail losses than the other. The VaR measure taken on its own would incorrectly suggest that both positions were equally risky.

Fortunately, we can sometimes ameliorate these problems by using more VaR information. For example, the trader who spikes his firm might be detected if the VaR of his position were also estimated at very high confidence levels. A solution to our earlier problems is, therefore, to look at the curve of VaR against confidence level, and not just to look at a single VaR figure — which is in effect to look at the VaR at only one point on its surface.

2.2.3.2   VaR Can Create Perverse Incentive Structures

But it is not always feasible to use information about VaRs at multiple confidence levels, and where it is not, the failure of VaR to take account of losses in excess of itself can create some perverse outcomes. For instance, a rational investor using a VaR risk measure can easily end up with perverse positions precisely because a VaR-based risk–return analysis fails to take account of the magnitude of losses in excess of VaR. If a particular investment has a higher expected return at the expense of the possibility of a higher loss, a VaR-based decision calculus will suggest that we should make that investment if the higher loss does not affect (i.e., and therefore exceeds) the VaR, regardless of the size of the higher expected return and regardless of the size of the higher possible loss. Such a categorical acceptance of any investment that increases expected return — regardless of the possible loss, provided only that it is insufficiently probable — makes a mockery of risk–return analysis, and the investor who makes decisions in this way is asking for trouble.[9] Admittedly, this example is rather extreme, because the VaR itself will often rise with the expected return, but the key point is that we cannot expect a VaR-based rule to give us good risk–return decisions except in particular circumstances (i.e., to be precise, unless risks are elliptically distributed or are rankable by first-order stochastic dominance, which is a very demanding and empirically unusual condition;[10] see, e.g., Yoshiba and Yamai (2001, pp. 16–17)).

If an investor working on his/her own behalf can easily end up with perverse positions, there is even more scope for mischief where decision-making is decentralised and traders or asset managers are working to VaR-constrained targets or VaR-defined remuneration packages. After all, traders or asset managers will only 'spike' their firm if they work to an incentive structure that encourages them to do so. If traders face a VaR-defined risk target, they will often have an incentive to sell out-of-the-money options to increase 'normal' profits and hence their bonus; the downside is that the institution takes a bigger hit once in a while, but it is difficult to design systems that force traders to care about these bigger hits: the fact that VaR does not take account of what happens in 'bad' states can distort incentives and encourage traders or managers to 'game' a VaR target (and/or a VaR-defined remuneration package), and promote their own interests at the expense of the interests of the institutions they are supposed to be serving.

---

[9]There is also a related problem. The VaR is not (in general) a convex function of risk factors, and this makes it difficult to program portfolio optimisation problems involving VaR: the optimisation problem has multiple local equilibria, and so forth (see, e.g., Mausser and Rosen (1998) or Yamai and Yoshiba (2001b, p. 15)).

[10]See note 1 above.

2.2.3.3 VaR Can Discourage Diversification

Another drawback is that VaR can discourage diversification, and a nice example of this effect is provided by Eber *et al.* (1999). Suppose there are 100 possible future states of the world, each with the same probability. There are 100 different assets, each earning reasonable money in 99 states, but suffering a big loss in one state. Each of these assets loses in a different state, so we are certain that one of them will suffer a large loss. If we invest in one of these assets only, then our VaR will be negative at, say, the 95% confidence level, because the probability of incurring a loss is 1%. However, if we diversify our investments and invest in all assets, then we are certain to incur a big loss. The VaR of the diversified portfolio is therefore much larger than the VaR of the undiversified one. So, a VaR measure can discourage diversification of risks because it fails to take into account the magnitude of losses in excess of VaR.

2.2.3.4 VaR Not Sub-additive

But there is also a deeper problem with VaR. In order to appreciate this problem, we need first to introduce the notion of sub-additivity. A risk measure $\rho(\cdot)$ is said to be sub-additive if the measured risk of the sum of positions A and B is less than or equal to the sum of the measured risks of the individual positions considered on their own, i.e.:

$$\rho(A + B) \leq \rho(A) + \rho(B) \tag{2.9}$$

Sub-additivity means that aggregating individual risks does not increase overall risk. Sub-additivity matters for a number of reasons:

- If risks are sub-additive, then adding risks together would give us an overestimate of combined risk, and this means that we can use the sum of risks as a conservative estimate of combined risk. This facilitates decentralised decision-making within a firm, because a supervisor can always use the sum of the risks of the units reporting to him as a conservative risk measure. But if risks are not sub-additive, adding them together gives us an underestimate of combined risks, and this makes the sum of risks effectively useless as a risk measure. In risk management, we want our risk estimates to be unbiased or biased conservatively.
- If regulators use non-sub-additive risk measures to set capital requirements, a financial firm might be tempted to break itself up to reduce its regulatory capital requirements, because the sum of the capital requirements of the smaller units would be less than the capital requirement of the firm as a whole.
- Non-sub-additive risk measures can also tempt agents trading on an organised exchange to break up their accounts, with separate accounts for separate risks, in order to reduce their margin requirements. This could be a matter of serious concern for the exchange because the margin requirements on the separate accounts would no longer cover the combined risks.

Sub-additivity is thus a highly desirable property for any risk measure. Unfortunately, VaR is not generally sub-additive, and can only be made to be sub-additive if we impose the (usually) implausible assumption that P/L (or returns) are normally (or slightly more generally, elliptically) distributed (Artzner et al. (1999, p. 217)).

A good counter-example that demonstrates the non-sub-additivity of VaR is a portfolio consisting of two short positions in very-out-of-the-money binary options. Suppose each of our binary options has a 4% probability of a payout (to us) of −$100, and a 96% probability of a payout of zero. The underlying variables (on which the payouts depend) are independently distributed, so the payout on

Table 2.1   Non-sub-additive VaR

<table>
<tr><td colspan="4" align="center">(a) Option Positions Considered Separately</td></tr>
<tr><td colspan="2" align="center">Position A</td><td colspan="2" align="center">Position B</td></tr>
<tr><td align="center">Payout</td><td align="center">Probability</td><td align="center">Payout</td><td align="center">Probability</td></tr>
<tr><td align="center">−100</td><td align="center">0.04</td><td align="center">−100</td><td align="center">0.04</td></tr>
<tr><td align="center">0</td><td align="center">0.96</td><td align="center">0</td><td align="center">0.96</td></tr>
<tr><td align="center">VaR at 95% cl</td><td align="center">0</td><td align="center">VaR at 95% cl</td><td align="center">0</td></tr>
</table>

<table>
<tr><td colspan="2" align="center">(b) Option Positions Combined</td></tr>
<tr><td align="center">Payout</td><td align="center">Probability</td></tr>
<tr><td align="center">−200</td><td align="center">$0.04^2 = 0.0016$</td></tr>
<tr><td align="center">−100</td><td align="center">$2(0.04)0.96 = 0.0768$</td></tr>
<tr><td align="center">0</td><td align="center">$0.96^2 = 0.9216$</td></tr>
<tr><td align="center">VaR at 95% cl</td><td align="center">100</td></tr>
</table>

one binary option is independent of the payout on the other. If we take the VaR confidence level to be 95% and the holding period to be equal to the period until the options expire, then each of our positions has a VaR of 0 at the 95% level. If we combine the two positions, however, the probability of a zero payout falls to less than 95% and the VaR is positive (and, in this case, equal to $100). The VaR of the combined position is therefore greater than the sum of the VaRs of the individual positions; and the VaR is not sub-additive (Table 2.1).

2.3 EXPECTED TAIL LOSS

2.3.1 Coherent Risk Measures

At this point, it is a good idea to step back and reconsider what we expect of our risk measures. At the very least, we surely want risk measures that correctly reflect diversification effects and facilitate decentralised decision-making by satisfying the sub-additivity condition. But how do we find such measures?

The answer is to be found in the theory of coherent risk measures developed by Artzner *et al.* (1997, 1999). If X and Y are the future values of two risky positions, a risk measure $\rho(\cdot)$ is said to be coherent if it satisfies the following properties:

$$\rho(X) + \rho(Y) \leq \rho(X + Y) \quad \text{(sub-additivity)} \tag{2.10a}$$

$$\rho(tX) = t\rho(X) \quad \text{(homogeneity)} \tag{2.10b}$$

$$\rho(X) \geq \rho(Y), \text{if } X \leq Y \quad \text{(monotonicity)} \tag{2.10c}$$

$$\rho(X + n) = \rho(X) - n \quad \text{(risk-free condition)} \tag{2.10d}$$

for any number n and positive number t. The first condition is the sub-additivity condition already covered. The second and third are reasonable conditions to impose a priori, and together imply that the function $\rho(\cdot)$ is convex. The last condition means that the addition of a sure amount n to our position will decrease our risk by the same amount, because it will increase the value of our end-of-period portfolio.

Artzner *et al.* go on to prove that any coherent risk measure can be regarded as the maximum expected loss on a set of 'generalised scenarios', where a generalised scenario is a set of loss values and their associated probabilities (Artzner *et al.* (1999, p. 219)). This is a very powerful result with far-reaching implications. Suppose that we assume the P/L follows a particular distribution function (e.g., a normal distribution). Given this distribution, we can produce a set of possible loss values, each of whose probability obeys the assumed distribution. This set of loss values constitutes a distinct scenario, and we can define a risk measure — the expected tail loss (ETL) — given by the expected value of these losses. This ETL can also be regarded as the coherent risk measure associated with a single distribution function. Now suppose that we do the same again with another distribution function, leading to an alternative ETL. The maximum of the two ETLs is itself a coherent risk measure. And so forth: if we have a set of comparable ETLs, each of which corresponds to a different distribution function for P/L, then the maximum of these ETLs is also a coherent risk measure.

Another coherent risk measure is the highest loss, or the highest loss among a subset of considered scenarios. Moreover, because coherent risk measures involve scenarios, we can also regard the outcomes of stress tests as coherent risk measures as well. The theory of coherent risk measures therefore provides a theoretical justification for stress testing!

In short, the highest loss from a set of possible outcomes, the expected tail loss, the highest ETL from a set of comparable ETLs based on different distribution functions, and loss estimates from scenario analyses are all coherent risk measures — and the VaR, of course, is not coherent.

2.3.2   The Expected Tail Loss

The ETL is perhaps the most attractive coherent risk measure.[11] This measure often goes by different names in the literature — including expected shortfall, conditional VaR,[12] tail VaR, tail conditional expectation, and worst conditional expectation, all of which are much the same[13] — but the basic concept itself is very simple.[14] The ETL is the expected value of our losses, L, if we get a loss in excess of VaR:

$$ETL = E[L \mid L > VaR] \tag{2.11}$$

---

[11] A brief heuristic proof of the coherence of ETL is suggested by Eber *et al.* (1999). Imagine a very simple world with 100 equiprobable states tomorrow, a list X of 100 possible numbers, and a confidence level of 95%. The ETL is minus the average of the five smallest numbers. Now consider choosing five states from the 100 available, and for each such choice assign 0.20 to each state, and 0 to every other state: this defines a probability p or generalised scenario on the state space. We now consider all such choices of five states from the 100 available, and this gives us a set P of probabilities. Next, note that searching for the average of the five biggest numbers is the same as searching for the biggest number of all averages of five possible numbers. This establishes that the ETL can be represented as the biggest value from a given set of scenarios, and application of Artzner *et al*'s representation theorem (proposition 4.1 in Artzner *et al.* (1999, p. 219)) then establishes that the ETL is coherent.

[12] As if the ETL (or whatever we call it) didn't have enough names, one of its names sometimes means something quite different. The term 'conditional VaR' can also mean VaR itself conditional on something else, such as a set of exogenous variables (e.g., as in the conditional autoregressive VaR or CAViaR of Engle and Manganelli (1999)). When meeting this term, we must make certain from the context what it actually refers to. Naturally, this ambiguity disappears if we have conditional conditional VaR — or conditional ETL, for those who have no sense of humour.

[13] There are some subtle variations in precise definitions, but I prefer to avoid these complications here. These different definitions and their implications are discussed further in Acerbi and Tasche (2001a).

[14] The ETL risk measure has also been familiar to insurance practitioners for a long time: it is very similar to the measures of conditional average claim size that have long been used by casualty insurers. Insurers are also very familiar with the notion of the conditional coverage of a loss in excess of a threshold (e.g., in the context of reinsurance treaties). For more on ETL and its precursors, see Artzner *et al.* (1999, pp. 223–224).

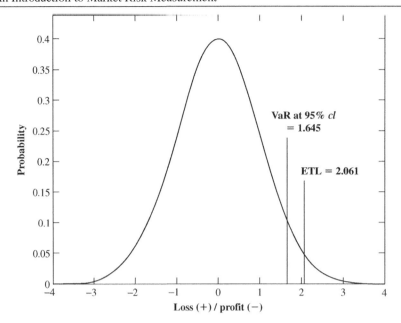

Figure 2.10 Expected tail loss.

Note: Produced using the 'normaletlfigure' function.

The VaR tells us the most we can expect to lose if a bad (i.e., tail) event does *not* occur, and the ETL tell us what we can expect to lose if a tail event *does* occur.[15]

An illustrative ETL is shown in Figure 2.10. If we express our data in loss/profit terms (i.e., we multiply P/L by minus 1, to make the loss terms positive), the VaR and ETL are shown on the right-hand side of the figure: the VaR is 1.645 and the ETL is (about) 2.061. Both VaR and ETL obviously depend on the underlying parameters and distributional assumptions, and these particular figures are based on a 95% confidence level and 1-day holding period, and on the assumption that daily P/L is distributed as standard normal (i.e., with mean 0 and standard deviation 1).

Since the ETL is conditional on the same parameters as the VaR itself, it is immediately obvious that any given ETL figure is only a point on an ETL curve or ETL surface. The ETL/confidence level curve is shown in Figure 2.11. This curve is similar to the earlier VaR curve shown in Figure 2.7 and, like it, tends to rise with the confidence level. There is also an ETL/holding period curve corresponding to the VaR/holding period curve shown in Figure 2.8.

There is also an ETL surface, illustrated in Figure 2.12, which shows how ETL changes as both confidence level and holding period change. In this case, as with its VaR equivalent in Figure 2.9, the surface rises with both confidence level and holding period, and spikes as both parameters approach their maximum values.

In short, the ETL has many of the same attractions as the VaR: it provides a common consistent risk measure across different positions, it takes account of correlations in a correct way, and it has many of the same uses as VaR. However, the ETL is also a better risk measure than the VaR for at least five different reasons:

---

[15]For those who want one, a thorough comparison of VaR and ETL is given in Pflug (2000).

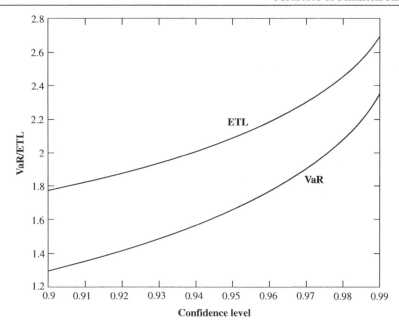

Figure 2.11   ETL and the confidence level.

Note: Produced using the 'normalvaretlplot2D_cl' function.

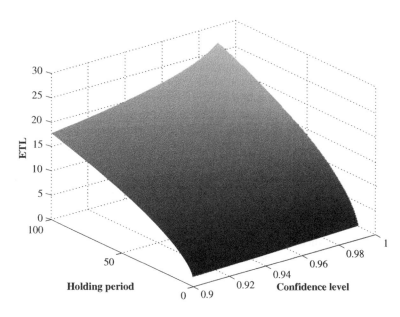

Figure 2.12   The ETL surface.

Note: Produced using the 'normaletlplot3D' function.

- The ETL tells us what to expect in bad (i.e., tail) states — it gives an idea of how bad bad might be — whilst the VaR tells us nothing other than to expect a loss higher than the VaR itself.
- An ETL-based risk–expected return decision rule is reliable under more general conditions than a VaR-based risk–expected return decision rule: in particular, the ETL-based rule is consistent with expected utility maximisation if risks are rankable by a second-order stochastic dominance rule, whilst a VaR-based rule is only consistent with expected utility maximisation if risks are rankable by a (much) more stringent first-order stochastic dominance rule (see Yoshiba and Yamai (2001, pp. 21–22)).[16]
- Because it is coherent, the ETL always satisfies sub-additivity, whilst the VaR does not. The ETL therefore has the various attractions of sub-additivity, and the VaR does not.
- The ETL does not discourage risk diversification, and the VaR sometimes does.
- Finally, the sub-additivity of ETL implies that the portfolio risk surface will be convex, and convexity ensures that portfolio optimisation problems using ETL measures, unlike ones that use VaR measures, will always have a unique well-behaved optimum (see, e.g., Uryasev (2000, p. 1), Pflug (2000), Acerbi and Tasche (2001b, p. 3)). In addition, as Rockafeller and Uryasev (2000) and Uryasev (2000) demonstrate, this convexity ensures that portfolio optimisation problems with ETL risk measures can be handled very efficiently using linear programming techniques.[17]

The ETL thus dominates the VaR as a risk measure, and users of VaR would be well advised, where practicable, to use ETL measures instead.

Box 2.4   Other Coherent Risk Measures

There are other coherent risk measures besides the ETL. One of these is the outcome of a worst-case scenario analysis (Boudoukh *et al.* (1995), Bahar *et al.* (1997)). We would normally carry out this analysis using a simulation method: if we take a confidence level of, say, 99%, we would run a simulation trial of 100 drawings from our chosen P/L distribution, and pick the minimum value; we then run M such trials to obtain a set of M comparable minimum values, change the sign on these to make losses positive, and so obtain a simulated distribution of worst-case losses. Our risk measure would then typically be a prespecified high quantile of this distribution (e.g., the quantile associated with the 95% confidence level, which cuts off the top 5% of worst-case losses from the bottom 95% of such losses). Alternatively, our risk measure might be the mean of this distribution, in which case our risk measure is the expected worst-case scenario, which is equivalent to the ETL. Leaving this special case aside, a worst-case scenario analysis based on a high quantile will produce a risk measure that exceeds the ETL, which in turn of course exceeds the VaR — and this risk measure is coherent.

Another coherent risk measure is provided by the Chicago Mercantile Exchange's Standard Portfolio Analysis of Risk (SPAN) methodology, which is used to derive the margin requirements for positions in the interest-rate futures market (see, e.g., Artzner *et al.* (1999, p. 212)). The system considers 14 scenarios where volatility can go up or down, and where the futures price can remain the same or take one of three possible upward or downward movements. In addition,

---

[16]See also note 2 above.

[17]One might also add that there is some evidence that ETL might be less prone to sampling error than VaR, so estimates of ETL might be more accurate than estimates of VaR (Mausser and Rosen (2000, p. 218)).

it also considers two extreme upwards or downwards movements of the futures price. The prices of securities in each scenario are then generated by an appropriate model (e.g., the Black model) and the measure of risk is the maximum loss incurred, using the full loss for the first 14 scenarios, and 35% of the loss for the last two extreme scenarios. This risk measure can be interpreted as the maximum of the expected loss under each of 16 different probability measures, and is therefore a coherent risk measure.

2.4 CONCLUSIONS

Work on risk measurement over the last decade has focused on the notion of VaR, and the VaR framework provides an approach to risk measurement that goes beyond earlier approaches in a number of important respects: in particular, we can apply a VaR approach using any P/L or return distribution. However, VaR also has serious limitations, and those who continue to use VaR should take account of these.

The VaR also faces a superior rival. Unlike the VaR, the ETL satisfies the conditions for a coherent risk measure, and coherent risk measures have a number of attractive features. Unless the ETL is significantly more difficult to estimate — which, to anticipate later chapters, will rarely if ever be the case — we must conclude that the ETL dominates the VaR, and users of VaR would be well advised to switch over.

2.5 RECOMMENDED READING

Artzner *et al.* (1997, 1999); Bahar *et al.* (1997); Boudoukh *et al.* (1995); Danielsson (2001); Danielsson *et al.* (2001); Duffie and Pan (1997); Linsmeier and Pearson (1996); Pflug (2000); Schachter (1997); Yoshiba and Yamai (2001).

3

Basic Issues in Measuring Market Risk

This chapter looks at some basic issues involved in measuring market risk. Our main concerns are:

- Preliminary data issues — dealing with data in profit/loss form, rate-of-return form, etc.
- How to estimate VaR, and how VaR estimation depends on assumptions about data and data distributions.
- How to estimate ETL.

We begin with the data issues.

3.1 DATA

3.1.1 Profit/Loss Data

Our data can come in various forms. Perhaps the simplest is in terms of profit/loss (or P/L). The P/L generated by an asset (or portfolio) over the period t, P/L_t, can be defined as the value of the asset (or portfolio) at the end of t plus any interim payments D_t minus the asset value at the end of $t - 1$:

$$P/L_t = P_t + D_t - P_{t-1} \tag{3.1}$$

If data are in P/L form, positive values indicate profits and negative values indicate losses.

If we wish to be strictly correct, we should evaluate all payments from the same point of time (i.e., we should take account of the time value of money), and we can do so in one of two ways. The first is to take the present value of P/L_t evaluated at the end of the previous period, $t - 1$:

$$\text{Present value } (P/L_t) = (P_t + D_t)/(1 + d) - P_{t-1} \tag{3.2}$$

where d is the discount rate and we assume for convenience that D_t is paid at the end of t. The alternative is to take the forward value of P/L_t evaluated at the end of period t:

$$\text{Forward value } (P/L_t) = P_t + D_t - (1 + d)P_{t-1} \tag{3.3}$$

which involves compounding P_{t-1} by d. The differences between these measures depend on the discount rate d, and will be small if the periods themselves are short. We will ignore these differences to simplify the discussion, but the reader should keep in mind that they do sometimes matter.

3.1.2 Loss/Profit Data

When estimating VaR and ETL, it is sometimes more convenient to deal with data in loss/profit (or L/P) form. L/P data are a simple transformation of P/L data:

$$L/P_t = -P/L_t \tag{3.4}$$

L/P data are thus equivalent to P/L data, except for changing signs: they assign a positive value to losses and a negative value to profits. L/P data are sometimes more convenient for VaR and ETL purposes because the VaR and ETL are themselves denominated in units of L/P.

3.1.3 Arithmetic Returns Data

Data can also come in the form of arithmetic returns. The arithmetic return is defined as:

$$r_t = (P_t + D_t - P_{t-1})/P_{t-1} \tag{3.5}$$

which is the same as the P/L over period t divided by the value of the asset at the end of $t - 1$.

In using arithmetic returns, we implicitly assume that the interim payment D_t does not earn any return of its own. However, this assumption will seldom be appropriate over long periods because interim income is usually reinvested. Hence, arithmetic returns are best used when we are concerned with relatively short horizon periods.

3.1.4 Geometric Returns Data

Returns can also be expressed in geometric form. The geometric return is:

$$R_t = \log[(P_t + D_t)/P_{t-1}] \tag{3.6}$$

The geometric return implicitly assumes that interim payments are continuously made and reinvested. The relationship of the two types of return can be seen by rewriting Equation (3.6) as:

$$R_t = \log[(P_t + D_t)/P_{t-1}] = \log(1 + r_t) \tag{3.7}$$

from which we can see that $R_t \approx r_t$ provided that returns are 'small'.

Which return should we use? One answer is that the difference between the two will be negligible provided returns are small, and returns will be small if we are dealing with a short horizon period. In those circumstances, we should use whichever return is more convenient. However, we should also bear in mind that the geometric return has certain advantages over the arithmetic return:

- It is more meaningful economically, because it ensures that the asset price (or portfolio value) is never negative even if the returns themselves are unbounded. With arithmetic returns, a low realised return — or a high loss — implies that the asset value P_t is negative, and a negative asset price seldom makes economic sense; on the other hand, a very low geometric return implies that the asset price P_t falls towards zero but is still positive.
- The geometric return makes more sense over long horizon periods because it allows for interim income to earn returns, whilst the arithmetic return implicitly assumes that interim income earns a zero return. Over long horizons, the returns on interim income will be important because of compounding, so we should use geometric rather than arithmetic returns when dealing with long horizon periods.

3.2 ESTIMATING HISTORICAL SIMULATION VAR

The simplest way to estimate VaR is by means of historical simulation (HS), which estimates VaR by means of ordered L/P observations.

Suppose we have 100 L/P observations and are interested in the VaR at the 95% confidence level. Since the confidence level implies a 5% tail, we know that there are five observations in the tail, and we can take the VaR to be the sixth highest L/P observation.

Assuming that our data are in L/P form, we can therefore estimate the VaR on a spreadsheet by ordering our data and reading off the sixth largest observation from the spreadsheet. We can also

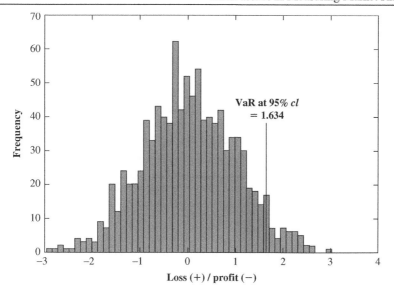

Figure 3.1 Historical simulation VaR.

Note: Based on 1,000 random numbers drawn from a standard normal L/P distribution, and estimated with the 'hsvarfigure' function.

estimate it more directly by using the 'Large' command in Excel, which gives us the kth largest value in an array. Thus, if our data are an array called 'Loss_data', our VaR is given by the Excel command 'Large(Loss_data,6)'. If we are using MATLAB, we first order the L/P data using the 'Sort()' command (i.e., by typing 'Loss_data=Sort(Loss_data)') and then derive the VaR by typing in 'Loss_data(6)' at the command line.

More generally, if we have n observations, and our confidence level is cl, we would want the $(1 - cl) n + 1$ highest observation, and we would use the commands 'Large(Loss_data, $(1 - cl)*n + 1$)' using Excel, or 'Loss_data($(1 - cl)*n + 1$)' using MATLAB, provided in the latter case that our 'Loss_data' array is already sorted into ordered observations.

An example of an HS VaR is given in Figure 3.1. This figure shows the histogram of 1,000 hypothetical L/P observations, and the VaR at the 95% confidence level. The figure is generated using the 'hsvarfigure' command in the IMRM Toolbox. The VaR is 1.634 and separates the top 5% from the bottom 95% of observations.

3.3 ESTIMATING PARAMETRIC VaR

We can also estimate VaR using parametric approaches, the distinguishing feature of which is that they require us to specify explicitly the statistical distribution from which our data observations are drawn. We can think of parametric approaches as fitting curves through the data and then reading off the VaR from the fitted curve.

In making use of a parametric approach, we therefore need to take account of both the statistical distribution and the type of data to which it applies. We now discuss some of the more important cases that we might encounter in practice.

3.3.1   Estimating VaR with Normally Distributed Profits/Losses

If we are using P/L data to estimate VaR under the assumption that P/L is normally distributed, our VaR is:

$$VaR = -\alpha_{cl}\sigma_{P/L} - \mu_{P/L} \tag{3.8}$$

where $\mu_{P/L}$ and $\sigma_{P/L}$ are the mean and standard deviation of P/L, and α_{cl} is the standard normal variate corresponding to our chosen confidence level. Thus, if we have a confidence level cl, we define α_{cl} as that value of the standard normal variate such that $1 - cl$ of the probability density lies to the left, and cl of the probability density lies to the right. For example, if our confidence level is 95%, our value of α_{cl} will be -1.645.[1]

In practice, $\mu_{P/L}$ and $\sigma_{P/L}$ would be unknown, and we would have to estimate VaR based on estimates of these parameters. Our VaR estimate would then be:

$$VaR^e = -\alpha_{cl}s_{P/L} - m_{P/L} \tag{3.9}$$

where $m_{P/L}$ and $s_{P/L}$ are estimates of the mean and standard deviation of P/L.

Figure 3.2 shows the VaR at the 95% confidence level for a normally distributed P/L with mean 0 and standard deviation 1. Since the data are in P/L form, the VaR is indicated by the negative of the cut-off point between the lower 5% and the upper 95% of P/L observations. The actual VaR is the negative of -1.645, and is therefore 1.645.

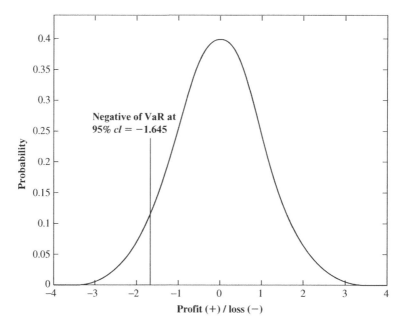

Figure 3.2   VaR with normally distributed profit/loss data.

Note: Obtained from Equation (3.9) with $\mu_{P/L} = 0$ and $\sigma_{P/L} = 1$. Estimated with the 'normalvarfigure' function.

---

[1]There is also an interesting special case: the VaR is proportional to the standard deviation of P/L whenever the mean P/L is zero and the P/L is elliptically distributed. However, it would be unwise to get into a habit of identifying the standard deviation and the VaR too closely, because these conditions will often not be met.

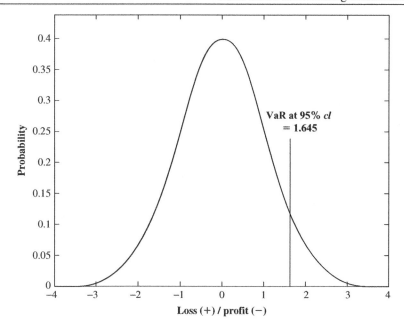

Figure 3.3 VaR with normally distributed loss/profit data.
Note: Obtained from Equation (3.10a) with $\mu_{L/P} = 0$ and $\sigma_{L/P} = 1$.

If we are working with normally distributed L/P data, then $\mu_{L/P} = -\mu_{P/L}$ and $\sigma_{L/P} = \sigma_{P/L}$, and it immediately follows that:

$$VaR = -\alpha_{cl}\sigma_{L/P} + \mu_{L/P} \qquad (3.10a)$$
$$VaR^e = -\alpha_{cl}s_{L/P} + m_{L/P} \qquad (3.10b)$$

Figure 3.3 illustrates the corresponding VaR. In this case, the VaR is given by the cut-off point between the upper 5% and the lower 95% of L/P observations. The VaR is again 1.645, as we would (hopefully) expect.

This figure also shows why it is sometimes more convenient to work with L/P rather than P/L data when estimating VaR: with L/P data the VaR is immediately apparent, whereas with P/L data the VaR is shown as the negative of a (usually) negative quantile. The information given is the same in both cases, but is more obvious in Figure 3.3.

3.3.2 Estimating VaR with Normally Distributed Arithmetic Returns

We can also estimate VaR making assumptions about returns rather than P/L. Suppose then that we assume arithmetic returns are normally distributed with mean μ_r and standard deviation σ_r. To derive the VaR, we begin by obtaining the critical value of r_t, r^*, such that the probability that r_t exceeds r^* is equal to our chosen confidence level. r^* is therefore:

$$r^* = \mu_r + \alpha_{cl}\sigma_r \qquad (3.11)$$

We know that the return r_t is related to the negative of the loss/profit divided by the earlier asset value, P_{t-1}:

$$r_t = (P_t - P_{t-1})/P_{t-1} = -Loss_t/P_{t-1} \qquad (3.12)$$

This gives us the relationship between r^*, the critical value of P_t, P^*, corresponding to a loss equal to VaR, and the VaR itself:

$$r_t^* = (P_t^* - P_{t-1})/P_{t-1} = -VaR/P_{t-1} \qquad (3.13)$$

Substituting Equation (3.11) into Equation (3.13) and rearranging then gives us the VaR:

$$VaR = -(\mu_r + \alpha_{cl}\sigma_r)P_{t-1} \qquad (3.14)$$

Equation (3.14) will give us equivalent answers to our earlier VaR equations. For example, if we set $cl = 0.95$, $\mu_r = 0$, $\sigma_r = 1$ and $P_{t-1} = 1$, which correspond to our earlier illustrative P/L and L/P parameter assumptions, our VaR is 1.645: these three approaches give the same results, because all three sets of underlying assumptions are equivalent.

3.3.3 Estimating Lognormal VaR

Unfortunately, each of these approaches also assigns a positive probability of the asset value, P_t, becoming negative. We can avoid this drawback by working with geometric returns rather than arithmetic returns. As noted already, the geometric return is:

$$R_t = \log[(P_t + D_t)/P_{t-1}]$$

Now assume that geometric returns are normally distributed with mean μ_R and standard deviation σ_R. If we assume that D_t is zero or reinvested continually in the asset itself (e.g., as with profits reinvested in a mutual fund), this assumption implies that the natural logarithm of P_t is normally distributed, or that P_t itself is lognormally distributed. A lognormal asset price is shown in Figure 3.4: observe that the price is always non-negative, and its distribution is skewed with a long right-hand tail.

If we now proceed as we did earlier with the arithmetic return, we begin by deriving the critical value of R, R^*, that is the direct analogue of r^*, i.e.:

$$R^* = \mu_R + \alpha_{cl}\sigma_R \qquad (3.15)$$

We then use the definition of the geometric return to unravel the critical value P^* (i.e., the value of P_t corresponding to a loss equal to our VaR), and thence infer our VaR:

$$R^* = \log P^* - \log P_{t-1} \Rightarrow \log P^* = R^* + \log P_{t-1}$$
$$\Rightarrow P^* = \exp[R^* + \log P_{t-1}] = \exp[\mu_R + \alpha_{cl}\sigma_R + \log P_{t-1}]$$
$$\Rightarrow VaR = P_{t-1} - P^* = P_{t-1} - \exp[\mu_R + \alpha_{cl}\sigma_R + \log P_{t-1}] \qquad (3.16)$$

This gives us the lognormal VaR, which is consistent with normally distributed geometric returns. The formula for lognormal VaR is more complex than the earlier VaR equations, but the lognormal VaR has the attraction over the others of ruling out the possibility of negative asset (or portfolio) values.

The lognormal VaR is illustrated in Figure 3.5, based on the hypothetical assumptions that $\mu_R = 0$, $\sigma_R = 1$, and $P_{t-1} = 1$. In this case, the VaR at the 95% confidence level is 0.807. The figure also

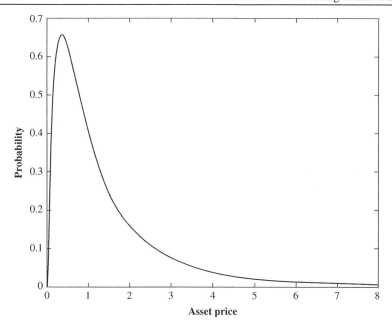

Figure 3.4   A lognormally distributed asset price.

Note: Estimated with mean and standard deviation equal to 0 and 1 respectively, using the 'lognpdf' function in the Statistics Toolbox.

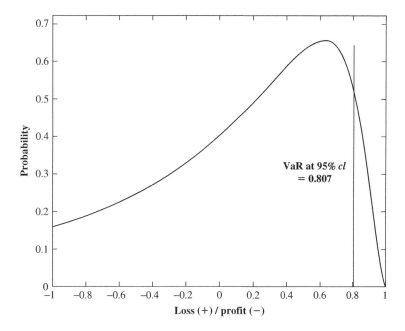

Figure 3.5   Lognormal VaR.

Note: Estimated assuming the mean and standard deviation of geometric returns are 0 and 1, and for an initial investment of 1. The figure is produced using the 'lognormalvarfigure'.

shows that the distribution of L/P is the mirror image of the distribution of P/L, which is in turn a reflection of the distribution of P_t shown earlier in Figure 3.4.

It is also worth stressing that lognormal VaR can never exceed P_{t-1} because the L/P is bounded above by P_{t-1}, and (as we have seen) this is a generally desirable property because it ensures that we cannot lose more than we invest.

3.4   ESTIMATING EXPECTED TAIL LOSS

We turn now to ETL estimation. The ETL is the probability-weighted average of tail losses, or losses exceeding VaR, and a normal ETL is illustrated in Figure 3.6. In this particular case, the ETL is (about) 2.061, corresponding to our earlier normal VaR of 1.645.

The fact that the ETL is a probability-weighted average of tail losses suggests that we can estimate ETL as an average of tail VaRs.[2] The easiest way to implement this approach is to slice the tail into a large number n of slices, each of which has the same probability mass, estimate the VaR associated with each slice, and take the ETL as the average of these VaRs.

To illustrate this method, suppose we wish to estimate an ETL at the 95% confidence level, on the assumption that P/L is normally distributed with mean 0 and standard deviation 1. In practice,

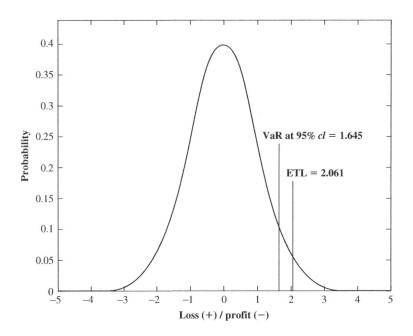

Figure 3.6   Normal VaR and ETL.

Note: Estimated with the mean and standard deviation of P/L equal to 0 and 1 respectively, using the 'normaletlfigure' function. Note that the 'normaletlfigure' gives an ETL estimate of 2.061 instead of the 'true' figure of 2.062 because of discretisation error (i.e., more precisely, because it divides the tail into 'only' 1,000 equal-probability slices).

---

[2]The obvious alternative is to seek a 'closed-form' solution, which we could use to estimate the ETL, but easy ETL formulas only exist for a small number of parametric distributions, and the 'average tail VaR' method is very easy to implement and can be applied to any ETLs we might encounter, parametric or otherwise.

Table 3.1 Estimating ETL as a weighted average of tail VaRs

Tail VaRs	Tail VaR values
VaR at 95.5% *cl*	1.6954
VaR at 96.0% *cl*	1.7507
VaR at 96.5% *cl*	1.8119
VaR at 97.0% *cl*	1.8808
VaR at 97.5% *cl*	1.9600
VaR at 98.0% *cl*	2.0537
VaR at 98.5% *cl*	2.1701
VaR at 99.0% *cl*	2.3263
VaR at 99.5% *cl*	2.5758
Average of tail VaRs	**1.9870**

Note: VaRs estimated assuming the mean and standard deviation of P/L are 0 and 1, using the 'normalvar' function.

Table 3.2 ETL estimates as a function of the number of tail slices

Number of tail slices	ETL
$n = 10$	1.9870
$n = 25$	2.0273
$n = 50$	2.0432
$n = 100$	2.0521
$n = 250$	2.0580
$n = 500$	2.0602
$n = 1,000$	2.0614
$n = 2,500$	2.0621
$n = 5,000$	2.0624

Note: VaRs estimated assuming the mean and standard deviation of P/L are 0 and 1.

we would use a high value of n and carry out the calculations on a spreadsheet or using appropriate software. However, to illustrate the procedure manually, let us work with a value of $n = 10$. This value gives us nine (i.e., $n - 1$) tail VaRs, or VaRs at confidence levels in excess of 95%. These VaRs are shown in Table 3.1, and vary from 1.6954 (for VaR at a confidence level of 95.5%) to 2.5758 (for VaR at a confidence level of 99.5%). Our estimated ETL is the average of these VaRs, which is 1.9870.

In using this method for practical purposes, we should of course use a value of n large enough to give accurate results. To give some idea of what this might be, Table 3.2 reports some alternative ETL estimates obtained using this procedure with varying values of n. These results show that the estimated ETL rises with n, and gradually converges to a value in the region of 2.062. If we take the latter to be the 'true' ETL value, our results also show that the estimated ETL is within 1% of this value when n reaches 50, so our ETL estimation procedure seems to be reasonably accurate even for quite small values of n. Any decent computer should therefore be able produce fairly accurate ETL estimates quickly in real time.

3.5 SUMMARY

It is important to pay attention to data issues and be clear about the implications of what we assume about our data. Assumptions about the distribution of our data have a critical bearing on how we should estimate our VaRs. To illustrate this, we looked at four different cases each corresponding to a different set of assumptions — namely, VaR for normally distributed profit/loss, VaR for normally distributed loss/profit, VaR for normally distributed arithmetic returns, and lognormal VaR. Naturally, there are many other possible cases, but these are some of the more important ones and give an indication of the main issues involved.

In estimating ETLs, we should keep in mind that 'closed-form' solutions for ETL are often lacking. However, we can always estimate the ETL as an average of tail VaRs, so estimation of ETL is easy once we know how to estimate our VaRs.

Appendix

Mapping Positions to Risk Factors

Portfolio returns (or P/L) are derived from the returns (or P/L) to individual positions, and we have taken for granted up to now that we are able to model the latter directly: that each position i has a return r_i, and we can model the process that generates r_i. However, it is not always possible or even desirable that we model each and every asset return in this direct manner. To appreciate the issues involved we must distinguish between individual positions and individual risk factors: our positions are particular investments or instruments; but our risk factors are the stochastic (i.e., risky) variables that determine our returns. So far, we have implicitly assumed that each position had its 'own' unique corresponding risk factor, and could be 'projected' onto it. Unfortunately, this is often not feasible or desirable in practice. Instead, we will often project our positions, not onto 'their' own individualised risk factors, but onto some set of benchmark risk factors: we will project our n individual instruments onto some (typically) smaller number, m, of risk factors. This requires that we describe our positions in terms that relate to those risk factors, as approximate combinations of standard building blocks. This process of describing our 'real' positions in terms of these standard building blocks is known as mapping.

There are three main reasons why we might want to engage in mapping. The first and most important is to cut down on the dimensionality of our covariance matrices. If we have n different instruments in our portfolio, we would need data on n separate volatilities, one for each instrument, plus data on $n(n-1)/2$ correlations — a total altogether of $n(n+1)/2$ pieces of information. As new instruments are added to our portfolio, the additional amount of correlation data needed therefore grows geometrically. As n gets large, the amount of data needed becomes enormous, and it becomes increasingly difficult to collect and process the data involved. For practical purposes, there is obviously a limit on the size of covariance matrix we can handle. In any case, as explained elsewhere, we would not normally want to work with very high dimension matrices, even if we had all the data: we need to keep the dimensionality of our covariance down to reasonable levels if we are not to run into serious computational problems (see Box T7.3).

The second reason is closely related to the first: if we try to handle risk factors that are closely correlated (or worse, perfectly correlated), there is a danger (or, in the case of perfect correlation, a certainty) of running into rank problems with the covariance matrix. Either our algorithms will not work or — if we are really unlucky — they will work but produce pathological estimates. If we are to avoid these problems, we have to ensure that our risk factors are not too closely related to each other, and this requires us to select an appropriate set of risk factors and map our instruments onto them.

The third reason is a very simple and obvious one: we might want to map our instruments because we do not have enough data. We might have an emerging market instrument that has a very short track record, and this means that we don't have enough 'direct' data on it; or we might have a new type of derivatives instrument that has no track record at all. In such circumstances we might map our instrument to some comparable instrument for which we do have sufficient data.

The process of mapping generally involves three stages. The first is to construct a set of benchmark instruments or factors and collect data on their volatilities and correlations. The benchmark instruments might include key bonds, equities, commodities, and so on. Having established a set of core instruments or factors and collected the necessary data, the next step is to derive synthetic substitutes for each instrument we hold, made up of positions in the core instruments. This synthetic substitution is the actual mapping. The final stage is to calculate VaR and/or ETL using the mapped instruments (i.e., the synthetic substitutes) instead of the actual instruments we hold. Put differently, we pretend that we are holding the synthetic portfolio composed only of core instruments, and we estimate its VaR or ETL, which we take to be an estimate of the 'true' VaR or ETL that we seek to estimate.

A3.1   SELECTING CORE INSTRUMENTS OR FACTORS

A3.1.1   Selecting Core Instruments

The usual approach in mapping is to select a set of core instruments — key money market and equity instruments, key currencies, etc. — that can be regarded as representative of the broad types of instruments actually held. The ideal is to have a rich enough set of core instruments to be able to provide good proxies for the instruments in our portfolio, whilst not having so many core instruments that we run into the high-dimensionality and related problems that we wish to avoid.[3]

The best-known approach — that used by RiskMetrics — uses the following set of core instruments:[4]

- Equity positions are represented by equivalent amounts in terms of equity indices in each of the core currencies.
- Fixed-income positions are represented by combinations of cash flows of a limited number of specified maturities in a given currency.[5]
- Foreign-exchange (FX) positions are represented by the relevant amounts in terms of a certain number of 'core' currencies, and FX forward positions are mapped as equivalent fixed-income positions in their respective currencies.
- Commodity positions are represented by amounts of selected standardised futures contracts traded on organised exchanges.

RiskMetrics uses a broad set of core instruments to be able to map a correspondingly broad range of different positions. However, most users of VaR and ETL have more specialised portfolios and would therefore work with some subset of the RiskMetrics core to reduce dimensionality problems and speed up calculations. If they wanted, they could also add new cores of their own (e.g., fixed-income instruments with new maturities, or sector-specific equity indices).

---

[3]A nice introduction to mapping is provided by Beder *et al.* (1998, pp. 291–296), who examine a variety of different mapping approaches and illustrate the strengths and weaknesses of each. They also show how the required sophistication of the VaR mapping methodology largely depends on the complexity of the portfolio being modelled, which means that we can't select a mapping methodology independently of the particular use to which it is to be put.

[4]The reader who wants further information on the RiskMetrics approach to mapping is referred to Phelan (1997) and to the RiskMetrics *Technical Document* (1996, ch. 6.2), which both contain extensive discussions of the RiskMetrics mapping system and the issues behind it.

[5]Positions are also differentiated by their credit standing, i.e., government (which is assumed to be free of default risk) and non-government (which is not). This categorisation obviously fails to do any real justice to credit risk, but we can always make more serious adjustments for credit risk if we wish to do so.

A3.1.2 Selecting Core Factors

An alternative is to select core factors, rather than core instruments, and map to those instead. These factors can be identified by principal components analysis (PCA), which is a quantitative procedure that identifies the independent sources of movement within a group of time series. These series in our case would be a set of prices or returns. Each principal component/factor is constructed to be independent of the others, so all have zero covariance with each other, and we will usually find that a small number of principal components is sufficient to explain a very large proportion of the movement in our price or return series. These procedures can therefore cut down drastically on the dimensionality of our system. Moreover, because the principal components are independent of each other, the only non-zero elements of the principal components variance–covariance matrix will be the volatilities, which cuts down even further on the number of parameters we would need.

PCA is generally suited to portfolios with a large number of different instruments that tend to be closely correlated with each other, reflecting the presence of common influences. Perhaps the best examples are portfolios of money market instruments and bonds, which typically show very high degrees of correlation with each other. These approaches offer enormous potential benefits in terms of parameter reduction. Thus, if we had, say, 50 different instruments in a bond portfolio and we were to work with those instruments directly (i.e., without mapping), we would need to handle a 50×50 covariance matrix with $50(51)/2 = 1,275$ separate volatility and correlation parameters. But if we used a principal components analysis, we could probably proxy the overwhelming proportion of bond price movements by three principal components, and the only variance–covariance parameters needed would be the volatilities of the three principal components. We would reduce the number of variance–covariance parameters needed from 1,275 to only 3! Once we have our principal components, each individual instrument can then be mapped as a linear combination of these components.

A3.2 MAPPING POSITIONS AND VaR ESTIMATION

We now consider how to map and estimate VaR for specific types of position. Naturally, there is a huge variety of different financial instruments, but the task of mapping them and estimating their VaRs can be simplified tremendously by recognising that most instruments can be decomposed into a small number of more basic, primitive instruments. Instead of trying to map and estimate VaR for each specific type of instrument, all we need to do is break down each instrument into its constituent building blocks — a process known as reverse engineering — to give us an equivalent portfolio of primitive instruments. We then map this portfolio of primitive instruments.

A3.2.1 The Basic Building Blocks

A3.2.1.1 Basic FX Positions

There are four types of basic building block, and the easiest of these are basic FX positions (e.g., holdings of non-interest-bearing foreign currency). FX positions are particularly simple to handle where the currencies involved (i.e., our own and the foreign currency) are included as core currencies in our mapping system.[6] We would then already have the exchange rate volatilities and correlations that we require for variance–covariance analysis. If the value of our position is x in foreign currency units and the exchange rate is E, the value of the position in domestic currency units — or the mapped position, if you like — is xE. Since there is no foreign interest rate being paid, x is constant, and so the only risk attaches to E.

We can then calculate the VaR (or ETL) in the usual way. For example, if the exchange rate is normally distributed with zero mean and standard deviation σ_E, then the VaR is:

$$VaR^{FX} = -\alpha_{cl}\sigma_E x E \tag{A3.1}$$

The VaR is minus the confidence level parameter (α_{cl}) times the standard deviation of the exchange rate (σ_E) times the size of the position in domestic currency units (xE).

A3.2.1.2   Basic Equity Positions

The second type of primitive position is equity, and handling equity positions is slightly more involved. Imagine we hold an amount x_A invested in the equity of firm A, but lack this particular firm's volatility and correlation data. However, we can reasonably suppose that the firm's return to equity, R_A, is related to the equity market return, R_m, by the following sort of equation:

$$R_A = \alpha_A + \beta_A R_m + \varepsilon_A \tag{A3.2}$$

where α_A is a firm-specific constant, β_A relates R_A to the market return R_m, and ε_A is a firm-specific random element. The variance of the firm's return is then:

$$\sigma_A^2 = \beta_A^2 \sigma_m^2 + \sigma_\varepsilon^2 \tag{A3.3}$$

where σ_A^2 is the variance of R_A, and so on. The variance of the firm's return therefore consists of a market-based component $\beta_A^2 \sigma_m^2$ and a firm-specific component σ_ε^2. Assuming zero-mean normality for the sake of argument, the VaR of the equity position is:

$$VaR_A = -\alpha_{cl}\sigma_A x_A = -\alpha_{cl} x_A \sqrt{\beta_A^2 \sigma_m^2 + \sigma_\varepsilon^2} \tag{A3.4}$$

Estimates of both σ_m^2 and β_A should be publicly available, so we can easily estimate $\beta_A^2 \sigma_m^2$. If we also have data on the firm-specific variance σ_ε^2, we can estimate Equation (A3.4) directly, and all is well and good.

But what do we do if we don't have information on σ_ε^2? The answer depends on how well diversified our portfolio is: if our portfolio is well diversified, the firm-specific risks will largely net out in the aggregate portfolio and we could estimate VaR as if σ_ε^2 were zero. Our VaR would then be:

$$VaR_A \approx -\alpha_{cl}\beta_A\sigma_m x_A \tag{A3.5}$$

In short, we map the equity risk to the market index, and use Equation (A3.5) to estimate the VaR of the mapped equity return. It is important to note that the only volatility information used is the market

---

[6]Where currencies are not included as core currencies, we need to proxy them by equivalents in terms of core currencies. Typically, non-core currencies would be either minor currencies (e.g., the Hungarian forint) or currencies that are closely tied to some other major currency (e.g., the Dutch guilder which was tied very closely to the German mark in its later years). Including closely related currencies as separate core instruments would lead to major collinearity problems: the variance–covariance matrix would fail to be positive-definite, etc. The mapping of non-core currencies to baskets is much the same in principle as the mapping of individual equities to equity indices as described in the next section. The reader who wants more specific material on mapping currencies is referred to Laubsch (1996).

volatility, and the only firm-specific information we need is the firm's market beta. This 'market beta' mapping allows us to approximate equity VaRs with very little firm-specific information.

The market beta approach also extends naturally to multi-asset equity portfolios, and enables us to estimate the VaR of such portfolios without needing to bother with covariance matrices. To illustrate the point, if we have a portfolio of two equities, A and B, and again assume that their expected returns are zero, the VaR of our mapped portfolio would be:

$$VaR = -\alpha_{cl}\beta_A\sigma_m x_A - \alpha_{cl}\beta_B\sigma_m x_B = -\alpha_{cl}\sigma_m(\beta_A x_A + \beta_B x_B) \tag{A3.6}$$

There is no covariance matrix because both equities are mapped to the same risk factor, namely, the market risk. This approach is highly convenient — to say the least — when dealing with equity portfolios.

The only real problem with this 'market beta' mapping procedure is that if we hold an undiversified portfolio, then the estimate of VaR given by Equation (A3.5) will understate the true VaR because it ignores the firm-specific risk. However, if we wish to do so, we can refine the VaR estimate by using an adjustment — explained in Box A3.1 — that takes account of the extent to which the portfolio is imperfectly diversified.

Box A3.1   Adjusting Equity VaRs for Firm-specific Risk

A drawback with the market beta approach to estimating equity VaRs is that it can underestimate VaR because it ignores firm-specific risk. One way to adjust for this bias is to multiply the beta-based VaR (i.e., $-\alpha_{cl}\beta_A\sigma_m x_A$) by an adjustment factor that reflects the degree to which the portfolio is *imperfectly* diversified. This adjustment factor is:

$$\phi + (1-\phi)\sigma_p^u/(\beta_A\sigma_m)$$

where σ_p^u is a hypothetical portfolio variance based on the assumption that risks are completely undiversified (i.e., perfectly correlated), and ϕ is a diversification index given by:

$$\phi = (\sigma_p^u - \sigma_p)/(\sigma_p^u - \sigma_m)$$

where σ_p is an estimate of the portfolio variance as it is. If the portfolio is perfectly diversified, then $\sigma_p = \sigma_m$ and $\phi = 1$. The adjustment factor is therefore also 1, and the VaR is exactly as given in Equation (A3.5). At the other extreme, if the portfolio is not diversified at all, then $\sigma_p = \sigma_p^u$ and $\phi = 0$. The adjustment is now $\sigma_p^u/(\beta_A\sigma_m)$ and the VaR is $-\alpha_{cl}\sigma_p^u x_A$, which is easily verified as the correct expression in the absence of any diversification. Finally, if the portfolio is imperfectly diversified, ϕ takes a value between 0 and 1 and we get a VaR somewhere between $-\alpha_{cl}\beta_A\sigma_m x_A$ and $-\alpha_{cl}\sigma_p^u x_A$. We thus have an adjustment factor that leads to correct VaRs at the extremes of perfect and zero diversification, and makes some allowance for the extent of diversification of intermediate portfolios.

It only remains to find ways of estimating σ_p^u and σ_p when we have very little information about the volatilities and correlations of specific assets. However, if the portfolio is totally undiversified, then σ_p^u is just the average standard deviation of the individual assets. We can therefore estimate σ_p^u by taking such an average. Estimating σ_p is only slightly more involved. The portfolio variance can be written as:

$$\sigma_p^2 = \sum_{i=1}^{N} w_i^2\sigma_i^2 + \sum_{i=1}^{N}\sum_{j=1}^{N} w_i w_j\sigma_{ij}^2$$

where w_i is the weight of stock i in the portfolio. If we now assume for convenience that the portfolio is equally weighted in the different assets (i.e., $w_i = 1/N$), then the portfolio variance becomes:

$$\sigma_p^2 = (1/N)\bar{\sigma}_i^2 + [(N-1)/N]\bar{\sigma}_{ij}$$

which means that we can approximate the portfolio variance if we have data on the average variance and average covariance of the individual stocks in our portfolio. Provided we have these data, we can estimate both σ_p^u and σ_p and make our adjustment for the effect of imperfect portfolio diversification.[7]

A3.2.1.3 Zero-coupon Bonds

The third type of primitive instrument is a zero-coupon bond, known as a zero. Assuming for convenience that we are dealing with instruments that have no default risk, our task is then to map a default-free zero-coupon bond against a set of default-free reference instruments. Let us also suppose that we are using a mapping procedure of the RiskMetrics sort. The core or reference assets might be 1-month zeroes, 3-month zeroes, and so on. This means that we will have volatility and correlation data on zeroes of these particular maturities, but not on zeroes of other maturities. We will therefore lack volatility and correlation data for the particular bonds we hold, except in the fortuitous special cases where our instruments happen to be reference ones. We might hold bonds with maturities varying from 50 to 90 days, say, and yet the nearest reference bonds might be 30-day and 90-day bonds. In this case, we would have the data we want for 30-day or 90-day bonds, but not for any of the others.

So how then do we estimate the VaR of, say, an 80-day bond? The answer is that we estimate the 80-day VaR from the mapped equivalent of our 80-day bond — that is to say, from its equivalent in terms of some combination of 30-day and 90-day bonds. We can then estimate the volatility and whatever other parameters we need from the parameters for the 30-day and 90-day bonds.

Unfortunately, there is no simple way to map such bonds. We therefore need to begin by deciding on criteria that the mapping procedure should satisfy, and the best criteria seem to be those used by RiskMetrics. They suggest that the mapped position should have the same value and same variance as the old one, and should consist of cash flows of the same sign.[8] We can illustrate this procedure with an example adapted from pp. 117–121 of the 1996 edition of the *Technical Document*. Suppose we have a cash flow coming in 6 years' time, but the nearest reference instruments are comparable bills maturing in 5 and 7 years. The mapped 6-year instrument (I_6^{mapped}) is then a combination of the 5- and 7-year instruments, I_5 and I_7:

$$I_6^{mapped} = \omega I_5 + (1 - \omega)I_7 \tag{A3.7}$$

---

[7]There are also other ways to reduce the degree of understatement of VaR that arises from a portfolio being imperfectly diversified. One solution is to use more than one price index. Instead of using the overall stock market index, we might use more specific indices such as those for energy stocks, manufacturing stocks, and so on. These sector-specific indices would pick up more of the movement in each stock return, and thereby reduce the amount of risk left unaccounted for as firm-specific. σ_ε^2 would then be lower relative to σ_m^2 and so result in a smaller understatement of VaR.

[8]See RiskMetrics *Technical Document* (1996, p. 118). The obvious alternative criteria are that the mapped position should have the same value and same duration as the old one. However, the duration approach only gives an exact measure of bond price volatility if the yield curve is horizontal and movements of the yield curve are strictly parallel. A mapped position that has the same duration as the original position will therefore have a different exposure to changes in the slope or shape of the yield curve.

The problem is then to find some way of choosing ω. Since the mapped asset is a linear combination of the other two, we know that the variance of its return, σ_6^2, is:

$$\sigma_6^2 = \omega^2 \sigma_5^2 + (1 - \omega)^2 \sigma_7^2 + 2\omega(1 - \omega)\rho_{5,7}\sigma_5\sigma_7 \tag{A3.8}$$

where $\rho_{5,7}$ is the correlation coefficient and the other terms are obvious. We could solve for ω if we knew all the other terms, and the only one we don't know is σ_6^2. Longerstaey *et al.* now suggest estimating a proxy for σ_6^2 from a simple linear average for σ_6, i.e.:

$$\sigma_6 = \hat{\omega}\sigma_5 + (1 - \hat{\omega})\sigma_7, \quad 0 \le \hat{\omega} \le 1 \tag{A3.9}$$

where the weight $\hat{\omega}$ is proportional to the relative distance between the maturity of the mapped instrument and the maturities of the reference ones (i.e., in this case, 0.5). We then substitute Equation (A3.9) into Equation (A3.8) and solve the resulting equation for ω. Since this equation is quadratic, there are two solutions for ω, i.e.:[9]

$$\omega = \left[-b \pm \sqrt{b^2 - 4ac} \right]/2a \tag{A3.10}$$

where:

$$a = \sigma_5^2 + \sigma_7^2 - 2\rho_{5,7}\sigma_5\sigma_7$$
$$b = 2\rho_{5,7}\sigma_5\sigma_7 - 2\sigma_7^2 \tag{A3.11}$$
$$c = \sigma_7^2 - \sigma_6^2$$

We then choose the solution that satisfies our earlier criteria (i.e., in practice, the one that gives us an ω value between 0 and 1), and substitute this value into Equation (A3.7) to give us our mapped position.[10]

Once our bond is mapped, we estimate its VaR by estimating the VaR of the mapped bond (i.e., the portfolio of 5- and 7-year zeroes, with weights ω and $1 - \omega$). This latter VaR is estimated in the same way we would estimate the VaR of any other zero-coupon bonds for which we have adequate volatility and correlation data (e.g., by using a duration approximation, etc.).

This mapping approach extends naturally to multi-instrument portfolios. The size of the covariance matrix needed will depend on how the maturities of the included bonds map against the maturities of the reference instruments, but we do at least know that it cannot exceed the size of the reference covariance matrix. So, for example, if we have n different zero-coupon bonds, and m fixed-income reference instruments, the size of the covariance used in our mapping process can never exceed $m \times m$, regardless of how big n might become. After all, we only ever deal with the reference covariance matrix or some subset of it—*not* the covariance matrix for our n different instruments.

A3.2.1.4 Basic Forward/Futures

The fourth building block is a forward/futures position. As any derivatives textbook will explain, a forward contract is an agreement to buy a particular commodity or asset at a specified

---

[9]See, e.g., RiskMetrics *Technical Document* (1996, p. 120).

[10]This description of mapping zero-coupon bonds ignores certain complications peculiar to bonds. One of these is the tendency of bond prices to move towards par as maturity approaches (the 'pull to par' effect). The other is the associated tendency of bond price volatility to decline as a bond approaches maturity (the 'roll down' effect). These effects imply that the standard procedures to infer VaR estimates over longer horizons from VaR estimates over shorter horizons will tend to overstate the true amounts at risk, and some illustrative exercises carried out by Finger (1996, p. 7) suggest that the errors involved can be quite substantial, especially for longer holding periods. However, Finger also suggests some simple modifications to correct for these errors.

future date at a price agreed now, with the price being paid when the commodity/asset is delivered; and a futures contract is a standardised forward contract traded on an organised exchange. There are a number of differences between these contracts, but for our purposes here these differences are seldom important. We can therefore run the two contracts together and speak of a generic forward/futures contract. To illustrate what is involved, suppose we have a forward/futures position that gives us a daily return dependent on the movement of the end-of-day forward/futures price. If we have x contracts each worth F, the value of our position is xF. If F is normal with standard deviation σ_F, the VaR of our position is approximately:[11]

$$VaR \approx -\alpha_{cl}\sigma_F xF \qquad (A3.12)$$

assuming again for convenience that the expected return is zero. The VaR is approximately $-\alpha_{cl}$ times the standard deviation of the forward/futures price (σ_F) times the value of our position (xF).

The only problem is that we may need to map the forward/futures position. How we do so would depend on the reference data available, but if we were using a RiskMetrics-style mapping system, we would have data on a number of points along a forward/futures maturity spectrum: the spot price, the 1-month forward/future price, the 3-month forward/future price, and so on. We could then map our position against these reference assets. If our position has a 4-month maturity, say, we might map it against reference contracts with maturities of 3 months and 6 months, and do so in much the same way as we previously mapped zero-coupon bonds. The mapped 4-month contract (I_4^{mapped}) would be a combination of the 3- and 6-month instruments, I_3 and I_6:

$$I_4^{mapped} = \omega I_3 + (1 - \omega)I_6 \qquad (A3.13)$$

We then map this position as we did the earlier zero-coupon bonds and take the position's VaR to be the estimated VaR of its mapped equivalent, and we can handle multiple-instrument positions in the same way as we would handle multiple bonds.

A3.2.2   More Complex Positions

Having set out our building blocks, we can now map more complex positions. We do so by reverse-engineering them — we produce synthetic equivalents for them, using our building blocks. We already know how to map these equivalent positions, and so we can take their VaRs to be approximations of the VaRs of our original positions. The main points to keep in mind are the following, which draw on established results in financial-engineering theory:

- *Coupon-paying bonds.* A coupon bond can be regarded as a portfolio of zero-coupon bonds, each maturing on a different maturity date. We can therefore map coupon bonds by regarding them as portfolios of zero-coupon bonds and mapping each individual zero-coupon bond separately. The VaR of our coupon bond is then equal to the VaR of its mapped equivalent in zero-coupon bonds.
- *Forward-rate agreements.* An FRA is equivalent to a portfolio long in the zero-coupon bond with the longer maturity and short in the zero-coupon bond with the shorter maturity, or vice versa. We can therefore map and estimate their VaRs in the usual way.
- *Floating-rate instruments.* Since a floating rate note re-prices at par with every coupon payment, we can think of it as equivalent to a hypothetical zero-coupon bond whose maturity is equal to the

---

[11]One reason for the approximation is that, with either contract, the investor is likely to face collateral or margin requirements, and the cost of maintaining these margin positions will usually be interest-sensitive. With forward markets, a second source of approximation is the illiquidity of secondary forward markets. A forward VaR is based on a price in a thin market, and any estimated forward price/VaR is subject to considerable liquidity risk.

period until the next coupon payment. We can then map this hypothetical bond as we would map any other zero-coupon bond.

- *Vanilla interest-rate swaps.* A vanilla interest-rate swap is equivalent to a portfolio that is long a fixed-coupon bond and short a floating-rate bond, or vice versa, and we already know how to map these instruments. All we therefore need to do is map a portfolio that is long one instrument and short the other, and the VaR follows in the standard manner.
- *Structured notes.* These can be produced synthetically by a combination of interest-rate swaps and conventional floating-rate notes, and we can leverage up by entering into more swaps.[12]
- *FX forwards.* A foreign-exchange forward is the equivalent of a long position in a foreign currency zero-coupon bond and a short position in a domestic currency zero-coupon bond, or vice versa.
- *Commodity, equity and FX swaps.* These can be broken down into some form of forward/futures contract on the one hand, and some other forward/futures contract or bond contract on the other.

We could extend this list ad nauseam, but the main point is very clear: subject to a reservation to be discussed below, we can map a great many different instruments using a small number of building blocks and some elementary financial engineering theory.

And what is the reservation? Optionality. The instruments just covered all have in common the point that their returns or P/L are linear or nearly linear functions of the underlying risk factors. Mapping is then fairly straightforward, and our results should be reasonable. Naturally, mapping involves approximation and hence error, but in the presence of linear risk factors there is no reason to be unduly concerned about such errors provided we are reasonably conscientious.

However, once we have significant optionality in any of our positions, we can easily get into serious trouble. The problem is not so much that we can't map options positions — we can map them using any of the delta, delta–gamma and similar approaches discussed in the Appendix to Chapter 5 — but the mischief caused by the non-linearity of options' payoffs relative to the underlying risk factors. We will have more to say on these issues later, but it suffices for the moment to be aware that this non-linearity can seriously undermine the accuracy of any standard (i.e., linear) mapping procedure. We should therefore be very careful — if not downright wary — of using linear-based mapping systems in the presence of significant optionality. In any case, even if they were initially fairly sound, linear-based mappings of options positions can rapidly degenerate in the face of market developments: for instance, a gamma-based approximation can rapidly become useless for an expiring at-the-money vanilla option, because the gamma of such an option approaches infinity. It follows that the mapping of options positions needs to be regularly updated to reflect current market positions: mapping options is thus a dynamic process, as well as a difficult one.

A3.3   RECOMMENDED READING

Beder *et al.* (1998); Henrard (2000); Phelan (1997); RiskMetrics *Technical Document*, 4th edition (1996).

---

[12]There is a very small amount of embedded optionality in basic structured note instruments, which we can ignore. However, more sophisticated structured notes can have a great deal of optionality — an example is the accrual super-floating rate note which revolves around an embedded digital option (see Chew (1996, pp. 184–187)) — and such positions can only be dealt with properly by coming to terms with their embedded options.

4

Non-parametric VaR and ETL

This chapter looks at some of the most popular approaches to the estimation of VaR and ETL — the non-parametric approaches, which seek to estimate VaR or ETL without making strong assumptions about the distribution of P/L or returns. The essence of these approaches is that we try to let the P/L data speak for themselves as much as possible, and use the recent *empirical* distribution of P/L — not some assumed theoretical distribution — to estimate our VaR and ETL.

All non-parametric approaches are based on the underlying assumption that the near future will be sufficiently like the recent past that we can use the data from the recent past to forecast risks over the near future — and this assumption may or may not be valid in any given context.

The first and most popular non-parametric approach is historical simulation (HS). HS is, loosely speaking, a histogram-based approach, and it is conceptually simple, easy to implement, very widely used, and has a fairly good historical record. However, we can also carry out non-parametric estimation using bootstrap methods, non-parametric density estimation methods (e.g., kernels), and principal components analysis methods. The latter methods are sometimes useful when dealing with high-dimensionality problems (i.e., when dealing with portfolios with very large numbers of risk factors).

We begin by discussing how to assemble the P/L data to be used for VaR and ETL estimation. We then discuss the key points in HS VaR and ETL estimation — the basic histogram approach, and the estimation of VaR or ETL curves and surfaces. Section 4.3 discusses how we can estimate confidence intervals for HS VaR and ETL, and includes a discussion of order statistics and bootstrap methods. Section 4.4 addresses how we might weight our data to capture the effects of observation age, changing volatility, and similar factors. Section 4.5 then reviews the main advantages and disadvantages of historical simulation, and Section 4.6 looks at the principal components approach. Section 4.7 offers some conclusions.

4.1 COMPILING HISTORICAL SIMULATION DATA

The first task is to assemble a suitable P/L series for our portfolio, and this requires a set of historical P/L or return observations on the positions in our current portfolio. These P/Ls or returns will be measured over a particular frequency (e.g., a day), and we want a reasonably large set of historical P/L or return observations over the recent past. For example, suppose we have a portfolio of N assets, and for each asset i we have the observed return for each of n sub-periods (e.g., daily sub-periods) in our historical sample period. If $R_{i,t}$ is the (possibly mapped) return on asset i in sub-period t, and if w_i is the amount currently invested in asset i, then the simulated portfolio P/L over the sub-period t is:

$$P/L_t = \sum_{i=1}^{N} w_i R_{i,t} \qquad (4.1)$$

Equation (4.1) gives us an historically simulated P/L series for our current portfolio, and is the basis of HS VaR and ETL. Observe, too, that this series will *not* generally be the same as the P/L *actually* earned on our portfolio — because our portfolio may have changed in composition over time or be subject to mapping approximations, and so on. Instead, the historical simulation P/L is the P/L we *would have* earned on our current portfolio had we held it throughout the historical sample period.[1]

4.2   ESTIMATION OF HISTORICAL SIMULATION VaR AND ETL

4.2.1   Basic Historical Simulation

Having obtained our historical simulation P/L data, we can estimate VaR by plotting the P/L or L/P on a simple histogram and then reading off the VaR from the histogram. To illustrate, suppose we have 100 observations in our HS P/L series and we plot the L/P histogram shown in Figure 4.1. If we choose our VaR confidence level to be, say, 95%, our VaR is given by the *x*-value that cuts off the upper 5% of very high losses from the rest of the distribution. Given 100 observations, we can take this value (i.e., our VaR) to be the sixth highest loss value, or 1.475.[2] The ETL is then the average of the five highest losses, or 1.782.

However, as explained in the previous chapter, we can also estimate the HS VaR more directly (i.e., without bothering with the histogram) by using a spreadsheet function that gives us the sixth highest loss value (e.g., the 'Large' command in Excel), or we can sort our L/P data with highest losses ranked first, and then obtain the VaR as the sixth observation in our sorted loss data.

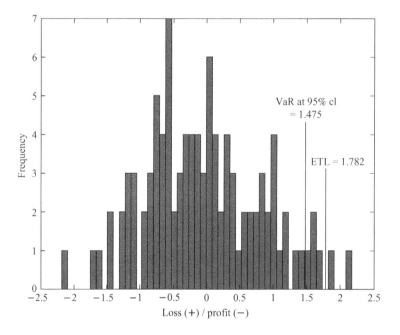

Figure 4.1   Basic historical simulation VaR and ETL.

Note: This figure and associated VaR and ETL estimates are obtained using the 'hsetlfigure' function.

---

[1]To be more precise, the historical simulation P/L is the P/L we would have earned over the sample period had we rearranged the portfolio at the end of each trading day to ensure that the amount left invested in each asset was the same as at the end of the previous trading day: we take out our profits, or make up for our losses, to keep the w_i constant from one end-of-day to the next.

[2]Strictly speaking, we could also take our VaR to be any point between the fifth and sixth largest losses (e.g., such as their mid-point). However, it is easiest if we take the VaR at the 95% confidence level as the sixth largest loss, given we have 100 observations, and we will adhere throughout to this convention of taking the VaR to be the highest loss observation outside the tail.

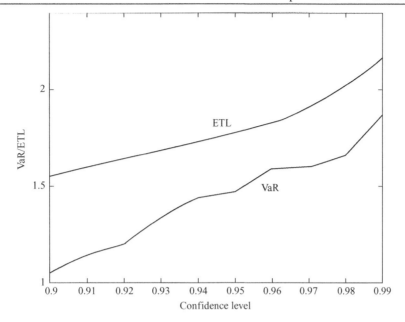

Figure 4.2 Plots of HS VaR and ETL against confidence level.

Note: Obtained using the 'hsvaretlplot2D_cl' function and the same hypothetical P/L data used in Figure 4.1.

4.2.2   Estimating Curves and Surfaces for VaR and ETL

We can use similar methods to estimate curves and surfaces for VaR and ETL. Given that we can estimate VaRs or ETLs for any confidence level, it is straightforward to produce plots of either variable against the confidence level. For example, our earlier hypothetical P/L data yield the curves of VaR and ETL against confidence level shown in Figure 4.2. Note that the VaR curve is fairly unsteady, as it reflects the randomness of individual loss observations, but the ETL curve is smoother, because each ETL is an average of tail losses.

It is more difficult constructing curves that show how VaR or ETL changes with the holding period. The methods discussed so far enable us to estimate the VaR or ETL at a single holding period equal to the frequency period over which our data are observed (e.g., they give us VaR or ETL for a daily holding period if P/L is measured daily). In theory, we can then estimate VaRs or ETLs for any other holding periods we wish by constructing an HS P/L series whose frequency matches our desired holding period: if we wanted to estimate VaR over a weekly holding period, say, we could construct a weekly P/L series and estimate the VaR from that. There is, in short, no theoretical problem as such with estimating HS VaR or ETL over any holding period we like.

However, there is a major practical problem: as the holding period rises, the number of observations rapidly falls, and we soon find that we don't have enough data. To illustrate, if we have 1,000 observations of daily P/L, corresponding to 4 years' worth of data at 250 trading days a year, then we obviously have 1,000 P/L observations if we use a daily holding period. If we have a weekly holding period, with 5 days to a week, each weekly P/L will be the sum of five daily P/Ls, and we end up with only 200 observations of weekly P/L; if we have a monthly holding period, we have only 50 observations of monthly P/L; and so forth. Given our initial data, the number of effective observations rapidly falls as the holding period rises, and the size of the data set imposes a major constraint on how large the holding period can practically be.

4.3 ESTIMATING CONFIDENCE INTERVALS FOR HISTORICAL SIMULATION VaR AND ETL

The methods considered so far are good for giving point estimates of VaR or ETL, but they don't give us any indication of the precision of these estimates or any indication of VaR or ETL confidence intervals. However, there are a number of methods to get around this limitation and produce confidence intervals for our risk estimates.

4.3.1 A Quantile Standard Error Approach to the Estimation of Confidence Intervals for HS VaR and ETL

One solution is to apply the theory of quantile standard errors. If a quantile (or VaR) estimate x has a density function with value f, a cumulative density function with value p, and we have a sample of size n, then the approximate standard error of our quantile estimate is:

$$se(x) = \sqrt{p(1-p)/(nf^2)} \qquad (4.2)$$

(see, e.g., Kendall and Stuart (1972, pp. 251–252)). We could therefore estimate confidence intervals for our VaR estimates in the usual textbook way, and the 95% confidence interval for our VaR would be:

$$[x + 1.96\,se(x), x - 1.96\,se(x)] \qquad (4.3)$$

This approach is easy to implement and plausible with large sample sizes. On the other hand:

- Results will be sensitive to the value of f, the relative frequency, whose estimated value depends a great deal on the bin size: our results are potentially sensitive to the value of what is essentially an ancillary and to some extent, arbitrary, parameter.
- The quantile standard error approach relies on asymptotic (i.e., limiting) theory, and can be unreliable with small sample sizes.
- This approach produces symmetric confidence intervals that can be misleading for VaRs at high confidence levels, where the 'true' confidence intervals are necessarily asymmetric because of the increasing sparsity of our data as we go further out into the tail.

4.3.2 An Order Statistics Approach to the Estimation of Confidence Intervals for HS VaR and ETL

An alternative is to estimate VaR and ETL confidence intervals using the theory of order statistics, explained in Tool No. 1: Estimating VaR and ETL Using Order Statistics. This approach gives us, not just a VaR (or ETL) estimate, but a complete VaR distribution function from which we can read off a VaR confidence interval. The median of this distribution function also gives us an alternative point estimate of our VaR. This approach is easy to program and very general in its application. Relative to the previous approach, it also has the advantages of not relying on asymptotic theory (i.e., is reliable with small samples) and of being less dependent on ancillary assumptions.

Applied to our earlier P/L data, the OS approach gives us estimates (obtained using the IMRM Toolbox 'hsvarpdfperc' function) of the 2.5% and 97.5% points of the VaR distribution function — that is, the bounds of the 95% confidence interval for our VaR — of 1.011 and 1.666. This tells us we can be 95% confident that the 'true' VaR lies in the range [1.011,1.666]. The median of the distribution — the 50th percentile — is 1.441, which is fairly close to our earlier VaR point estimate, 1.475.

The corresponding points of the ETL distribution function can be obtained (using the 'hsetldfperc' function) by mapping from the VaR to the ETL: we take a point on the VaR distribution function, and estimate the corresponding point on the ETL distribution function. Doing this gives us an estimated 95% confidence interval of [1.506,2.022] and an ETL median of 1.731, and the latter is not too far away from our earlier ETL point estimate of 1.782.[3]

4.3.3 A Bootstrap Approach to the Estimation of Confidence Intervals for HS VaR and ETL

A third approach is the bootstrap, covered in Tool No. 3: The Bootstrap. A bootstrap procedure involves resampling, with replacement, from our existing data set. If we have a data set of *n* observations, we create a new data set by taking *n* drawings, each taken from the whole of the original data set. Each new data set created in this way gives us a new VaR estimate. We then create a large number of such data sets and estimate the VaR of each. The resulting VaR distribution function enables us to obtain estimates of the confidence interval for our VaR. The bootstrap is very intuitive and easy to apply.

For example, if we take 1,000 bootstrapped samples from our P/L data set, estimate the VaR of each, and then plot them, we get the histogram shown in Figure 4.3. (By the way, the gaps and unevenness of the histogram reflect the small initial sample size (i.e., 100), rather than the bootstrap itself.) The 95% confidence interval for our VaR is [1.095,1.624], and the median of the distribution is 1.321.

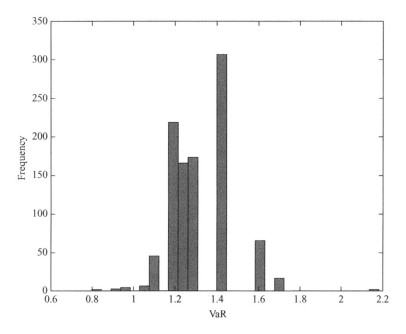

Figure 4.3 Bootstrapped VaR.

Note: Results obtained using the 'bootstrapvarfigure' function, and the same hypothetical data as in earlier figures.

---

[3]Naturally, the order statistics approach can be combined with more sophisticated non-parametric density estimation approaches. Instead of applying the OS theory to the histogram or naïve estimator, we could apply it to a more sophisticated kernel estimator, and thereby extract more information from our data. This approach has a lot of merit and is developed in detail by Butler and Schachter (1998). It is, however, also less transparent, and I prefer to stick with histograms if only for expository purposes.

Table 4.1   Confidence intervals for non-parametric VaR and ETL

Approach	Lower bound	Upper bound	% Range
VaR			
Order statistics	1.011	1.666	44.4%
Bootstrap	1.095	1.624	40.0%
ETL			
Order statistics	1.506	2.022	29%
Bootstrap	1.366	1.997	35.4%

Note: The VaR and ETL are based on a 95% confidence level, and the range is estimated as the difference between the upper and lower bounds, divided by the VaR or ETL point estimate.

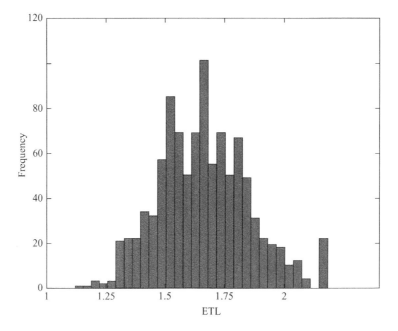

Figure 4.4   Bootstrapped ETL.

Note: Results obtained using the 'bootstrapetlfigure' function, and the same hypothetical data as in earlier figures.

We can also use the bootstrap to estimate ETLs in much the same way: for each new resampled data set, we estimate the VaR, and then estimate the ETL as the average of losses in excess of VaR. Doing this a large number of times gives us a large number of ETL estimates, and we can plot them in the same way as the VaR estimates. The plot of bootstrapped ETL values is shown in Figure 4.4, and it is more well-behaved than the VaR histogram in the last figure because the ETL is an average of tail VaRs. The 95% confidence interval for our ETL is [1.366,1.997].

It is also interesting to compare the VaR and ETL confidence intervals obtained by the two methods. These are summarised in Table 4.1, with the middle two columns giving the bounds of the 95% confidence interval, and the last column giving the difference between the two bounds standardised in terms of the relevant VaR or ETL point estimate. As we can see, the OS and bootstrap approaches give fairly similar results — a finding that is quite striking when one considers the very low sample size of only 100 observations.

4.4   WEIGHTED HISTORICAL SIMULATION

One of the most important features of traditional HS is the way it weights past observations. Recall that $R_{i,t}$ is the return on asset i in period t, and we are implementing HS using the past n observations. An observation $R_{i,t-j}$ will therefore belong to our data set if j takes any of the values $1, \ldots, n$, where j is the age of the observation (e.g., so $j = 1$ indicates that the observation is 1-day old, and so on). If we construct a new HS P/L series, P/L_t, each day, our observation $R_{i,t-j}$ will first affect P/L_t, then P/L_{t+1}, and so on, and finally P/L_{t+n}: our return observation will affect each of the next n observations in our P/L series. Also, other things (e.g., position weights) being equal, $R_{i,t-j}$ will affect each P/L in exactly the same way. But after n periods have passed, $R_{i,t-j}$ will fall out of the data set used to calculate the current HS P/L series, and will thereafter have no effect on P/L. In short, our HS P/L series is constructed in a way that gives any observation the *same* weight in our VaR estimate provided it is less than n periods old, and *no* weight (i.e., a zero weight) if it is older than that.

This weighting structure has a number of problems. One is that it is hard to justify giving each observation in our sample period the same weight, regardless of age, market volatility, or the value it takes (e.g., whether it is extreme). A good example of the difficulties this can create is given by Shimko *et al.* (1998). It is well known that natural gas prices are usually more volatile in the winter than in the summer, so a raw HS approach that incorporates both summer and winter observations will tend to average the summer and winter observations together. As a result, treating all observations as having equal weight will tend to underestimate true risks in the winter, and overestimate them in the summer.[4]

The equal-weight approach can also make risk estimates unresponsive to major events. For instance, a stock market crash might have no effect on VaRs except at a very high confidence level, so we could have a situation where everyone might agree that risk had suddenly increased, and yet that increase in risk would be missed by most HS VaR estimates. The increase in risk would only show up later in VaR estimates if the stock market continued to fall in subsequent days — a case of the stable door closing only well after the horse had bolted. That said, the increase in risk *would* show up in ETL estimates just after the first shock occurred — which is, incidentally, a good example of how ETL can be a more informative risk measure than VaR.

The equal-weight structure also presumes that each observation in the sample period is equally likely and independent of the others over time. However, this 'iid' assumption is unrealistic because it is well known that volatilities vary over time, and that periods of high and low volatility tend to be clustered together. The natural gas example just considered is a good case in point.

It is also hard to justify why an observation should have a weight that suddenly goes to zero when it reaches a certain age. Why is it that an old observation is regarded as having a lot of value (and, indeed, the same value as any more recent observation), but an observation just slightly older is regarded as having no value at all? Even old observations usually have *some* information content, and giving them zero value tends to violate the old statistical adage that we should never throw information away.

This weighting structure also creates the potential for distortions and ghost effects — we can have a VaR that is unduly high, say, because of a single loss observation, and this VaR will continue to be

---

[4] If we have data that show seasonal volatility changes, a solution — also suggested by Shimko *et al.* (1998) — is to weight the data to reflect seasonal volatility (e.g., so winter observations get more weight, if we are estimating a VaR in winter).

high until n days have passed and the observation has fallen out of the sample period. At that point, the VaR will fall again, but the fall in VaR is only a ghost effect created by the weighting structure and the length of sample period used.

4.4.1 Age-weighted Historical Simulation

We can respond to these problems by weighting our data to reflect their relative importance. One way of doing so is suggested by Boudoukh, Richardson and Whitelaw (BRW; 1998): instead of treating each observation for asset i as having the same implied probability as any other (i.e., $1/n$), we could weight their probabilities to discount the older observations in favour of newer ones. Thus, if $w(1)$ is the probability weight given to an observation 1 day old, then $w(2)$, the probability given to an observation 2 days old, could be $\lambda w(1)$; $w(3)$ could be $\lambda^2 w(1)$; and so on. The λ term is between 0 and 1, and reflects the exponential rate of decay in the weight or value given to an observation as it ages: a λ close to 1 indicates a slow rate of decay, and a λ far away from 1 indicates a high rate of decay. $w(1)$ is then set so that the sum of the weights is 1.

To implement age weighting, all we then do is replace the HS probabilities, $1/n$, with the new age-weighted probabilities, $w(i)$. Hence, our core information — the information input to the HS estimation process — is the paired set of P/L values and associated weights $w(i)$, instead of the traditional paired set of P/L values and associated equal weights $1/n$. We can then proceed as before, but with the new set of probability weights. For example, if we are using a spreadsheet, we can order our observations in one column, put their weights in the next column, cumulate these weights in a third column, and then go down that column until we reach our desired percentile. Our VaR is then the negative of the corresponding value in the first column, and if our desired percentile falls between two percentiles, we can take our VaR to be the (negative of the) interpolated value of the corresponding first-column observations.

This age-weighted approach has four major attractions.[5] First, it provides a nice generalisation of traditional HS, because we can regard traditional HS as a special case with zero decay, or $\lambda = 1$. If HS is like driving along a road looking only at the rear-view mirror, then traditional equal-weighted HS is only safe if the road is straight, but the age-weighted approach is also safe if the road bends — provided it doesn't bend too suddenly.

Second, a suitable choice of λ can make the VaR (or ETL) estimates much more responsive to large loss observations: a large loss event will receive a higher weight than under traditional HS, and the resulting next-day VaR would be higher than it would otherwise have been. This not only means that age-weighted VaR estimates are more responsive to large losses, but also makes them better at handling clusters of large losses.

Thirdly, age weighting helps to reduce distortions caused by events that are unlikely to recur, and helps to reduce ghost effects. As an observation ages, its probability weight gradually falls and its influence diminishes gradually over time. Furthermore, when it finally falls out of the sample period, its weight will fall from $\lambda^n w(1)$ to zero, instead of from $1/n$ to zero. Since $\lambda^n w(1)$ is likely to be less than $1/n$ for any reasonable values of λ and n, the shock — the ghost effect — will be less than it would be under equal-weighted HS.

Finally, we can also modify age weighting in a way that makes our risk estimates more efficient and effectively eliminates any remaining ghost effects. Since age weighting allows the impact of past

---

[5]Furthermore, these advantages are not just theoretical, as the empirical evidence of Boudoukh *et al.* (1998) confirms that their age-weighting approach can generate significantly better VaR estimates than unweighted HS or basic variance–covariance approaches.

extreme events to decline as past events recede in time, it gives us the option of letting our sample size grow over time. (Why can't we do this under equal-weighted HS? Because we would be stuck with ancient observations whose information content was assumed never to date.) Age weighting allows us to let our sample period grow with each new observation, and so never throw potentially valuable information away. This would improve efficiency and eliminate ghost effects, because there would no longer be any 'jumps' in our sample resulting from old observations being thrown away.

However, age weighting also reduces the effective sample size, other things being equal, and a sequence of major profits or losses can produce major distortions in its implied risk profile (Hull and White (1998b, p. 9)). In addition, Pritsker (2001, pp. 7–8) shows that even with age weighting, VaR estimates can still be insufficiently responsive to changes in underlying risk.[6] Furthermore, there is the disturbing point that the BRW approach is ad hoc and, except for the special case where $\lambda = 1$, we cannot point to any asset-return process for which the BRW approach is theoretically correct (Pritsker (2001, p. 15)). The moral of the story seems to be that age weighting can improve on traditional unweighted HS, but does not really do justice to some of the risk changes implied by changing volatilities.

4.4.2 Volatility-weighted Historical Simulation

We can also weight our data in other ways, and one such approach is to weight them by volatility. The basic idea — suggested by Hull and White (HW; 1998b) — is to update return information to take account of recent changes in volatility. For example, if the current volatility in a market is 1.5% a day, and it was only 1% a day a month ago, then data a month old understates the changes we can expect to see tomorrow. On the other hand, if last month's volatility was 2% a day, month-old data will overstate the changes we can expect tomorrow.

Suppose we are interested in forecasting VaR for day T. Let $r_{t,i}$ be the historical return to asset i on day t in our historical sample, $\sigma_{t,i}$ be the historical GARCH (or EWMA) forecast of the volatility of the return to asset i for day t, made at the end of day $t-1$, and $\sigma_{T,i}$ be our most recent forecast for the volatility of asset i. We then replace the returns in our data set, $r_{t,i}$, with volatility-adjusted returns, given by:

$$r^*_{t,i} = \sigma_{T,i} r_{t,i} / \sigma_{t,i} \tag{4.4}$$

Actual returns in any period t are therefore increased (or decreased), depending on whether the current forecast of volatility is greater (or less than) the estimated volatility for period t. We now calculate the HS P/L using Equation (4.4) instead of the original data set $r_{t,i}$, and then proceed to estimate HS VaRs or ETLs in the traditional way (i.e., with equal weights, etc.).

The HW approach has a number of advantages relative to the traditional equal-weighted and/or the BRW age-weighted approaches:

- It takes account of volatility changes in a natural and direct way, whereas equal-weighted HS ignores volatility changes and the age-weighted approach treats volatility changes in a restrictive way.

---

[6]If VaR is estimated at the confidence level cl, the probability of an HS estimate of VaR rising on any given day is equal to the probability of a loss in excess of VaR, which is of course $1 - cl$. However, if we assume a standard GARCH(1,1) process and volatility is at its long-run mean value, then Pritsker's proposition 2 shows that the probability that HS VaR should increase is about 32% (Pritsker (2001, pp. 7–9)). In other words, most of the time HS VaR estimates should increase (i.e., when risk rises), they fail to.

- It produces risk estimates that are appropriately sensitive to current volatility estimates, and so enables us to incorporate information from GARCH forecasts into HS VaR and ETL estimation.
- It allows us to obtain VaR and ETL estimates that can exceed the maximum loss in our historical data set: in periods of high volatility, historical returns are scaled upwards, and the HS P/L series used in the HW procedure will have values that exceed actual historical losses. This is a major advantage over traditional HS, which prevents the VaR or ETL from being any bigger than the losses in our historical data set.
- Empirical evidence presented by HW indicates that their approach produces superior VaR estimates to the BRW one (Hull and White (1998b, p. 19)).

The HW approach is also capable of various extensions. For instance, we can combine it with the age-weighted approach if we wish to increase the sensitivity of risk estimates to large losses, and to reduce the potential for distortions and ghost effects. We can also combine the HW approach with the bootstrap to estimate confidence intervals for our VaR or ETL — that is, we would resample with replacement from the HW-adjusted P/L, rather than the traditional HS portfolio P/L series.

Box 4.1   General Approaches to Weighted Historical Simulation

There are also more general approaches to weighted historical simulation. Duffie and Pan (1997, p. 30) describe a method to adjust a set of historical scenarios so that they reflect current market conditions. If $\mathbf{R}$ is an $m \times 1$ set of historical scenarios reflecting a covariance matrix Σ, but current market conditions indicate a currently prevailing covariance matrix $\bar{\Sigma}$, they suggest that we obtain a set of adjusted scenarios by applying the transformation $\bar{\Sigma}^{1/2}\Sigma^{-1/2}$ to $\mathbf{R}$. The returns adjusted in this way will then have the currently prevailing variance–covariance matrix $\bar{\Sigma}$. This approach is a major generalisation of the HW approach, because it gives us a weighting system that takes account of correlations as well as volatilities.

But perhaps the best and most general approach to weighted historical simulation is suggested by Holton (1998, 1999). He suggests that we choose weights to reflect current market estimates, not only of means, volatilities and correlations, but also of skewness, kurtosis and higher moments. To do so, he suggests a linear programming routine that should produce a reasonable set of weights provided we have enough data to work with. This approach is conceptually simple and easy to program, and yet it is very flexible and extremely general. It also has the additional attraction that it can be applied to Monte Carlo as well as historical simulation.

4.4.3   Filtered Historical Simulation

Another promising alternative is the filtered historical simulation (FHS) approach proposed in a series of recent papers by Barone-Adesi, Bourgoin, Giannopoulos and Vosper (e.g., Barone-Adesi *et al.* (1998, 1999)). As we have seen, traditional HS approaches fail to come fully to terms with conditionally varying volatilities. The natural way to handle these volatilities would be to model them using a GARCH model, but a GARCH model requires us to specify the return process, which does not sit well with a non-parametric approach. The earlier literature therefore suggests that we could either keep a non-parametric approach, and settle for a fairly simple treatment of volatility, or we could sacrifice the benefits of a non-parametric approach in return for a more sophisticated treatment of volatility. This is exactly where FHS comes in: FHS seeks the best of both worlds, and combines the benefits of HS with the power and flexibility of conditional volatility models such as GARCH. It does so by bootstrapping returns within a conditional volatility (e.g., GARCH) framework, where the bootstrap preserves the non-parametric nature of HS, and the volatility model gives us a sophisticated treatment of volatility.

Suppose we wish to use FHS to estimate the VaR of a single-asset portfolio over a 1-day holding period. The first step in FHS is to fit, say, a GARCH model to our portfolio-return data. We want a model that is rich enough to accommodate the key features of our data, and Barone-Adesi and colleagues recommend an asymmetric GARCH, or AGARCH, model. This not only accommodates conditionally changing volatility, volatility clustering, and so on, but also allows positive and negative returns to have differential impacts on volatility, a phenomenon known as the leverage effect (Black (1976)). The AGARCH postulates that portfolio returns obey the following process:

$$r_t = \mu + \varepsilon_t \tag{4.5a}$$
$$\sigma_t^2 = \omega + \alpha(\varepsilon_{t-1} + \gamma)^2 + \beta\sigma_{t-1}^2 \tag{4.5b}$$

The daily return in Equation (4.5a) is the sum of a mean daily return (which can often be neglected in volatility estimation) and a random error ε_t. The volatility in Equation (4.5b) is the sum of a constant and terms reflecting last period's 'surprise' and last period's volatility, plus an additional term γ that allows for the surprise to have an asymmetric effect on volatility, depending on whether the surprise is positive or negative.

The second step is to use the model to forecast volatility for each of the days in a sample period. These volatility forecasts are then divided into the realised returns to produce a set of standardised returns. These standardised returns should be independently and identically distributed (iid), and therefore be suitable for HS.

Assuming a 1-day VaR holding period, the third stage involves bootstrapping from our data set of standardised returns: we take a large number of drawings from this data set, which we now treat as a sample, replacing each one after it has been drawn, and multiply each random drawing by the AGARCH forecast of tomorrow's volatility. If we take M drawings, we therefore get M simulated returns, each of which reflects current market conditions because it is scaled by today's forecast of tomorrow's volatility.

Finally, each of these simulated returns gives us a possible end-of-tomorrow portfolio value, and a corresponding possible loss, and we take the VaR to be the loss corresponding to our chosen confidence level.

We can easily modify this procedure to encompass the obvious complications of a multi-asset portfolio or a longer holding period. If we have a multi-asset portfolio, we would fit a multivariate GARCH (or AGARCH) to the set or vector of asset returns, and standardise this vector of asset returns. The bootstrap would then select, not just a standardised portfolio return for some chosen past (daily) period, but the standardised vector of asset returns for the chosen past period. This is important because it means that our simulations would keep any correlation structure present in the raw returns. The bootstrap thus maintains existing correlations, without having to specify an explicit multivariate pdf for asset returns.

The other obvious extension is to a longer holding period. If we have a longer holding period, we would first take a drawing and use Equations (4.5a and b) to get a return for tomorrow; we would then use this drawing to update our volatility forecast for the day after tomorrow, and take a fresh drawing to determine the return for that day; and carry on in the same manner — taking a drawing, updating our volatility forecasts, taking another drawing for the next period, and so on — until we had reached the end of our holding period. At that point we would have enough information to produce a single simulated P/L observation; and we would repeat the process as many times as we wished in order to produce the histogram of simulated P/L observations from which we can estimate our VaR.

FHS has a number of attractions. (1) It enables us to combine the non-parametric attractions of HS with a sophisticated (e.g., GARCH) treatment of volatility. (2) It is fast, even for large portfolios. (3) As with the earlier HW approach, FHS allows us to get VaR and ETL estimates that can exceed the maximum historical loss in our data set. (4) It maintains the correlation structure in our return data without relying on knowledge of the variance–covariance matrix or the conditional distribution of asset returns. (5) It can be modified to take account of autocorrelation or past cross-correlations in asset returns. (6) It can be modified to produce estimates of VaR or ETL confidence intervals, by combining it with an OS or bootstrap approach to confidence interval estimation.[7] (7) There is evidence that FHS works well and clearly dominates traditional HS (Barone-Adesi and Giannopoulos (2000, p. 17)). (8) Last but not least, FHS is readily applicable to many derivatives positions, including positions in futures, options and swaps. Provided the underlying variable(s) can be suitably modelled, we can apply this approach to estimate the risks of derivatives positions by revaluing the derivative(s) at each step in the simulation process, bearing in mind that the value(s) of our derivative(s) depends on the simulated values of the underlying variable(s).[8]

4.5   ADVANTAGES AND DISADVANTAGES OF HISTORICAL SIMULATION

4.5.1   Advantages

It is perhaps a good idea at this point to pause and summarise the main advantages and disadvantages of HS approaches. They have a number of attractions:

- They are intuitive and conceptually simple. Indeed, basic HS is very simple, although some of the more refined HS approaches such as HW, FHS, Duffie-Pan or Holton are a little more involved.
- HS approaches are (in varying degrees, fairly) easy to implement on a spreadsheet.
- They use data that are (often) readily available, either from public sources (e.g., Bloomberg) or from in-house data sets (e.g., collected as a by-product of marking positions to market).
- They provide results that are easy to report, and easy to communicate to senior managers and interested outsiders (e.g., bank supervisors or rating agencies).
- Since they do not depend on parametric assumptions about P/L, they can accommodate fat tails, skewness, and any other non-normal features that can cause problems for parametric approaches.
- They dispense with any need to handle variance–covariance matrices, and therefore avoid the many problems associated with such matrices.

---

[7]The OS approach would require a set of paired P/L and associated probability observations, so we could apply this to FHS by using a P/L series that had been through the FHS filter. The bootstrap is even easier, since FHS already makes use of a bootstrap. If we want M bootstrapped estimates of VaR, we could produce, say, 100*M or 1,000*M bootstrapped P/L values; each set of 100 (or 1,000) P/L series would give us one HS VaR estimate, and the histogram of M such estimates would enable us to infer the bounds of the VaR confidence interval.

[8]However, FHS does have potential problems. In his thorough simulation study of FHS, Pritsker (2001, pp. 22–24) comes to the tentative conclusions that FHS VaR might not pay enough attention to extreme observations or time-varying correlations, and Barone-Adesi and Giannopoulos (2000, p. 18) largely accept these points. A partial response to the first point would be to use ETL instead of VaR as our preferred risk measure, and the natural response to the second concern is to develop FHS with a more sophisticated past cross-correlation structure. Pritsker (2001, p. 22) also presents simulation results that suggest that FHS VaR tends to underestimate 'true' VaR over a 10-day holding period by about 10%, but this finding conflicts with results reported by Barone-Adesi and Giannopoulos (2000) based on real data. The evidence on FHS is thus mixed.

- They can accommodate any type of position, including derivatives positions.
- We can easily produce confidence intervals for HS VaR and ETL.
- HS approaches can easily be modified to allow for age weighting (as in BRW), volatility weighting (as in HW), or GARCH volatility forecasts (as in FHS) or other features of current market conditions (as in Duffie-Pan or Holton). HS approaches are thus capable of considerable refinement.
- There is a widespread perception among risk practitioners that HS works quite well empirically, although formal empirical evidence on this issue is inevitably mixed.

4.5.2 Disadvantages

4.5.2.1 Total Dependence on the Data Set

Naturally, HS approaches also have their weaknesses, and perhaps their biggest potential weakness is that their results are completely dependent on the data set.[9] This dependence on the data set can lead to a number of problems:

- If our data period was unusually quiet, HS will often produce VaR or ETL estimates that are too low for the risks we are actually facing.
- If our data period was unusually volatile, HS will often produce VaR or ETL estimates that are too high for the risks we are actually facing.
- HS approaches can have difficulty handling shifts that take place during our sample period. For example, if there is a permanent change in exchange rate risk, it will usually take time for the HS VaR or ETL estimates to reflect the new exchange rate risk.
- HS approaches are sometimes slow to reflect major events, such as the increases in risk associated with sudden market turbulence.
- If our data set incorporates extreme losses that are unlikely to recur, these losses can dominate our HS risk estimates — particularly ETL ones — even though we don't expect them to recur.
- Most forms of HS are subject to the phenomenon of ghost or shadow effects.[10]
- In general, HS estimates of VaR or ETL make no allowance for plausible events that might occur, but did not actually occur, in our sample period.
- HS estimates of VaR and ETL are to a greater or lesser extent constrained by the largest loss in our historical data set. In the simpler versions of HS, we cannot extrapolate from the largest historical loss to anything larger that might conceivably occur in the future — and this is clearly a major limitation when trying to use HS to deal with low-probability, high-loss events. In most sophisticated versions of HS, such as FHS, or those suggested by HW, Duffie and Pan, or Holton (see Box 4.1), this constraint takes a softer form, and in periods of high volatility (or, depending on the approach used, high correlation, etc.) we can get VaR or ETL estimates that exceed our largest historical loss. Yet, even so, the fact remains that estimates of VaR or ETL are still constrained by the largest loss in a way that parametric estimates are not, and this means that HS methods are not well suited to handling extremes, particularly with small- or medium-sized samples.

---

[9]There can also be problems getting the data set. We need time series data on all current positions, and such data are not always available (e.g., if the positions are in emerging markets). We also have to ensure that data are reliable, compatible, and delivered to the risk estimation system on a timely basis.

[10]However, Holton (1999) suggests a promising way to deal with these effects. He suggests using 'mirror scenarios' — to each historical scenario in our sample, we add its mirror image (i.e., so a large loss would become a large profit, and so on). Correctly implemented, this should eliminate ghost effects and also increase the accuracy of our results by a factor of $1/\sqrt{2}$.

However, we can often ameliorate these problems by suitable refinements: we can ameliorate volatility, market turbulence, correlation and other problems by the adjustments just suggested; and we can ameliorate ghost effects by age weighting our data and allowing our sample size to rise over time, or by using Holton's 'mirror scenarios' approach (see note 10). In short, most (though not all) problems associated with the dependence of HS results on the historical data set are capable of some amelioration using more refined versions of HS.

4.5.2.2 *Problems of Data Period Length*

There can also be problems associated with the length of our data period. We need a reasonably long data period to have a sample size large enough to get reasonable risk estimates — and in particular, reasonably precise ones. Nonetheless, a very long data period can also create problems of its own:

- The longer the data set, the more difficult it is to defend the maintained assumption that all data are equally relevant for VaR or ETL estimation (i.e., the bigger the problem with aged data).
- The longer the sample period, the longer the period over which results will be distorted by unlikely-to-recur past events, and the longer we will have to wait for ghost effects to disappear.
- The longer the sample size, the more the news in current market observations is likely to be drowned out by older observations — and the less responsive our risk estimates to current market conditions.
- A long sample period can lead to data collection problems. This is a particular concern with new or emerging market instruments, where long runs of historical data don't exist and are not necessarily easy to proxy.

Fortunately, we can deal with most of these problems (except the last) by appropriate modifications to HS — in particular, by age weighting to deal with distortions, ghost and news effects. In practice, our main concerns are usually to obtain a long enough run of historical data, and as a broad rule of thumb, most experts believe that to get reliable results, we usually need at least a year's worth of daily observations (i.e., 250 observations, at 250 trading days to the year), and often more.

4.6   PRINCIPAL COMPONENTS APPROACHES TO VAR AND ETL ESTIMATION

Some alternative non-parametric approaches to VaR and ETL estimation are provided by principal components analysis (PCA). These are covered in Tool No. 4: Principal Components Analysis, and are non-parametric methods that provide a simpler representation of the risk factors present in a data set. They are useful because they enable us to reduce the dimensionality of problems and reduce the number of variance–covariance parameters we need to estimate, and can also be useful when cleaning and mapping data.

The standard textbook application of PCA for VaR and ETL estimation is to fixed-income portfolios whose values fluctuate with changes across the interest-rate term structure.[11] In such cases we have a large number of highly (but not perfectly) correlated risk factors, which would give rise to a high-dimension variance–covariance matrix, and the high collinearity of these risk factors can make it difficult to estimate the variance–covariance terms with any great precision. We might then resort to principal components analysis to identify the underlying sources of movement in our data. Typically, the first three such factors — the first three principal components — will capture 95% or thereabouts

---

[11]For some examples of applications of PCA to fixed-interest positions, see, e.g., Wilson (1994a), Golub and Tilman (1997), or Phoa (2000).

of the variance of our data, and so enable us to cut down the dimensionality of the problem and (sometimes drastically) cut down the number of parameters to be estimated. However, PCA needs to be used with care because estimates of principal components can be unstable (e.g., Wilson (1994a)).

Factor analysis (FA) is a related method that focuses on explaining correlations rather than (as PCA does) explaining variances, and is particularly useful when investigating correlations among a large number of variables. When choosing between PCA and FA, a good rule of thumb is to use PCA when dealing with instruments that are mainly volatility-dependent (e.g., when dealing with portfolios of interest-rate caps or floors), and to use FA when dealing with problems that are mainly correlation-dependent (e.g., portfolios of diff swaps).

These methods do not as such give us estimates of the confidence intervals attached to our VaRs or ETLs. However, we can estimate these confidence intervals by supplementing PCA or FA methods with order statistics or bootstrap approaches. For example, we could use PCA to produce 'synthetic' portfolio P/L data, and then apply an OS or bootstrap approach to that data, and so estimate both VaR (or ETL) and the associated confidence interval.

4.7 CONCLUSIONS

Non-parametric methods are widely used and in many respects highly attractive approaches to VaR and ETL estimation. They have a reasonable track record and are often superior to parametric approaches based on simplistic assumptions such as normality. They are also capable of considerable refinement to deal with some of the weaknesses of more basic non-parametric approaches. As a general rule, they work fairly well if market conditions remain reasonably stable, and are also capable of considerable refinement. Nonetheless, users should keep their limitations in mind:

- They can be unreliable if market conditions change.
- Results are totally dependent on the data set, and tell us little or nothing about possible losses from 'what if' events that are not reflected in our sample period.
- Non-parametric estimates of VaR or ETL can be badly affected by distortions from one-off events, and from ghost effects.
- Non-parametric approaches are not much use when dealing with extremes, particularly if we don't have a large sample size.
- HS estimates of VaR or ETL can be imprecise given the small sample periods often available, and there seems to be a general feeling among practitioners that one needs at least a year or more of daily observations to get results of acceptable accuracy.

In short, non-parametric approaches have many uses, but they also have their limitations. It is often a good idea to supplement them with other approaches to VaR and ETL estimation and, where possible, complement all risk estimates by stress testing to gauge our vulnerability to 'what if' events. We should never rely on non-parametric methods alone.

Box 4.2   Non-parametric Functions in MATLAB

MATLAB has a number of functions that are useful for non-parametric risk estimation. MATLAB itself has the 'hist' and 'histc' functions that are useful when dealing with histograms, and the Statistics Toolbox has many other functions useful for non-parametric analysis, including a variety of useful principal components functions ('princomp', 'pcacov', 'pcares', etc.).

The IMRM Toolbox also has some useful non-parametric functions. These include the functions 'hsvar' and 'hsetl', which estimate HS VaR and ETL, 'hsvardfperc' and 'hsetldfperc', which estimate percentiles from the VaR and ETL distribution functions using order statistics theory, 'hsvarfigure' and 'hsetlfigure', which produce pdf figures with HS VaR and ETL, 'hsvarplot2D_cl', 'hsetlplot2D_cl' and 'hsvaretlplot2D_cl', which plot HS VaR and/or ETL against the confidence level. The IMRM Toolbox also includes the quantile standard error functions discussed in Section 4.3.1 and the bootstrap VaR and ETL functions discussed in Section 4.3.3.

4.8 RECOMMENDED READING

Barone-Adesi and Giannopoulos (2000); Barone-Adesi *et al.* (1998, 1999); Boudoukh *et al.* (1998); Butler and Schachter (1998); Golub and Tilman (1997); Holton (1998, 1999); Hull and White (1998b); Phoa (2000); Prinzler (1999); Pritsker (2001); Ridder (1997, pp. 5–12); Scaillet (2000b); Shimko *et al.* (1998); Taylor (2000).

5

Parametric VaR and ETL

This chapter looks at parametric approaches to VaR and ETL. These approaches estimate risk by fitting probability curves to the data, and then inferring the VaR or ETL from the fitted curve. Parametric approaches are more powerful than non-parametric ones, because they make use of additional information contained in the assumed density or distribution function. They are also very easy to use, because they give rise to straightforward VaR and sometimes ETL formulas. However, they are vulnerable to error if the assumed density function does not adequately fit the data.

This chapter discusses parametric VaR and ETL at two different levels — at the portfolio level, where we are dealing with portfolio P/L or returns, and at the sub-portfolio or individual-position level, where we are dealing with the P/L or returns to individual positions. Beginning at the portfolio level, Sections 5.1–5.4 discuss alternative parametric approaches based on the normal, Student t, lognormal and extreme value distributions, respectively. After that, we turn to the position level, and deal with the variance–covariance approach where individual asset returns are assumed to follow a multivariate normal distribution. Some conclusions are offered in Section 5.6.

The Appendix deals with the use of delta–gamma and related approximations to deal with non-linear risks (e.g., such as those arising from options).

Box 5.1 Unconditional vs. Conditional Approaches

When fitting parametric distributions to financial profit or loss, or rates of return, there is an important distinction between unconditional and conditional coverage. If we fit a distribution unconditionally, we are saying that the distribution 'fits' the behaviour of the random variable concerned — that P/L is normally distributed, or whatever.

However, it is often good practice to fit distributions conditionally — to adjust our data, and then fit the distribution to the adjusted data. Conditional coverage allows us to take account of factors that unconditional coverage ignores. For example, we might want to adjust daily P/L to take out seasonal or holiday effects: the adjusted data would then fit the chosen distribution better than the raw data with their seasonal or holiday effects still included. We might also want to adjust our raw data by dividing them by the corresponding daily volatility forecast: if volatilities are changing, the standardised data should fit the chosen distribution better, because we are making some allowance for the changing volatility. More generally, we can also adjust the data by first regressing them against data for other variables that are believed to affect them; we then clean our P/L or return data by subtracting the deterministic part of the regression from them (i.e., thus taking out the effects of the other variables); and we fit the parametric distribution to the 'cleaned' residuals. A good example is where we might fit a GARCH process to our data, and then apply a parametric distribution to the residuals from the GARCH process.

When estimating VaR and ETL, we should always begin by asking whether and — if so — how we should adjust our data, and there is almost always some reason why we might wish to do so. But if we do adjust our data, we must remember that our results may relate to adjusted VaR or ETL, and we may need to un-adjust these figures to unravel the 'true' VaR or ETL.

5.1 NORMAL VAR AND ETL

5.1.1 General Features

The normal (or Gaussian) distribution was briefly introduced in Chapter 3. It is very widely used, and has plausibility in many contexts because of the central limit theorem. Loosely speaking, this theorem says that if we have a random variable from an unknown but well-behaved distribution, then the means of samples drawn from that distribution are asymptotically (i.e., in the limit) normally distributed. Consequently, the normal distribution is often used when we are concerned about the distribution of sample means and, more generally, when we are dealing with quantiles and probabilities near the centre of the distribution.

The normal distribution is also attractive because it has only two independent parameters — a mean, μ, and a standard deviation, σ (or its square, the variance, σ^2). The third moment of the normal distribution, the skewness, is zero (i.e., so the normal distribution is symmetric) and the fourth moment, the kurtosis (which measures tail fatness), is 3. To apply the normal distribution, we therefore need estimates of only μ and σ.

The normal distribution is also convenient because it produces straightforward formulas for both VaR and ETL. If we apply a normal distribution to P/L,[1] then the VaR and ETL[2] are respectively:

$$VaR = -\alpha_{cl}\sigma_{P/L} - \mu_{P/L} \tag{5.1a}$$

$$ETL = \sigma_{P/L}\phi(-\alpha_{cl})/F(\alpha_{cl}) - \mu_{P/L} \tag{5.1b}$$

where $\mu_{P/L}$ and $\sigma_{P/L}$ have their obvious meanings, α_{cl} is the standard normal variate corresponding to our chosen confidence level (e.g., $\alpha_{cl} = -1.645$ if we have a 95% confidence level), and $\phi(\cdot)$ and $F(\cdot)$ are the values of the normal density and distribution functions. However, in most cases the mean and standard deviation are not known, so we have to work with estimates of them, m and s. Our estimates of VaR and ETL are therefore:[3]

$$VaR^e = -\alpha_{cl}s_{P/L} - m_{P/L} \tag{5.2a}$$

$$ETL^e = s_{P/L}\phi(-\alpha_{cl})/F(\alpha_{cl}) - m_{P/L} \tag{5.2b}$$

Figure 5.1 shows the standard normal L/P pdf curve and normal VaR and ETL at the 95% confidence level. The normal pdf has a distinctive bell-shaped curve, and the VaR cuts off the top 5% tail whilst the ETL is the probability-weighted average of the tail VaRs.

One of the nice features of parametric approaches is that the formulas they provide for VaR (and, where they exist, ETL) also allow us to estimate these risk measures at any confidence level or holding period we like. In the normal case, we should first note that Equations (5.1a and b) give the VaR and ETL formulas for a confidence level reflected in the value of α_{cl}, and for a holding period equal to the period over which P/L is measured (e.g., a day). If we change the

---

[1] As discussed already in Chapter 3, we can apply a normality assumption to portfolio P/L, L/P or arithmetic returns. The formulas then vary accordingly: if we assume that L/P is normal, our VaR and ETL formulas are the same as in Equations (5.1a and b), except for the mean terms having a reversed sign; if we assume that arithmetic returns are normal, then the μ and σ terms refer to returns, rather than P/L, and we need to multiply our VaR and ETL formulas by the current value of our portfolio.

[2] Following on from the last footnote, if L/P is normal, with mean $\mu_{L/P}$ and standard deviation $\sigma_{L/P}$, then our ETL is $\sigma_{L/P}\phi(-\alpha_{cl})/F(\alpha_{cl}) + \mu_{L/P}$; and if our portfolio return r is normal, with mean μ_r and standard deviation σ_r, our ETL is $[\sigma_r\phi(-\alpha_{cl})/F(\alpha_{cl}) - \mu_r]P$, where P is the current value of our portfolio.

[3] The normality assumption has the additional attraction of making it easy for us to get good estimators of the parameters. As any econometrics text will explain, under normality, least squares (LS) regression will give us best linear unbiased estimators of our parameters, and these are also the same as those we would get using a maximum likelihood approach.

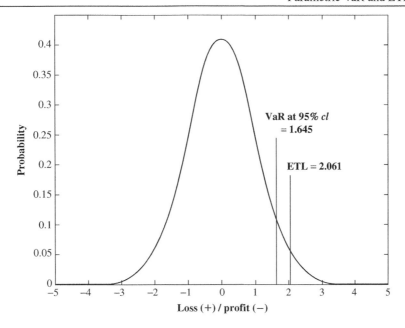

Figure 5.1   VaR and ETL for normal loss/profit.

Note: Based on a 1-day holding period with L/P having a mean 0 and standard deviation 1. The figure is obtained using the 'normaletlfigure' function.

confidence level, we therefore change the value of α_{cl} to correspond to the new confidence level: for example, if we change the confidence level from 95% to 99%, α_{cl} changes from -1.645 to -2.326.

To take account of a change in the holding period, we need formulas for the mean and standard deviation of P/L over arbitrary periods. If we now define $\mu_{P/L}$ and $\sigma_{P/L}$ as the mean and standard deviation of P/L over a given period (e.g., a day), then the mean and standard deviation of P/L over hp such periods are:

$$\mu_{P/L}(hp) = hp\,\mu_{P/L} \tag{5.3a}$$

$$\sigma^2_{P/L}(hp) = hp\,\sigma^2_{P/L} \Rightarrow \sigma_{P/L}(hp) = \sqrt{hp}\,\sigma_{P/L} \tag{5.3b}$$

We now substitute these into Equations (5.1a and b) to get the formulas for VaR and ETL over an arbitrary holding period hp and confidence level cl:

$$VaR(hp, cl) = -\alpha_{cl}\sqrt{hp}\,\sigma_{P/L} - hp\,\mu_{P/L} \tag{5.4a}$$

$$ETL(hp, cl) = \sqrt{hp}\,\sigma_{P/L}\phi(-\alpha_{cl})/F(\alpha_{cl}) - hp\,\mu_{P/L} \tag{5.4b}$$

These formulas make it very easy to measure VaR and ETL once we have values (or estimates) of $\mu_{P/L}$ and $\sigma_{P/L}$ to work with. These formulas tell us that VaR and ETL will rise with the confidence level, as shown earlier in Figure 2.7. However, the effects of a rising holding period are ambiguous, as the first terms in each formula rise with hp, but the second terms fall as hp rises. Since the first terms relate to σ, and the second to μ, the effects of a rising hp on VaR or ETL depend on the relative sizes of σ and μ. Furthermore, since the first terms rise with the square root of hp, whilst the second terms rise proportionately with hp, we also know that the second terms will become more

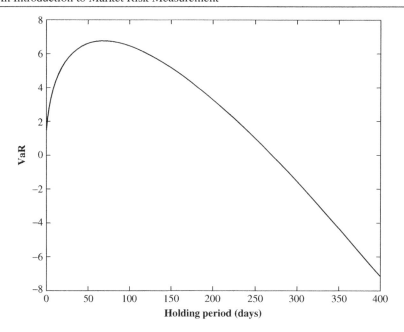

Figure 5.2   Normal VaR and holding period.

Note: This figure is obtained using the 'normalvarplot2D_hp' function and shows the VaR at the 95% confidence level for a normal P/L distribution with mean 0.1 and standard deviation 1.

prominent as *hp* gets larger. If we assume plausible parameter values (e.g., a confidence level of 95% and μ positive but 'small' relative to σ), then we get the following:

- When *hp* is very low, the first term dominates the second, so the VaR and ETL are positive.
- As *hp* gets bigger, the second terms grow at a faster rate, so VaR and ETL will rise but at a diminishing rate.
- As *hp* continues to rise, VaR and ETL will turn down, and eventually become negative.
- Thereafter, they will move further away from zero as *hp* continues to rise.

Figure 5.2 gives an example of how VaR behaves under these conditions. (We get a similar looking chart for the ETL.) In this particular case (with daily parameters of $\mu = 0.1$ and $\sigma = 1$), the VaR peaks at a holding period of around 70 days, and becomes negative at a holding period of around 250 days. VaRs beyond that holding period move further and further away from zero as the holding period continues to rise.

As an aside, this VaR–holding period chart is very different from the one we would get under the well-known 'square root rule', which is now enshrined in the Basle regulations on bank capital adequacy. According to this rule, we can obtain VaRs over longer holding periods by taking a VaR measured over a short holding period and scaling it up by the square root of the longer holding period. If our VaR over a 1-day holding period is $VaR(1,cl)$, say, then the VaR over a holding period of *hp* days, $VaR(hp,cl)$, is given by:

$$VaR(hp,cl) = \sqrt{hp}\, VaR(1,cl) \tag{5.5}$$

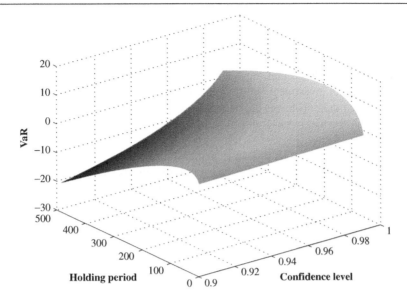

Figure 5.3   A normal VaR surface.

Note: This figure shows the VaR surface for a normal P/L distribution with daily mean 0.1 and daily standard deviation 1. It is produced using the 'normalvarplot3D' function.

This formula produces a VaR that always rises as the holding period increases, although at a decreasing rate, as illustrated earlier in Figure 2.8. If we compare the two figures, we can see that the 'true' normal VaR becomes increasingly strongly negative, whilst the 'square root VaR' becomes increasingly strongly positive as hp gets large. It follows, then, that we should never use the 'square root' extrapolation rule, except in the special case where $\mu = 0$ — and even then, the 'square root VaR' will only be correct for certain P/L distributions. My advice is to forget about it altogether, and use the correct parametric VaR formula instead.

It is often useful to look at VaR and ETL surfaces, as these convey much more information than single point estimates or even curves such as Figure 5.2. The usual (i.e., $\mu > 0$ case) normal VaR surface is shown in Figure 5.3. (Again, the ETL equivalent is similar.) The magnitudes will vary with the parameters, but we always get the same basic shape: the VaR rises with the confidence level, and initially rises with the holding period, but as the holding period continues to rise, the VaR eventually peaks, turns down and becomes negative; the VaR is therefore highest when the confidence level is highest and the holding period is high but not too high. Away from its peak, the VaR surface also has nicely curved convex isoquants: these are shown in the figure by the different shades on the VaR surface, each representing a different VaR value.

Again, it is instructive to compare this surface with the one we would obtain if $\mu = 0$ (i.e., where the square root approach is valid). The zero-μ normal VaR surface was shown earlier in Figure 2.9, and takes a very different shape. In this case, VaR rises with both confidence level and holding period. It therefore never turns down, and the VaR surface spikes upwards as the confidence level and holding period approach their maximum values. It is important to emphasise that the difference between the surfaces in Figures 2.9 and 5.3 is due entirely to the fact that μ is zero in the first case and positive in the second. The lesson? The mean μ makes a big difference to the risk profile.

5.1.2 Disadvantages of Normality

The normality assumption—whether applied to P/L or returns—also has a number of potential disadvantages. The first is that it allows P/L (or returns) to take any value, and this means that it might produce losses so large that they more than wipe out our capital: we could lose more than the value of our total investment. However, it is usually the case (e.g., due to limited liability and similar constraints) that our losses are bounded, and the failure of the normality assumption to respect constraints on the maximum loss can lead to gross overestimates of what we really stand to lose.

A second potential problem is one of statistical plausibility. As mentioned already, the normality assumption is often justified by reference to the central limit theorem, but the central limit theorem applies only to the central mass of the density function, and not to its extremes. It follows that we can justify normality by reference to the central limit theorem only when dealing with more central quantiles and probabilities. When dealing with extremes—that is, when the confidence level is either very low or very high—we should refer to the extreme value theorem, and that tells us very clearly that we should *not* use normality to model extremes.

A third problem is that most financial returns have excess kurtosis, or fatter than normal tails, and a failure to allow for excess kurtosis can lead to major problems. The implications of excess kurtosis are illustrated in Figure 5.4. This figure shows both the standard normal pdf and a particular type of fat-tailed pdf, a Student t pdf with five degrees of freedom. The impact of excess kurtosis is seen very clearly in the tails: excess kurtosis implies that tails are heavier than normal, and this means that VaRs (at the relatively high confidence levels we are usually interested in) will be bigger. For example, if we take the VaR at the 95% confidence level, the standard normal VaR is 1.645,

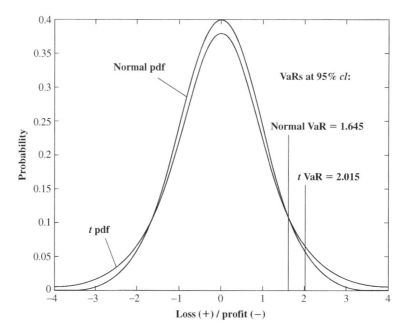

Figure 5.4   Normal VaR vs. fat-tailed VaR.

Note: This figure shows VaRs at the 95% confidence level for standard normal P/L and Student t P/L, where the latter has five degrees of freedom.

but the t VaR is 2.015 — which is 22% bigger.[4] Furthermore, it is obvious from the figure that the proportional difference between the two VaRs gets bigger with the confidence level (e.g., at the 99% confidence level, the normal VaR is 2.326, but the t VaR is 3.365, which is almost 44% bigger). What this means is that if we assume that P/L is normal when it is actually fat-tailed, then we are likely to underestimate our VaRs (and, indeed, ETLs), and these underestimates are likely to be particularly large when dealing with VaRs at high confidence levels.

Box 5.2   The Cornish–Fisher Approximation

If our distribution is not normal, but the deviations from normality are 'small', we can approximate our non-normal distribution using the Cornish–Fisher expansion, which tells us how to adjust the standard normal variate α_{cl} to accommodate non-normal skewness and kurtosis. To use it, we therefore replace the standard variate α_{cl} in our normal VaR or ETL formula by:

$$\alpha_{cl} + (1/6)(\alpha_{cl}^2 - 1)\rho_3 + (1/24)(\alpha_{cl}^3 - 3\alpha_{cl})\rho_4 - (1/36)(2\alpha_{cl}^3 - 5\alpha_{cl})\rho_3^2$$

When using the Cornish–Fisher approximation, we should keep in mind that it will only provide a 'good' approximation if our distribution is 'close' to being normal, and we cannot expect it to be much use if we have a distribution that is too non-normal.

5.2   THE STUDENT t-DISTRIBUTION

As we have just seen, one way to accommodate excess kurtosis is to use a Student t-distribution instead of a normal one. A Student t-distribution with υ degrees of freedom has a kurtosis of $3(\upsilon - 2)/(\upsilon - 4)$, provided $\upsilon \geq 5$, so we can approximate an observed kurtosis of up to 9 by a suitable choice of υ. If we want a relatively high excess kurtosis, we would choose a relatively low value for υ, and if we want a relatively low excess kurtosis, we would choose a high value for υ. This gives us considerable scope to accommodate excess kurtosis, so long as the kurtosis is not too extreme. For risk measurement purposes, we would work with a generalised Student t-distribution that allows us to specify the mean and standard deviation (or variance) of our P/L or return distribution, as well as the number of degrees of freedom. Using the same notation as before, our VaR is then:

$$VaR(hp,cl) = -\alpha_{cl,\upsilon}\sqrt{hp}\,\sqrt{(\upsilon - 2)/\upsilon}\,\sigma_{P/L} - hp\,\mu_{P/L} \tag{5.6}$$

The t VaR formula differs from the earlier normal VaR formula, Equation (5.4a), in that the confidence level term, $\alpha_{cl,\upsilon}$, now refers to a Student t-distribution instead of a normal one, and so depends on υ as well as cl. The t VaR formula also includes the additional multiplier term $\sqrt{(\upsilon - 2)/\upsilon}$, which moderates the effect of the standard deviation on the VaR.

Since the Student t-distribution converges to the normal distribution as υ gets large, we can regard the Student t as a generalization of the normal that produces higher than normal kurtosis when υ is finite. However, as υ gets large, $\alpha_{cl,\upsilon}$ approaches its normal equivalent α_{cl}, $\sqrt{(\upsilon - 2)/\upsilon}$ approaches 1, and the t VaR, Equation (5.6), approaches the normal VaR, Equation (5.4a).

The t VaR is very closely related to the normal VaR, and has many of the same properties. In particular, it behaves in much the same way as normal VaR in the face of changes in cl or hp: it

---

[4]The reason for the t VaR being higher is, in part, because the t has a higher standard deviation: with $\upsilon = 5$, its standard deviation is $\sqrt{\upsilon/(\upsilon - 2)} = 1.291$. However, as we go further out into the tail, even the t VaR we would get with a unit standard deviation is bigger, and increasingly bigger, than the standard normal VaR.

rises with cl; for $\mu_{P/L} > 0$, it tends to rise initially with hp, and then peak and fall; and so forth. Consequently, it produces curves and surfaces that are similar to the normal ones we have seen in Figures 2.7, 5.2 and 5.3.

The great advantage of the t over the normal is its ability to handle reasonable amounts of excess kurtosis.[5] However, the t also has its problems. Like the normal, it fails to respect constraints on maximum possible losses, and can produce misleadingly high-risk estimates as a result. When used at very high or very low confidence levels, it also has the drawback, like the normal, of not being consistent with extreme value theory: we should therefore avoid using a Student t-distribution at extreme confidence levels.

5.3   THE LOGNORMAL DISTRIBUTION

Another popular alternative is to assume that geometric returns are normally distributed. As explained in Chapter 3, this is tantamount to assuming that the value of our portfolio at the end of our holding period is lognormally distributed. Hence, this case is often referred to as lognormal. The pdf of the end-period value of our portfolio is illustrated in Figure 5.5. The value of the portfolio is always positive, and the pdf has a distinctive long tail on its right-hand side.

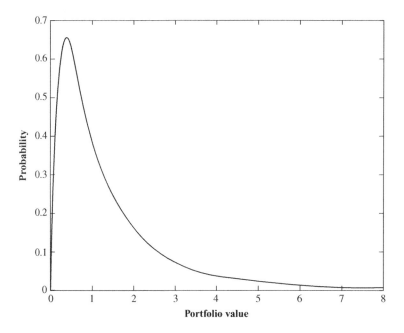

Figure 5.5   A lognormally distributed portfolio.

Note: Estimated with mean and standard deviation equal to 0 and 1, and a current portfolio value of $1, using the 'lognpdf' function in the Statistics Toolbox.

---

[5]We might also use the t-distribution for another reason: if we have a normal P/L, but don't know the parameters μ and σ, then we would have to work with estimates of these parameters instead of their true values. In these circumstances we might sometimes use a t-distribution instead of a normal one, where the number of degrees of freedom is equal to the number of observations in our sample minus 2. For more on this use of the Student t-distribution, see Wilson (1993). However, this exception aside, the main reason for using a t-distribution is to accommodate excess kurtosis, as explained in the text.

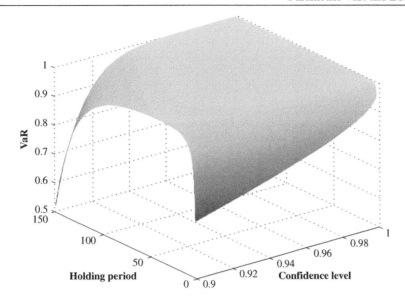

Figure 5.6   A lognormal VaR surface.

Note: Estimated with the 'lognormalvarplot3D' function, assuming the mean and standard deviation of daily geometric returns are 0.1 and 1, and with an initial investment of $1.

The lognormal VaR is given by the following formula:

$$VaR = P_{t-1} - \exp[hp\,\mu_R + \alpha_{cl}\sqrt{hp}\,\sigma_R + \log P_{t-1}] \tag{5.7}$$

where P_{t-1} is the current value of our portfolio. Equation (5.7) generalises the earlier lognormal VaR equation (i.e., Equation (3.16)) by allowing for an arbitrary holding period *hp*. The lognormal assumption has the attraction of ruling out the possibility of a positive-value portfolio becoming a negative-value one: in this case, the VaR can never exceed the value of our portfolio.

The lognormal VaR was illustrated earlier in Figure 3.5, and the typical lognormal VaR surface — that is, the VaR surface with positive μ_R — is shown in Figure 5.6. The VaR initially rises with the confidence level and holding period until it reaches an upper bound. This bound is given by the initial value of our portfolio, assumed here to be $1. The surface then flattens out along this ceiling for a while. As *hp* continues to rise, the surface eventually turns down again, enters negative territory, and then becomes ever more strongly negative as the holding period gets bigger. As we would expect, the surface falls off at lower confidence levels first, and it can take a long time for it to fall off at higher confidence levels. However, the VaR surface always turns down eventually, regardless of the confidence level, so long as the mean return is positive. The reason for this is the same as with normal VaR: as the holding period continues to rise, the mean term becomes more important than the standard deviation term because it grows at a faster rate; eventually, therefore, it kicks in to pull the VaR down, then make it negative, and subsequently make it ever more strongly negative as the holding period continues to rise.[6]

---

[6]Of course, the parameter values on which Figure 5.6 is based are merely illustrative and are not meant to be empirically realistic. However, the general surface will always take the form shown in Figure 5.6 provided the mean is positive, and the only real issue is how long it takes for the surface to start falling as *hp* continues to rise. Note also that the identification of our basic time period as a day is merely a convention, and our time period could be any length we choose.

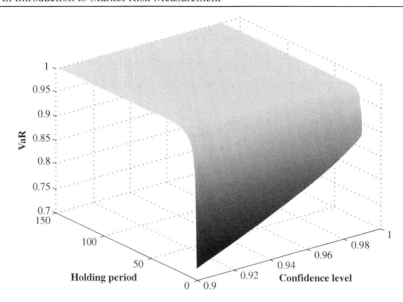

Figure 5.7   A lognormal VaR surface with zero mean return.

Note: Estimated with the 'lognormalvarplot3D' function, assuming the mean and standard deviation of geometric returns are 0 and 1, and with an initial investment of $1.

Once again, the mean term is important in determining the shape of the VaR surface. A lognormal VaR surface with a zero mean term would, by contrast, have the VaR rise — and rise more quickly — to hit its ceiling and then stay there for ever. This is shown in Figure 5.7, which is the direct analogue to the normal zero-mean case shown in Figure 2.9. Again, the mean term can make a big difference to estimated risks, particularly over long holding periods.

One other point to note about a lognormal distribution is its asymmetry, which is obvious from Figure 5.5. One important implication of any asymmetric P/L or return distribution is that long and short positions have asymmetric risk exposures. A long position loses if the market goes down, and a short position loses if the market goes up, but with any symmetric distribution the VaR on a long position and the VaR on a short position are mirror images of each other, reflecting the symmetry of the lower and upper tails of the distribution.

The situation can be very different with asymmetric distributions. With the lognormal, for example, the worst the long position can do is lose the value of its investment — the VaR and ETL are bounded above in a natural way — but a short position can make much larger losses. To illustrate, Figure 5.8 shows the VaRs for long and short positions in a lognormally distributed asset. The long position loses when the market falls, but the fall in the market is limited by the value of the initial investment. A $1 investment — a long position — has a VaR of 0.807. However, the corresponding short position — a short $1 position has a VaR of 4.180. The short side has a potentially unlimited VaR, and its VaRs will be particularly high because it gets hit very hard by the long right-hand tail in the asset price, shown in Figure 5.5 — a tail that translates into very high profits for the long position, and very high losses for the short position.

In short, the lognormal approach has the attraction of taking account of maximum loss constraints on long positions. It also has the advantage of being consistent with a geometric Brownian motion

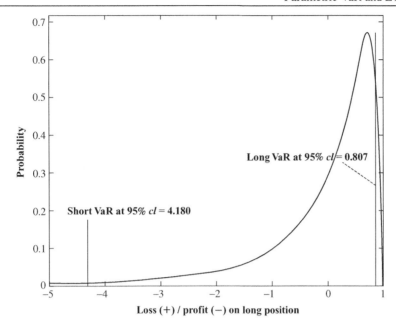

Figure 5.8 Lognormal VaRs for long and short positions.

Note: Estimated with the 'lognormalvarfigure' function, assuming the mean and standard deviation of geometric returns are 0 and 1, and with initial positions worth plus or minus $1.

process for the underlying asset price—a process that has a number of nice features and is widely used in the derivatives industry. However, it also has potential disadvantages, of which the most important are that it does not accommodate fat tails in (geometric) returns,[7] and extreme value (EV) theory tells us that it is not suitable for VaR and ETL at extreme confidence levels.

5.4 EXTREME VALUE DISTRIBUTIONS

If we are concerned about VaRs and ETLs at extreme confidence levels, the best approach is to use an EV distribution (see Tool No. 5: Extreme Value VaR and ETL). In a nutshell, EV theory tells us that we should use these—and only these—to estimate VaRs or ETLs at extreme confidence levels.

5.4.1 The Generalised Extreme Value Distribution

EV theory offers a choice of two approaches. The first of these is to work with a generalised extreme value (GEV) distribution. The choice of this distribution can be justified by reference to the famous

---

[7]This criticism also applies to geometric Brownian motion. However, one straightforward solution is to replace the assumption that geometric returns are normally distributed with the assumption that they are distributed as a Student *t*-distribution. This 'log-*t*' approach combines the benefits of the lognormal with the fatter geometric return tails of the *t*.

Fisher–Tippett theorem, which tells us that if X has a suitably 'well-behaved' distribution function $F(x)$, then the distribution function of extreme values of X converges asymptotically to the GEV distribution function:

$$H_{\xi,a,b} = \begin{cases} \exp[-(1 + \xi(x - a)/b)^{-1/\xi}] & \\ \exp[-\exp(-(x - a)/b)] & \end{cases} \text{if} \quad \begin{matrix} \xi \neq 0 \\ \xi = 0 \end{matrix} \tag{5.8}$$

where $1 + \xi(x - a)/b > 0$, a and b are location and scale parameters, and ξ is the tail index. The relationship of the location and scale parameters to the mean and variance is explained in Tool No. 5.

We are usually interested in two special cases of this distribution: the Gumbel distribution (if $\xi = 0$) and the Fréchet distribution (if $\xi > 0$). The Gumbel and Fréchet VaRs are:

$$VaR = \begin{cases} a - (b/\xi)[1 - (-\log cl)^{-\xi}] & \\ a - b \log(\log(1/cl)) & \end{cases} \text{if} \quad \begin{matrix} \xi > 0 \\ \xi = 0 \end{matrix} \tag{5.9}$$

We can estimate these VaRs by inserting estimates of the parameters into the relevant formulas, and obtain parameter estimates by ML or semi-parametric methods.

In estimating EV VaR, we must also take care to use the correct formula(s). For example, the formulas given in Equation (5.9) could apply to P/L, L/P or just high losses. However, as they involve no variable representing the size of our portfolio or the amount invested — we should multiply them by the value of such a variable when our data are in rate-of-return form: if we have a \$1 investment, we would multiply Equation (5.9) by 1, if we had a \$2 investment, we would multiply Equation (5.9) by 2, etc.

We should also take care to apply the (correct) formula(s) in the correct way: we need to decide whether we are fitting losses, profits/losses, returns, etc., to the EV distribution, and in doing so, we need to take account of any constraints on the values that our data can take; we need to be clear which tail of the EV distribution — the lower tail or the upper tail — we are interested in; and we need to take account of whether our position is a long or a short one, which is also one factor in determining which tail we should be interested in.

These decisions will have a critical effect on the VaR and on the shape of the VaR surface. And, as we might expect from the earlier cases, the shape of the VaR surface will also depend in an important way on the mean parameter. For example, if we apply the Gumbel to P/L, and take the mean to be positive, we get the Gumbel VaR surface shown in Figure 5.9. This surface is reminiscent of the normal positive-mean VaR surface shown in Figure 5.3, and has much the same explanation (i.e., the mean term becomes more important as the holding period rises, and eventually pulls the VaR down, etc.). However, if we assume a zero mean, we get a Gumbel VaR surface reminiscent of Figure 2.9, in which the VaR continues to rises as the holding period increases. We would also get a different VaR surface if we apply the Gumbel to, say, geometric returns, because geometric returns imply that the VaR of any positive-value position is limited by the value of that position: we would then get VaR surfaces reminiscent of the lognormal VaR surfaces in Figures 5.6 and 5.7. In short, the shape of the VaR surface depends on how we apply EV theory, and on the parameter values involved.

5.4.2   The Peaks Over Threshold (Generalised Pareto) Approach

We can also apply EV theory to the distribution of excess losses over a (high) threshold. This leads us to the peaks over threshold (POT) or generalised Pareto approach. If X is a suitable random loss

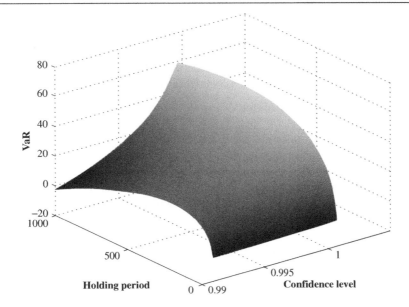

Figure 5.9   A Gumbel VaR surface.

Note: Estimated with the 'gumbelvarplot3D' function, assuming the mean and standard deviation of P/L are 0.1 and 1.

with distribution function $F(x)$, and u is a threshold value of X, then we can define a distribution of excesses over u as:

$$F_u(y) = \Pr\{X - u \le y \mid X > u\} \tag{5.10}$$

This gives the probability that a loss exceeds the threshold u by at most y, given that it does exceed the threshold. The distribution of X itself can be any of the commonly used distributions, but as u gets large, the distribution $F_u(y)$ converges to a generalised Pareto distribution:

$$G_{\xi,\beta}(x) = \begin{cases} 1 - (1 + \xi x/\beta)^{-1/\xi} & \text{if} \quad \xi \ne 0 \\ 1 - \exp(-x/\beta) & \qquad \xi = 0 \end{cases} \tag{5.11}$$

where $\beta > 0$ is a scale parameter, ξ is a shape or tail parameter (see, e.g., McNeil (1999a, p. 4)). We are usually interested in the case where $\xi > 0$, corresponding to our returns being fat-tailed.

As discussed in Tool No. 5: Extreme Value VaR and ETL, the POT approach gives rises to the following formulas for VaR and ETL:

$$VaR = u + (\beta/\xi)\{[(n/N_u)(1 - cl)]^{-\xi} - 1\} \tag{5.12a}$$

$$ETL = [VaR + (\beta - \xi u)]/(1 - \xi) \tag{5.12b}$$

provided that $\xi < 1$, where n is the sample size and N_u is the number of excess values.

In applying the POT approach, we should also take account of the same ancillary factors as we would if we were using a GEV approach: which variable — excess loss, excess return, etc. — we are fitting to the GP distribution; the need to multiply the formulas by a position size variable if we are dealing with rates of return; the need to decide which tail we should be interested in; and the need to take account of whether our position is long or short.

Box 5.3   Estimating Confidence Intervals for Parametric VaR and ETL

There are various ways we can estimate confidence intervals for parametric VaR. Leaving aside simple cases where we can easily derive confidence intervals analytically — for an example see Chappell and Dowd (1999) — we can obtain confidence intervals using the following approaches:

- We can estimate confidence intervals for VaR using the quantile standard error approach outlines in Section 4.3.1
- We can obtain confidence intervals using order statistics theory, explained in Tool No. 1: Estimating VaR and ETL Using Order Statistics, and Section 4.3.2. The OS approach is also useful for estimating confidence intervals for ETL.
- We can obtain confidence intervals for VaR or ETL using Monte Carlo simulation: we run a batch of n trials, obtain the VaR or ETL of each batch, and estimate the confidence interval from the sample on n VaR or ETL estimates.
- We can obtain confidence intervals using profile likelihood approaches: we use estimates of the likelihood function of the assumed distribution function to determine the range of VaR values consistent with a given data set at a chosen probability level (e.g., as in McNeil (1998)).

5.5   THE MULTIVARIATE NORMAL VARIANCE–COVARIANCE APPROACH

We now consider parametric VaR and ETL from the individual position level, where we make parametric assumptions about individual asset returns (or P/L) rather than assumptions about portfolio returns (or P/L). In many respects the obvious assumption to make — or at least the assumption we would like to be able to make — is that individual asset returns are distributed as multivariate normal. This assumption is the counterpart to the earlier assumption that portfolio returns (or P/L) are normal — and, indeed, the assumption that individual asset returns are multivariate normal implies that portfolio returns will be normal.

Suppose we have a portfolio consisting of n different assets, the (arithmetic) returns to which are distributed as multivariate normal with mean μ and variance–covariance matrix Σ, where μ is an $n \times 1$ vector and Σ is an $n \times n$ matrix with variance terms down its main diagonal and covariances elsewhere. The $1 \times n$ vector $\mathbf{w}$ gives the proportion of our portfolio invested in each asset (i.e., the first element w_1 gives the proportion of the portfolio invested in asset 1, and so on, and the sum of the w_i terms is 1). Our portfolio return therefore has an expected value of $\mathbf{w}\mu$, a variance of $\mathbf{w}\Sigma\mathbf{w}^T$, where $\mathbf{w}^T$ is the $n \times 1$ transpose vector of $\mathbf{w}$, and a standard deviation of $\sqrt{\mathbf{w}\Sigma\mathbf{w}^T}$. If the current value of our portfolio is P, then its VaR over holding period hp and confidence level cl is:

$$VaR(hp,cl) = -\left[\alpha_{cl}\sqrt{hp}\,\sqrt{\mathbf{w}\Sigma\mathbf{w}^T} + hp\,\mathbf{w}\mu\right]P \tag{5.13}$$

Equation (5.13) is the multivariate normal equivalent of our earlier normal VaR, Equation (5.4a), and the α_{cl} term again refers to the relevant quantile from a standard normal distribution. The 'P' term arises because we are applying multivariate normality to returns, rather than P/L. It follows, too, that our ETL is:

$$ETL(hp,cl) = \left[\sqrt{hp}\,\sqrt{\mathbf{w}\Sigma\mathbf{w}^T}\phi(-\alpha_{cl})/F(\alpha_{cl}) - hp\,\mathbf{w}\mu\right]P \tag{5.14}$$

which is the multivariate normal equivalent of the normal ETL, Equation (5.4b). Note that in

Equation (5.14), as in Equation (5.4b), the $\phi(-\alpha_{cl})$ and $F(\alpha_{cl})$ terms are both from the univariate standard normal distribution.

The variance–covariance matrix Σ — or covariance matrix for short — captures the interactions between the returns to the different assets. It is also closely related to the $n \times n$ correlation matrix. If we define σ as an $n \times n$ matrix consisting of standard deviations along its main diagonal and zeros elsewhere, then $\Sigma = \sigma C \sigma$, where C is the $n \times n$ correlation matrix. This matrix has ones down its main diagonal — these can be interpreted as each return's correlation with itself — and the correlations between different asset returns elsewhere.

The values of these covariance or correlation terms have a critical bearing on the VaR. To see these effects in their simplest form, suppose our portfolio consists of two assets, 1 and 2, with a relative amount $w_1 = 0.5$ held in asset 1, and a relative amount $w_2 = 0.5$ held in asset 2. If each asset has a return with mean 0 and standard deviation 1, the standard deviation of the portfolio return σ_p is:

$$\sigma_p = \sqrt{w_1^2 \sigma_1^2 + w_2^2 \sigma_2^2 + 2\rho w_1 w_2 \sigma_1 \sigma_2} = \sqrt{(1 + \rho)/2} \qquad (5.15)$$

where ρ is the correlation between the returns to the two assets. If we now take the value of our portfolio to be 1, and set the holding period to be 1 as well, then our VaR is:

$$VaR = -\alpha_{cl} \sigma_p = -\alpha_{cl} \sqrt{(1 + \rho)/2} \qquad (5.16)$$

which shows very clearly the dependence of the VaR on the value of the correlation coefficient.

The correlation coefficient can vary over the range $[-1, +1]$, and there are three important special cases:

- If ρ takes its minimum value of -1, the portfolio standard deviation is zero, and so, too, is the VaR. The explanation is that the shocks to the two returns perfectly offset each other, so the portfolio return is certain; the standard deviation of the portfolio return and the VaR are therefore both zero.
- If ρ is 0, the portfolio standard deviation is $\sqrt{1/2} = 0.707$, and the VaR is 1.163. In this case the returns are independent of each other, and the portfolio VaR is less than the VaR we would get (i.e., 1.645) if we invested our portfolio entirely into one asset or the other. This result reflects the well-known idea that if returns are independent, a portfolio of two assets will be less risky than a portfolio consisting of either asset on its own.
- If ρ reaches its maximum value of 1, the portfolio standard deviation is 1 and the VaR is 1.645, which is the same as the VaR we would have obtained investing entirely in either asset. If asset returns are perfectly correlated, the portfolio variance is the sum of the variances of the individual returns, and there is no risk diversification.

More generally, the main points are that the portfolio VaR falls as the correlation coefficient falls and, except for the special case where the correlation coefficient is 1, the VaR of the portfolio is less than the sum of the VaRs of the individual assets.

These insights extend naturally to portfolios with more than two assets. If we have n assets in our portfolio and invest equally in each, and if we assume for convenience that all correlations take the same value ρ and all asset returns have the same standard deviation σ, then the standard deviation of the portfolio return is:

$$\sigma_p = \sigma \sqrt{\frac{1}{n} + \frac{(n-1)\rho}{n}} \qquad (5.17)$$

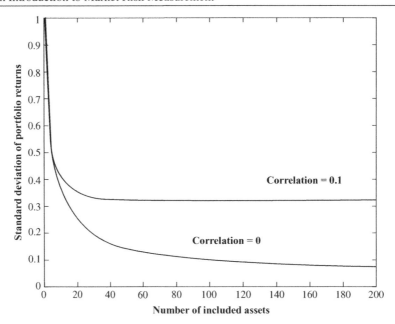

Figure 5.10   Portfolio standard deviation and the number of included assets.

Note: Estimated assuming that individual assets have the same standard deviation σ, equal to 1, and all correlations take the same value.

(see, e.g., Elton and Gruber (1995, p. 60)). Except for the special case where $\rho = 1$ — in which case σ_p is always σ — the portfolio standard deviation falls as n gets bigger. The behaviour of the portfolio standard deviation as n changes is illustrated in Figure 5.10. The portfolio standard deviation falls rapidly at first — which indicates substantial reductions in portfolio risk as n initially rises — but then levels out and thereafter falls much more slowly.

This figure also has other interpretations. The curves in the figure are the portfolio standard deviations taking account of diversification effects, divided by the portfolio standard deviation if we take no account of diversification effects (i.e., and invest entirely in one asset). The curves can therefore be regarded as measuring the extent to which diversification reduces overall risk, dependent on the number of included assets and the correlation. The curves tell us that diversification reduces risk more, the more assets are included and the lower the correlation ρ.

Furthermore, given the parameters assumed in Figure 5.10, these same curves also give us the ratio of diversified to undiversified VaR — they give the VaR taking account of diversification, divided by the VaR taking no account of diversification (i.e., the VaR we would get if we invested only in one asset). Again, we see that the extent to which VaR is reduced by diversification depends on the number of assets and the correlation. However, we can also see that even a small amount of diversification can have big effects on the VaR, and these effects are particularly strong if the correlation coefficient is relatively low.

5.6   CONCLUSIONS

As we have seen, parametric approaches are very diverse, and can be applied at both the portfolio level and the position level. Their main attraction is that they give us a lot of VaR and ETL information on the basis of relatively limited assumptions. Their main weakness, of course, is that they depend on those assumptions, and can lead to serious errors if we get those assumptions wrong. In using parametric approaches, it is therefore important to choose parametric assumptions that fit the problems to hand. Some fairly obvious points then follow:

- We should think carefully about the range of permissible values that returns or P/L can take. For example, do we want losses or returns to be bounded?
- If we have fat tails in our data, we shouldn't use normal distributions. We should also bear in mind that appeals to the central limit theorem don't cut much ice when dealing with quantiles and probabilities well away from the mean. Instead, we should use a suitable fat-tailed distribution, and there are a number of these to choose from.
- If we are especially concerned with VaR or ETL at very high confidence levels, we should pay attention to extreme value theory, and use an EV approach rather than an ad hoc one.

In short, the key to success in parametric risk estimation is to get the parametric assumptions right: once we have these sorted out, everything else follows easily.

Box 5.4   Parametric VaR and ETL Functions in MATLAB

The Statistics Toolbox has a number of functions that are useful for parametric VaR and ETL. These include, among others, the various functions that derive the quantiles or inverse distribution functions: 'norminv', 'logninv', 'tinv', etc., for the normal, lognormal, Student t, and other cases.

For its part, the IMRM Toolbox has a large number of parametric VaR and ETL routines. If we take normal VaR as an instance, we have the functions 'normalvar', 'normalvarconfidenceinterval', 'normalvardfperc', 'normalvarfigure', 'normalvarplot2D_cl', 'normalvarplot2D_hp' and 'normalvarplot3D'. The first three of these estimate normal VaR, normal VaR confidence intervals, and percentiles of the normal VaR distribution function. The others plot a normal VaR figure, and produce 2D and 3D curves or surfaces showing how normal VaR changes with confidence level and/or holding period.

There are some similar functions for normal ETL ('normaletl', etc.), other parametric VaRs (e.g., 'gumbelvar', 'frechetvar', 'lognormalvar', 'tvar', 'logtvar', 'gparetovar', etc.) and other parametric ETLs (e.g., 'gumbeletl', 'frechetetl', 'lognormaletl', 'tetl', 'logtetl', 'gparetoetl', etc.).

The IMRM Toolbox also has the functions 'cornishfishervar' and 'cornishfisheretl' which estimate VaR and ETL using the Cornish–Fisher expansion.

At the position level, the Toolbox also has the functions 'variancecovariancevar' and 'variancecovarianceetl', which estimate VaR and ETL from the position level, assuming that returns are multivariate normally distributed, and the functions 'adjustedvariancecovariancevar' and 'adjustedvariancecovarianceetl', which use a variance–covariance approach and then adjust the results using a Cornish–Fisher adjustment for the non-normality of portfolio returns.

5.7   RECOMMENDED READING

Bauer (2000); Duffie and Pan (1997); Eberlein and Prause (2000); Eberlein *et al.* (1998); Embrechts *et al.* (1997); Engle and Manganelli (1999); Huisman *et al.* (1998); Hull and White (1998a); Jackson *et al.* (1997); Malevergne and Sornette (2001); McNeil (1998); Rachev and Mittnik (2000); Ridder (1997, pp. 12–20); RiskMetrics *Technical Document* (1996); Venkataraman (1997); Wilson (1994b, 1996); Zangari (1996a–c).

Appendix
Delta–Gamma and Related Approximations

As we have seen, if all positions are linear in underlying risk factors — and preferably, though not necessarily, linear in normal risk factors — then mapping and VaR estimation is quite straightforward. But how do we handle positions that are *not* linear in underlying risk factors?

A5.1 DELTA–NORMAL APPROACHES

Such non-linearity is particularly common when dealing with options, but is also common with positions in fixed-income instruments (e.g., where a bond's price–yield relationship exhibits convexity). One possible response is to work with linear approximations: we replace the 'true' positions with these linear approximations, and handle the linearly approximated positions in the same way as genuine linear positions in (typically) normal (or lognormal) risk factors.[8] This is the delta–normal approach, which effectively assumes that the non-linearity is sufficiently limited that we can ignore it and still get sufficiently accurate VaR estimates to be useful.

Imagine we have a straightforward equity call option of value c. The value of this option depends on a variety of factors (e.g., the price of the underlying stock, the exercise price of the option, the volatility of the underlying stock price, etc.), but in using the delta–normal approach we ignore all factors other than the underlying stock price, and handle that by taking a first-order Taylor series approximation of the change in the option value:

$$\Delta c \approx \delta \Delta S \tag{A5.1}$$

where $\Delta c = c - \bar{c}$ and $\Delta S = S - \bar{S}$, S is the underlying stock price, δ is the option's delta, and the lines above c and S refer to the current values of these variables. If we are dealing with a very short holding period (i.e., so we can take δ as if it were approximately constant over that period), the option VaR is:

$$VaR^{option} \approx \delta VaR^S \tag{A5.2}$$

where VaR^S is the VaR of a unit of underlying stock.[9] The VaR is thus δ times the VaR of the underlying stock. If S is normally distributed and the holding period is sufficiently short that we can ignore the expected return on the underlying stock — an assumption we will make throughout this Appendix, and which is not unreasonable in the context — then the option VaR is:

$$VaR^{option} \approx \delta VaR^S \approx -\delta \alpha_{cl} \sigma S \tag{A5.3}$$

where σ is the volatility of S.

---

[8] Any approach to approximate options risks works better with a shorter holding period. The smaller the time period, the smaller the change dS and, hence, the smaller the squared change $(dS)^2$. We can therefore sometimes get away with the delta–normal approximation when dealing with relatively short holding periods, but it is more difficult defending this assumption with longer holding periods.

[9] We are also assuming that the option position is a long one. If the option position is short, the option VaR would be approximately $-\delta VaR^S$. However, these approximations only hold over very short time intervals. Over longer intervals, the long and short VaRs become asymmetric, and the usefulness of these approximations is, to say the least, highly problematic.

This approach has a number of attractions. (1) It gives us a tractable way of handling option positions that retains the benefits of linear normality. (2) It does so without adding any new risk factors. (3) The new parameter introduced into the calculation, the option's δ, is readily available for any traded option, so the delta–normal approach requires minimal additional data. (4) It relies on a premise — normality — that is often plausible, and particularly so:

> if the time horizon is very short, e.g., intraday, and if the products themselves have a relatively linear pay-off profile, or, because it is easy to calculate, if a quick and dirty method is required. Thus, it may be very well suited for measuring and controlling intraday risks of a money market or foreign exchange book with few option positions.
>
> (Wilson (1996, p. 220))

We can handle the non-linearities of bond portfolios in a comparable way, using the duration approximation discussed in Section 1.2.2.

However, these first-order approaches — whether based on delta–normal or duration approximations — are only likely to be reliable when our portfolio is close to linear in the first place, since only then can a linear approximation be expected to produce an accurate VaR estimate.[10] We can therefore get away with delta–normal techniques only if there is very limited non-linearity (e.g., optionality or convexity) in our portfolio, but we should be very wary of resorting to such techniques when dealing with positions with considerable optionality or other non-linear features.

Box A5.1   Instruments with Embedded Optionality

Many otherwise straightforward instruments have embedded optionality. Many bonds have embedded call options that allow the issuer to call (i.e., repurchase) them before maturity on prespecified terms. Bonds can also be convertible, giving the holder the right to convert them into the issuer's equity on prespecified terms, or puttable, giving the holder the right to sell back to the issuer.

The existence of an embedded option can have a major impact on an instrument's price and volatility behaviour. Where a call option is embedded in a bond, the bond price cannot rise too far without leading the issuer to call the bond. (The issuer would call the bond to profit from the difference between the high market price and the (low) call price.) Similarly, if the issuer's share price rose too high, the holder of a convertible bond would have an incentive to exercise his option to convert. Hence, the price/volatility behaviour of a callable or convertible bond can be quite different from that of a corresponding 'straight' bond.

Handling instruments with embedded options is straightforward. The rule of zero arbitrage should ensure that the price of any instrument with an embedded option is the same as the price of the corresponding straight instrument plus or minus the price of the embedded option. For example, the price of a callable bond would be:

$$p_B^{callable} = p_B - c$$

where $p_B^{callable}$ is the price of the callable bond, p_B is the price of its straight equivalent, and c is the price of the option. In theory, we can therefore handle the callable bond by working with its synthetic equivalent consisting of a long straight bond and a short call, and we already know how to map these positions and estimate their VaRs.

---

[10]If there is any doubt on this issue — which there shouldn't really be — this supposition is confirmed by the simulation results of Estrella *et al.* (1994, p. 39), which suggest that linear approximations can 'seriously underestimate' the VaRs of option positions precisely because they ignore second-order risk factors (i.e., gamma risks).

A5.2   DELTA–GAMMA APPROACHES

A5.2.1   The Delta–Gamma Approximation

An obvious alternative is to take a second-order approach — to accommodate non-linearity by taking a second-order Taylor series approximation rather than a first-order one. This second-order approximation is usually known in finance as a delta–gamma approximation, and taking such an approximation for a standard European call option gives us the following:

$$\Delta c \approx \delta \Delta S + (\gamma/2)(\Delta S)^2 \tag{A5.4}$$

This second-order approximation takes account of the gamma risk that the delta–normal approach ignores (cf. Equation (A5.1)).[11] The improvement over the delta–normal approach is particularly marked when the option has a high (positive or negative) gamma (e.g., as would be the case with at-the-money options that are close to maturity).[12] However, once we get into second-order approximations the problem of estimating VaR becomes much more difficult, as we now have the squared or quadratic terms to deal with.[13]

A5.2.2   The Delta–Gamma Normal Approach

One tempting but flawed response to this problem is to use a delta–gamma normal approach, the essence of which is to regard the extra risk factor $(\Delta S)^2$ as equivalent to another independently distributed normal variable to be treated in the same way as the first one (i.e., ΔS). We can then regard the change in option value as if driven by two risk factors, ΔS and ΔU:

$$\Delta c \approx \delta \Delta S + (\gamma/2)\Delta U \tag{A5.5}$$

where ΔU equals $(\Delta S)^2$. When estimating VaR, we treat the option as equivalent to a portfolio that is linear in two normal risk factors. The option VaR is therefore equal to $-\alpha_{cl}$ times the 'portfolio'

---

[11]However, as is clear from the Black–Scholes equation, both delta–normal and delta–gamma approximations can also run into problems from other sources of risk. Even if the underlying price S does not change, a change in expected volatility will lead to a change in the price of the option and a corresponding change in the option's VaR: this is the infamous problem of vega risk, or the volatility of volatility. Similarly, the option's value will also change in response to a change in the interest rate (the rho effect) and in response to the passing of time (the theta effect). In principle, these effects are not too difficult to handle because they do not involve higher-order (e.g., squared) terms, and we can tack these additional terms onto the basic delta–normal or delta–gamma approximations if we wish to. However, vega in particular can be notoriously badly behaved.

[12]There can also be some difficult problems lurking beneath the surface here. (1) The second-order approximation can still be inaccurate even with simple instruments such as vanilla calls. Estrella (1996, p. 360) points out that the power series for the Black–Scholes approximation formula does not always converge, and even when it does, we sometimes need very high-order approximations to obtain results of sufficient accuracy to be useful. However, Mori *et al.* (1996, p. 9) and Schachter (1995) argue on the basis of plausible parameter simulations that Estrella is unduly pessimistic about the usefulness of Taylor series approximations, but even they do not dispute Estrella's basic warning that results based on Taylor series approximations can be unreliable. (2) We might be dealing with instruments with more complex payoff functions than simple calls, and their payoff profiles might make second-order approximations very inaccurate (e.g., as is potentially the case with options such as knockouts or range forwards) or just intractable (as is apparently the case with the mortgage-backed securities considered by Jakobsen (1996)).

[13]Nonetheless, one way to proceed is to estimate the moments of the empirical P/L or return distribution, use these to fit the empirical distribution to a fairly general class of distributions such as Pearson family or Johnson distributions, and then infer the VaR from the fitted distribution (see, e.g., Zangari (1996c), Jahel *et al.* (1999)). This type of approach can easily accommodate approximations involving the Greeks, as well as other features such as stochastic volatility (Jahel *et al.* (1999)). We will consider such approaches in Section A5.2.4.

standard deviation, where the latter is found by applying the usual formula, i.e.:

$$\sigma_p = \sqrt{\delta^2\sigma^2 + (\gamma/2)^2\sigma_U^2} = \sqrt{\delta^2\sigma^2 + (1/4)\gamma^2\sigma^4} \tag{A5.6}$$

where σ, as before, is the volatility of the stock and σ_U is the volatility of the hypothetical instrument U. Consequently, the option VaR is:

$$VaR^{option} = -\alpha_{cl}\sigma_p S = -\alpha_{cl}\sigma S\sqrt{\delta^2 + (1/4)\gamma^2\sigma^2} \tag{A5.7}$$

The delta–gamma normal approach thus salvages tractability by forcing the model back into the confines of linear normality, so that we can then apply a modified delta–normal approach to it. Unfortunately, it also suffers from a glaring logical problem: ΔS and $(\Delta S)^2$ *cannot* both be normal. If ΔS is normal, then $(\Delta S)^2$ is chi-squared and Δc, as given by Equation (A5.5), is the sum of a normal and a chi-squared. The delta–gamma normal approach consequently achieves tractability by compromising its logical coherence, and it can lead to seriously flawed estimates of VaR.[14]

A5.2.3 Wilson's Delta–Gamma Approach

An alternative approach was proposed by Wilson (1994b, 1996). This procedure goes back to the definition of VaR as the maximum possible loss with a given level of probability. Wilson suggests that this definition implies that the VaR is the solution to a corresponding optimisation problem, and his proposal is that we estimate VaR by solving this problem.[15] In the case of a single call option, the VaR can be formally defined as the solution to the following problem:[16]

$$VaR = \max_{\{\Delta S\}} [-\Delta c], \quad \text{subject to } (\Delta S)^2\sigma_S^{-2} \leq \alpha_{cl}^2 \tag{A5.8}$$

In words, the VaR is the maximum loss (i.e., the maximum value of $-[\Delta c]$) subject to the constraint that underlying price changes occur within a certain confidence interval. The bigger the chosen confidence level, the bigger α_{cl} and the bigger the permitted maximum price change ΔS.[17] In the present context we also take the option price change Δc to be proxied by its delta–gamma approximation:

$$\Delta c \approx \delta\Delta S + \gamma(\Delta S)^2/2 \tag{A5.9}$$

---

[14] A good example is the option position just considered, since the delta–gamma estimate of VaR is actually *worse* than the delta–normal one. Equation (A5.7) implies that the delta–gamma normal procedure gives an estimate of VaR that is even higher than the delta–normal estimate, and the delta–normal estimate is already too big. (Why? If the underlying stock price falls, the corresponding fall in the option price is cushioned by the gamma term. The true VaR of the option position is then less than would be predicted by a linear delta approximation that ignores the gamma effect. Hence, the delta–normal approach overestimates the option's VaR.) Since the delta–normal estimate is already too high, the delta–gamma one must be even higher. In this particular case, we would have a better VaR estimate if we ignored the gamma term completely — a good example that shows how treacherous the delta–gamma normal approach can be.

[15] Wilson himself calls his risk measure 'capital at risk' rather than value at risk, but it is clear from his discussion that he sees 'capital at risk' as conceptually similar to VaR and I prefer to use the more conventional term. However, there are in fact major differences between the VaR (or whatever else we call it) implied by a quadratic programming approach (of which Wilson's is an example) and conventional or 'true' VaR (see Britten-Jones and Schaefer (1999, appendix)), and we will come back to these differences a little later in the text.

[16] See, e.g., Wilson (1996, pp. 205–207).

[17] In the case of our call option, the constraint could equally have been written in the more intuitive form $(\Delta S)\sigma_S^{-1} \leq \alpha_{cl}$. However, more generally, the maximum loss could occur for positive or negative values of ΔS depending on the particular position. Writing the constraint in squared form is a convenient way to capture both positive and negative values of ΔS in a single constraint.

In general, this approach allows for the maximum loss to occur with $(\Delta S)^2$ taking any value in the range permitted by the constraint, i.e.:

$$0 \leq (\Delta S)^2 \leq \alpha_{cl}^2 \sigma_S^2 \tag{A5.10}$$

which in turn implies that:

$$\alpha_{cl}\sigma_S \leq \Delta S \leq -\alpha_{cl}\sigma_S \tag{A5.11}$$

However, in this case, we also know that the maximum loss occurs when ΔS takes one or other of its permitted extreme values, i.e., where $\Delta S = \alpha_{cl}\sigma_S$ or $\Delta S = -\alpha_{cl}\sigma_S$. We therefore substitute each of these two values of ΔS into Equation (A5.11) and the VaR is the bigger of the two losses.

The Wilson approach also applies to portfolios with more than one instrument, but in doing so it unfortunately loses its easiness. In this more general case, the VaR is given by the solution to the following quadratic programming (QP) optimisation problem:

$$VaR = \max_{\{\Delta \mathbf{S}\}} -[\boldsymbol{\delta}^{\mathrm{T}}\Delta \mathbf{S} + \Delta \mathbf{S}^{\mathrm{T}}\boldsymbol{\gamma}\Delta \mathbf{S}/2], \quad \text{subject to } \Delta \mathbf{S}^{\mathrm{T}}\boldsymbol{\Sigma}^{-1}\Delta \mathbf{S} \leq \alpha_{cl}^2 \tag{A5.12}$$

where $\boldsymbol{\delta}$ is a vector of deltas, $\boldsymbol{\gamma}$ is a matrix of gamma and cross-gamma terms, the superscript 'T' indicates a transpose, and we again use bold face to represent the relevant matrices (Wilson (1996, p. 207)). This problem is a standard quadratic programming problem, and one way to handle it is to rewrite the problem in Lagrangian form:

$$L = -[\boldsymbol{\delta}^{\mathrm{T}}\Delta \mathbf{S} + \Delta \mathbf{S}^{\mathrm{T}}\boldsymbol{\gamma}\Delta \mathbf{S}/2] + \lambda[\Delta \mathbf{S}^{\mathrm{T}}\boldsymbol{\Sigma}^{-1}\Delta \mathbf{S} - \alpha_{cl}] \tag{A5.13}$$

We then differentiate L with respect to each element of $\Delta \mathbf{S}$ to arrive at the following set of Kuhn–Tucker conditions, which describe the solution:

$$[-\boldsymbol{\gamma} - \lambda\boldsymbol{\Sigma}^{-1}]\Delta \mathbf{S} = \boldsymbol{\delta}$$
$$\Delta \mathbf{S}^{\mathrm{T}}\boldsymbol{\Sigma}^{-1}\Delta \mathbf{S} \leq \alpha_{cl}^2 \tag{A5.14}$$
$$\lambda\left(\Delta \mathbf{S}^{\mathrm{T}}\boldsymbol{\Sigma}^{-1}\Delta \mathbf{S} - \alpha_{cl}^2\right) = 0 \quad \text{and} \quad \lambda \geq 0$$

where λ is the Lagrange multiplier associated with the constraint, which indicates how much the VaR will rise as we increase the confidence level (Wilson (1996, p. 208)). The solution, $\Delta \mathbf{S}^*$, is then:

$$\Delta \mathbf{S}^* = A(\lambda)^{-1}\boldsymbol{\delta} \tag{A5.15}$$

where $A(\lambda) = -[\boldsymbol{\gamma} + \lambda\boldsymbol{\Sigma}^{-1}]$. Solving for $\Delta \mathbf{S}^*$ therefore requires that we search over each possible λ value and invert the $A(\lambda)$ matrix for each such value. We also have to check which solutions satisfy our constraint and eliminate those that do not satisfy it. In so doing, we build up a set of potential $\Delta \mathbf{S}^*$ solutions that satisfy our constraint, each contingent on a particular λ value, and then plug each of them into Equation (A5.15) to find the one that maximises L.[18]

---

[18]That said, implementing this procedure is not easy. We have to invert bigger and bigger matrices as the number of risk factors gets larger, and this can lead to computational problems (e.g., matrices failing to invert). We can ameliorate these problems if we are prepared to make some simplifying assumptions, and one useful simplification is to assume that the $A(\lambda)$ matrix is diagonal. If we make this assumption Equation (A5.15) gives us closed-form solutions for $\Delta \mathbf{S}^*$ in terms of λ without any need to worry about matrix inversions. Computations become much faster, and the gain in speed is particularly large when we have a big $A(\lambda)$ matrix (Wilson (1996, p. 210)). But even this improved procedure can be tedious, and the diagonal $A(\lambda)$ simplification still does not give us the convenience of a closed-form solution for VaR.

Unfortunately, this QP approach also suffers from a major conceptual flaw. Britten-Jones and Schaefer (1999, pp. 184–187) point out that there is a subtle but important difference between the 'true' VaR and the QP VaR: the 'true' VaR is predicated on a confidence region defined over portfolio value changes, whilst the QP VaR is predicated on a confidence region defined over (typically multidimensional) factor realisations. There are several problems with the latter approach, but perhaps the most serious is that it is generally not possible to use confidence regions defined over factors to make inferences about functions of those factors. To quote Britten-Jones and Schaefer:

> Simply because a point lies within a 95% confidence region does not mean that it has a 95% chance of occurrence. A point may lie within some 95% region, have a negligible chance of occurring and have a massive loss associated with it. The size of this loss does not give any indication of the true VaR. In short the QP approach is conceptually flawed and will give erroneous results under all but special situations where it will happen to coincide with the correct answer.
>
> (Britten-Jones and Schaefer (1999, p. 186))

Britten-Jones and Schaefer go on to prove that the QP VaR will, in general, exceed the true VaR, but the extent of the overstatement will depend on the probability distribution from which the P/L is generated.

So, in the end, all we have is a risk measure that generally overestimates the VaR by an amount that varies from one situation to another. It is therefore not too surprising that empirical evidence suggests the QP approach can give very inaccurate estimates of 'true' VaR, and is sometimes even less accurate than the delta–gamma normal approach (Pritsker (1997, p. 231)).

A5.2.4   Other Delta–Gamma Approaches

Fortunately, there are other delta–gamma approaches that work much better, and a large number of alternative approaches have been suggested:

- Zangari (1996a,c) estimates the moments of the portfolio P/L process and matches these against a Johnson family distribution, and obtains the VaR from that distribution with the same moments as the portfolio P/L. This method is fast and capable of generating considerably more accurate VaR estimates than a delta approach. Jahel *et al.* (1999) propose a somewhat similar approach, but one that uses a characteristic function to estimate the moments of the underlying vector process.
- Fallon (1996) takes a second-order Taylor series approximation of the portfolio P/L about the current market prices, and rearranges this expression to obtain a quadratic function of a multi-normal distribution. He then uses standard methods to calculate the moments of the approximated P/L distribution, and appropriate approximation methods to obtain the quantiles and, hence, the VaR, of this distribution. He also found that the Cornish–Fisher approach gave the best quantile approximations, and was both reliable and accurate.
- Rouvinez (1997) takes a quadratic approximation to the portfolio P/L and estimates its moments, and then obtains some bounds for the VaR expressed in terms of these moments. He goes on to use the characteristic function to estimate the value of the cdf, and then inverts this to obtain a VaR estimate. His methods are also fast and straightforward to implement.
- Cárdenas *et al.* (1997) and Britten-Jones and Schaefer (1999) obtain the usual delta–gamma approximation for portfolio P/L, estimate the second and higher moments of the P/L distribution using orthogonalisation methods, and then read off the VaR from appropriate chi-squared tables. These methods are also fairly fast.
- Studer (1999) and Mina (2001) describe procedures by which the quadratic approximation is estimated by least squares methods: we select a set of scenarios, value the portfolio in each

of these scenarios to produce 'true' P/Ls, and then choose the delta and gamma parameters to provide a best-fitting approximation to the 'true' P/L. These methods produce fairly accurate and fast delta–gamma approximations to 'true' VaR.

- Albanese *et al.* (2001) use a 'fast convolution' or fast Fourier transform method that enables the user to obtain accurate VaR estimates very quickly. This method also gives the portfolio's marginal VaRs, and is therefore very useful for risk decomposition.
- Feuerverger and Wong (2000) propose a saddlepoint approximation method that uses formulas derived from the moment-generating function to obtain highly accurate delta–gamma approximations for VaR.

Box A5.2   A Duration–convexity Approximation to Bond Portfolios

The second-order approximation approach used to handle non-linearity in options positions can also be used to handle non-linearity in bonds. Suppose we take a second-order approximation of a bond's price–yield relationship:

$$P(y + \Delta y) \approx P(y) + (dP/dy)\Delta y + (1/2)(d^2P/dy^2)\Delta y^2$$

We know from standard fixed-income theory that:

$$dP/dy = -D^m P \quad \text{and} \quad d^2P/dy^2 = CP$$

where D^m is the bond's modified duration and C its convexity (see Tuckman (1995, pp. 123, 126)). The percentage change in bond price is therefore:

$$\Delta P/P \approx -D^m \Delta y + (1/2)C(\Delta y)^2$$

which is the second-order approximation for bond prices corresponding to the delta–gamma approximation for option prices given by Equation (A5.4).

A5.3   CONCLUSIONS

So where does this leave us? On the plus side, delta–gamma and related approaches have some limited usefulness, if used carefully, and research findings suggest that taking account of the higher-order terms can generate improvements — sometimes very substantial ones — in the accuracy of VaR estimates. However, on the negative side, some of these approaches can be inaccurate and involve a lot of work.

I would also like to add a further point. These approaches were developed to deal with non-linearity at a time when there were few, if any, practicable alternatives. Practitioners knew that variance–covariance and historical simulation methods were not really up to the job, and the simulation packages that existed were much slower and much less user-friendly than those available today. The delta–normal and delta–gamma approaches were therefore designed to fill the gap. Practitioners knew that these approaches were limited and often unreliable, but they didn't have many other alternatives.

Since then the situation has changed drastically, and the need for such methods is far less than it used to be. Numerical and simulation methods are improving rapidly — they are becoming both more sophisticated and much faster — and are much better suited to estimating the VaR of options positions than crude delta–normal and delta–gamma approaches. As they continue to improve, as they surely will, the need for Greek-based approaches to VaR estimation will continue to diminish, and at some point, may disappear altogether.[19]

A5.4 RECOMMENDED READING

Albanese *et al.* (2001); Britten-Jones and Schaefer (1999); Duffie and Pan (1997, pp. 23–27, 30–32); Jahel *et al.* (1999); Estrella (1996); Estrella *et al.* (1994); Fallon (1996); Mina (2001); Pritsker (1997); Rouvinez (1997); Studer (1999); Wilson (1994b, 1996); Zangari (1996c).

---

[19] However, as discussed elsewhere (e.g., in Tool No. 6: Monte Carlo Simulation Methods), we sometimes also need Greek approximations to provide preliminary VaR estimates for use as control variates in simulation methods and in importance sampling simulation methods. But these (possible) exceptions aside, I very much doubt that there will be any other need for Greek-based VaR approximations in a few years' time.

6
Simulation Approaches to
VaR and ETL Estimation

This chapter examines how we can estimate VaR and ETL using simulation methods. These methods are extremely flexible and powerful, and can be applied to many different types of VaR or ETL estimation problem. They are particularly good at dealing with complicating factors — such as path-dependency, fat tails, non-linearity, optionality and multidimensionality — that often defeat analytical approaches. On the other hand, simulation methods are less easy to use than some alternatives, require a lot of calculations, and can have difficulty with early-exercise features.

This chapter looks at some of the more important VaR (or ETL) estimation problems to which simulation methods are suited:

- Using simulation methods to estimate the risks of options positions.
- Estimating risks using principal components simulation methods.
- Using simulation methods to estimate the risks of fixed-income positions, and positions in fixed-income derivatives.
- Using simulation methods to estimate risks in the face of dynamic portfolio management strategies (i.e., when we relax the assumption that the portfolio is given over the holding period).
- Using simulation methods to estimate credit-related risks.
- Using simulation methods to estimate the risks of insurance portfolios.
- Using simulation methods to estimate pension risks.

In each of these cases, the best approach is to construct tailor-made solutions to each specific problem. Not only are these problems extremely diverse, but effective simulation requires that we make good use of the variance-reduction methods available for that problem — and discussed in Tool No. 6: Monte Carlo Simulation Methods, the feasibility and usefulness of many variance-reduction techniques are extremely problem-specific.

6.1 OPTIONS VAR AND ETL

6.1.1 Preliminary Considerations

We begin with the estimation of options VaR and ETL. Perhaps the first point to appreciate about using simulation methods for such purposes is that we should not use them when better alternatives are available (e.g., such as analytical solutions for the VaRs of Black–Scholes equations).[1] We should therefore only use simulation methods to estimate the VaR or ETL of options in more difficult cases, where straightforward solutions are not available — and this would include many portfolios of heterogeneous options, as well as positions in individual options that are not amenable to more straightforward methods. When using simulation methods for estimating options VaR or ETL, a natural (although computationally expensive) approach is 'simulation within simulation': we

---

[1] For more on such solution methods, see Dowd (2002, ch. 5, app. 2).

simulate paths of the underlying, simulate the option value at discrete points over (or at the end of) each simulated underlying path, and then infer the VaR (or ETL) from the simulated option P/L values prevailing at the end of the holding period. In cases where it is not easy to use simulation methods to value the option (e.g., as with certain types of American option), we might still simulate the underlying variable, but in such cases we might use a binomial or other numerical approach to price the option at points along each simulated underlying path: we have tree option valuation within a simulation framework for the underlying.[2] Once we have option values for the end of the holding period, we can then obtain the VaR/ETL from the option P/L in the usual manner.

In these cases, the accuracy of our results depends on the number of trials M and (sometimes also on) the number of increment steps N, and we face the usual trade-offs between speed and accuracy. Furthermore, because we are also simulating or tree-pricing within our simulations, these trade-offs can become particularly acute because such exercises inevitably involve a large number of calculations. It is therefore important to use whatever refinements we can — to make use of control variates, stratified sampling, or whatever other refinements are appropriate, as well as to choose good values for M and N — to speed up calculations and/or cut down on the number of calculations needed.[3]

6.1.2   An Example: Estimating the VaR and ETL of an American Put

To illustrate, suppose we wish to estimate the VaR and ETL of an American put. To do so using simulation methods, we need to embed an appropriate option-pricing method (i.e., one that takes account of the option's early and exercise feature) within the underlying stock-price simulation path. The easiest such method is a simple binomial tree. Hence, at each discrete point in the stock-price simulation path, we value the option using the prevailing stock price and a binomial tree. If we take our test parameter values as $S(0) = X = 1, r = \mu = 0, \sigma = 0.25$, option maturity $= 1$ year (or 360 days), $cl = 0.95$, $hp = 1$ day, plus values of $N = 20$ (i.e., 20 discrete steps in the tree) and $M = 1,000$ trials, then the function 'americanputvar_sim' tells us that a \$1 investment in a portfolio of identical American puts has a simulated VaR estimate of 0.021. The corresponding ETL estimate is 0.026.

We also want to estimate the accuracy of these estimates, and gauging the accuracy of MCS VaR estimates is somewhat different from gauging that of MCS derivatives values. With derivatives values, each trial run produces its own simulated derivative value, so all we need to do is run a large number of trials, estimate the sample standard deviation of these derivative values, and then invoke the central limit theorem to get the confidence interval. But with VaR (or ETL) we only get one VaR estimate from the whole simulation exercise, so we don't have a histogram of VaR estimates to work with. However, we can still estimate confidence intervals for VaR (or ETL) by treating the sample of option P/L values as an empirical pdf and then estimating the confidence interval using order statistics theory. If we apply this approach to our American put position, we then get an estimated 95% confidence interval for our VaR of [0.019,0.022], and a comparable ETL confidence interval of

---

[2]It is no longer the case that early exercise features pose insurmountable problems for simulation methods, and a number of recent papers have proposed innovative ways of handling American-style securities in simulation frameworks. These include, among others, the stochastic mesh approach of Broadie and Glasserman (1997), and the least-squares simulation approach of Longstaff and Schwartz (2001). For more on the pricing of American-style options by simulation, see also Boyle *et al.* (1997, pp. 1309–1315).

[3]The comparative slowness of simulation methods can be a major nuisance when we want to estimate a full VaR or ETL surface. Estimating a VaR surface by simulation methods can involve many times more calculations than estimating a VaR at a single point. Yet, ironically, it is precisely in the more complicated problems where we need to resort to simulation that it is especially important to look at the whole VaR surface and not just at a single-point VaR. The only realistic way to deal with these problems is to make maximum use of variance-reduction and other methods (e.g., principal components methods) to improve accuracy and so enable us to cut back on the number of calculations we need to run.

[0.025,0.026]. When estimating confidence intervals, we should also keep in mind that the estimated interval will tend to narrow as M gets bigger, so if we want narrow confidence intervals we should choose high values of M.

6.1.3 Refining MCS Estimation of Options VaR and ETL

Clearly, we can improve the accuracy of our estimates and reduce computational time by making appropriate refinements. Possible refinements include:

- *Control variates.* We should use control variates where we reasonably can, but whether we can find good controls depends largely on the specifics of the problem at hand. For example, if we are dealing with reverse knock-outs, good controls are hard to come by, because the option is not well correlated with obvious candidate controls such as vanilla options or the underlying. On the other hand, an arithmetic Asian option has many good controls, including geometric Asian options, some of the standard approximations to arithmetic Asians (e.g., Turnbull and Wakeman, etc.), vanilla options, and the underlying itself.
- *Importance sampling.* IS methods are very well suited to VaR and ETL estimation, particularly at high confidence levels, and can produce very large variance reductions. However, their usefulness depends on being able to find a good preliminary VaR estimate, such as a good quadratic approximation.
- *Stratified sampling.* Stratified sampling methods are also well suited to VaR and ETL estimation, particularly if we target the allocation of our strata around the VaR (or the tail, if we are estimating ETL). On the other hand, basic stratified sampling can run into difficulties in high-dimensional problems, and in such cases we might want to make use of Latin hypercube or Brownian bridge approaches. Another problem of stratified sampling is that it complicates the estimation of confidence intervals, and forces us to obtain such estimates using batch methods.
- *Moment matching.* These methods are easy to implement and have the potential to reduce variance by respectable amounts; however, their results can be biased and we have to obtain estimates of confidence intervals by batch methods.

Many of these methods can often be used together to produce very substantial cumulative reductions in variance.

6.2 ESTIMATING VaR BY SIMULATING PRINCIPAL COMPONENTS

We turn now to the estimation of VaR (or ETL) by simulating principal components. This type of approach is well suited to problems where we have a large number of possibly highly correlated risk factors, such as a series of points along a spot rate (or zero-coupon rate) curve. Simulating the principal components can then produce large gains in efficiency, because we have fewer random variables to handle.

6.2.1 Basic Principal Components Simulation

To simulate PCA applied to, say, a fixed-income portfolio, we begin by choosing a vector of n key zero-coupon rates, $[r_1, r_2, \ldots, r_n]$, each with its own different maturity. We then postulate a stochastic process for each rate, such as the simple geometric Brownian motion process suggested by Jamshidian and Zhu (1997):

$$dr_i/r_i = \mu_i(t)dt + \sigma_i dz_i(i) \tag{6.1}$$

where $z_i(i) \sim N(0, \sqrt{t})$ and the $z_i(i)$ would in general be correlated with each other.[4] We will usually find that the first three principal components of a spot rate curve will explain around 95% or more of the movement in it, and that these have ready spot rate interpretations: the first principal component can be interpreted as its shift factor, the second as its slope or twist factor, and the third as its curvature or butterfly factor. These findings suggest that we might wish to focus on the first three principal components.

We now determine the principal components. If we let $\mathbf{C} = [\rho_{i,j}]_{i,j=1,\ldots,n}$ be the $n \times n$ correlation matrix of the n key rates, and let the jth eigenvector of $\mathbf{C}$ be $\boldsymbol{\beta}_j = [\beta_{1,j}, \ldots, \beta_{n,j}]^{\mathrm{T}}$, then, by the definition of an eigenvector:

$$\mathbf{C}\boldsymbol{\beta}_j = \lambda_j \boldsymbol{\beta}_j, \quad j = 1, \ldots, n \tag{6.2}$$

where λ_j is the jth eigenvalue. We now normalise the $\boldsymbol{\beta}$ so that $|\boldsymbol{\beta}_j|^2 = \sum_{i=1}^{n} \beta_{i,j}^2 = \lambda_j$, and re-label the λ_i terms so that λ_1 is no less than λ_2, λ_2 no less than λ_3, and so on. The jth principal component is then β_j.

We can now write dz_i in terms of the principal components:

$$dz_i = \sum_{j=1}^{n} \beta_{i,j} dw_j \approx \beta_{i,1} dw_1 + \beta_{i,2} dw_2 + \beta_{i,3} dw_3, \quad i = 1, \ldots, n \tag{6.3}$$

where $E[w_k, w_j] = 0$ for $k \neq j$ and $dw_j = \sqrt{dt}$, and assuming that the fourth and further principal components are not particularly significant. Using this approximation, Equation (6.1) then becomes:

$$dr_i/r \approx \mu_i(t)dt + \sigma_i \beta_{i,1} dw_1 + \sigma_i \beta_{i,2} dw_2 + \sigma_i \beta_{i,3} dw_3 \tag{6.4}$$

(see, e.g., Jamshidian and Zhu (1997, pp. 45–47)). The dimensionality of the problem is reduced from n to 3 and, because the principal components are independent, we now have a correlation matrix with three terms rather than the $n(n + 1)/2$ terms we had before.

We would now simulate the principal components and derive our VaR (or ETL) estimate(s): we would run trials for dw_1, dw_2 and dw_3, each trial would (via Equation (6.4)) produce a set of dr_i/r_i values, and we would use these to estimate our VaR (or ETL) in the usual way.

6.2.2 Scenario Simulation

This PCA procedure can still involve a large number of calculations, but we can cut down on the number of calculations using the 'scenario simulation' approach suggested by Jamshidian and Zhu (1997).[5] Each of our three principal components, dw_1, dw_2 and dw_3, is allowed to take one of a limited number of states, and we can determine which state occurs by taking a random drawing from a multinomial distribution. Thus, if a particular principal component is allowed to take one of $m + 1$

---

[4]This process has the drawback that it fails to allow for mean reversion in interest rates, but we can easily modify it to allow for mean reversion if we wish to do so (Jamshidian and Zhu (1997, pp. 50–51)).

[5]This approach is very closely related to the 'factor-based interest-rate scenario' approach suggested a little earlier by Frye (1996). The only detectable difference between these is a relatively trivial one — that Jamshidian and Zhu use the first three principal components, whilst Frye uses the first four — and this is a minor difference in application, not a difference in the basic approach.

states, the probability of state i, $P(i)$, is:

$$P(i) = 2^{-m} \frac{m!}{i!(m-i)!}, \quad i = 0, \ldots, m \tag{6.5}$$

So, for example, if we have five states, their corresponding probabilities are:

$$\frac{1}{16}, \frac{1}{4}, \frac{3}{8}, \frac{1}{4}, \frac{1}{16} \tag{6.6}$$

The middle state is more likely than either of the adjacent states, and these in turn are more likely than the extreme states. Hence, the middle state might be 'no change' in the principal component concerned, the adjacent states might be 'moderate up' and 'moderate down' changes, and the other two might be 'extreme up' or 'extreme down' changes. Since the first principal component is more important than the second, and the second more important than the third, it would make sense to allow the first principal component to have more states than the second, and the second more than the third. Jamshidian and Zhu suggest that we might allow seven states for the first component, five for the second, and three for the third. We can then define a spot rate curve scenario to be a set of states for each of our principal components, and the total number of scenarios is equal to the product of the number of different states (so, e.g., if the first component has seven different states, the second five and the third three, the total number of scenarios is $7 \times 5 \times 3 = 105$). Moreover, since the states are independent, their probability is equal to the product of the multinomial probabilities in Equation (6.5). In other words, if the first principal component has $m_1 + 1$ possible states, the second has $m_2 + 1$ possible states, and the third has $m_3 + 1$ possible states, then the scenario (i, j, k), in which the first principal component takes state i, the second takes state j, and the third takes state k, occurs with probability:

$$P(\text{component } 1 = i) \times P(\text{component } 2 = j) \times P(\text{component } 3 = k)$$

$$= \left[2^{-m_1} \frac{m_1!}{i!(m_1 - i)!} \right] \times \left[2^{-m_2} \frac{m_2!}{j!(m_2 - j)!} \right] \times \left[2^{-m_3} \frac{m_3!}{k!(m_3 - k)!} \right] \tag{6.7}$$

So, basically, we randomly select scenarios using Equation (6.7), and each scenario gives us a particular spot rate curve, and a particular P/L on our portfolio. If we take a reasonable number of trials, we should be able to get a good VaR estimate from the sample of trial P/L values. Observe, too, that we only ever have to make $(m_1 + 1)(m_2 + 1)(m_3 + 1)$ evaluations (i.e., one for each scenario), regardless of the number of trials. As each trial only involves the selection of a scenario using Equation (6.7), but not its evaluation, it follows that the trials are not computer-intensive, and this suggests that even a large number of trials should be calculated quickly. We would therefore expect scenario simulation to perform very well compared to principal components MCS, and the results reported by Jamshidian and Zhu confirm this expectation.[6]

The scenario simulation approach also has other attractive features. First, it allows us to pay attention to extreme moves. For example, in Jamshidian and Zhu's own example with 105 separate scenarios, some of these occur with a probability of only 0.024% (Jamshidian and Zhu (1997, p. 56)). These low-probability scenarios occur because of the compounding of low-probability states. Second, if we want more extreme scenarios, we can obtain them by increasing the number of states, and so get a better handle on extreme outcomes. Third, the results of our PC analysis give us an

---

[6]The scenario simulation approach can also be adapted to estimate the VaR or ETL of multi-currency portfolios in which we have to model more than one spot rate curve (Jamshidian and Zhu (1997, pp. 52–56)), and also to estimate potential losses from credit exposures (Jamshidian and Zhu (1997, pp. 60–65)).

indication of the way in which our portfolio is exposed to interest-rate movements: for instance, we might see that our portfolio is sensitive to rising interest rates or a steepening of the spot rate curve (Frye (1996, p. 3)). Fourth, the method can be used to give us a fairly quick way of determining the impact of additional trades on our overall risk, and this can be very useful, not only when trading, but also when determining hedge strategies (Frye (1996, p. 3)). And, finally, the ability of scenario simulation to target tail events makes it easier to play with tails by conducting 'what if' experiments in which we make certain changes to state outcomes (or state probabilities) and see how they affect the VaR. This can make simulation very useful for stress-testing purposes.[7]

6.3   FIXED-INCOME VaR AND ETL

6.3.1   General Considerations

Our third topic is the estimation of the risks of positions in interest-sensitive instruments, usually known as fixed-income instruments: these are bonds, floating-rate notes, structured notes, interest-rate derivatives such as interest rate swaps and futures, and swaptions. However, fixed-income problems can be difficult to handle using analytical or algorithmic methods because they usually involve a range of spot rates across the term structure, not just one or two spot interest rates, and fixed-income problems can be particularly difficult to handle where they involve interest-rate options, because of the extra complications of optionality (e.g., the need to take account of volatilities, etc.). But, fortunately, fixed-income problems are often also very amenable to simulation methods.[8]

When estimating the fixed-income VaR or ETL, we generally have to take account of two distinctive features of fixed-income positions: the types of stochastic processes governing interest rates, and the term structure.

6.3.1.1   Stochastic Processes for Interest Rates

Interest-rate processes differ from stock-price processes in that interest rates are usually taken to be mean-reverting — if interest rates are high, they have a tendency to fall, and if interest rates are low, they have a tendency to rise. This means that interest rates are expected to fall if they are relatively high, and are expected to rise if they are relatively low. In this respect interest rates differ from stock prices which show no mean reversion: for instance, under the archetypal assumption of a random walk or martingale, the best forecast of a future stock price is today's stock price, regardless of how high (or low) that price might be. There is a considerable literature on interest-rate processes (see, e.g., Hull (2000, ch. 20–21), James and Webber (2000, ch. 3 and 7), etc.), but one of the most popular of these processes is the Cox–Ingersoll–Ross (CIR) process:

$$dr = k(\mu - r)\,dt + \sigma\sqrt{dt}\,\sqrt{r}\,dz \tag{6.8}$$

where μ is the long-run mean interest rate, or the reversion level to which interest rates tend to revert, σ is the annualised volatility of interest rates, k indicates the speed with which interest rates tend

---

[7]However, we should also be careful with scenario simulation: the results of Abken (2000, p. 27) suggest that the performance of scenario simulation can sometimes be erratic and results can be significantly biased compared to those of standard Monte Carlo simulation and principal components simulation approaches. Convergence can also be slow for some types of portfolio, and Abken recommends that users of scenario simulation should periodically check its results against those of standard methods.

[8]There is a very diverse specialist literature on fixed-income VaR, and I haven't space in this book to cover it properly. However, a good starting point is D'Vari and Sosa (2000), Niffikeer *et al.* (2000) and Vlaar (2000). For those who are interested in the VaR of mortgage-backed securities, see Jakobsen (1996).

to revert to their mean values, and dz is a standard normal random variable (Cox *et al.* (1985)). This process is popular because it captures the three major stylised facts of empirical interest-rate processes[9] — namely, that interest rates are stochastic, positive and mean-reverting.[10]

6.3.1.2   *The Term Structure of Interest Rates*

The other distinctive feature of fixed-income positions is more important, and harder to deal with. Most fixed-income positions involve payments that are due on multiple future dates, so the valuation of fixed-income instruments requires us to take account of a number of different points along the spot rate term structure. For example, if we have a coupon-paying bond that pays a coupon every 6 months, we can only price this bond if we have information about the spot rates at 6-monthly intervals along the term structure.[11] There are exceptions — most notably those relating to zero-coupon bonds, which can be priced with only one spot rate — but the main point is inescapable: in general, we need information about the spot rate term structure, and not just about one individual spot rate, to be able to price interest-sensitive instruments.

From the perspective of VaR (or ETL) estimation, this means that we need information about the *prospective* term structure *at the end of the holding period*. The VaR depends on the P/L, and the P/L depends on how the prices of our instruments change over the holding period. We must already know the current prices of our fixed-income instruments, but their prices at the end of the holding period will depend on the spot rate term structure that prevails at that time, and possibly on other future variables as well. So we need a prospective future term structure to price our instruments at the end of the holding period, so that we can then estimate prospective P/L and hence estimate VaR and ETL.

6.3.2   A General Approach to Fixed-income VaR and ETL

So how do we estimate fixed-income VaR and ETL? At first sight, this is quite a daunting prospect, because fixed-income positions are very diverse and some fixed-income problems are extremely difficult. However, most of these difficulties actually relate to pricing, and most pricing problems have now been resolved. Indeed, the state of the art has advanced to the point where the vast majority of fixed-income positions can now be priced both accurately and quickly. Since pricing is the key to VaR (and ETL) estimation, it follows that, if we can price positions, then we can also estimate their VaRs; consequently, there are — in theory — few real obstacles to VaR estimation. If we encounter any problems, they would be the usual practical issues of accuracy and calculation time.

To estimate the VaR (or ETL) of a fixed-income position, we therefore need to simulate the distribution of possible values of a fixed-income portfolio at the end of the holding period. If we are dealing with the simpler fixed-income instruments — such as bonds, floating-rate notes or swaps — then a terminal term structure provides us with enough information to price the instruments and, hence, value the portfolio, at the end of the holding period. The term structure information is sufficient

---

[9]However, none of the simpler models of interest-rate processes can fully capture the dynamics of interest rates. We tend to find that after a model has been fitted to the data, the goodness of the fit then tends to deteriorate over time, and this makes the use of such models for pricing purposes somewhat problematic unless they are frequently recalibrated. For more on these issues and how to deal with them, see, e.g., James and Webber (2000).

[10]That said, it is still an open question how much mean reversion really matters when it comes to VaR estimation — but when in doubt, it is usually best to play safe and put a reasonable mean-reversion term into our interest-rate process.

[11]I realise that we can also price such a bond if we have the yield to maturity, but the yield to maturity is only a (bad) surrogate for the term structure anyway, and we can't calculate the yield in the first place without the term structure information I am referring to. So one way or the other, we still need the term structure to price the bond.

because we can value these instruments using standard pricing methods based on present-value calculations of the remaining payments due.

However, if we are dealing with interest-rate options — such as interest-rate calls, puts, floors, ceilings, etc. — then information *only* about the term structure of spot rates will *not* be enough to value our instruments. To value positions involving interest-rate options, we also generally need information about the terminal volatility term structure (i.e., we want the volatilities associated with each of a number of spot rates). Moreover, in these circumstances, we can no longer price our instruments using simple present-value methods, and we need to resort to an appropriate option pricing model as well.

There is a very large literature on such models, and the models themselves vary a great deal in their sophistication and flexibility.[12] Fortunately, given the availability these days of good software, it is no longer difficult to implement some of the better models, including the Heath–Jarrow–Morton (HJM) model.[13] The only problem then remaining is how to obtain the terminal volatilities, and we can forecast these volatilities either by assuming that the terminal volatilities are equal to the currently prevailing volatilities (which is permissible if we can assume that volatilities are random walks or martingales, which are best predicted by their current values) or by using GARCH or similar approaches.

Since accuracy and calculation time are often significant issues in fixed-income problems, it also makes sense to look for ways of improving accuracy and/or reducing computation time. We should therefore explore ways to use variance-reduction methods and/or principal components methods.

A good approach for these problems is scenario simulation, which is, as we have seen, a form of speeded-up principal components simulation. If we follow Jamshidian and Zhu (1997) and have three principal components, with seven possible states for the first principal component, five for the second, and three for the third, then we would have 105 distinct principal component scenarios. This would also give us 105 spot rate (or term structure) scenarios, and the only simulation required would be to pick a random scenario from the multinomial scenario-selection process. The random number generation should therefore be very quick.

We now have to come up with plausible principal component scenarios, and these are best obtained by combining information on principal component volatilities with the state probabilities specified in Equation (6.5). For example, if a principal component has five possible states, then Equation (6.5) implies that the probabilities of these states are $1/16$, $1/4$, $3/8$, $1/4$ and $1/16$, and we might then say that the middle scenario reflected no change in the principal component, the two adjacent states reflected changes of minus or plus, say, one standard deviation, and the other two states reflected changes of, say, two standard deviations.

Box 6.1   Estimating the VaR and ETL of Coupon Bonds

Suppose we wish to estimate the VaR and ETL at the 95% confidence level of a \$1 position in a coupon-paying bond with 10 years to maturity, with a coupon rate of 5%, over a holding period of 1 year. These coupon payments should be accounted for in our P/L, and one simple way of

---

[12]These models are covered in textbooks such as Hull (2000, ch. 21–22), James and Webber (2000, part 2) or Rebonato (1998, part 4).

[13]The HJM model is highly flexible, and can price the vast majority of fixed-income instruments, including options, based on information about term-structure spot rates and term-structure volatilities. HJM can also be implemented in MATLAB using the HJM functions in the Financial Derivatives Toolbox.

doing so is to assume that coupon payments are reinvested at the going spot rate until the end of the holding period. We assume for convenience that the term structure is flat at 5%, so all spot rates are 5%. We also assume that the spot interest-rate process is a CIR process like that given in Equation (6.8), with $\mu = 0.05$, $k = 0.01$ and $\sigma = 0.05$, and discretise this process into $N = 10$ steps, so $dt = 1/10$ measured in years, and assume a number of trials, M, equal to 1,000. Given these parameters, our estimated VaR and ETL — estimated with the function 'bondvaretl' — turn out to be 0.011 and 0.014 respectively.

6.4   ESTIMATING VaR AND ETL UNDER A DYNAMIC PORTFOLIO STRATEGY

We turn now to some more specialised applications of simulation methods. When dealing with such applications, we should aim to design a tailor-made VaR (or ETL) simulation routine to meet the specific circumstances of each problem, as the most appropriate solution to any given problem will usually be very specific to the problem itself. This is important because we wish to (and sometimes must!) get accurate answers in good time, without large numbers of unnecessary calculations: skill in designing problem-specific simulation routines is therefore very useful, and sometimes indispensable.

We begin with the problem of estimating VaR (or ETL) in the presence of a dynamic portfolio strategy. The estimation of dynamic VaR is a difficult problem to handle using analytical methods, but is ideally suited to simulation methods. The method is simple: we specify the dynamic portfolio management strategy, run a simulation exercise taking this strategy into account, obtain a simulated P/L sample, and derive the VaR in the usual way from the simulated P/L histogram.

To illustrate the general approach, we consider two alternative dynamic portfolio strategies: a stop-loss strategy, and a filter rule strategy.

A stop-loss strategy is one in which we exit the market and move into something safer as soon as our loss reaches a specified level. In this particular case, we assume for simplicity that the safer asset is risk-free, and that the initial portfolio is invested entirely in a single risky asset whose (arithmetic) return is distributed as a standard lognormal. A stop-loss strategy is contingent on a new parameter, the stop-loss limit, and the impact of this limit is illustrated in Figure 6.1.

The impact of the stop-loss strategy on the VaR depends on the size of the loss limit: if the loss limit is low, the probability of running into the limit will be relatively high, and the maximum likely loss at this confidence level will be the loss limit itself; the higher the limit, the less likely it is to be breached; and if the limit is sufficiently high, the VaR will fall below the loss limit and be close to the static portfolio VaR we would have obtained with no stop-loss strategy at all.[14] The stop-loss strategy can therefore have a big impact on the VaR, depending on the value of the loss limit.

A filter rule strategy can be applied where we have two assets, one riskier than the other. The strategy postulates that we increase the proportion of the portfolio held in the more risky asset as the value of our portfolio rises, and decrease that proportion as the value of our portfolio falls. In this

---

[14]Of course, this treatment of loss limits is rather simplistic and makes additional assumptions that we might sometimes be wary of making in practice: most particularly, the assumption that we can 'cut and run' without incurring any further costs, and this (rather optimistically) presupposes that the market for our asset is fully liquid. We will come back to liquidity issues in Chapter 8.

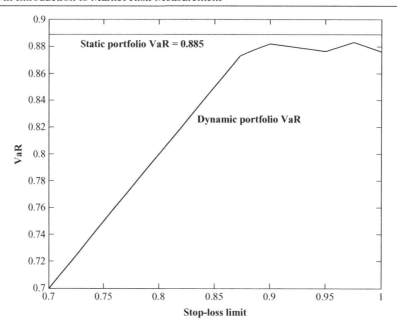

Figure 6.1   VaR with a stop-loss portfolio management strategy.

Note: Based on an assumed investment of $1, annualized arithmetic returns of mean 0 and standard deviation 1, lognormally distributed, 5,000 MCS trials, 100 incremental time steps in each trial, and VaR predicated on a confidence level of 0.95 and holding period of 1 day.

particular case, we again assume that the alternative asset is risk-free, and that the portfolio is initially divided equally between the risky and risk-free assets. We also assume that when the portfolio value rises (or falls), $\alpha\%$ of the increase (or decrease) in the portfolio value is invested in (or disinvested from) holdings of the risky asset. The parameter α, sometimes known as a participation rate, indicates the degree of responsiveness of the portfolio composition to the change in the value of the portfolio: if α is low, then the portfolio responds relatively sluggishly to changes in the value of the portfolio; if α is high, the portfolio responds more aggressively to such changes; and the special case where $\alpha = 0$ (i.e., no change) corresponds to the usual static portfolio strategy often assumed in VaR exercises.

The impact of a filter rule strategy on VaR is illustrated in Figure 6.2, which plots an illustrative VaR against varying values for the participation rate. A participation rate of zero (i.e., a static portfolio) gives a VaR of almost 0.45; however, as the participation rate rises, the VaR falls in a negative-exponential pattern, and a participation rate of 1 produces a VaR of little over 0.05. The participation rate therefore has a very considerable, negative, effect on the VaR. The explanation is that a bigger participation rate implies a larger cut back on loss-making positions, and hence a lower loss and lower VaR.

In short, a dynamic portfolio management strategy can have a very large impact on the VaR, although the impact also depends critically on the type of dynamic strategy and the values of the strategic parameters concerned.[15]

---

[15]For more on the impact of such strategies on VaR, see Fusai and Luciano (1998).

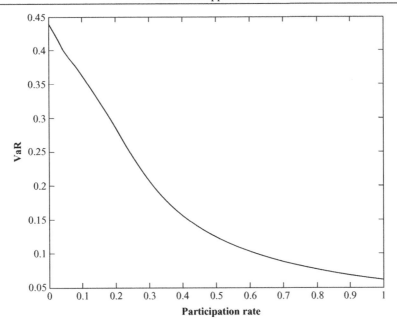

Figure 6.2   VaR with a filter rule portfolio management strategy.

Note: Based on an assumed investment of $1, initially divided equally between two assets, a lognormally distributed asset with annualized arithmetic returns of mean 0 and standard deviation 1, and a zero-mean risk-free asset, 5,000 MCS trials, and VaR predicated on a confidence level of 0.95 and holding period of 1 day.

6.5   ESTIMATING CREDIT-RELATED RISKS WITH SIMULATION METHODS

Simulation approaches to VaR (or ETL) estimation are also often very good for positions with credit-related risks. Credit-related or default risks arise in a huge variety of contexts, ranging from portfolios of simple default-risky bonds, at one extreme, to portfolios of sophisticated, credit-sensitive, interest-rate derivatives, including credit derivatives, at the other.[16] Credit-related risks involve at least three possible complicating factors:

- The first is the need to model the default process. Since a default event is a binary variable (i.e., it takes a value 1 if default occurs, and 0 if it does not), this means that we are dealing with a risk factor, or set of risk factors, that is very non-normal. The P/L associated with default losses is therefore also non-normal, except in unusual cases where we have a lot of 'small' independent default risks that allow us to appeal to the central limit theorem.
- The second complicating factor is the need to take account of how the risk of default affects the prices of instruments concerned. Market risk is not independent of credit risk, and the price difference (or, if we prefer, the yield spread difference) between default-risky and default-free bonds will depend on the default risk in a complex way. We might also want to take account of

---

[16]For obvious reasons, I can't do justice here to the very large literature on credit-risk measurement. However, for those who wish to pursue these issues in detail, I recommend Saunders (1999) and Crouhy *et al.* (2001, ch. 7–11).

the way in which the default probability might change over time (i.e., we should account for its transition process). We should also take account of the recovery rate and how that might change over time as well. Furthermore, since default probabilities and recovery rates depend on other factors (e.g., the stage of the business cycle, sector-specific changes, etc.), we might also want to model default probabilities and recovery rates as dependent random variables, and take account of the factors on which they depend.

- With many credit-related positions, there are also various institutional or contractual factors to consider, and these can have an important bearing on the actual losses we might suffer in the event of default. These factors include netting agreements, collateral requirements, credit triggers, recouponing features, credit guarantee arrangements, and mutual termination options.[17] These 'credit-enhancement' features help institutions manage their credit risks, but also make risks more complicated, and in the process complicate the estimation of market risks and liquidity risks as well.

As we might expect, these complicating features make credit-related problems amenable to simulation methods in ways that analytical or algorithmic methods are often not.[18] And, as with many other simulation problems with complex problem-specific features, the strategy is to build a model that is tailor-made to the specific problem at hand.

We can illustrate the basic issues by considering the simple problem of estimating the VaR of a coupon bond with default risk. To make this concrete, suppose we have a bond with 1 year to run, with coupon payments due in 6 and 12 months. The coupon rate is c, and bonds of this credit rating are assumed to have a flat spot rate curve with a universal spot rate r. If the issuer defaults, the holder is assumed to recover a fraction δ of the current market value of the bond, and the probability of default is p. If the issuer defaults in 6 months' time, the holder obtains the recovery value and is assumed to invest it at the risk-free rate until the end of the holding period, which is assumed to coincide with the maturity period of the bond. We now write a program to estimate the VaR of our bond portfolio, and the details can be found in the function 'defaultriskybondvar'. This function estimates the VaR once we specify the values of the parameters concerned: for example, if $r = c = 0.05$, $r_f = 0$, $\sigma = 0.25$, $p = 0.05$, $\delta = 0.5$, $hp = 360$, $cl = 0.95$, with an amount invested of \$1, then a 1,000-trial MCS exercise gives us a VaR estimate of 0.452.

This type of methodology is also useful for shedding light on how our risks vary with underlying parameters. For example, a key parameter for a default-risky bond is the recovery rate: the higher the recovery rate, the less we lose in the event of default and the lower the VaR. We can examine the impact of the recovery rate by plotting the VaR against a range of recovery rates, as in Figure 6.3. This plot shows that the recovery rate has a big impact on the VaR, and confirms that the VaR falls as the recovery rate improves. Observe, too, that as the recovery rate approaches 1, the default-risky VaR approaches the VaR we would get with a default-free bond (which is as we should expect).[19]

---

[17]For more on credit-enhancement methods, see, e.g., Wakeman (1998).

[18]That said, Jarrow and Turnbull (1998) provide a lattice approach to credit-risk estimation that is able to accommodate a reasonable range of problems, and Duffie and Pan (1999) provide an algorithmic approach that is applicable to many credit-related VaR problems. However, neither approach is as user-friendly or as flexible as simulation.

[19]We can also perform similar exercises for the other parameters — the risk of default p, the term to maturity, the holding period, and so on. Obviously, with more complicated instruments, there will also be more parameters or other distinguishing features to be considered.

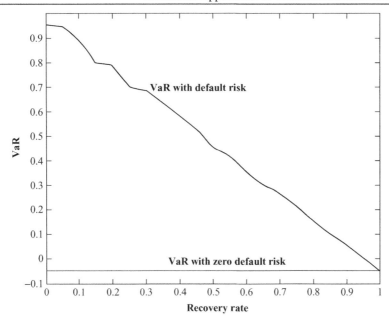

Figure 6.3   VaR and the recovery rate for a default-risky bond.

Note: Obtained using the 'defaultriskybondvar' function with $r = c = 0.05, r_f = 0, \sigma = 0.25, p = 0.05, \delta = 0.5, hp = 360,$ $cl = 0.95$, an amount invested of $1, and 1,000 MCS trials.

6.6   ESTIMATING INSURANCE RISKS WITH SIMULATION METHODS

Another application of simulation approaches is to the measurement of the VaR (or ETL) of insurance portfolios.[20] To illustrate the potential of simulation methods to solve insurance problems, suppose we wish to estimate the VaR of an insurance company portfolio consisting of a large number of identical insurance contracts. To be specific, let us assume:

- There are n contracts, each paying a fixed premium to the insurance company, and these contracts are priced so the insurance company expects to make a target profit of θ on each contract in the portfolio.
- The insurable loss events are independent of each other, and each occurs with probability p.
- When any of these events occur, the associated loss L is determined by a drawing from a lognormal distribution, and log L has mean μ and standard deviation σ.
- Each contract has a deductible D, and we assume that there are no 'no claims' bonuses or similar inducements to encourage policyholders not to recover losses from the insurance company. Hence, when a loss occurs, the contract holder will bear the whole loss if $L \leq D$ and a loss of D if $L > D$; the insurance company will bear a loss of 0 if $L \leq D$ and a loss of $L - D$ if $L > D$.

---

[20]For more on insurance VaR, see Panning (1999). Many insurance (and, indeed, pensions) problems also involve very long-term horizons, and long-term VaR issues are covered in more detail in, e.g., Kim *et al.* (1999) and Dowd *et al.* (2001).

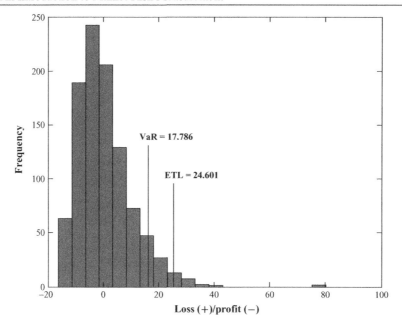

Figure 6.4   Insurance VaR.

Note: Obtained using the 'insurancevaretl' function with $\mu = 0$, $\sigma = 1$, $p = 0.2$, $n = 100$, $\theta = 0.1$, $D = 1$, 1000 trials, and $cl = 0.95$.

Obviously, many real-world insurance contracts will be much more complicated, and we would often be interested in measuring the risks of portfolios with many different insurance contracts.

We can solve this problem by writing a suitable program to estimate the VaR, the details of which can be found in the function 'insurancevar'. The gist of the program is that in each trial, we take a random drawing from a binomial distribution for each contract to determine if it incurs a loss; for each loss event, we also take a random drawing from a lognormal distribution to determine the size of the loss. We then adjust the losses for the deductible and pricing policies, and determine the VaR and ETL from the sample of adjusted losses. A parameterised example is given in Figure 6.4, which shows the histogram of simulated L/P values and the associated VaR and ETL estimates — in this case, the L/P histogram has a long right-hand tail (which is in fact characteristic of the lognormal) and the VaR and ETL are respectively equal to 17.786 and 24.601.

We can also adapt this approach for related purposes: we can change parameters and examine the resulting impact on VaR, and so on.

6.7   ESTIMATING PENSIONS RISKS WITH SIMULATION METHODS

Some final applications of simulation approaches are to the measurement of pensions risks. With pensions, the general method is to build a model that allows the pension fund to grow in line with pension-fund contributions and the (risky) returns made on past pension-fund investment. If the model is sophisticated, it would also allow for the effects of the pension-fund portfolio management strategy, which might also be dynamic, and for the possibility of interrupted contributions (e.g., due to the holder of the pension scheme being unemployed). When the holder retires, one of two things might happen, depending on whether the pension scheme is a defined-benefit scheme or a defined-contribution scheme:

- With a defined-benefit (DB) scheme, the holder gets a predefined retirement income, usually specified in terms of a certain proportion of their final salary or the average of their last few years' salary, plus possible add-ons such as inflation adjustment.[21] In these schemes, the pension-plan provider bears a considerable amount of risk, because the holder's pension benefits are defined and yet their (and, where applicable, their employers') contributions might not cover the provider's pension liability. In such cases, the pension risk we are interested in is related to the probability and magnitude of the holder's accumulated pension fund falling short of the amount needed to meet the costs of the holder's defined pension benefits. Pension risk in this context is the risk of the pension provider's assets falling short of its liabilities.
- With a defined-contribution (DC) scheme, the holder gets a pension based on the value of their accumulated fund and the way in which, and terms on which, the fund is converted to an annual retirement income.[22] Usually, the accumulated fund would be converted into an annual retirement income by purchasing an annuity, in which case the retirement income depends not just on the value of the accumulated fund, but also on the going interest rate and the holder's expected mortality. With these schemes, the holder bears the pension risk, and the risk we are interested in is the risk of a low pension relative to some benchmark (e.g., such as final salary). Pensions risk in this context is the risk of the holder having a low pension.

We now consider each of these two types of scheme in turn.

6.7.1 Estimating Risks of Defined-benefit Pension Plans

To estimate the risks of a defined-benefit pension scheme, we must first clarify the precise features of the scheme concerned, and it is helpful to do so focusing on the pension provider's assets and liabilities.

On the asset side, we need to make assumptions about the starting and ending dates of the scheme, the amounts contributed to the pension fund, the unemployment (or other contribution interruption) risk, and the way in which the pension fund is invested. To illustrate, we might assume that the pension-plan holder:

- Starts contributing at age 25 and aims to retire at age 65.
- Has a salary of $25,000 at age 25, contributes 20% of gross income to the fund, and expects salary to grow at 2% a year in real terms until retirement.
- Faces a constant unemployment risk of 5% a year, and contributes nothing to the scheme when unemployed.[23]
- Does not benefit from any employer contributions to their pension fund.

---

[21] For more on DB schemes, see, e.g., Blake (2000, 2003) and Gupta *et al.* (2000).

[22] The reader who is interested in the mechanics and simulation of DC pension schemes might wish to explore the 'pensionmetrics' work of Blake *et al.*, and particularly Blake *et al.* (2001a), where the pensionmetrics methodology and associated simulation issues are discussed in detail.

[23] These assumptions are unrealistically precise, but we need to make these or similar assumptions to estimate the risks involved, and these rather simple assumptions help to illustrate the approach. In practice, we might want to modify them in many ways: we might want to use a variety of alternative assumptions about start/end dates or contribution rates, real income growth rates, and so on. We might also wish to make real income growth stochastic, or allow a wage profile that peaks before retirement age and possibly depends on the holder's profession, or we might allow unemployment risk to vary with age or profession (e.g., as in Blake *et al.* (2001c)).

We also assume that the fund is invested entirely in one risky asset (e.g., equities), and that the return to this asset is normally distributed with annualised mean and standard deviation both equal to 0.1.[24]

On the liability side, we can think of the pension provider as being obliged to purchase an annuity when the holder retires to give him/her a specified retirement income, and the provider's liability is the cost of this annuity plus the cost of any add-ons such as guarantees against inflation. The provider's liability therefore depends on the final salary (or the last few years' average salary), the formula used to determine retirement income, the annuity rate, and the holder's life expectancy conditional on reaching retirement. It follows, then, that in general the provider's liability is subject to (at least) five (!) different sources of risk:

- Risk arising from uncertainty about the holder's salary at or near retirement.
- Risk arising from uncertainty about the exact timing of retirement.
- Risk arising from uncertainty about employment, which creates uncertainty about the number of years the holder will contribute to the scheme.
- Risk arising from uncertainty about the annuity rate at retirement. This is important, because the annuity rate determines the cost of the annuity necessary to provide a given retirement income: the lower the annuity rate, the greater the cost of the annuity, other things being equal.
- Risk arising from uncertainty about the holder's life expectancy on retirement, and this is also important because of its effect on the cost of the annuity.

To make the analysis as transparent as possible, we now make the following illustrative assumptions:

- The pension is equal to the final salary times the proportion of years in which the holder has contributed to the fund. This implies that if the holder has worked and contributed throughout his/her working life, then he/she will get a pension equal to his/her final salary.
- The annuity rate on retirement is taken as 4%[25]
- There are no add-ons, so the provider's liability is only the cost of the annuity.

Having established the structure of our model, we now program it, and one way to do so is provided by the function 'dbpensionvar'. Leaving aside details, the programming strategy is to model the asset and liability sides separately, work out the terminal values of each under each simulation trial, and take the pension provider's P/L to be the difference between the two. Once we have a set of simulated sample P/L values, we can then estimate VaR or ETL in the usual way. With the asset side, we build up the value of the pension fund over time, bearing in mind that the fund is equal to current contributions plus the last period's fund value plus the return earned on last period's fund value, and pension-fund contributions depend on whether the holder is working that period. We therefore need to take random drawings to determine the rate of return earned on previous pension-fund

---

[24]This assumption is also unrealistic in that it ignores the diversity of assets invested by pension funds, and ignores the possibility of dynamic investment strategies such as the lifestyling or threshold strategies followed by many pension funds (and which are explained, e.g., in Blake *et al.* (2001a)).

[25]We therefore assume away uncertainty associated with both the annuity rate life expectancy. In practical applications we would certainly want to make the annuity rate stochastic, but would also want to ensure that the rate used was consistent with other contemporaneous rates. The correct way to treat the annuity rate is discussed in detail in Blake *et al.* (2001a).

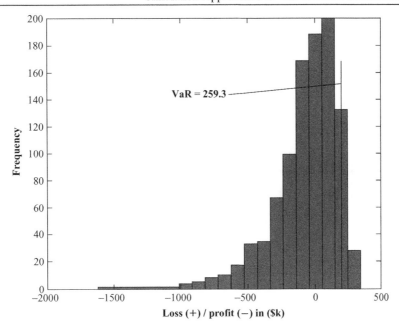

Figure 6.5   VaR of defined-benefit pension scheme.

Note: Obtained using the 'dbpensionvar' function with initial income $25k, income growth rate of 0.02, conditional life expectancy 80 years, contribution rate 0.15, $\mu = 0.1$, $\sigma = 0.1$, $p = 0.05$, annuity rate 0.04, 1000 trials, and $cl = 0.95$.

investments and to determine whether the holder is working in the current period. On the liability side, we determine the final salary value and the number of contribution years, use these to determine the pension entitlement, and then apply the annuity rate and life expectancy to obtain the value of the pension annuity.

After all of this, we now choose our confidence level and run the program to estimate our VaR. Given the assumptions made, our VaR at the 95% confidence level turns out to be 259,350. This is shown in Figure 6.5, which also shows the provider's simulated L/P. Perhaps the most striking feature of this figure is the very wide dispersion in the L/P series: the provider can get outcomes varying from a loss of $400k to a profit of over $1.5m. The business of providing DB pensions is clearly a very risky one. The other point that stands out is that the VaR itself is quite high, and this in part is a reflection of the high risks involved. However, the high VaR is also partly illusory, because these prospective outcomes are 40 years' off in the future, and should be discounted to obtain their net present values. If we then discount the future VaR figure at, say, a 5% annual discount rate, we obtain a 'true' VaR of about 36,310 — which is about 14% of the amount shown in the figure. When dealing with outcomes so far off into the future, it is therefore very important to discount future values and work with their present-value equivalents.

6.7.2   Estimating Risks of Defined-contribution Pension Plans

Defined-contribution pension schemes share much the same asset side as DB schemes; however, they differ in not having any distinct liability structure. Instead of matching assets against specified

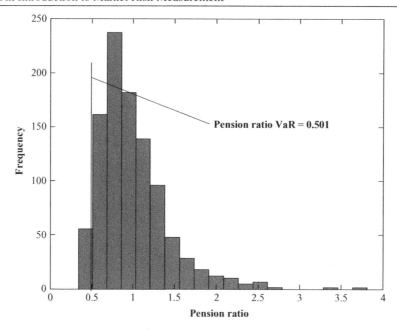

Figure 6.6 VaR of defined-contribution pension scheme.

Note: Obtained using the 'dcpensionvar' function with initial income \$25k, income growth rate of 0.02, conditional life expectancy 80 years, contribution rate 0.15, $\mu = 0.1$, $\sigma = 0.1$, $p = 0.05$, annuity rate 0.04, 1000 trials, and $cl = 0.95$.

liabilities, they (usually) convert the assets available into an annuity to provide the pension.[26] This implies that the pension is determined by the size of the fund built up, and by the terms on which that fund can be annuitised.

To model a DC scheme, we would therefore have the same asset structure as the earlier DB scheme: hence, we can assume that our pension-plan holder starts contributing at age 25, aims to retire at 65, has a starting salary of \$25,000, and so on. Once he/she reaches retirement age, the accumulated fund is converted into an annuity at the going rate, and the pension obtained will also depend on the prevailing annuity rate and the holder's life expectancy at that time.[27] To complete the model, we need assumptions about the annuity rate and the life expectancy on retirement, and we may as well make the same assumptions about these as we did before. However, with DC schemes, the notion of pensions risk refers to the value of the pension itself, not to a possible pension-fund shortfall, and it is convenient to express this risk in terms of the pension divided by the final salary.

We now program the model, and a program is provided by the IMRM function 'dcpensionvar'. The programming strategy is to model the terminal value of the pension fund under each simulation

---

[26] The practice of annuitising funds on retirement is however not necessarily the best way to convert the fund into a pension. These issues are explored in more detail in Blake *et al.* (2001b) and Milevsky (1998).

[27] As viewed from the time when the scheme is first set up, this means that the pension is subject to a number of sources of risk — leaving aside retirement age and contribution rate risks, there are also risks arising from the returns earned on pension-fund investments, risks arising from the possibility of unemployment and interrupted contributions, and risks arising from uncertainty about the annuity rate and life expectancy that will prevail at the time of retirement. Furthermore, these risks are borne entirely by the plan holder, and not by the pension-plan provider, who essentially bears no risk.

trial, annuitise each trial fund value at the going rate, and then divide these by the final salary to obtain a set of normalised pension values. The distribution of these pension values then gives us an indication of our pension risks.

If we carry out these calculations, we find that the pension ratio has a sample mean of 0.983 and a sample standard deviation of 0.406 — which should indicate that DC schemes can be very risky, even without looking at any VaR analysis. The pension VaR — the likely worst pension outcome at the relevant (and in this case, 95%) confidence level — is 0.501, and this indicates that there is a 95% chance of a pension ratio higher than 0.501, and a 5% chance of a lower pension ratio.

6.8 CONCLUSIONS

This chapter has looked at a considerable number of illustrative applications of simulation methods to risk measurement. Our discussion suggests two broad conclusions:

- Simulation methods can be extremely effective for many problems that are too complicated or too messy for analytical or algorithmic approaches, and simulation methods are particularly good at handling complications like fat tails, path-dependency, non-linearity or optionality, and multiple dimensions.
- In applying simulation methods, we should think in terms of programming particular solutions to particular problems, and do so making good use of variance-reduction techniques.

However, we should also keep in mind that simulation methods can be time-consuming, and are not well suited to problems with significant early-exercise features.

Box 6.2   MATLAB Simulation Risk Measurement Functions

The IMRM Toolbox includes a number of tailor-made functions for particular risk measurement problems. These include: 'americanputvar_sim', which uses MCS to estimate the VaRs of American put positions; 'bondvaretl', which estimates the VaR and ETL of a coupon bond; 'stoplosslognormalvar' and 'filterstrategylognormalvar', which estimate the VaR of positions in lognormal assets in the presence of stop-loss and filter rule dynamic portfolio management strategies; 'defaultriskybondvar', which estimates the VaR of the default-risky coupon bond in Section 6.5; 'insurancevaretl', which estimates the VaR and ETL of the insurance portfolio in Section 6.6; and 'dbpensionvar' and 'dcpensionvar', which estimate the defined-benefit and defined-contribution pension risks discussed in Section 6.7.

6.9 RECOMMENDED READING

Abken (2000); Blake *et al.* (2001a); Boyle *et al.* (1997); Broadie and Glasserman (1998); Frye (1996); Glasserman *et al.* (1999a,b; 2000a,b); Holton (1998); Jakobsen (1996); Jamshidian and Zhu (1997); Morokoff *et al.* (1997); Niffikeer *et al.* (2000); Vlaar (2000).

7

Incremental and Component Risks

This chapter considers risk addition and decomposition — how changing our portfolio alters our risk, and how we can decompose our portfolio risk into constituent or component risks.[1] We are therefore concerned with the following:

- *Incremental risks*. These are the changes in risk when some factor changes. To give an example, we might want to know how VaR changes when we add a new position to our portfolio, and in this case the incremental VaR or IVaR is the change in VaR associated with the addition of the new position to our portfolio.
- *Component risks*. These are the component or constituent risks that make up a certain total risk. For instance, if we have a portfolio made up of particular positions, the portfolio VaR can be broken down into components, known as component VaRs or CVaRs, that tell us how much each position contributes to the overall portfolio VaR.

Measures of IVaR can be used as an aid in risk–return decision-making (e.g., we can use IVaRs to determine the required returns on prospective investments; see, e.g., Dowd (1998a, ch. 8)) and to set position limits (see, e.g., Garman (1996b)).

For their part, CVaRs can be used to decompose portfolios into their constituent risks. They are useful for identifying high sources of risk and their opposite, natural hedges (or positions that reduce overall risk), and for setting position limits, making investment decisions, determining capital requirements, and so forth (see, e.g., Litterman (1996) or Dowd (1998a, p. 163)).

7.1 INCREMENTAL VaR

7.1.1 Interpreting Incremental VaR

If VaR gives us an indication of portfolio risks, IVaR gives us an indication of how those risks change when we change the portfolio itself. In practice, we are often concerned with how the portfolio risk changes when we take on a new position, in which case the IVaR is the change in portfolio VaR associated with adding the new position to our portfolio.

The relationship of the IVaR to the new position is very informative. This relationship is illustrated in Figure 7.1, which plots the IVaR against the size of the new position relative to the size of the existing portfolio. There are three main cases to consider:

- *High IVaR*. A high positive IVaR means that the new position adds substantially to portfolio risk. Typically, the IVaR not only rises with relative position size, but also rises at an increasing rate. The reason for this is that as the relative position size continues to rise, the new position has an

---

[1]The literature on incremental and component risks focuses on the VaR as the baseline risk measure; however, it should be obvious by now that we can translate the analysis of incremental and component VaRs so that it applies to the ETL as well. We can estimate the incremental ETL using the 'before and after' approach discussed in the text below or using estimates of marginal ETL comparable to the marginal VaRs that are dealt with in the text. The latter will then also suffice to give us estimates of the component ETLs.

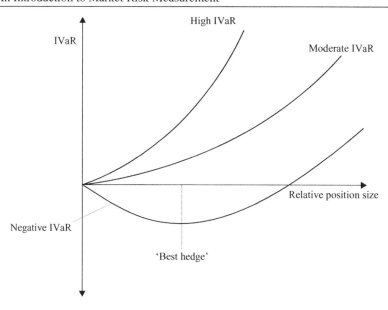

Figure 7.1   Incremental VaR and relative position size.

ever-growing influence on the new portfolio VaR, and hence the IVaR, and increasingly drowns out diversification effects.

- *Moderate IVaR*. A moderate positive IVaR means that the new position adds moderately to portfolio risk, and once again, the IVaR typically rises at an increasing rate with relative position size.
- *Negative IVaR*. A negative IVaR means that the new position reduces overall portfolio risk VaR, and indicates that the new position is a natural hedge against the existing portfolio. However, as its relative size continues to rise, the IVaR must eventually rise because the IVaR will increasingly reflect the VaR of the new position rather than the old portfolio. This implies that the IVaR must have a shape similar to that shown in the figure — it initially falls, but bottoms out, and then rises at an increasing rate. So any position is only a hedge over a limited range of relative position sizes, and ceases to be a hedge when the position size gets too large. The point (or relative position) at which the hedge effect is largest is known as the 'best hedge', and is a useful benchmark for portfolio risk management.[2]

7.1.2   Estimating IVaR by Brute Force: The 'Before and After' Approach

The most obvious way to estimate IVaR is a brute force, or 'before and after', approach. This approach is illustrated in Figure 7.2. We start with our existing portfolio p, map the portfolio, and then input

---

[2]Although IVaRs are good for telling us the impact of trades on VaR — a positive IVaR means that the trade increases VaR, a negative IVaR tells us that it decreases VaR, etc. — they give us a rather incomplete basis for comparing alternative trades. The point is that we can always alter the IVaR by altering the size of the trade: if position A has a lower IVaR than position B, we can usually reverse the ranking simply by changing the sizes of the trades. We therefore need to standardise or normalise the basis of comparison so we can make more meaningful comparisons between alternative trades. The key to this is to nail down what we mean by a trade's size, and we can define a trade's size in various ways: in terms of the amount invested, the notional principal, its standalone VaR, its expected returns, and so on (see, e.g., Garman (1996b, pp. 62–63; 1996c, pp. 4–5)). Each of these alternatives has its own strengths and weaknesses, and we should take care to use one that is appropriate to our situation.

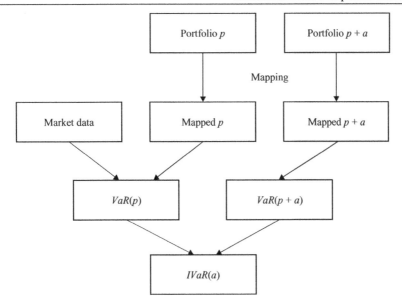

Figure 7.2   The 'before and after' approach to IVaR estimation.

Note: Adapted with permission from Garman (1996c, figure 1).

market data to obtain our portfolio VaR, *VaR(p)*. We then consider the candidate trade *a*, construct
the hypothetical new portfolio that we would have if we went ahead with the trade, and do the same
for that portfolio. This gives us the new portfolio VaR, *VaR(p + a)*, say. The IVaR associated with
trade/position *a*, *IVaR(a)*, is then estimated as the difference between the two:

$$IVaR = VaR(p + a) - VaR(p) \tag{7.1}$$

However, this 'before and after' approach has a fairly obvious drawback. If we have a large number of
different positions — and particularly if we have a lot of optionality or other forms of non-linearity —
then estimating each VaR will take time. Many financial institutions often have tens of thousands
of positions, and re-evaluating the whole portfolio VaR can be a time-consuming process. Because
of the time they take to obtain, IVaR estimates based on the 'before and after' approach are often of
limited practical use in trading and real-time decision-making.

7.1.3   Estimating IVaR Using Marginal VaRs

7.1.3.1   Garman's 'delVaR' Approach

An elegant way to reduce the computational burden is suggested by Garman (1996a–c). His suggestion is that we estimate IVaR using a Taylor-series approximation based on marginal VaRs (or, if we
like, the mathematical derivatives of our portfolio VaR). Again, suppose we have a portfolio *p* and
wish to estimate the IVaR associated with adding a position *a* to our existing portfolio. We begin by
mapping *p* and *a* to a set of *n* instruments. The portfolio *p* then has a vector of (mapped) position
sizes in these instruments of $[w_1, \ldots, w_n]$ (so w_1 is the size of our mapped position in instrument 1,
etc.) and the new portfolio has a corresponding position-size vector of $[w_1 + \Delta w_1, \ldots, w_n + \Delta w_n]$.
If *a* is 'small' relative to *p*, we can approximate the VaR of our new portfolio (i.e., *VaR(p + a)*) by

taking a first-order Taylor-series approximation around $VaR(p)$, i.e.:

$$VaR(p + a) \approx VaR(p) + \sum_{i=1}^{n} \frac{\partial VaR}{\partial w_i} dw_i \qquad (7.2)$$

where $dw_i \approx \Delta w_i$ (see Garman (1996b, p. 61)). The IVaR associated with position a, $IVaR(a)$, is then:

$$IVaR(a) = VaR(p + a) - VaR(p) \approx \sum_{i=1}^{n} \frac{\partial VaR}{\partial w_i} dw_i \qquad (7.3)$$

where the partial derivatives, $\partial VaR/\partial w_i$, give us the marginal changes in VaR associated with marginal changes in the relevant cash-flow elements. If we wish, we can rewrite Equation (7.3) in matrix notation as:

$$IVaR(a) \approx \nabla \mathbf{VaR(p)dw} \qquad (7.4)$$

where $\mathbf{dw}$ is the transpose of the $1 \times n$ vector $[dw_1, \ldots, dw_n]$ and $\nabla \mathbf{VaR(p)}$, known as 'delVaR' is the $1 \times n$ vector of partial derivatives of $VaR(p)$ with respect to the w_i.[3] Equation (7.4) gives us an approximation to the IVaR associated with position a given information on the $\nabla \mathbf{VaR(p)}$ and $\mathbf{dw}$ vectors: the latter is readily obtained from mapping the position, and the former (which depends only on the existing portfolio p) can be estimated at the same time that $VaR(p)$ is estimated. This means that we can approximate the IVaR associated with position a using only one set of initial estimates — those of $VaR(p)$ and $\nabla \mathbf{VaR(p)}$ — relating only to the original portfolio, and the only information we need about the position itself is its (readily available) mapped position-size vector $[dw_1, \ldots, dw_n]$. This, in turn, means that we can estimate as many different IVaRs as we like, given only one set of estimates of $VaR(p)$ and $\nabla \mathbf{VaR(p)}$. This 'delVaR' approach is very useful because it enables us to estimate and so use IVaRs in real time — for instance, when assessing investment risks and specifying position limits.

The process of estimating IVaR using the delVaR approach is illustrated in Figure 7.3. We begin by mapping our portfolio and using market data to estimate the portfolio VaR and delVaRs. Observe, too, that these depend on the portfolio we already have, and not on any candidate trades. Once we have the portfolio VaR and delVaRs, we can then take any candidate trade a, map the trade, and use the mapped trade and delVaRs to estimate the IVaR associated with that candidate trade.

The only question that remains is how to estimate $\nabla \mathbf{VaR(p)}$, and we can always estimate the terms in this vector by suitable approximations — we can estimate $\partial VaR/\partial w_i$ by estimating the VaR for position sizes w_i and $w_i + \Delta w_i$, and taking $\partial VaR/\partial w_i \approx (VaR(p|w_i + \Delta w_i) - VaR(p|w_i))/\Delta w_i$, where $VaR(p|w_i)$ is the VaR of p with position size i equal to w_i, etc.

In some cases, we can also solve $\nabla \mathbf{VaR(p)}$ algebraically. For example, where P/L is normally distributed with mean vector $\boldsymbol{\mu}$ and variance–covariance matrix Σ, $\nabla \mathbf{VaR(p)}$ is:

$$\nabla \mathbf{VaR(p)} = -\boldsymbol{\mu} + \frac{\Sigma \mathbf{w}\alpha_{cl}}{[\mathbf{w}^{\mathrm{T}} \Sigma \mathbf{w}]^{1/2}} \qquad (7.5)$$

---

[3]My exposition differs from Garman's in that I prefer to deal in terms of position sizes whilst he couches his discussion in terms of cash-flow vertices. The two are much the same, but I believe positions sizes are easier for most people to follow. The 'delVaR' approach has since been patented by Financial Engineering Associates under the tradename 'VaRDelta', and further details can be found on their website, www.fea.com.

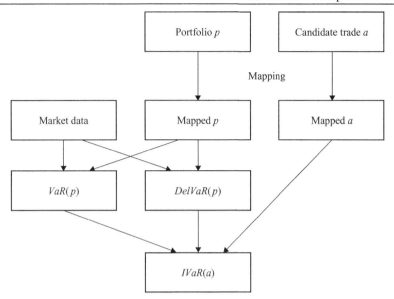

Figure 7.3   The delVaR approach to IVaR estimation.

Note: Adapted with permission from Garman (1996c, figure 3).

(see, e.g., Gourieroux *et al.* (2000, p. 228),[4] and Garman (1996b)). Equation (7.5) allows us to estimate $\nabla\mathbf{VaR(p)}$ making use of information about the position size vectors for the existing portfolio (**w**) and the new position (**dw**), the mean vector $\boldsymbol{\mu}$ and the variance–covariance matrix $\boldsymbol{\Sigma}$ — all of which are readily available or already known.

The delVaR approach could be implemented on a daily cycle. At the start of each trading day, we would estimate both the VaR and delVaR of our existing portfolio. As we require our various IVaR estimates throughout the day, we would obtain them using Equation (7.4) and Equation (7.5), as appropriate. These estimates could be based on our initial daily estimates of *VaR(p)* and $\nabla\mathbf{VaR(p)}$, and could be done extremely quickly without the arduous process of re-estimating portfolio VaRs throughout the day, as we would have to do using a 'before and after' approach. Experience suggests that this approximation is pretty good for most institutions most of the time.

Box 7.1   Estimating IVaR

We can estimate IVaR (and CVaR) by any of the standard methods: parametric estimation methods, non-parametric (e.g., HS) methods, or simulation methods:

- Parametric methods are appropriate when we can solve for the delVaRs (e.g., as we can for normal VaR).
- We can apply HS methods by using a 'before and after' approach using HS to estimate the 'before' and 'after' portfolio VaRs.

---

[4]Gourieroux *et al.* (2000) also provide a more general approach to delVaR applicable for other parametric assumptions, and Scaillet (2000b) does the same for non-parametric ETL.

- We can also apply simulation methods using a 'before and after' approach, but this can be inaccurate if the user is not careful. If we run two separate 'before' and 'after' paths, the variance of the IVaR (or CVaR) estimator will behave much like the variance of an option-delta estimator in such circumstances: the variance will get very large as the 'increment' gets small (see Boyle *et al.* (1997, p. 1304)). The solution is to run one set of price paths, and infer the 'before' and 'after' portfolio VaRs from that. This estimator is of order 1, and will therefore get small as the increment gets small. We can also apply simulation methods to estimate the original portfolio VaR and the delVaR terms, and can then plug these estimates into Equation (7.4) to obtain our IVaRs.

7.1.3.2 *Potential Drawbacks of the delVaR Approach*

Nonetheless, the delVaR approach only approximates IVaR, and is therefore only as good as the approximation itself. When the position or trade considered is 'small' relative to the size of the original portfolio, the approximation should be a good one and we could expect the delVaR approach to be reliable. However, there are two circumstances in which this procedure might not be reliable:

- If we are dealing with very large trades, the first-order Taylor series might not give us a good approximation for the VaR of the new portfolio, and in this case the resulting IVaR approximation might be poor.
- If we have a large number of small trades accumulating during the day, the sum of daily trades will cause the intra-day portfolio to drift away from the start-of-day portfolio, and the VaR and delVaRs of the latter will be increasingly poor proxies for the VaR and delVaRs of the former. Inaccurate VaR and delVaR estimates can then lead to inaccurate IVaR estimates due to drift in the portfolio composition, even if individual trades are all 'small'.

Whether these problems are significant will depend on our circumstances, but if we wish to make our IVaR estimates more accurate, we can do so by re-estimating the portfolio VaR and delVaR more frequently: for instance, we can re-estimate VaR and delVaR after a particularly big trade, or after a specified number of trades have taken place, or every so often (e.g., every few minutes) during the trading day.

7.2 COMPONENT VaR

7.2.1 Properties of Component VaR

We turn now to consider the component VaR, CVaR, and begin by considering the properties that we want CVaR to satisfy. The two main properties we want are:

- *Incrementality.* We want the component VaR to be, at least to a first order of approximation, equal to the IVaR — the increase or decrease in VaR experienced when the relevant component is added to or deleted from the portfolio.
- *Additivity.* We want the arithmetic sum of component VaRs to be equal to the VaR of the total portfolio. This ensures that however we decompose the VaR, all the constituents, the component VaRs, collectively add up to the whole of the VaR.

We can obtain our component VaR as follows. We first select the decomposition criteria — whether we wish to decompose VaR by instrument, asset class, desk, etc.). The portfolio VaR will be a linearly homogeneous function of the positions in the instruments (or asset classes, etc.) concerned.[5] This linear homogeneity allows us to apply Euler's theorem, which tells us that:

$$VaR = \sum_{i=1}^{n} w_i \frac{\partial VaR}{\partial w_i} = \nabla\mathbf{VaR(p)w} \tag{7.6}$$

If we now define the component VaR for instrument i, $CVaR_i$, as:

$$CVaR_i = w_i \frac{\partial VaR}{\partial w_i} \tag{7.7}$$

we can substitute Equation (7.6) into Equation (7.7) to get:

$$VaR = \sum_{i=1}^{n} CVaR_i \tag{7.8}$$

which gives us a breakdown of the VaR into component VaR constituents that satisfies both incrementality and additivity properties.[6] The key to CVaR is thus Equation (7.7), which specifies the $CVaR_i$ in terms of the position sizes (i.e., the w_i) and the marginal VaRs or mathematical first derivatives of the VaR with respect to the w_i.

It is sometimes more convenient to express CVaRs in percentage terms, and we can do so by dividing Equation (7.8) throughout by the VaR itself:

$$1 = \frac{1}{VaR} \sum_{i=1}^{n} CVaR_i = \sum_{i=1}^{n} \%CVaR_i \tag{7.9}$$

The percentage CVaRs, the $\%CVaR_i$ terms, give us the component VaRs expressed as percentages of total VaR.

Component VaRs give us a good idea of the distribution of risks within our portfolio and, as with incremental VaR, we can distinguish between three main cases:

- *High contributions to risk.* High CVaRs represent high pockets of risk, which contribute strongly to overall portfolio VaR.
- *Moderate contributions to risk.* Moderate positive CVaRs represent moderate pockets of risk.
- *Negative contributions to risk.* Negative CVaRs represent natural hedges that offset some of the risk of the rest of the portfolio. Natural hedges are very useful, because they indicate where and how we can reduce overall risks.

It is important to note that these CVaRs reflect marginal contributions to total risk, taking account of all relevant factors, including correlations and volatilities as well as position sizes. As a result, we cannot really predict CVaRs using only position-size information or volatility information alone:

- A position might be relatively large in size and have a small or negative CVaR, and another position might be relatively small and have a large CVaR, because of volatility and correlation effects.
- A position in a high-volatility instrument might have a low or negative CVaR and a position in a low-volatility instrument might have a high CVaR, because of correlation and position-size effects.

---

[5] A function $y = (x_1, \ldots, x_n)$ is linearly homogeneous if multiplying the inputs by some positive constant λ leads to the output multiplying by the same proportion (i.e., $\lambda y = (\lambda x_1, \ldots, \lambda x_n)$).

[6] The latter is obvious; the other is a useful exercise.

The impact of correlation factors can also be appreciated by considering an important special case. If P/L or arithmetic returns are normal, we can show that $CVaR_i$ is approximately:

$$CVaR_i \approx \omega_i \beta_i VaR(p) \qquad (7.10)$$

where ω_i is the relative share of instrument i in the portfolio, and is assumed to be 'small', β_i is the beta coefficient of instrument i in the portfolio, or $\sigma_{i,p}/\sigma_p^2$, where $\sigma_{i,p}$ is the covariance between the returns to i and p (see, e.g., Dowd (1998b, p. 32) or Hallerbach (1999, pp. 8–9)). As we might expect in a normal world, the CVaR for instrument i reflects that instrument's beta: other things being equal, a high beta implies a high CVaR, a low beta implies a low CVaR, and a negative beta implies a negative CVaR. Correlations therefore have important effects on CVaRs — and because of the complicated ways in which correlations interact with each other, these effects are seldom obvious at first sight.[7]

However, we should also keep in mind that the CVaR risk decomposition outlined in Equations (7.6)–(7.9) has an important limitation: it is a linear marginal analysis. The component risks add up to total VaR because of linear homogeneity working through Euler's theorem, but the price we pay for this additivity property is that we have to take each component VaR to be simply the position size multiplied by the marginal VaR. This is restrictive, because it implies that the component VaR is proportional to the position size: if we change the size of the position by $k\%$, the component VaR will also change by $k\%$. Strictly speaking, this linear-proportionality is only guaranteed if each position is very small relative to the total portfolio; and where the position size is significant relative to the total portfolio, the component VaR estimated in this way is likely, at best, to give only an approximate idea of the impact of the position on the portfolio VaR. If we want a 'true' estimate of the latter, we would have to resort to the IVaR, and take the difference between the VaRs of the portfolio with and without the position concerned. The IVaR then gives us an exact estimate of the impact of the portfolio. Unfortunately, this exactness also has its price: we lose the additivity property, and the component VaRs no longer add up to the total VaR, which makes it difficult to interpret these IVaR-CVaRs (or whatever else we call them) as decompositions of the total risk. In short, when positions are significant in size relative to the total portfolio, we can only hope for our CVaRs to give approximate estimates of the effects of the positions concerned on the portfolio VaR.[8]

7.2.2 Uses of Component VaR

7.2.2.1 'Drill-down' Capability

The additivity of component VaRs is, as we have seen, very useful for 'explaining' how the VaR can be broken down into constituent components. Yet it also enables us to break down our risks at multiple levels, and at each stage the component risks will correctly add up to the total risk of the unit at the next level up. We can break down the firm-wide risk into component risks associated with large

---

[7]The IVaR also depends on the relative position size as well (as reflected here in the position size or ω_i terms), but does not depend particularly on any individual instrument or asset volatility.

[8]This can cause problems for capital allocation purposes in particular. If we want to use component VaRs to allocate capital, we want the component VaRs to be accurate and to satisfy additivity, but we can't in general satisfy both conditions. This leaves us with an awkward choice: we can satisfy additivity and base our capital requirements on potentially inaccurate component risk measures; or we can make our IVaR-CVaR estimates accurate, and then they don't add up properly. In the latter case, we could find that the component VaRs add up to more than the total VaR, in which case a bottom-up approach to capital requirements would leave us excessively capitalised at the firm-wide level; or, alternatively, we might find that the components add up to less than the total VaR, in which case we would have a capital shortfall at the aggregate level. Either way, we get into messy overhead allocation problems, and any solution would inevitably be ad hoc — and therefore probably inaccurate anyway. Additive accurate CVaRs would certainly make life much easier.

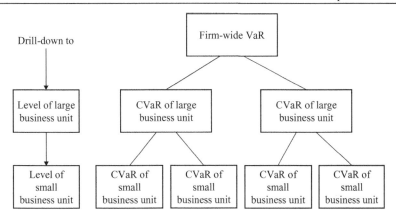

Figure 7.4   Multiple-level risk decomposition and drill-down capability.

business units (e.g., by country or region); we can break these down in turn to obtain the component risks associated with smaller units (e.g., individual branches); and so forth, right down to the level of individual desks or traders. This breakdown is illustrated in Figure 7.4. The key point is that the component risks correctly add up, and this implies that we can break down our risks to obtain the component VaRs at any level we choose: we can break down our firm-wide VaR into component VaRs at the level of large business units, at the level of smaller units, or at any other level, including the level of the individual desk, the individual trader, or the individual instrument. The additivity of component VaRs therefore gives rise to a 'drill-down' capability — an ability to decompose a risk figure, or identify its components, down to any level we choose. So, for example, an institution might use drill-down to establish how each and every unit, at each and every level — each trader, instrument, asset class, desk, branch, region, or whatever — contributes to overall risk. Drill-down capability is, needless to say, of immense practical usefulness — for determining the positions or units that need attention, identifying hidden sources of risk, setting limits, making investment or trading decisions, determining capital requirements, establishing remuneration schedules, and so on.

7.2.2.2   *Reporting Component VaRs*

Given especially that many component risks are less than obvious, it is very important to report component risks meaningfully, and in ways that interested parties (e.g., senior managers, etc.) can understand without too much difficulty. This suggests that:

- We should 'slice and dice' component VaRs, and report them accordingly, in ways geared to each particular audience, business unit, etc.
- Reports should be as short and straightforward as possible, and avoid unnecessary information that can distract from the key points to be communicated.
- Reports should identify key assumptions and spell out possible consequences if those assumptions are mistaken.

It follows, then, that there are many possible ways of reporting CVaR information. These might include, among many others, reports of CVaR by asset class (e.g., equities, commodities, etc.), market risk factors, individual trades or positions, types of counterparty (e.g., government counterparties, swap counterparties, etc.), individual counterparties, and so on, and each of these is good for its own particular purpose.

CVaR and IVaR information can also be presented in the form of 'hot spots', 'best hedges', 'best replicating portfolios' and 'implied views' reports:

- Hot spots reports give the CVaRs ranked in terms of their size — the top-ranking CVaRs are the 'hot spots', or the biggest sources of portfolio risk — and these give a very immediate indication of where the portfolio risks are coming from.
- Best hedges reports give the best hedges — for each instrument or asset, the trade (long or short) that would minimise portfolio VaR. For a position with a negative IVaR, the best hedge would involve a further purchase or investment; for a positive IVaR, the best hedge would involve a sale or short position. Best hedges are very useful benchmarks for portfolio management (see, e.g., Litterman (1997b, p. 40)).
- Best replicating portfolios (BRPs) are those portfolios, made up of small numbers of positions, that best replicate the risks of our 'real' portfolio: we select a small number of assets n, estimate the BRP using regression analysis (see Litterman (1997b, pp. 40–41)), and report the BRPs of a range of n-values. Best replicating portfolios are very useful for identifying macro portfolio hedges — hedges against the portfolio as a whole. They also help us to understand the risks we face: if we have a very large portfolio, it can be difficult to understand what is going on, but if we can replicate the portfolio with one that has only a small number of different assets, we can get a much better picture of the risks involved. BRP reports are therefore particularly useful when dealing with very large or very complex portfolios.
- Implied views are the views about future returns that make the current portfolio an optimal one. Comparing implied views about returns with actual views is a useful tool in helping to understand how portfolios can be improved. They are also useful in helping to macro manage a portfolio whose composition is subject to delegated decision-making. A good example, suggested by Litterman (1997b, p. 41), is in big financial institutions whose portfolios are affected by large numbers of traders operating in different markets: at the end of each day, the implied views of the portfolio can be estimated and compared to the actual views of, say, in-house forecasters. Any differences between actual and implied views can then be reconciled by taking positions to bring the implied views into line.

7.3 CONCLUSIONS

Both IVaR and CVaRs (and, of course, their ETL equivalents) are extremely useful measures in portfolio risk management: amongst other uses, they give us new methods of identifying sources of risk, finding natural hedges, defining risk limits, reporting risks and improving portfolio allocations.

In theory, we can always estimate IVaRs (or IETLs) by brute force 'before and after' approaches, but these methods can be impractically time-consuming. Fortunately, there exist good approximation methods based on marginal VaRs — most notably the delVaR approach pioneered by Garman — that can estimate IVaRs or IETLs much more rapidly, and similar methods can also be used to estimate component VaRs and component ETLs.

7.4 RECOMMENDED READING

Aragonés *et al.* (2001); Blanco (1999a); Dowd (1999); Garman (1996b,c, 1997); Gourieroux *et al.* (2000); Hallerbach (1999); Ho *et al.* (1996); Litterman (1996, 1997a,b); Mausser and Rosen (1998, 2000).

8

Estimating Liquidity Risks

We have implicitly assumed so far that markets are liquid — that is, we can liquidate or unwind positions at going market prices, usually taken to be the mean of bid and ask prices, without too much difficulty or cost. This assumption is very convenient and provides a nice justification for the practice of marking positions to market prices. However, it is often empirically questionable, and where it does not hold, we need to revise the way we estimate market risks to allow for the effects of illiquidity.

This chapter looks at liquidity issues and how they affect market risk measurement. Liquidity issues affect market risk measurement not just through their impact on our standard measures of market risk, VaR and ETL, but also because effective market risk management involves an ability to measure and manage liquidity risk itself. We therefore need to be able to measure liquidity risk — or liquidity at risk, if you will. Furthermore, since liquidity problems are particularly prominent in market crises, we also need to address how to measure crisis-related liquidity risks. In short, the main themes of this chapter are:

- The nature of market liquidity and illiquidity, and their associated costs and risks.
- Measuring VaR and ETL in illiquid or partially liquid markets — liquidity-adjusted VaR (or LVaR) and liquidity-adjusted ETL (or LETL).
- Measuring liquidity at risk (LaR).
- Measuring crisis-related liquidity risks.

8.1 LIQUIDITY AND LIQUIDITY RISKS

The notion of liquidity refers to the ability of a trader to execute a trade or liquidate a position with little or no cost, risk or inconvenience. Liquidity is a function of the market, and depends on such factors as the number of traders in the market, the frequency and size of trades, the time it takes to carry out a trade, and the cost (and sometimes risk) of transacting. It also depends on the commodity or instrument traded, and more standardised instruments (e.g., such as FX or equities) tend to have more liquid markets than non-standardised or tailor-made instruments (e.g., such as over-the-counter (OTC) derivatives). Markets vary greatly in their liquidity: markets such as the FX market and the big stock markets are (generally) highly liquid; but other markets are much less so, particularly those for many OTC instruments and instruments that are usually held to maturity (and, hence, are rarely traded once initially bought). However, even the 'big' standardised markets are not perfectly liquid — their liquidity fluctuates over time,[1] and can fall dramatically in a crisis — so we cannot take their liquidity for granted.

---

[1] We can estimate market liquidity if we have good transactions data, and such data are now becoming available. Using such data, Froot *et al.* (2001) regress returns on cross-border purchases and sales and use the coefficients from these exercises to estimate a 'liquidity index', which gives us an estimate of the price impact of trades (see also Persaud (2000)). Results suggest that market liquidity was very hard hit in the summer of 1998, and thereafter took a long time to recover: for example, cross-border equity liquidity was still less in 2000 than it was in 1997, and liquidity in some emerging markets was even lower in 2000 than during the turbulence of 1998.

Our first concern is with liquidity issues as they affect the estimation of VaR and ETL. We therefore begin by focusing on liquidity costs and liquidity risks, both of which are very relevant for market risk measurement.

The main source of liquidity costs is the bid–ask spread. When a trader undertakes a trade, he or she does not get 'the' going market price. Instead, there are two going market prices — an ask price, which is the price at which the trader sells, and a (lower) bid price, which is the price at which the trader buys. The 'market' price often quoted is just an average of the bid and ask prices, and this price is fictional because no one actually trades at this price. The difference between the two — which is equal to half the bid–ask spread — is a cost of liquidity, and in principle we should allow for this cost in calculating our VaR and ETL.

The bid–ask spread also has an associated risk, because the spread itself is a random variable. This means there is some risk associated with the price we can obtain, even if the fictional mid-spread price is given. Other things being equal, if the spread rises, the costs of closing out our position will rise, so the risk that the spread will rise should be factored into our risk measures along with the usual 'market' price risk.

We should also take account of a further distinction. If our position is 'small' relative to the size of the market (e.g., because we are a very small player in a very large market), then our trading should have a negligible impact on the market price. In such circumstances we can regard the bid–ask spread as exogenous to us, and can assume that the spread is determined by the market beyond our control. However, if our position is large relative to the market, our activities will have a noticeable effect on the market itself, and can affect both the 'market' price and the bid–ask spread. If we suddenly unload a large position, for instance, we should expect the 'market' price to fall and the bid–ask spread to widen.[2] In these circumstances the 'market' price and the bid–ask spread are to some extent endogenous (i.e., they respond to our trading activities) and we should take account of how the market reacts or might react to us when estimating liquidity costs and risks. Other things again being equal, the bigger our trade, the bigger the impact we should expect it to have on market prices.

In sum, we are concerned with both liquidity costs and liquidity risks, and we need to take account of the difference between exogenous and endogenous liquidity. We now consider some of the approaches available to adjust our estimates of VaR and ETL to take account of these factors.[3]

8.2 ESTIMATING LIQUIDITY-ADJUSTED VAR AND ETL

8.2.1 A Transactions Cost Approach

One approach is to adjust VaR and ETL for liquidity effects through an examination of the impact of transactions costs on our P/L. Given our earlier discussion of liquidity, we can plausibly assume that transactions costs rise with the size of the transaction relative to the market size for the instrument concerned (i.e., because of adverse market reactions due to limited liquidity) and with the bid–ask spread. We can also assume that transactions costs fall with the length of time taken to liquidate the

---

[2]There is an extensive financial economics literature on this subject, but broadly speaking, the literature suggests two reasons why market prices might move against the trader. The first is the liquidity effect already alluded to, namely, that there is a limited market, and prices must move to induce other traders to buy. The other reason is a little more subtle: large trades often reveal information, and the perception that they do will cause other traders to revise their views. For example, a large sale may encourage other traders to revise downwards their assessment of the prospects for the instrument concerned, and this will further depress the price.

[3]There is in fact no need to say much about adjusting ETL estimates. Once we can estimate the VaR, we can easily estimate the ETL by using the average tail VaR approach outlined in Chapter 3: we adjust the VaR for liquidity factors, and then estimate the liquidity-adjusted ETL as the tail average of liquidity-adjusted VaRs. There is therefore no need to say anything further about ETL estimation in the presence of liquidity adjustments.

position, because we can expect to get better prices if we are prepared to take longer to complete our transactions.[4] A functional form with these properties is the following:

$$TC = [1 + PS/MS]^{\lambda_1}(AL \times spread/2)\exp(-\lambda_2 hp) \qquad (8.1)$$

where TC are transactions costs, PS and MS are the position size and market size (so that PS/MS is an indicator of position size relative to the market), AL is the amount liquidated at the end of the holding period hp, $spread$ is the bid–ask spread (so $spread/2$ is the difference between the quoted mid-spread price and the actual transaction price), and λ_1 and λ_2 are positive parameters. We can easily show that λ_1 is closely related to the elasticity of transactions costs, TC, with respect to relative position size, PS/MS, and this is helpful because we can apply some economic intuition to get an idea of what the value of this elasticity might be (e.g., a good elasticity of this sort might be in the range from a little over 0 to perhaps 2). For its part, λ_2 has the interpretation of a rate of decay — in this particular case, the rate of decay (measured in daily units) of TC as hp rises — and this is useful in putting a plausible value to this second parameter (e.g., λ_2 might be, say, 0.20 or thereabouts).

The first square-bracketed term in Equation (8.1) gives us an indicator of the effect of relative position size on transactions costs: this term will generally be bigger than 1, but goes to 1 as PS/MS goes to zero and our relative position size becomes insignificant. The second term gives the effect of the bid–ask spread on transactions costs, scaled by the amount liquidated at the end of the holding period. The third term in Equation (8.1) gives us the impact of the holding period on transactions costs, and says that this impact declines exponentially with the length of the holding period, other things being equal. Equation (8.1) thus captures our transactions cost story in a way that allows us to quantify transactions costs and assign plausible values to the parameters concerned.

This framework now gives us the market risk measures (i.e., the $LVaR$ and, using obvious terminology, the $LETL$) associated with any chosen holding period taking into account the transactions costs involved. Noting that if we make a loss equal to the $LVaR$, the amount liquidated (AL) at the end of the holding period will be equal to the initial position size (PS) minus the $LVaR$, we get:

$$\begin{aligned} TC &= [1 + PS/MS]^{\lambda_1}(AL \times spread/2)\exp(-\lambda_2 hp) \\ &= [1 + PS/MS]^{\lambda_1}[(PS - LVaR) \times spread/2]\exp(-\lambda_2 hp) \end{aligned} \qquad (8.2)$$

which gives us TC in terms of $LVaR$. The $LVaR$, in turn, is equal to the VaR we would have obtained in the absence of transactions costs plus the transactions costs themselves:

$$LVaR = VaR + TC \qquad (8.3)$$

We now solve these two equations to obtain our expression for $LVaR$, i.e.:

$$LVaR = \frac{VaR + kPS}{1 + k} \qquad (8.4)$$

---

[4] This transactions cost story is similar to that of Lawrence and Robinson (1995b,c), which was the first published analysis of LVaR. However, they did not report a precise (i.e., operational) specification for the transactions cost function, which makes their results impossible to reproduce, and they also used transactions costs as only one element of a broader notion of liquidation costs, the other elements of their liquidation costs being exposure (or capital) costs and hedging costs. I do not believe that these latter costs really belong in a liquidation cost function (i.e., it is best to focus more narrowly on transactions costs) and I believe that their including these costs, the former especially, leads them to the mistaken notion that there is an 'optimal' liquidation period which minimises liquidation costs. This is inplausible, as liquidation costs should continue to fall indefinitely as the holding or liquidation period continues to rise, until they become negligible. I also have serious doubts about some of the results they report (see Lawrence and Robinson (1995b, p. 55; 1995c, p. 26)): of their four main sets of results, two involve VaRs that are less than the LVaRs, which makes no sense given that liquidation or transactions costs must be non-negative; and one set of results gives LVaR estimates that are about 10 times their corresponding traditional (or unadjusted) VaRs, which seems excessively high.

where:

$$k = [1 + PS/MS]^{\lambda_1}(spread/2)\exp(-\lambda_2 hp) \qquad (8.5)$$

which can be interpreted as a (positive) transactions cost rate (i.e., it gives transactions costs per unit position involved). For low values of hp, k has an order of magnitude of around half the spread rate, and as hp gets high, k goes towards zero. The impact of transactions costs on VaR can readily be appreciated by considering the $LVaR/VaR$ ratio:

$$\frac{LVaR}{VaR} = \frac{1 + kPS/VaR}{1 + k} \qquad (8.6)$$

The impact of transactions therefore depends critically on the transactions cost rate k and on the ratio PS/VaR, which should also be greater than 1.

If k is very low (e.g., $k \approx 0$), then $LVaR/VaR \approx 1$ and transactions costs have a negligible effect on VaR — a result that makes sense because the transactions costs themselves will be negligible. On the other hand, if k is (relatively) high (e.g., $k = 0.025$ and PS is high relative to VaR (e.g., $PS/VaR \approx 20$?), then $LVaR/VaR \approx 1.46$. So if we take $k \approx 0$ as one extreme, and $k = 0.025$ and $PS/VaR = 20$ as a plausible characterisation of the other, we might expect a transactions cost adjustment to alter our VaR estimate by anything in the range from 0 to nearly 50%.

The impact of transactions costs on $LVaR$ also depends on the holding period, and this impact is illustrated in Figure 8.1, which plots the $LVaR/VaR$ ratio against the holding period for a fairly reasonable set of parameter values. In this case, a holding period of 1 day leads to an $LVaR/VaR$ ratio of about 1.22, but the ratio falls with hp and is under 1.01 by the time hp reaches 20 days. Clearly,

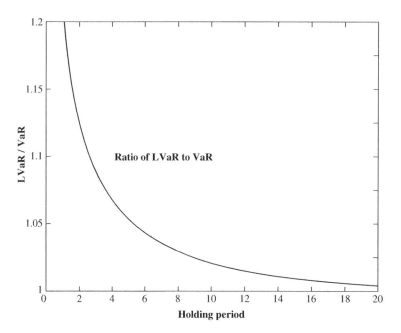

Figure 8.1   The impact of holding period on LVaR.

Note: Based on normal P/L with assumed values of $\mu = 0$, $\sigma = 1$, $spread = 0.05$, $\lambda_1 = 1$, $\lambda_2 = 0.1$, relative position size 0.05, and initial position size 10 times VaR at the 1-day holding period.

if we take a holding period long enough, we can effectively eliminate the impact of transactions costs on *LVaR*.

Box 8.1   Liquidation Strategies

A trader who wishes to liquidate a position over a certain period has a number of ways to do so. Typically, a strategy of selling quickly will involve high transactions costs — the more rapid the sale, the more pressure the trader puts on the market, and the worse the price he/she gets, and so on — but it also means that the trader rapidly reduces his/her exposure to loss from adverse price movements. On the other hand, a more leisurely strategy generally involves lower transactions costs, but a greater exposure over a longer period. There is therefore a trade-off between transactions costs and exposure costs.

A solution to the optimal liquidation problem is suggested by Almgren and Chriss (1999, 2000). They suggest that we begin by identifying this trade-off and estimating the set of efficient trading strategies that produce the minimum remaining risk exposure at any given point in time, for any given expected (mainly transactions) cost. Once we have identified the efficient trading strategies, we choose one that best fits our risk-aversion. If we are risk averse, we would choose a strategy that rapidly reduces our exposure, but at the cost of accepting a high expected cost; and if we are less risk averse, we would choose a strategy that leaves us more exposed, but is not expected to be so expensive.

8.2.2   The Exogenous Spread Approach

An alternative (and simpler) approach is suggested by Bangia *et al.* (1999). If our position is sufficiently small relative to the market, we can regard our liquidity risk as exogenous to us (or independent of the extent of our own trading), for any given holding period. In such cases, they suggest that we think of liquidity risk in terms of the bid–ask spread and its volatility. If the spread has a mean μ_{spread} and a volatility σ_{spread}, and we conveniently assume that the spread itself is normally distributed, we can be 95% confident, say, that the closing-out cost will be no more than $((\mu_{spread} + 1.645\sigma_{spread})/2)$ of the amount liquidated, measured relative to a benchmark of the mid-point of the expected bid–ask spread. (Of course, we can assume other confidence levels and other distributions besides the normal, and Bangia *et al.* actually assume a lognormal spread, but the story is easier to follow if we assume a normal spread instead.) The *LVaR* is then given by:

$$LVaR = [1 + (\mu_{spread} + 1.645\sigma_{spread})/2]VaR \tag{8.7}$$

and is easily computed by inputting appropriate parameter values. For example, if $\mu_{spread} = 0.05$ and $\sigma_{spread} = 0.02$, then $LVaR = 1.042 \times VaR$, and the liquidity spread adjustment increases the VaR by a little over 4%.[5] Naturally, other distributions and other confidence levels could produce somewhat bigger liquidity spread adjustments; however, it is difficult to see how these spreads

---

[5]Those, if any, who enjoy these sorts of details might note that this *LVaR* is predicated, not on one, but on two confidence levels: the original confidence level *cl* on which all VaRs are predicated, and a second confidence level, which may or may not be the same, expressed in terms of the distribution of the bid–ask spread. Strictly speaking, we should therefore refer to this *LVaR* as predicated on the VaR confidence level *cl* and on the 95% bid–ask spread confidence level. Purists will, I hope, not be too harsh on me if I sweep all this under the rug.

could plausibly be as large as some of the spreads obtainable under the previous transactions cost approach.

8.2.3   The Market Price Response Approach

If the last approach ignores the possibility of the market price responding to our trading, the next approach, suggested by Berkowitz (2000b) and Cosandey (2001), focuses on it to the exclusion of everything else. If we have a trader who must dispose of a certain amount of his/her portfolio, and the market price responds to the trade, then this response creates an additional loss, relative to the case where the market price is given, and their suggestion is that we simply add this extra loss to our VaR. We can estimate this extra loss on the basis of assumptions or estimates of the coefficients of linear demand equations or of demand elasticities in conjunction with ancillary factors (e.g., the size of the sale relative to the size of the market). Other things being equal, the liquidity adjustment will depend on the responsiveness of market prices to our trade: the more responsive the market price, the bigger the loss.

This approach is easy to implement, but also rather narrow in focus and entirely ignores bid–ask spreads and transactions costs. For instance, if the market responsiveness is zero (i.e., we have purely exogenous liquidity risk), then this approach gives us liquidity costs of zero, regardless of the spread cost, the spread risk, and so forth.

8.2.4   Derivatives Pricing Approaches

There are also related approaches that focus on the market's response to the trading of derivatives securities. One of these is suggested by Krakovsky (1999a,b).[6] His approach is suitable for liquidity-adjusting derivatives prices, but in this case the adjustment is made for the impact of trading on the market price for the underlying security. We start by defining a liquidity variable L as the inverse of the partial derivative of the underlying price S with respect to the amount traded, N (i.e., $L = 1/(\partial S/\partial N)$). We now assume that S obeys the following process:

$$dS = \mu dt + \sigma dx_t + \frac{1}{L}dN \tag{8.8}$$

where the terms concerned have their usual interpretations. Equation (8.8) differs from standard processes by the inclusion of the last term reflecting the impact of trading in the underlying on the underlying price. However, if liquidity L is very high, the last term is insignificant and Equation (8.8) reduces to the standard GBM process. We then go through the usual hoops in stochastic differentiation to produce the relevant equation of motion. For example, if we were interested in vanilla calls or puts, we would derive the liquidity-adjusted Black–Scholes equation:

$$\frac{\partial V}{\partial t} + rS\frac{\partial V}{\partial S} + \frac{\sigma^2}{2\left[1 + \dfrac{1}{L}\dfrac{\partial^2 V}{\partial S^2}\right]^2}\frac{\partial^2 V}{\partial S^2} - rV = 0 \tag{8.9}$$

where V is the option price and so forth (see Krakovsky (1999b, p. 66)). This equation differs from the traditional Black–Scholes equation because of the presence of the L-related term in the

---

[6]Krakovsky (1999a) discusses how liquidity affects the prices (and, hence, the loss) on credit-related derivatives, and he particularly focuses on leveraged notes, which are a form of credit derivative. By contrast, Krakovsky (1999b) deals with the impact of liquidity factors on the prices of vanilla options, and is discussed at further length in this section of the text.

denominator. Since this term involves the second derivative of the option price with respect to the underlying, we can immediately see that the impact of the liquidity adjustment is very closely related — in fact, proportional to — the option's gamma. This equation cannot be solved analytically even for a vanilla European option, but can be solved easily using appropriate (e.g., finite difference) methods.

Once we can price our liquidity-adjusted options, then liquidity-adjusted VaR (and ETL) calculations are straightforward: we use a Monte Carlo or some other method to price our derivatives at the end of the holding period, taking account of liquidity, and thence derive a simulated portfolio P/L series from which a (liquidity-adjusted) VaR is easily obtained. However, we should keep in mind that this approach, like the last, is narrow in focus and completely ignores bid–ask risks and transactions costs.[7]

8.2.5   The Liquidity Discount Approach

A broader and more flexible, but also more demanding, alternative is the liquidity discount approach of Jarrow and Subramanian (1997) and Subramanian and Jarrow (1998). They consider a trader who faces an optimal liquidation problem — the trader must liquidate his or her position within a certain period of time to maximise expected utility, and seeks the best way to do so. Their approach encompasses both exogenous and endogenous market liquidity, and they model their optimisation problem as a stochastic impulse control problem that generates both the optimal liquidation policy and the liquidity discount information that is used to make the liquidity adjustment for our VaR.

Their analysis suggests that we should modify the traditional VaR in three ways. First, instead of using some arbitrary holding period, we should use an optimal holding period determined by the solution to the trader's expected utility optimization problem, which takes into account liquidity considerations and the possible impact of the trader's own trading strategy on the market. Second, they suggest we should add the average liquidity discount to the trader's losses (or subtract it from our prices) to take account of the expected loss from selling at the bid price rather than the mid-spread price. And, third, we should add the volatility of the time to liquidation and the volatility of the discount factor itself to the volatility of the market price.

In their analysis, these liquidity discounts are expressed in terms of proportionality factors, $c(s)$, which are functions of the amounts traded (i.e., s). These are the liquidity-discounted prices relative to the mid-spread price, so $c(s) = 1$ implies no liquidity discount and $c(s) < 1$ implies a positive discount. If we now assume away the volatility of the time to liquidation, which is often small anyway, and translate their results into a normal VaR framework,[8] their liquidity-adjusted VaR becomes:

$$LVaR = -\mu hp - \mu_{\log c(s)} - \alpha_{cl}\sigma\sqrt{hp} + 2\sigma_{\log c(s)} \tag{8.10}$$

which can readily be compared to its traditional, liquidity-unadjusted, equivalent:

$$VaR = -\mu hp - \alpha_{cl}\sigma\sqrt{hp} \tag{8.11}$$

---

[7]There are also other VaR approaches that seek to make adjustments for the illiquidity of the underlying security. For example, Frey (2000) focuses on the impact of a dynamic hedging strategy on the price of an underlying security. His model is essentially a liquidity-adjusted Black–Scholes model, and the liquidity adjustment is related to the gamma of the derivative instrument. On the other hand, Cherubini and Della Lunga (2000) suggest making the adjustment using a fuzzy logic approach in which illiquidity is reflected in a fuzzified future option price.

[8]Strictly speaking, the Subramanian–Jarrow model actually presupposes lognormality, as does that of Bangia *et al.*, but the normal translation makes the basic ideas easier to see, and clarity is more important here than literal accuracy.

To make Equation (8.10) operational, we need to specify the values of the included parameters: μ and σ are obviously no problem, but we also need to specify values for $\mu_{\log c(s)}$ and $\sigma_{\log c(s)}$. Subramanian and Jarrow suggest that these latter parameters can be estimated from trading experience, but we can also estimate these parameters using ad hoc methods. If we take the holding period as given, one such method is to assume an appropriate distribution for $c(s)$ — and a good choice would be a beta distribution, which is bounded between 0 and 1 — draw random numbers from this distribution and log them, and then estimate the mean and standard deviation of the logged random numbers. A reasonably plausible choice might be beta(20,1), which has a mean of 0.953 and a standard deviation of 0.045, and the log of this distribution has a mean and standard deviation of –0.050 and 0.050 respectively. If we take these as our estimates of $\mu_{\log c(s)}$ and $\sigma_{\log c(s)}$, and take $\mu = 0$, $\sigma = 1$, $cl = 0.95$ and $hp = 1$, our LVaR estimate is $LVaR = 1.795$. Since our 'traditional' VaR estimate is 1.645, the liquidity adjustment increases our VaR estimate by about 9%. The liquidity discount approach would thus appear to make a noticable difference to our VaR estimates, and we would expect bigger adjustments if $\mu_{\log c(s)}$ and $\sigma_{\log c(s)}$ were larger.

8.2.6 A Summary and Comparison of Alternative Approaches

Before moving on, it might be a good idea to pause at this point to compare these different approaches. A summary of their main features is given in Table 8.1. The features compared are their coverage (or not) of spread cost, spread risk, exogenous liquidity, endogenous liquidity, whether they deal with transactions costs, whether they have a variable or endogenous holding period, and whether they incorporate an endogenous liquidation strategy (i.e., whether they tell us how to liquidate, or whether they take the liquidation strategy as given). The main findings are:

- The transactions cost approach fares well by all criteria except those on spread risk and endogenous liquidation strategy.
- The exogenous spread approach fares well by most criteria, but fails to cover endogenous liquidity and does not really tackle holding-period issues.
- The market response and derivative pricing approaches fare well by one criterion — endogenous liquidity — and effectively fail all the others.
- The liquidity discount approach does well by all criteria. The only reservation about this approach is that it can be difficult to implement the way its authors recommend; however, even that drawback can be largely avoided by using the simpler implementation method suggested above.

In short, the more promising approaches are the transactions costs and liquidity discount approaches, followed by the exogenous spread and then the market response and derivative pricing approaches. We should note, though, that all these approaches are very simplistic, and a lot more work needs

Table 8.1 The main features of alternative approaches to liquidity VaR adjustment

Feature/approach	Spread cost	Spread risk	Exogenous liquidity	Endogenous liquidity	Deals with transactions costs	Variable or endogenous holding period	Endogenous liquidation strategy
Transactions cost	Yes	No	Yes	Yes	Yes	Yes	Not really
Exogenous spread	Yes	Yes	Yes	No	Yes	Not really	No
Market price response	No	No	Not really	Yes	No	No	No
Derivative pricing	No	No	Not really	Yes	No	No	No
Liquidity discount	Yes	Yes	Yes	Yes	Yes	Yes	Yes

to be done to establish how best to model liquidity factors and their implications for measures of market risk.

However, it is best to avoid trying to focus on one 'best' approach to the exclusion of the others. Each approach has some merit, and practitioners would be advised to select the two or three approaches they feel are most appropriate to their particular concerns. Since some of these approaches complement each other (e.g., the exogenous spread approach complements the market response and derivative pricing approaches), it might also make sense to combine them together to produce more comprehensive liquidity adjustments. But in the final analysis, as any experienced market trader — or even an academic economist — would know, liquidity issues are much more subtle than they look, and there is no established consensus on how we should deal with them. So the best advice is for risk measurers to hedge their bets: they should not rely on any one approach to the exclusion of the others, and they should use different approaches to highlight different liquidity concerns.

8.3   ESTIMATING LIQUIDITY AT RISK (LaR)

We turn now to liquidity at risk (or LaR), sometimes also known as cash flow at risk (or CFaR). LaR (or CFaR) relates to the risk attached to prospective cash flows over a defined horizon period, and can be defined in terms analogous to the VaR.[9] Thus, the LaR is the maximum likely cash outflow over the horizon period at a specified confidence level: for example, the 1-day LaR at the 95% confidence level is the maximum likely cash outflow over the next day, at the 95% confidence level, and so forth. A positive LaR means that the likely 'worst' outcome, from a cash-flow perspective, is an outflow of cash; and a negative LaR means that the likely worst outcome is an inflow of cash. The LaR is the cash-flow equivalent to the VaR, but whereas VaR deals with the risk of losses (or profits), LaR deals with the risk of cash outflows (or inflows).

These cash-flow risks are quite different from the risks of liquidity-related losses.[10] Nonetheless, they are closely related to these latter risks, and we might use LaR analysis as an input to evaluate them. Indeed, the use of LaR for such purposes is an important liquidity management tool.[11]

An important point to appreciate about LaR is that the amounts involved can be very different from the amounts involved with VaR. Suppose for the sake of illustration that we have a large market-risk position that we hedge with a futures hedge of much the same amount. If the hedge is a good one, the basis or net risk remaining should be fairly small, and our VaR estimates should reflect that low basis risk and be relatively small themselves. However, the futures hedge leaves us exposed to the possibility of margin calls, and our exposure to margin calls will be related to the size of the futures

---

[9] There are a number of short articles on CFaR and LaR, and I particularly recommend McNew (1996), Shimko (1996), Turner (1996), Gilmour (1997) and Singer (1997).

[10] The link between cash-flow risks and risks of loss associated with cash-flow risks is important, and anyone who has any doubts on this needs to re-examine the Metallgesellschaft debacle of 1993. In the early 1990s, a US subsidiary of MG, MG Refining and Marketing (MGRM), had sold a large number of long-term guarantees on the oil price, and it hedged the resulting oil-price risk using futures and swaps. However, when oil prices fell in 1993, its hedge positions lost a lot of value, and MGRM faced large margin and collateral calls on them. These created a huge cash-flow drain, and the firm ended up making a loss of about $1.3 bn. The MG case is still controversial, and Culp and Miller (1995) have argued that the hedging strategy was fundamentally sound, and that the loss arose because the institution unwound its positions when it should have maintained them. I believe that Culp and Miller are correct, but be this as it may, the MG case shows very clearly that cash-flow problems can easily lead to 'real' losses — and potentially very large ones too.

[11] Measuring these risks is critical if we are to manage them: it gives us an indication of our potential liquidity needs, so we can then arrange to meet them (e.g., by arranging lines of credit, etc.). With liquidity risks, it is also very important to have estimates of LaR over the whole of the foreseeable business horizon period — over the next day, week, month, etc. Failing to anticipate cash-flow needs is one of the most serious (and, in many cases, also most elementary) errors that firms can make, and a good LaR (or equivalent cash-flow risk) system is an essential risk management tool.

position, which corresponds to the gross size of our original position. Thus, the VaR depends largely on the netted or hedged position, whilst the LaR depends on the larger gross position. If the hedge is a good one, the basis risk (or the VaR) will be low relative to the gross risk of the hedge position (or the LaR), and so the LaR can easily be an order of magnitude greater than the VaR. On the other hand, there are also many market-risk positions that have positive VaR, but little or no cash-flow risk (e.g., a portfolio of long European option positions, which generates no cash flows until the position is sold or the options expire), and in such cases the VaR will dwarf the LaR. So the LaR can be much greater than the VaR or much less than it, depending on the circumstances.

As we might expect, the LaR is potentially sensitive to any factors or activities, risky or otherwise, that might affect future cash flows. These include:

- Borrowing or lending, the impact of which on future cash flows is obvious.
- Margin requirements on market-risk positions that are subject to daily marking-to-market.
- Collateral obligations, such as those on swaps, which can generate inflows or outflows of cash depending on the way the market moves. Collateral obligations can also change when counterparties like brokers alter them in response to changes in volatility, and collateral requirements on credit-sensitive positions (e.g., such as default-risky debt or credit derivatives) can change in response to credit events such as credit-downgrades.
- Unexpected cash flows can be triggered by the exercise of options, including the exercise of convertibility features on convertible debt and call features on callable debt.
- Changes in risk management policy: for instance, a switch from a futures hedge to an options hedge can have a major impact on cash-flow risks, because the futures position is subject to margin requirements and marking-to-market whilst a (long) option position is not.

Two other points are also worth emphasizing here. The first is that obligations to make cash payments often come at bad times for the firms concerned, because they are often triggered by bad events. The standard example is where a firm suffers a credit-downgrade, and so experiences an increase in its funding costs, and yet this very event triggers a higher collateral requirement on some existing (e.g., swap) position and so generates an obligation to make a cash payment. It is axiomatic in many markets that firms get hit when they are most vulnerable. The second point is that positions that might be similar from a market-risk perspective (e.g., such as a futures hedge and an options hedge) might have very different cash-flow risks. The difference in cash-flow risks arises, not so much because of differences in market-risk characteristics, but because the positions have different *credit*-risk characteristics, and it is the measures taken to manage the credit risk — the margin and collateral requirements, etc. — that generate the differences in cash-flow risks.

We can estimate LaR using many of the same methods used to estimate VaR and ETL.[12] One strategy, suggested by Singer (1997), is to use our existing VaR estimation tools to estimate the VaRs of marginable securities only (i.e., those where P/L translates directly into cash flows), thus allowing us to infer a LaR directly from the VaR. We could then combine this LaR estimate with comparable figures from other sources of liquidity risk within the organization (e.g., such as estimates of LaR arising from the corporate treasury) to produce an integrated measure of firm-wide liquidity risk. The beauty of this strategy is that it makes the best of the risk measurement

---

[12]We can also estimate liquidity risks using the old spreadsheet methods (e.g., such as gap analysis) originally developed to look at bank interest-rate risk in the days before we had any substantial computer power. Such methods are useful for giving ballpark figures (e.g., much like duration figures can give us ballpark figures for interest-rate risk), but are certainly not a substitute for more sophisticated approaches. These days there is no excuse — except perhaps laziness — for relying on such primitive methods when much better ones are now readily available.

capabilities that already exist within the firm, and effectively tweaks them to estimate liquidity risks.[13]

However, this strategy is also fairly rough and ready, and cannot be relied upon when the firm faces particularly complex liquidity risks. In such circumstances, it is often better to build a liquidity-risk measurement model from scratch, and we can start by setting out the basic types of cash flow to be considered. These might include:

- Known certain (or near certain) cash flows (e.g., income from government bonds, etc.): these are very easy to handle because we know them in advance.
- Unconditional uncertain cash flows (e.g., income from default-risky bonds, etc.): these are uncertain cash flows, which we model in terms of the pdfs (i.e., we choose appropriate distributions, assign parameter values, etc.).
- Conditional uncertain cash flows: these are uncertain cash flows that depend on other variables (e.g., a cash flow might depend on whether we proceeded with a certain investment, and so we would model the cash flow in terms of a pdf, conditional on that investment); other conditioning variables that might trigger cash flows could be interest rates, exchange rates, decisions about major projects, and so forth.

Once we specify these factors, we can then construct an appropriate engine to carry out our estimations. The choice of engine would depend on the types of cash-flow risks we have to deal with. For instance, if we had fairly uncomplicated cash flows we might use an HS or variance–covariance approach, or some specially designed term-structure model; however, since some cash flows are likely to be dependent on other factors such as discrete random variables (e.g., such as downgrades or defaults), it might not be easy 'tweaking' such methods to estimate LaRs with sufficient accuracy. In such circumstances, it might be better to resort to simulation methods, which are much better suited to handling discrete variables and the potential complexities of cash flows in larger firms.

8.4   ESTIMATING LIQUIDITY IN CRISES

We now consider liquidity in crisis situations. As we all know, financial markets occasionally experience major crises — these include, for example, the stock market crash of 1987, the ERM crisis of 1992, and the Russian default crisis of the summer of 1998. Typically, some event occurs which is, or triggers, a large price fall. This event triggers a huge number of sell orders and makes traders reluctant to buy, and the bid–ask spread then rises dramatically. At the same time, the flood of sell orders can overwhelm the market and drastically slow down the time it takes to get orders executed. Selling orders that would take minutes to execute in normal times instead take hours, and the prices eventually obtained are often much lower than sellers had anticipated, so market liquidity dries up at the very time market operators need it most. Assumptions about market liquidity that hold in 'normal' market conditions can thus break down when markets experience crises, and this means that estimating crisis liquidity is more than just a process of extrapolation from LaR under more normal market conditions. We therefore need to estimate crisis-liquidity risks using methods that

---

[13] Another alternative is to use scenario analysis. We can specify liquidity scenarios, such as those arising from large changes in interest rates, default by counterparties, the redemption of putable debt, calls for collateral on repos and derivatives, margin calls on swaps or futures positions, and so forth. We would then (as best we could) work through the likely/possible ramifications of each scenario, and so get an idea of the liquidity consequences associated with each scenario. Such exercises can be very useful, but, as with all scenario analyses, they might give us an indication of what could happen if the scenario occurs, but don't as such tell us anything about the probabilities associated with those scenarios or the LaR itself.

take into account the distinctive features of a crisis — large losses, high bid–ask spreads, and so forth.[14]

One such method is the 'crashmetrics' approach suggested by Hua and Wilmott (1997) and Wilmott (2000, ch. 58) (see also Box 10.5). They suggest that we use some method to estimate the worst-case losses — they actually suggest a Greek-based approximation — and then infer the cash flows by applying margin requirements to the loss involved. To take a simple example, assume we have a position in a single derivatives instrument, and the profit/loss on this instrument is given by a delta–gamma approximation:

$$\Pi = \delta \, dS + 0.5\gamma(dS)^2 \tag{8.12}$$

where dS is the change in the stock price, and so forth. We can easily show that the maximum loss occurs when:

$$dS = -\gamma/\delta \tag{8.13}$$

and is equal to:

$$L^{\text{max}} = -\Pi^{\text{min}} = \delta^2/(2\gamma) \tag{8.14}$$

The worst-case cash outflow is therefore $m\delta^2/2\gamma$, where m is the margin or collateral requirement. This approach can also be extended to handle the other Greek parameters — the vegas, thetas, rhos, etc. However, it is open to criticism on the grounds that it relies heavily on the Greek approximations in circumstances where those approximations are not likely to be good.

Nonetheless, the basic idea — of identifying worst-case outcomes and then evaluating their liquidity consequences — is a good one and can be implemented in other ways as well. For example, we might identify the worst-case outcome as the expected outcome at a chosen confidence level, and we could estimate this (e.g., using extreme value methods) as the ETL at that confidence level. The cash outflow is then m times this ETL.[15]

Yet both these suggestions (i.e., Greek-based and EV ETL) are still rather simplistic, and with complicated risk factors — such as often arise with credit-related risks — we might want a more sophisticated model that was able to take account of the complications involved, such as:

- The discreteness of credit events.
- The interdependency of credit events.
- The interaction of credit- and market-risk factors (e.g., the ways in which credit events depend, in part, on market-risk factors).
- Complications arising from the use of credit-enhancement methods such as netting arrangements, periodic settlement, credit derivatives, credit guarantees, and credit triggers.[16]

These complicating factors are best handled using simulation methods tailor-made for the problems concerned.

The obvious alternative to probabilistic approaches to the estimation of crisis liquidity is to use crisis scenario analyses. (We shall come to scenario analysis in Chapter 10.) We would imagine a big liquidity event — a major market crash, the default of a major financial institution or government,

---

[14]For more on these methods, see Bank for International Settlements (2000).

[15]There are also other ways we can estimate crisis LaR. Instead of focusing only on the high losses associated with crises, we can also take account of the high bid–ask spreads and/or the high bid–ask spread risks associated with crises. We can do so by, for example, estimating these spreads (or spread risks), and inputting these estimates into the relevant liquidity-adjusted VaR models discussed in Section 8.2.

[16]For more on these methods and their liquidity implications, see, e.g., Wakeman (1998).

the outbreak of a war, or whatever—and work through the ramifications for the liquidity of the institution concerned. One attraction of scenario analysis in this context is that we can work through scenarios in as much detail as we wish, and so take proper account of complicated interactions such as those mentioned in the last paragraph. This is harder to do using probabilistic approaches, which are by definition unable to focus on any specific scenarios. However, as with all scenario analysis, the results of these exercises are highly subjective, and the value of the results is critically dependent on the quality of the assumptions made.

8.5 RECOMMENDED READING

Almgren and Chriss (1999); Bangia *et al.* (1999); Berkowitz (2000b); Cherubini and Della Lunga (2000); Cosandey (2001); Fiedler (2000); Frey (2000); Jarrow and Subramanian (1997); Krakovsky (1999b); Lawrence and Robinson (1995b); Persaud (2000); Singer (1997); Upper (2000).

9

Backtesting Market Risk Models

Before we can use risk models with confidence, it is necessary to validate them, and the critical issue in model validation is backtesting — the application of quantitative, typically statistical, methods to determine whether a model's risk estimates are consistent with the assumptions on which the model is based.

Backtests are a critical part of the risk measurement process, as we rely on them to give us an indication of any problems with our risk measurement models (e.g., such as misspecification, underestimation of risks, etc.).

This chapter deals with backtesting market risk models, and covers seven main topics:

- Preliminary data issues.
- Statistical backtests based on the frequency of tail losses, or losses in excess of VaR.
- Statistical backtests based on the sizes of tail losses.
- Forecast evaluation approaches to backtesting.
- Comparing alternative models.
- Assessing the accuracy of backtest results.
- Backtesting with alternative confidence levels, positions and data.

9.1 PRELIMINARY DATA ISSUES

9.1.1 Obtaining Data

The first requirement in backtesting is to obtain suitable data. One problem is that P/L data are typically calculated according to standard principles of accounting prudence, and this often means that assets are understated in value and fluctuations in their values are smoothed over. However, for risk measurement purposes it is often more important that our P/L data reflect underlying volatility rather than accounting prudence.

Our P/L data also need cleaning to get rid of components that are not directly related to current or recent market risk-taking. Such components include fee income, hidden profits/losses from trades carried out at prices different from the mid bid–ask spread, P/L earned from other forms of risk-taking (e.g., high yields on bonds with high credit risks), and unrealised P/L and provisions against future losses. We also need to take account of the impact of the internal funding regime that underlies the institution's trading activity, and of the impact of intra-day trading on both P/L and risk measures. (For more on all these issues, see Deans (2000, pp. 265–269).) To compare P/L against market risk, we should therefore either clean the P/L data so that they (as much as possible) reflect the P/L on end-of-day market risk positions, or use hypothetical P/L data obtained by revaluing trading positions from one day to the next.

Having obtained (reasonably) clean data, it can be very useful to draw up a chart like the one shown in Figure 9.1. This chart can be drawn up at institutional or business-unit level, and shows the time series (i.e., sequential values) of both daily P/L and risk measures (e.g., VaRs) delineating

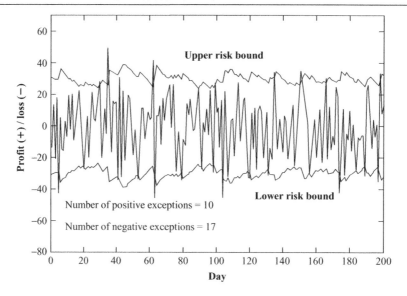

Figure 9.1 A backtesting chart.

'regular' profits or losses from more extreme ones. This chart shows how these series have behaved over time, and gives a good visual indication of the behaviour of the outliers or exceptions — the extremely high profits above the upper risk bound and the extremely large losses below the lower risk bound in the chart. It also shows how many exceptions there were, how big they were, and whether they show any pattern. Such a chart gives a good indication of possible underlying causes:

- A relatively large number of extreme observations indicates that our risk measures are probably too low.
- A relatively small number of tail observations, or none at all, indicates that our risk measures are probably too high.
- If there are major differences between high and low exceptions, then our P/L measures might be biased.
- If the risk lines show flatness, or excessive smoothness, risk measures are not being updated sufficiently quickly.
- If P/L is close to zero much of the time, then there is relatively little trading taking place, and this suggests that positions are illiquid.
- Abrupt changes in risk lines suggest changes in volatility or changes in the way the risks are estimated.

This particular figure shows a backtesting chart for a hypothetical portfolio daily P/L series and the associated VaRs at the 5% and 95% confidence levels, which generally lie on either side of the P/L series. All three series are fairly stable, and show no obvious deformities. Given the number of observations (200) and the VaR confidence levels, we would expect 10 positive and 10 negative exceptions, and we actually get 10 positive and 17 negative exceptions. The number of negative exceptions (or tail losses) is well above what we would expect, and the risk practitioner would be well advised to look into this further.

It is also good practice to supplement backtesting charts with P/L histograms, which sometimes give a clearer indication of the empirical distribution of P/L, and QQ or similar charts, which help to give a broad indication of whether the empirical P/L distribution is consistent with the risk model. In addition, it is a good idea to examine summary P/L statistics, including the obvious statistics of mean, standard deviation, skewness, kurtosis, volatility, range, etc. and basic statistics on the number and size of extreme observations. Such information can be very helpful in helping practitioners to get to know their data and develop a feel for any problems they might encounter.

9.2   STATISTICAL BACKTESTS BASED ON THE FREQUENCY OF TAIL LOSSES

Having completed our preliminary data analysis, we turn now to formal statistical backtesting. All statistical tests are based on the idea that we first select a significance level, and then estimate the probability associated with the null hypothesis being 'true'. Typically, we would accept the null hypothesis if the estimated value of this probability, the estimated prob-value, exceeds the chosen significance level, and we would reject it otherwise. The higher the significance level, the more likely we are to accept the null hypothesis, and the less likely we are to incorrectly reject a true model (i.e., to make a Type I error, to use the jargon). However, it also means that we are more likely to incorrectly accept a false model (i.e., to make a Type II error). Any test therefore involves a trade-off between these two types of possible error.[1]

In principle, we should select a significance level that takes account of the likelihoods of these errors (and, in theory, their costs as well) and strikes an appropriate balance between them. However, in practice, it is very common to select some arbitrary significance level such as 5% and apply that level in all our tests. A significance level of this magnitude gives the model a certain benefit of the doubt, and implies that we would reject the model only if the evidence against it is reasonably strong: for example, if we are working with a 5% significance level, we would conclude that the model was adequate if we obtained any prob-value estimate greater than 5%.

A test can be said to be reliable if it is likely to avoid both types of error when used with an appropriate significance level.

9.2.1   The Basic Frequency-of-tail-losses (or Kupiec) Test

Perhaps the most widely used test is the basic frequency-of-tail-losses test (see Kupiec (1995)). The idea behind this approach is to test whether the observed frequency of tail losses (or frequency of losses that exceed VaR) is consistent with the frequency of tail losses predicted by the model. In particular, under the null hypothesis that the model is 'good' (i.e., consistent with the data), the number of tail losses x follows a binomial distribution:

$$\text{Prob}(x \mid n, p) = \binom{n}{i} p^i (1-p)^{n-i} \tag{9.1}$$

---

[1] We should keep in mind that the critical value associated with the null hypothesis will depend on the alternative hypothesis (e.g., whether the alternative hypothesis is that the 'true' prob-value is different from, or greater than, or less than, the prob-value under the null hypothesis). However, in what follows we will assume that the alternative hypothesis is the last of these, namely, that the 'true' prob-value is less than the null-hypothesis prob-value.

where n is the number of P/L observations and p, the predicted frequency of tail losses, is equal to 1 minus the VaR confidence level. Given the values of the parameters n, p and x, the Kupiec test statistic is easily calculated using a suitable calculation engine (e.g., using the 'binomdist' function in Excel or the 'binocdf' function in MATLAB).

To implement the Kupiec test, we require data on n, p and x. The first two are easily found from the sample size and the VaR confidence level, and we can derive x from a set of paired observations of P/L and VaR each period. These paired observations could be the actual observations (i.e., observed P/L and associated VaR forecasts each period)[2] or historical simulation ones (i.e., the historical simulation P/L we would have observed on a given portfolio, had we held it over the observation period, and the set of associated VaR forecasts).

For example, suppose we have a random sample of $n = 1,000$ P/L observations drawn from a portfolio. We take the confidence level to be 95%, and our model predicts that we should get $np = 50$ tail losses in our sample. With this sample, the number of tail-loss observations, x, is 55. The Kupiec test then gives us an estimated prob-value estimate of 21%, where the latter is taken to be the estimated probability of 55 or more excess loss observations. At a standard significance level such as 5%, we would therefore have no hesitation in 'passing' the model as acceptable.

The Kupiec test has a simple intuition, is very easy to apply and does not require a great deal of information. However, it also has some drawbacks:

- The Kupiec test is not reliable except with very large sample sizes.[3]
- Since it focuses exclusively on the frequency of tail losses, the Kupiec test throws away potentially valuable information about the sizes of tail losses.[4] This suggests that the Kupiec test should be relatively inefficient, compared to a suitable test that took account of the sizes as well as the frequency of tail losses.[5]

---

[2]Note, therefore, that the Kupiec test allows the portfolio or the VaR to change over time. The same goes for the other tests considered in this chapter, although it may sometimes be necessary (e.g., as with the basic sizes of excess losses test considered below) to first apply some transformation to the data to make the tests suitably invariant. It should be obvious that any test that requires a fixed portfolio or constant VaR is seldom of much practical use.

[3]Frequency-of-tail-loss tests have even more difficulty as the holding period rises. If we have a longer holding period than a day, we can attempt to apply these tests in one of two ways: by straightforward temporal aggregation (i.e., so we work with P/L and VaR over a period of h days rather than 1 day), and by using rolling h-day windows with 1-day steps (see, e.g., Tilman and Brusilovskiy (2001, pp. 85–86)). However, the first route cuts down our sample size by a factor of h, and the second is tricky to implement. When backtesting, it is probably best to work with data of daily frequency — or more than daily frequency, if that is feasible.

[4]The Kupiec test also throws away useful information about the pattern of tail losses over time. If the model is correct, then not only should the observed frequency of tail losses be close to the frequency predicted by the model, but the sequence of observed indicator values — that is to say, observations that take the value 1 if the loss exceeds VaR and 0 otherwise — should be independently and identically distributed. One way to test this prediction is suggested by Engle and Manganelli (1999, pp. 9–12): if we define hit_t as the value of the indicator in period t minus the VaR tail probability, $1 - cl$, then hit_t should be uncorrelated with any other variables in the current information set. (In this case, the indicator variable takes the value 1 if an exception occurs that day, and the value 0 otherwise.) We can test this prediction by specifying a set of variables in our current information set and regressing hit_t against them: if the prediction is satisfied, these variables should have jointly insignificant regression coefficients.

[5]Nonetheless, one way to make frequency-of-tail-loss tests more responsive to the data is to broaden the indicator function. As noted already, in the case of a pure frequency-of-tail-losses test, the indicator function takes a value of 1 if we have a loss in excess of VaR and a value of 0 otherwise. We can broaden this function to award higher indicator values to higher tail losses (e.g., as in Tilman and Brusilovskiy (2001, pp. 86–87)), and so give some recognition to the sizes as well as the frequencies of tail losses. However, these broader indicator functions complicate the testing procedure, and I would suggest we are better off moving directly to sizes-of-tail-losses tests instead.

Box 9.1   Regulatory Backtesting Requirements

Commercial banks in the G-10 countries are obliged to carry out a set of standardised backtests prescribed by the 1996 Amendment to the 1988 Basle Accord, which lays down capital adequacy standards for commercial banks. The main features of these regulations are:[6]

- Banks must calibrate daily VaR measures to daily P/L observations, and these VaRs are predicated on a confidence level of 99%.
- Banks are required to use two different P/L series: actual net trading P/L for the next day; and the theoretical P/L that would have occurred had the position at the close of the previous day been carried forward to the next day.
- Backtesting must be performed daily.
- Banks must identify the number of days when trading losses, if any, exceed the VaR.

The results of these backtests are used by supervisors to assess the risk models, and to determine the multiplier (or hysteria) factor to be applied: if the number of exceptions during the previous 250 days is less than five, then the multiplier is 3; if the number of exceptions is five, the multiplier is 3.40, and so forth; and 10 or more exceptions warrant a multiplier of 4.

Leaving aside problems relating to the capital standards themselves, these backtesting rules are open to a number of objections:

- They use only one basic type of backtest, a Kupiec test, which is known to be unreliable except with very large samples.
- They ignore other backtests and don't make use of valuable information about the sizes of exceptions.
- Models can fail the regulatory backtests in abnormal situations (e.g., such as a market crash or natural disaster) and lead banks to incur unwarranted penalties.
- The rules relating the capital multiplier to the number of exceptions are arbitrary, and there are concerns that the high scaling factor could discourage banks from developing and implementing best practice.
- Backtesting procedures might discourage institutions from reporting their 'true' VaR estimates to supervisors.

However, even if these problems were dealt with or at least ameliorated, there would always remain deeper problems: any regulatory prescriptions would inevitably be crude, inflexible, probably counterproductive, and certainly behind best market practice. It would be better if regulators did not presume to tell banks how they should conduct their backtests, and did not make capital requirements contingent on the results of their own preferred backtest procedure — and a primitive one at that.

9.2.2   The Time-to-first-tail-loss Test

There are also related approaches. One of these is to test for the time when the first tail loss occurs (see Kupiec (1995, pp. 75–79)). If the probability of a tail loss is p, the probability of observing the first tail loss in period T is $p(1 - p)^{T-1}$, and the probability of observing the first tail loss by period T is $1 - (1 - p)^T$, which obeys a geometric distribution.

---

[6]For more on regulatory backtesting, see Crouhy *et al.* (1998, pp. 15–16).

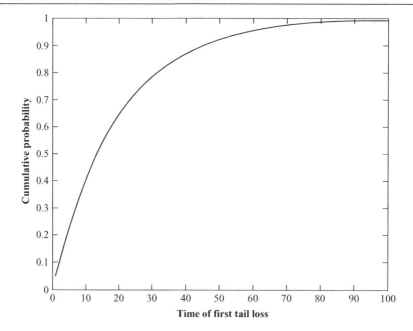

Figure 9.2   Probabilities for the time of first tail loss.

Note: Estimated for an assumed *p*-value of 5%, using the 'geocdf' function in MATLAB.

These probabilities are easily calculated, and Figure 9.2 shows a plot of the probability of observing our first tail loss by period T, for a *p*-value of 5%. The figure shows that the probability of observing our first loss by time T rises with T itself — for example, at $T = 5$, the probability of having observed a first tail loss is 22.6%; but for $T = 50$, the same probability is 92.3%.

However, this test is inferior to the basic Kupiec test because it uses less information: it only uses information since the previous tail loss, and in effect throws all our other information away. It is therefore perhaps best regarded as a diagnostic to be used alongside more powerful tests, rather than as a substitute for them.

9.2.3   A Tail-Loss Confidence-interval Test

A related alternative is to estimate a confidence interval for the number of tail losses, based on the available sample, and then check whether the expected number of tail losses lies within this sample. We can construct a confidence interval for the number of tail losses by using the inverse of the tail-loss binomial distribution (e.g., by using the 'binofit' function in MATLAB). For example, if we have $x = 55$ tail losses out of $n = 1,000$ observations, then the 95% confidence interval for the number of tail losses is [42, 71]. Since this includes the number of tail losses (i.e., 50) we would expect under the null hypothesis that the model is 'true', we can conclude that the model is acceptable.

This approach uses the same data as the Kupiec test and should, in theory, give the same model assessment as it.[7]

---

[7]The same goes for a final binomial alternative, namely, using binomial theory to estimate the confidence interval for the 'true' prob-value given the number of exceptions and the sample size.

9.2.4   The Conditional Backtesting (Christoffersen) Approach

A useful adaptation to these approaches is the conditional backtesting approach suggested by Christoffersen (1998). The idea here is to separate out the particular hypotheses being tested, and then test each hypothesis separately. For example, the full null hypothesis in a standard frequency-of-tail-losses test is that the model generates a correct frequency of exceptions and, in addition, that exceptions are independent of each other. The second assumption is usually subsidiary and made only to simplify the test. However, it raises the possibility that the model could fail the test, not because it generates the wrong frequency of failures, as such, but because failures are not independent of each other.

The Christoffersen approach is designed to avoid this problem. To use it, we break down the joint null hypothesis into its constituent parts, thus giving us two distinct sub-hypotheses: the sub-hypothesis that the model generates the correct frequency of tail losses, and the sub-hypothesis that tail losses are independent. If we make appropriate assumptions for the alternative hypotheses, then each of these hypotheses has its own likelihood ratio test, and these tests are easy to carry out. This means that we can test our sub-hypotheses separately, as well as test the original joint hypothesis that the model has the correct frequency of independently distributed tail losses.

The Christoffersen approach therefore helps us to separate out testable hypotheses about the dynamic structure of our tail losses from testable hypotheses about the frequency of tail losses. This is potentially useful because it not only indicates whether models fail backtests, but also helps to identify the reasons why.

9.3   STATISTICAL BACKTESTS BASED ON THE SIZES OF TAIL LOSSES

9.3.1   The Basic Sizes-of-tail-losses Test

Nonetheless, the tests considered so far all share one common feature: they focus on the frequency of tail losses, and effectively throw away information about the sizes of tail losses. Yet, information about the sizes of tail losses is potentially very useful for assessing model adequacy, and we might expect that tests using such information could be considerably more reliable than tests using only frequency-of-tail-loss information. This suggests that we should seek to test if the values (as opposed to mere frequencies) of tail losses are consistent with what we would expect from our model — in other words, we should compare the distribution of empirical tail losses against the tail-loss distribution predicted by our model.

One fairly obvious test procedure is as follows. We first take our sample of P/L observations, select a VaR confidence level and estimate our VaR. We then reverse the sign of our P/L observations (to make loss observations positive) and truncate the sample to eliminate all observations except those involving losses higher than VaR. This enables us to obtain the empirical distribution of tail-loss observations. We then use the distributional assumptions on which our risk model is based to predict the distribution of tail-loss observations, and test whether the two distributions are the same. We can then test the significance of the difference between these two distributions by using any one of the standard distribution-difference tests (e.g., the Kolmogorov–Smirnov or Kuiper tests, see Box 9.2).[8]

To illustrate, suppose we take a sample of, say, 1,000 P/L observations drawn from a Student *t*-distribution with five degrees of freedom, and we have a model that assumes the P/L distribution

---

[8]The results reported here are based on the most popular and straightforward of these, the Kolmogorov–Smirnov test. This is also the easiest to use with MATLAB, because we can make use of MATLAB's Kolmogorov–Smirnov function, 'kstest'.

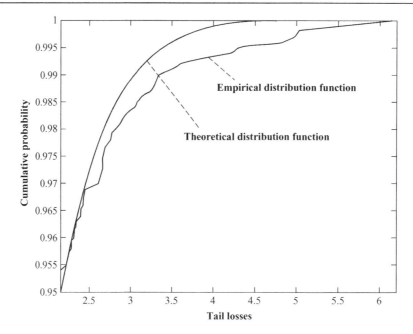

Figure 9.3 Predicted and empirical tail-loss distribution functions.

Note: Estimates obtained for a random sample size of 1,000 drawn from a Student *t*-distribution with five degrees of freedom. The model assumes that the P/L process is normal, and the confidence level is 95%.

is normal. If we select a 95% VaR confidence level, we would expect 5% of 1,000, or 50, loss observations exceeding our VaR. Given our sample, we estimate the VaR itself to be 2.153, and there are 47 tail-loss observations.

We now wish to assess the (in this case, incorrect) null hypothesis that the empirical and predicted distribution functions (DFs) are the same. We can form some idea of whether they are the same from the plot of the two tail-loss distributions shown in Figure 9.3, and casual observation would indeed suggest that the two distributions are quite different: the empirical DF is below the predicted DF, indicating that tail losses are higher than predicted. This casual impression is quite useful for giving us some 'feel' for our data, but we also need to check our impressions with a formal test of the distance between the two cdfs.

Perhaps the most straightforward formal test of this difference is provided by the Kolmogorov–Smirnov test, which gives us a test value of 0.2118 and gives the null hypothesis a probability value of 2.49%. If we take the standard 5% significance level, our test result is significant and we would (rightly) reject the null hypothesis. The Kupiec test, by contrast, would have accepted the null hypothesis as correct.

The main difference between these tests is that the sizes-of-tail-losses test takes account of the sizes of losses exceeding VaR and the Kupiec test does not. The Kupiec test will not be able to tell the difference between a 'good' model that generates tail losses compatible with the model, and a 'bad' one that generates tail losses incompatible with the model, provided that they have the right tail-loss frequencies. By contrast, our sizes-of-tail-losses approach does take account of the difference between the two models, and should be able to distinguish between them. We should therefore expect this test to be more discriminating and, hence, more reliable than the Kupiec test. Some simulations I ran to check this out broadly confirmed this expectation, and suggest that the new test is practically feasible given the amount of data we often have to work with.

Box 9.2   Testing the Difference between Two Distributions

There are often situations (e.g., when applying the Crnkovic–Drachman or other backtests) where we wish to test whether two distribution functions — an empirical distribution and a theoretical or predicted distribution — are significantly different from each other. We can carry out this type of test using a number of alternative test statistics.[9]

The most popular is the Kolmogorov–Smirnov (KS) test statistic, which is the maximum value of the absolute difference between the two distribution functions. The KS statistic is easy to calculate and its critical values can be approximated by a suitable program (e.g., using the routine described in Press *et al.* (1992, pp. 624–626)). We can also calculate both the test statistic and its significance using MATLAB's 'kstest' function. However, the KS statistic tends to be more sensitive around the median value of the distribution and less sensitive around the extremes. This means that the KS statistic is less likely to detect differences between the tails of the distributions than differences between their central masses — and this can be a problem for VaR and ETL estimations, where we are more concerned with the tails than the central mass of the distribution.

An alternative that avoids this latter problem is Kuiper's statistic, and it is for this reason that Crnkovic and Drachman prefer the Kuiper statistic over the KS one. The Kuiper statistic is the sum of the maximum amount by which each distribution exceeds the other, and its critical values can be determined in a manner analogous to the way in which we obtain the critical values of the KS statistic. However, Crnkovic and Drachman (1996, p. 140) also report that the Kuiper's test statistic is data-intensive: results begin to deteriorate with less than 1,000 observations, and are of little validity for less than 500.[10] Both these tests are therefore open to objections, and how useful they might be in practice remains controversial.

9.3.2   The Crnkovic–Drachman Backtest Procedure

Another size-based backtest is suggested by Crnkovic and Drachman (CD; 1995, 1996). The essence of their approach is to evaluate a market model by testing the difference between the empirical P/L distribution and the predicted P/L distribution, across their whole range of values.[11] Their argument is that each P/L observation can be classified into a percentile of the forecasted P/L distribution, and

---

[9] The tests discussed in Box 9.2 — the Kolgmorov–Smirnov and Kuiper tests — are both tests of the differences between two continuous distributions. However, if we are dealing with discrete distributions, we can also test for differences between distributions using more straightforward chi-squared test procedures (see, e.g., Press *et al.* (1992, pp. 621–623)). These tests are very easy to carry out — and we can always convert continuous distributions into discrete ones by putting the observations into bins. See also Section 9.3.3 below.

[10] One other cautionary point should be kept in mind: both these statistics presuppose that the parameters of the distributions are known, and if we use estimates instead of known true parameters, then we can't rely on these test procedures and we should strictly speaking resort to Monte Carlo methods (Press *et al.* (1992, p. 627)) or an alternative test, such as the Lillifors test (Lilliefors (1967)), which also examines the maximum distance between two distributions, but uses sample estimates of parameter values instead of parameter values that are assumed to be known.

[11] Since this test uses more information than the frequency-of-tail-losses test, we would also expect it to be more reliable, and this seems to be broadly confirmed by results reported by Crnknovic and Drachman (1995).

if the model is good, the P/L observations classified this way should be uniformly distributed and independent of each other. This line of reasoning suggests two distinct tests:

- A test of whether the classified observations have a uniform density function distributed over the range (0,1), which we can operationalise by testing whether the empirical distribution of classified observations matches the predicted distribution of classified observations.
- A test of whether the classified observations are independent of each other, which we can carry out by means of a standard independence test (e.g., the BDS test, as suggested by Crnkovic and Drachman).

The first of these is effectively a test of whether the predicted and empirical P/L (or L/P) distributions are the same, and is therefore equivalent to our earlier sizes-of-tail-losses test applied to all observations rather than just tail losses. This means that the main difference between the sizes-of-tail-losses test and the (first) Crnkovic–Drachman test boils down to the location of the threshold that separates our observations into tail observations and non-tail ones.[12]

The impact of the threshold is illustrated in Figure 9.4. If we take the threshold to be the VaR at the 95% confidence level, as we did earlier, then we get the high threshold indicated in the figure, with only 5% of expected observations lying in the tail to the right: 95% of the observations used

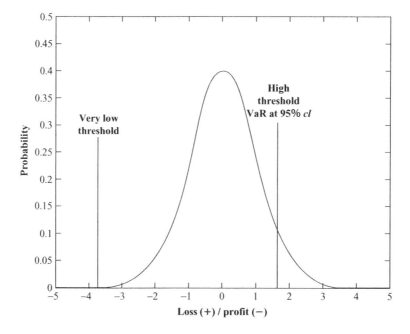

Figure 9.4   The impact of alternative thresholds on tail losses.

<hr />

[12]There are also certain minor differences. In particular, Crnkovic and Drachman suggest the use of Kuiper's statistic rather than the Kolmogorov–Smirnov statistic in testing for the difference between the predicted and empirical distributions. Nonetheless, the choice of distance test is ancillary to the basic procedure, and we could easily carry out the sizes-of-tail-losses test using Kuiper's statistic instead of the Kolmogorov–Smirnov one. Crnkovic and Drachman also suggest weighting Kuiper's statistic to produce a 'worry function' that allows us to place more weight on the deviations of large losses from predicted values. This is a good suggestion, because it enables us to take account of the economic implications of alternative outcomes, and if we wish to, we can easily incorporate a 'worry function' into any of the backtests discussed in the text.

by the CD test will be truncated, and there will be a large difference between the observation sets used by the two tests. However, if the threshold is sufficiently low (i.e., sufficiently to the left in the figure), we would expect all observations to lie to the right of it. In that case, we could expect the two tests to be indistinguishable.

The bottom line is that we can regard the first CD test as a special case of the sizes-of-tail-losses test, and this special case occurs when the sizes-of-tail-losses test is used with a very low threshold. This, in turn, implies that the sizes-of-tail-losses test can be regarded as a generalization of the (first) CD test.

But which test is more helpful? The answer depends in part on the relevance of the non-tail observations in our data set to the tail observations (or tail quantiles, such as VaRs) that we are (presumably) more interested in. If we believed that the central-mass observations gave us useful and unbiased information relevant for the estimation of tail probabilities and quantiles, then we might want to make use of them to get the benefits of a larger sample size. This might suggest making use of the whole P/L sample — which in turn suggests we should use the CD test. However, there are many circumstances in which we might wish to truncate our sample and use the sizes-of-tail-losses test instead. We might be concerned that the distribution fitted to the tail did not fit the more central observations so well (e.g., as would be the case if we were fitting an extreme value distribution to the tail), or we might be concerned that the distribution fitted to the central-mass observations was not providing a good fit for the tail. In either case, including the more central observations could distort our results, and we might be better off truncating them.

There is, in effect, a sort of trade-off between variance and bias: making the tail larger (and, in the limit, using the CD test) gives us more observations and hence greater precision (or a lower variance); but if the extreme observations are particularly distinctive for any reason, then including the central ones (i.e., working with a larger tail or, in the limit, using the CD test) could bias our results. Strictly speaking, therefore, we should only use the CD test if we are confident that the whole empirical distribution of P/L is relevant to tail losses we are concerned about. In terms of our variance–bias trade-off, this would be the case only if concerns about 'variance' dominated concerns about 'bias'. But if we are concerned about both variance and bias, then we should choose a tail size that reflects an appropriate balance between these factors — and this would suggest that we should use the sizes-of-tail-losses test with an appropriately chosen threshold.

Box 9.3   Tests of Independence

The second test in the Crnkovic–Drachman backtest procedure is a test of the independence of classified P/L observations. They suggest carrying this out with the BDS test of Brock *et al.* (1987). The BDS test is powerful but quite involved and data-intensive, and we might wish to test independence in other ways. For instance, we could use a likelihood ratio test (as in Christoffersen). Alternatively, we could estimate the autocorrelation structure of our classified P/L observations, and these autocorrelations should be (jointly) insignificant if the observations are independent. We can then test for independence by testing the significance of the empirical autocorrelations, and implement such tests using standard econometrics packages or MATLAB (e.g., using the 'crosstab' command in the Statistics Toolbox or the 'crosscor' command in the Garch Toolbox).

9.3.3   The Berkowitz Approach

There is also another, more useful, size-based approach to backtesting. Recall that the CD approach tells us that the distribution of classified P/L observations should be 'iid U(0,1)' distributed — both uniform over the range (0,1) and independently and identically distributed over time. Instead of testing these predictions directly, Berkowitz (2001) suggests that we transform these classified observations to make them normal under the null hypothesis, and we can obtain our transformed normal series by applying an inverse normal transformation to the uniform series (i.e., making use of the result that if x_t is iid U(0,1), then $z_t = \Phi^{-1}(x_t)$ is iid N(0,1)). What makes this suggestion so attractive is that once the data are transformed into normal form, we can apply much more powerful statistical tools than we can apply directly to uniform data. In particular, it now becomes possible to apply a battery of likelihood ratio tests and identify more clearly the possible sources of model failure.

One possible use of such a procedure is to test the null hypothesis (i.e., that z_t is iid N(0,1)) against a fairly general first-order autoregressive process with a possibly different mean and variance. If we write this alternative process as:

$$z_t - \mu = \rho(z_{t-1} - \mu) + \varepsilon_t \tag{9.2}$$

then the null hypothesis maintains that $\mu = 0$, $\rho = 0$, and σ^2, the variance of ε_t, is equal to 1. The log-likelihood function associated with Equation (9.2) is known to be:

$$-\frac{1}{2}\log(2\pi) - \frac{1}{2}\log[\sigma^2/(1-\rho)^2] - \frac{[z_1 - \mu/(1-\rho)]^2}{2\sigma^2/(1-\rho)^2} - \frac{(T-1)}{2}\log(2\pi) - \frac{(T-1)}{2}\log(\sigma^2)$$

$$-\left[z_{t-1} - \sum_{t=2}^{T} \frac{(z_t - \mu - \rho z_{t-1})^2}{2\sigma^2}\right] \tag{9.3}$$

(Berkowitz (2001, p. 468)). The likelihood ratio test statistic for the null hypothesis is then:

$$LR = -2[L(0, 1, 0) - L(\hat{\mu}, \hat{\sigma}^2, \hat{\rho})] \tag{9.4}$$

where $\hat{\mu}$, $\hat{\sigma}$ and $\hat{\rho}$ are maximum likelihood estimates of the parameters concerned. LR is distributed under the null hypothesis as $\chi^2(3)$, a chi-squared with three degrees of freedom. We can therefore test the null hypothesis against this alternative hypothesis by obtaining maximum likelihood estimates of the parameters, deriving the value of the LR statistic, and comparing that value against the critical value for a $\chi^2(3)$. This is a powerful test because the alternative hypothesis is quite a general one and because, unlike the last two approaches just considered, this approach captures both aspects of the null hypothesis — uniformity/normality and independence — within a single test.

We can also adapt the Berkowitz approach to test whether the sizes of tail losses are consistent with expectations under the null hypothesis. The point here is that if the underlying data are fatter tailed than the model presumes, then the transformed z_t will also be fatter tailed than the normal distribution predicted by the null hypothesis. We can test this prediction by transforming our tail-loss data and noting that their likelihood function is a truncated normal log-likelihood function (i.e., because we are dealing only with values of z_t corresponding to tail losses, rather than the whole range of possible z_t values). We then construct the LR test in the same way as before: we estimate the parameters, substitute these into the truncated log-likelihood function, substitute the value of the latter into the equation for the LR test statistic, Equation (9.4), and compare the resulting test value against the critical value bearing in mind that the test statistic is distributed as $\chi^2(3)$ under the null hypothesis.

Box 9.4   A Risk-return Backtest

Beder *et al.* (1998, pp. 302–303) suggest a rather different backtest based on the realised risk–return ratio. Assume for the sake of argument that we have normally distributed P/L, with mean μ and standard deviation σ. Our VaR is then $-\mu - \alpha_{cl}\sigma$, and the ratio of expected P/L to VaR is $-\mu/(\mu + \alpha_{cl}\sigma) = -1/[1 + \alpha_{cl}\sigma/\mu]$. If the model is a good one and there are no untoward developments over the backtesting period, we should find that the ratio of actual P/L to VaR is equal to this value give or take a (hopefully well-behaved) random error. We can test this prediction formally (e.g., using Monte Carlo simulation), or we can use the ratio of actual P/L to VaR as an informal indicator to check for problems with our risk model.

9.4   FORECAST EVALUATION APPROACHES TO BACKTESTING

9.4.1   Basic Ideas

We turn now to forecast evaluation, which is a very different approach to backtesting. The forecast evaluation approach was suggested by Lopez (1998, 1999) and is motivated by the evaluation methods often used to rank the forecasts of macroeconomic models. This approach allows us to rank models, but does not give us any formal statistical indication of model adequacy. In ranking them, it also allows us to take account of any particular concerns we might have: for example, we might be more concerned about higher losses than lower losses, and might therefore wish to give higher losses a greater weight. Furthermore, because they are not statistical tests, forecast evaluation approaches do not suffer from the low power of standard tests such as the Kupiec test: this makes them very attractive for backtesting with the small data sets typically available in real-world applications.[13]

A forecast evaluation process has four key ingredients, and a single output, a final score for each model.

The first ingredient is a set of n paired observations — paired observations of losses (or P/L) each period and their associated VaR forecasts.

The second ingredient is a loss function that gives each observation a score depending on how the observed loss (or profit) compares to the VaR forecast for that period. Thus, if L_t is the loss (or profit, if negative) made over period t, and VaR_t is the forecast VaR for that period, our loss function assigns the following value to the period-t observation:

$$C_t = \begin{cases} f(L_t, VaR_t) \\ g(L_t, VaR_t) \end{cases} \quad \text{if} \quad \begin{matrix} L_t > VaR_t \\ L_t \le VaR_t \end{matrix} \tag{9.5}$$

where $f(L_t, VaR_t) \ge g(L_t, VaR_t)$ to ensure that tail losses do not receive a lower value than other P/L observations.[14]

The third ingredient is a benchmark, which gives us an idea of the score we could expect from a 'good' model.

---

[13]It also seems to be quite effective: Lopez (1999, pp. 51–60) presents simulation results to suggest that his forecast evaluation approach seems to be better able to distinguish between good and bad models than the Kupiec test.

[14]If we wish it to, the loss function can incorporate asymmetries in the backtester's concerns about loss outcomes (e.g., it might treat losses in excess of VaR differently from losses below VaR). This makes the loss function comparable to the 'worry function' of Crnkovic and Drachman (see note 12), and is very useful because it allows us to take account of the economic as well as statistical consequences of high losses.

The fourth ingredient is a score function, which takes as its inputs our loss function and benchmark values. For example, if we take our benchmark to be the expected value of C_t under the null hypothesis that the model is 'good', then we might use a quadratic probability score (QPS) function, given by:

$$QPS = (2/n) \sum_{t=1}^{n} (C_t - p)^2 \qquad (9.6)$$

(see Lopez (1999, p. 47)). The QPS takes a value in the range [0,2], and the closer the QPS value to zero, the better the model. We can therefore use the QPS (or some similar score function) to rank our models, with the better models having the lower scores.

The QPS criterion also has the attractive property that it (usually) encourages truth-telling by VaR modellers: if VaR modellers wish to minimise their QPS score, they will (usually) report their VaRs 'truthfully' (Lopez (1999, pp. 47–48)). This is a useful property in situations where the backtester and the VaR modeller are different, and where the backtester might be concerned about the VaR modeller reporting false VaR forecasts to alter the results of the backtest.

9.4.2   The Frequency-of-tail-losses (Lopez I) Approach

To implement forecast evaluation, we need to specify the loss function, and a number of different loss functions have been proposed. Perhaps the most straightforward is the binomial loss function proposed by Lopez (1998, p. 121)), which gives an observation a value of 1 if it involves a tail loss, and a value of 0 otherwise. Equation (9.5) therefore takes the form:

$$C_t = \begin{cases} 1 \\ 0 \end{cases} \quad \text{if} \quad \begin{matrix} L_t > VaR_t \\ L_t \leq VaR_t \end{matrix} \qquad (9.7)$$

This 'Lopez I' loss function is intended for the user who is (exclusively) concerned with the frequency of tail losses. The benchmark for this loss function is p, the expected value of $E(C_t)$.[15]

9.4.3   The Size-adjusted Frequency (Lopez II) Approach

This loss function ignores the magnitude of tail losses. If we wish to remedy this defect, Lopez (1998, p. 122) himself suggests a second, size-adjusted, loss function:

$$C_t = \begin{cases} 1 + (L_t - VaR_t)^2 \\ 0 \end{cases} \quad \text{if} \quad \begin{matrix} L_t > VaR \\ L_t \leq VaR_t \end{matrix} \qquad (9.8)$$

This loss function allows for the sizes of tail losses in a way that Equation (9.7) does not: a model that generates higher tail losses would generate higher values of Equation (9.8) than one that generates lower tail losses, other things being equal. However, with this loss function, there is no longer a straightforward condition for the benchmark, so we need to estimate the benchmark by some other means (e.g., Monte Carlo simulation).[16]

---

[15]Although the Lopez procedures are not formal statistical tests, Haas (2001, p. 5) observes that they can be converted into such tests by simulating a large number of P/L series, calculating the C-value for each, and deriving the critical C-value that corresponds to a chosen confidence level. We then carry out our tests by comparing our actual C-values to these critical C-values. This is an interesting suggestion that is worth exploring further.

[16]One way to do so is suggested by Lopez (1998, pp. 123–24). He suggests that we assume the observed returns are independent and identically distributed (iid); we can then use this assumption to derive an empirical loss function and a value

9.4.4   The Blanco-Ihle Approach

However, the size-adjusted loss function (Equation (9.8)) has the drawback that it loses some of its intuition, because squared monetary returns have no ready monetary interpretation. Accordingly, Blanco and Ihle (1998) suggest a different size-loss function:

$$C_t = \begin{cases} (L_t - VaR_t)/VaR_t \\ 0 \end{cases} \quad \text{if} \quad \begin{matrix} L_t > VaR_t \\ L_t \leq VaR_t \end{matrix} \qquad (9.9)$$

This loss function gives each tail-loss observation a weight equal to the tail loss divided by the VaR. This has a nice intuition, and ensures that higher tail losses get awarded higher C_t values without the impaired intuition introduced by squaring the tail loss.

The benchmark for this forecast evaluation procedure is also easy to derive: the benchmark is the expected value of the difference between the tail loss and the VaR, divided by the VaR itself, and this is equal to the difference between the ETL and the VaR, divided by the VaR.[17]

9.4.5   An Alternative Sizes-of-tail-losses Approach

Yet the Blanco–Ihle loss function also has a problem: because Equation (9.9) has the VaR as its denominator, it is not defined if the VaR is zero, and will give mischievous answers if VaR gets 'close' to zero or becomes negative. It is therefore unreliable unless we can be confident of the VaR being sufficiently large and positive.

What we want is a size-based loss function that avoids the squared term in the Lopez II loss function, but also avoids denominators that might be zero-valued. A promising candidate is the tail loss itself:

$$C_t = \begin{cases} L_t \\ 0 \end{cases} \quad \text{if} \quad \begin{matrix} L_t > VaR_t \\ L_t \leq VaR_t \end{matrix} \qquad (9.10)$$

The expected value of the tail loss is of course the ETL, so we can choose the ETL as our benchmark, and use a quadratic score function such as:

$$QS = (2/n) \sum_{t=1}^{n} (C_t - ETL_t)^2 \qquad (9.11)$$

This approach penalises deviations of tail losses from their expected value, which makes intuitive sense. Moreover, because it is quadratic, it gives very high tail losses much greater weight than more 'normal' tail losses, and therefore comes down hard on very large losses.

---

of the final score; if we repeat the operation a large number of times, we can use the average final score as our estimate of the benchmark. However, if the VaR model is parametric, we can also use simpler and more direct approaches to estimate the benchmark: we simulate P/L data under the null hypothesis using Monte Carlo methods, and we can take the benchmark to be the average of our final scores.

[17] Blanco and Ihle also suggest a second approach that incorporates concerns about both the frequency and the size of tail losses. If we let $C_t^{frequency}$ be the Lopez I frequency-loss function (Equation (9.7)), and C_t^{size} be the Blanco–Ihle size-loss function (Equation (9.9)), they suggest an alternative loss function that is a weighted average of both, with the weighing factor reflecting our relative concern about the two sources of loss. This is an appealing idea, but this suggestion does not produce reliable rankings: $C_t^{frequency}$ and C_t^{size} are not defined in terms of the same underlying metric, so irrelevant changes (e.g., like redefining our monetary units: say, going from dollars to cents) can alter our scores, and so change our rankings. The idea of taking a weighted average is a good one, but we need a more reliable way of implementing it.

9.5   OTHER METHODS OF COMPARING MODELS

If we wish to compare alternative models, we can also do so using standard statistical measures: we take a group of models and compare their risk measures either to the average results for the group of models as a whole, or to those predicted by each individual model.[18] These risk measures would generally be the VaRs, although we could also use ETL risk measures too. Thus, if we compare risk measures to the model-average measures, we can get some feel for which models produce higher or more volatile risk estimates; and if we compare them to predicted measures, we can rank models by the closeness of their VaRs (or ETLs) to predicted values. These procedures are discussed at length by Hendricks (1996), and he lists nine alternative measures:

- *Mean relative bias*. The mean relative bias measures the extent to which estimated risks are higher than average (or predicted), measured as a percentage of the latter.
- *Root mean-squared relative bias*. The root mean-squared relative bias is the square root of the mean of squared relative biases.
- *Percentage volatility of risk measures*. This measures the volatility of our risk measures over time, and so enables us to rank risk measures in terms of their volatility.
- *Fraction of outcomes covered*. The fraction of outcomes covered is the empirical confidence level, which should equal the confidence level on which the model is predicated. The fraction of outcomes covered is of course equal to 1 minus the proportion of tail losses.
- *Multiple needed to attain desired coverage*. This is the multiple that needs to be applied to each model to produce the desired coverage. For example, a multiple of 1.1, say, indicates that our VaR estimates need to be multiplied by 1.1 to produce the desired coverage.
- *Average or expected tail loss to VaR*. This is the average tail loss or ETL divided by VaR.
- *Maximum tail loss to VaR*. This is the highest tail loss divided by VaR.
- *Correlations between risk measure and P/L*. This is the extent to which the model's risk measures track true risk, as reflected in the actual behaviour of P/L.
- *Mean relative bias for scaled risk measures*. This is the mean relative bias that results when risk measures are scaled to produce the coverage on which they are predicted.

Each of these measures looks at a different aspect of model performance, and we should not generally expect that these different measures would produce the same rankings of alternative models. However, they can give us a feel for the relative strengths and weaknesses of different models, and so help us come to a more informed view of model adequacy.

9.6   ASSESSING THE ACCURACY OF BACKTEST RESULTS

One problem with the standard statistical backtests is that they place a lot of weight on the estimated prob-value. After all, we have only an estimate of the prob-value to go on, and the 'true' probability we are really seeking will always remain unknown. This raises an obvious problem: we might get a poor prob-value estimate that leads us to make an incorrect judgement of the model and incorrectly reject a 'true' model or incorrectly accept a 'false' one. To make matters

---

[18] We can also rank models based on more formal tests, and can do so in one of two ways. The first and easiest is to take a statistical backtest procedure and rank models by means of their resulting prob-values: the better the model, the higher the prob-value. This approach is easy to carry out, but it is also statistically fast and loose, and not too reliable. A more sophisticated approach is suggested by Christoffersen *et al.* (2001). Their approach not only allows us to test models, but also allows us to make pairwise comparisons of models in a rigorous fashion using an appropriate statistical (i.e., non-nested hypothesis-testing) framework.

worse, we might never know that we are doing so, precisely because the 'true' prob-value will be unknown.

Suppose for example that we use the Kupiec procedure to backtest a VaR model against a set of P/L observations. This exercise will produce an estimated prob-value that the null hypothesis is true, and in the usual backtest procedure we would compare this test value to a standard significance level such as 5%, and pass or fail the model accordingly. However, the problem is that we would only have the one prob-value estimate to go on, and we don't really know whether this is accurate enough to provide a reliable conclusion.

To help avoid an incorrect conclusion, it would help if we could get some idea of the precision (or otherwise) of our estimated prob-value, and we can do so by bootstrapping the data. For each bootstrapped sample of observations, we get a new, typically different, estimated prob-value. If we draw a large number of such samples, we can get some idea of the distribution of these prob-value estimates. For instance, we might estimate a 95% confidence interval for the prob-value, and this would lead to one of three possible conclusions:

- The whole of the estimated confidence interval for the prob-value might lie above the critical prob-value at which we would reject the model (e.g., the estimated confidence interval might be [0.06, 0.35], which is well above the critical value of 5%). In this case, we can be at least 95% confident that the true prob-value is above the critical level, and we can pass the model with confidence.
- The whole of the estimated confidence interval for the prob-value might lie below the critical prob-value (e.g., the estimated confidence interval might be [0.01, 0.04]). In this case, we can be at least 95% confident that the true prob-value is below the critical level, and we can reject the model with confidence.
- The estimated confidence interval might straddle the critical prob-value at which we would reject the model (e.g., the estimated confidence interval might be [0.03, 0.06]), and in this case we cannot be 95% confident that the true prob-value lies either above or below the critical value: in other words, we cannot come to a firm conclusion either way — a more modest conclusion that does justice to the uncertainty in our data.

This illustrates that we cannot always arrive at binary conclusions. Instead of concluding that a model either 'passes' a backtest or 'fails' it, the correct conclusion is sometimes that we can't be confident whether the model passes or not. However, if that is what the data tell us, then so be it: better to conclude that we are not confident enough to judge the model one way or the other, and be right, than to come to confident conclusions and be wrong.[19]

9.7 BACKTESTING WITH ALTERNATIVE CONFIDENCE LEVELS, POSITIONS AND DATA

We can also get more information about the adequacy or otherwise of our risk model by backtesting with alternative inputs. Recall that the objective of any backtest procedure is to evaluate a given market risk model. However, as illustrated in the general backtesting framework outlined in Figure 9.5, in order to be able to do so, we also have to specify a particular VaR confidence level, particular positions in market instruments, and a particular set of market price/return data. Yet it

---

[19] An alternative is to simulate additional tail-loss observations using a Monte Carlo approach: we would make some assumption about the P/L or tail-loss distribution, carry out a large number of simulations based on the parameters estimated from our sample, and obtain the histogram of simulated prob-values. However, this approach requires us to specify the P/L or tail-loss distribution, and so exposes us to a potential source of error that is absent with the bootstrap backtest procedure.

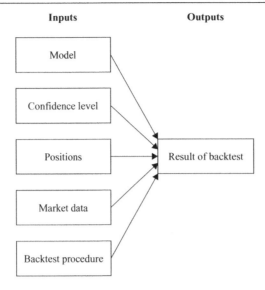

Figure 9.5 A general backtesting framework.

is the model that we are really interested in and the confidence level, positions and data are only supplementary, albeit necessary, inputs. Once we have the model, the confidence level, the positions and the market data, the only other input is the particular backtest procedure used — the Kupiec test, Crnkovic–Drachman test, or whatever. These then produce the output, which is a quantitative indication of the adequacy of the model.

So far, we have examined alternative backtests and taken the other inputs as given. However, we can also evaluate a model by varying the other inputs too: we can evaluate the model using different VaR confidence levels, different position data, and so on. This opens up new ranges of backtest possibilities.[20]

9.7.1 Backtesting with Alternative Confidence Levels

The first option is to carry out backtests using alternative confidence levels. In doing so, we should take account of two important factors:

- As the confidence level rises, we will have fewer tail or tail-loss observations to work with. Estimates of VaR and associated probabilities can then become less precise, and our tests less reliable.
- The choice of confidence level is usually constrained by a priori or theoretical considerations — for example, risk managers tend to be more interested in the quantities associated with relatively high confidence levels.

---

[20]We can also open up a vast array of additional backtesting possibilities by tuning into the large applied statistical literature on the properties of measures of distributional conformity as functions of risk factors. This literature is very relevant to the backtesting of market risk models, and uses methods based on a great variety of different assumptions, data structures, technical tools, and ancillary assumptions. The models involved include, among others, time series/cross-section models, generalised mixed models, vector autoregressive moving average exogenous variable (VARMAX) models, Kalman filter models, and neural networks. Tilman and Brusilovskiy (2001, pp. 87–89) provide a nice overview of this literature.

It should go without saying that we should not be surprised if our backtest results vary as we change the confidence level used: one model might be good at one confidence level, and another model good at a different confidence level.

9.7.2 Backtesting with Alternative Positions

We can also backtest our model on a large variety of alternative positions. These might include:

- The actual portfolio we are currently holding.
- Each of the different portfolios we held over some past time period.
- We can backtest at the business-unit level, as well as at the aggregate, institutional, level: we can backtest our equity positions separately from our fixed-income positions, and so on. We can also backtest at any business-unit level we want, right down to the level of the individual trader or asset manager, or the individual instrument held.
- We can carry out benchmark backtesting: we select a set of important or representative positions, which we regard as benchmarks, and backtest our model on these benchmarks. These benchmarks might be a typical stock market position, a typical FX options position, and so on (see also Barone-Adesi and Giannopoulos (2000)). Such benchmark backtesting can be very useful for comparison purposes.
- We can carry out simulation exercises in which we randomly select a large number of portfolios, backtest against each, and then focus on average results (as in Hendricks (1996, pp. 44–45)). This approach has the advantage of giving us some protection against results that might be specific to a particular portfolio.

9.7.3 Backtesting with Alternative Data

We can also carry out backtests using alternative sets of market price data. In particular:

- We can vary the historical time period used in our backtesting procedures, and we would typically want to do so to check that our results were not dependent on a particular choice of time period.
- For any given time period, we can bootstrap the data and work with bootstrapped data instead: the bootstrap then gives us the benefit of a potentially much larger data set.
- We can produce simulated data using Monte Carlo or other simulation methods, and parameterise such data on existing market price data or our beliefs about the values of the parameters concerned.

Thus, there are many ways in which we can multiply our data, and so increase our scope for backtesting. However, the biggest problem in practice is not so much how to obtain backtest results, but how to keep on top of the backtesting exercise and make sense of the plethora of (often conflicting) results that we would usually get.

9.8 SUMMARY

This chapter suggests the following conclusions:

- The first requirement in backtesting is to clean our data and carry out a preliminary data analysis. This analysis should include the use of a backtesting chart and some summary statistical analysis.
- The most straightforward tests are those based on a comparison of the actual and predicted frequencies of tail losses — the Kupiec test, etc. However, these can be unreliable, and throw away valuable information about tail losses.

- It is therefore better to use tests that make use of the sizes as well as the frequencies of tail losses, and there are a variety of such tests available.
- We can also compare alternative models using forecast evaluation methods (as in Lopez, etc.) or by comparing their risk measures against some standard (e.g., as in Hendricks (1996)).
- We should not rely on any one backtest, and if a particular procedure gives a strong result, either positive or negative, we should seek to confirm or disconfirm that result using other backtests.
- In any case, it is good practice to use a battery of whatever backtests are feasible, and to use their results to get a feel for the strengths and weaknesses of our risk measurement model.
- Sometimes the data do not admit of clear results about model adequacy (i.e., sometimes the correct result is not 'guilty' or 'innocent', but 'not proven'). We should therefore bootstrap our backtests to get a better idea of the distribution of prob-value estimates.
- We can also carry out additional backtests by changing other inputs besides the actual backtest procedure itself: we can change the VaR confidence level, and the positions and market data used. Additional backtests can tell us a lot about model adequacy that would not otherwise be apparent.

Box 9.5   Useful Backtesting Functions in MATLAB

The Statistics and IMRM Toolboxes have a number of commands that are useful in backtesting. The Statistics Toolbox includes 'binopdf' and 'binocdf' (which compute the binomial pdf and cdf), 'binofit' (which estimates parameters and confidence intervals for the binomial data), 'binoinv' (which computes the inverse of the binomial), 'geopdf' (which can be used to estimate the probability of the time of the first tail loss), and 'geocdf' (which can be used to estimate the cumulative probability of the time of the first tail loss).

The IMRM Toolbox includes functions for the Blanco–Ihle backtest, 'blancoihlebacktest' and the two Christoffersen backtests, 'christoffersen1backtest' and 'christoffersen2backtest', which estimate the likelihood ratio test probabilities for the unconditional frequency of tail losses and for the independence of tail losses. The IMRM Toolbox also includes functions for a modified version of the Crnkovic–Drachman test assuming normal P/L, 'modifiednormalCDbacktest', the Kupiec backtest, 'kupiecbacktest', the Lopez forecast evaluation backtest, 'lopezbacktest', the sizes-of-tail-losses statistical backtest for normal P/L, 'normaltaillossesbacktest', discussed in Section 9.3.1, and the sizes-of-tail-losses forecast evaluation score introduced in Section 9.4.5, 'tailloss-FEbacktest'.

9.9   RECOMMENDED READING

Berkowitz (2001); Blanco and Ihle (1998); Christoffersen (1998); Crnkovic and Drachman (1996); Deans (2000); Hendricks (1996); Kupiec (1995); Lopez (1998, 1999); Tilman and Brusilovskiy (2001).

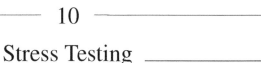

10
Stress Testing

This chapter examines stress testing — procedures that attempt to gauge the vulnerability of our portfolio to hypothetical events. Financial institutions have used stress testing in some form or another for many years, particularly for gauging their exposure to interest-rate risk. Early stress tests were often little more than 'back of the envelope' exercises, but the methodology has improved over the years, thanks in large part to improvements in spreadsheet technology and computing power and, though still limited in many respects, modern stress testing is much more sophisticated than its predecessors.

There has in the past often been a tendency to see stress testing as secondary to other methods of risk estimation, such as those based on Greek parameter estimation in the derivatives field or VaR more generally. This is due in part to the fact that the methodology of stress testing is not as developed as risk measurement methodologies in the proper sense of the term. Prior to 1996, most stress testing was also done at the desk level, and relatively few firms carried out stress testing at the corporate-wide level. However, since then, corporate-wide stress testing has become much more common and more sophisticated, and stress tests are now routinely applied to credit and liquidity shocks, as well as market ones.[1] As Schachter points out:

> The events of October 1997 represent a watershed of sorts for stress testing. The attention given to stress tests by regulators and banks has increased dramatically since that event. In some respects, the event has kindled a love affair with stress testing. Yet the theory behind stress testing is still ill developed, more so than value at risk, which itself is an immature risk management tool.
>
> (Schachter (1998, p. 5F-10))

So stress testing is now getting much more attention, fuelled in large part by the belated recognition that good stress testing might have helped institutions to avoid some of the painful losses of recent years.[2]

Stress testing is particularly good for quantifying what we might lose in crisis situations where 'normal' market relationships break down and VaR and ETL risk measures can be very misleading. Stress tests can identify our vulnerability to a number of different crisis phenomena:

- *Breakdowns in 'normal' correlation relationships.* In crises, correlations often swing to extreme values, and losses can be much greater than suggested by VaR estimates based on 'normal' correlation assumptions.
- *Sudden decreases in liquidity.* Markets can suddenly become very illiquid in crisis situations, bid–ask spreads and order execution times can increase dramatically, and risk management strategies

---

[1] The current state of the art in stress testing is reflected in a BIS survey of leading financial institutions' stress testing procedures, carried out on May 31, 2000. For more on this survey and its results, see Bank for International Settlements (2000) or Fender and Gibson (2001).

[2] The importance of stress testing is also recognised in the Amended Basle Accord on bank capital adequacy requirements. This specifies that banks that seek to have their capital requirements based on their internal models should also have in place a 'rigorous and comprehensive' stress testing programme, and this programme should include tests of the portfolio against past significant disturbances and a bank's own stress tests based on the characteristics of its portfolio.

(e.g., such as those based on dynamic trading) can become unhinged, leading to much bigger losses than anticipated.

- *Concentration risks*. Stress tests can sometimes reveal that we might have a much larger exposure to a single counterparty or risk factor than we had realised, taking into account the unusual conditions of a crisis. VaR or ETL measures can overlook such concentration risks because they tend not to pay much attention to crisis conditions.
- *Macroeconomic risks*. Stress tests are also better suited for gauging our exposure to macroeconomic factors such as the state of the business cycle, the economic condition of a particular country, and so on.

Although the principles behind stress testing are straightforward, there are a huge variety of different categories of stress test depending on the *type of event* (i.e., normal, extreme, contingent, sea change, liquidity, etc.), the *type of risk* involved (market risk, liquidity risk, credit risk, and combinations of these risks), the *risk factors* (e.g., equity risks, yield curve risks, FX risks, default risks, etc.), the *country or region* (e.g., North America, Japan, etc.), the stress test *methodology* (i.e., scenario analysis, factor push, maximum loss optimisation, etc.), the *model assumptions* (e.g., relating to yield curves, the distributions of risk factors, default parameters, etc.), the *book* (i.e., trading book, banking book, off-balance sheet), the *instruments* concerned (e.g., basic equities or bonds, futures, options, etc.), the *level* of the test (desk level, business-unit level, or corporate level), data requirements (e.g., desk-level data, corporate-wide data, etc.) and the *complexity of our portfolio*. Stress testing is thus simple in principle but complex in practice.

Stress testing is a natural complement to probability-based risk measures such as VaR and ETL. Recall that the VaR gives us the maximum likely loss at a certain probability, but gives us no idea of the loss we might suffer in 'bad' states where we would get a loss in excess of VaR. ETL is a little better because it gives us the expected value of a loss in excess of VaR, but even ETL tells us nothing else about the distribution of 'tail losses' other than the expected value. By contrast, stress testing can give us a lot of information about bad states — and, indeed, stress testing is explicitly *designed* to give us information about losses in bad states. However, stress testing does not (usually) tell us, and is not as such designed to tell us, the *likelihood* of these bad states. So VaR and ETL are good on the probability side, but poor on the 'what if' side, whereas stress tests are good for 'what if' questions and poor on probability questions. The two approaches — the probabilistic approaches, VaR and ETL, and stress tests — are therefore natural complements to each other, each highlighting what the other tends to miss.

Broadly speaking, we can distinguish between two main approaches to stress testing:

- Scenario analyses, in which we evaluate the impact of specified scenarios (e.g., such as a particular fall in the stock market) on our portfolio. The emphasis is on specifying the scenario and working out its ramifications.
- Mechanical stress tests, in which we evaluate a number (and often a large number) of mathematically or statistically defined possibilities (e.g., such as increases and decreases of market risk factors by a certain number of standard deviations) to determine the most damaging combination of events and the loss it would produce.

We will consider these presently, but we begin by looking at the benefits and difficulties of stress testing.

Box 10.1   Using Stress Tests

In the right hands, stress testing can be a very important and useful risk management tool, and stress tests can be used for risk management in at least three ways. The first is as a source of information, and the results of stress tests can be disseminated to all levels of management or decision-makers. Stress test results can be a particularly effective means of communicating risk information because the underlying conceptual experiment — i.e., what if . . . happens? — is easy to understand and free of any dependence on the probability notions that are inescapable when using VaR or ETL risk measures. However, it is important not to swamp recipients with unnecessary data, so it is best to give each level of manager or decision-maker only the stress test information relevant to them. When used in this way, stress tests can help to assess risks in the context of the firm's risk appetite, as well as identify major contributors to the firm's overall exposure and reveal hidden sources of risk that might not otherwise be apparent. If they are to provide up-to-date information, stress tests also need to be carried out on a reasonably frequent basis (e.g., every week or month).

The second main use of stress tests is to guide decision-making and, in particular, to help with setting position limits, allocating capital, and managing funding risks. The usefulness of stress tests for setting positions and allocating capital is self-evident, and stress tests can help manage funding risks by identifying the circumstances in which firms might get bad headlines and run into funding problems, so that managers can take appropriate pre-emptive action.

The third use of stress testing is to help firms design systems to protect against bad events — for example, to provide a check on modelling assumptions, to help design systems to protect against stress events (e.g., to protect the firm's liquidity in a liquidity crisis), and to help with contingency planning.

10.1   BENEFITS AND DIFFICULTIES OF STRESS TESTING

10.1.1   Benefits of Stress Testing

Stress testing (ST) is ideal for showing up the vulnerability of our portfolio (and of our VaR calculations) to otherwise hidden risks or sources of error. Schachter (1998) suggests five different ways in which ST can provide valuable information to risk managers that may not otherwise be available to them:

- Since stress events are unlikely, the chances are that the data used to estimate VaR (or ETL) will not reveal much about stress events.
- The short holding period often used for VaR will often be too short to reveal the full impact of a stress event, so it is important to carry out stress events on longer holding periods.
- If stress events are rare, they are likely to fall in the VaR tail region, and VaR will tell us nothing about them. As noted earlier, ETL fares a little better because it would tell us the expected (i.e., average) value of tail losses, but even ETL does not really tell us a great deal about prospective bad events.
- Assumptions that help to value non-linear positions in normal times might be wide of the mark in a stress situation, so a stress test with full revaluation could reveal considerably more than, say, a second-order approximation VaR.

- A stress test could take account of the unusual features of a stress scenario (e.g., such as radicalised correlations, etc.), and so help to reveal exposures that a VaR procedure would often overlook.

We can give many examples where stress testing highlights exposures that probabilistic approaches to risk measurement might easily overlook. An important example is in helping to identify an institution's breaking point — it helps to identify those types of scenario (in terms of severity and conjunction of events, etc.) that would force the institution into insolvency. To quote the Federal Reserve chairman, Alan Greenspan:

> In estimating necessary levels of risk capital, the primary concern should be to address those distur-bances that occasionally do stress institutional solvency — the negative tail of the loss distribution that is so central to modern risk management. As such, the incorporation of stress scenarios into formal risk modelling would seem to be of first-order importance.
>
> (Greenspan (2000, p. 2))

A stress test could identify these scenarios much more explicitly than other methods, and so give management a much clearer idea of the scenarios that they had to worry about. Once these scenarios are identified, it becomes much easier to develop hedging or other risk management strategies to protect against them.

A stress test is also very good for identifying and quantifying liquidity exposures: a stress test can identify liquidity risk factors that might not otherwise be apparent. Liquidity effects — such as connections between interest rates and collateral requirements or credit triggers, the impacts of widening bid–ask spreads and increasing execution times, etc. — can be quite subtle. VaR systems cannot really do them justice, but they are quite amenable to well-designed stress tests. As with solvency tests, the information provided by liquidity stress tests can be crucial in determining how to deal with the risks concerned.

A stress test can be useful in identifying the consequences of large market moves. For example, given the leverage involved in options positions, a firm that delta hedges could be covered against a very small market move and destroyed by a very large one, and the only way to detect this sort of exposure is to run stress tests based on very large hypothesised market moves (e.g., moves of 5–10 standard deviations, or more). We might also use stress tests to examine some of the other potential consequences of a large market move, including the consequences of a drying up of market liquidity, or the possible funding consequences if positive-valued derivatives positions suddenly become major liabilities and force us to put up collateral or meet margin calls.

Stress testing is also good for examining the consequences of changes in volatility. Estimates of volatility based on historical data can be unreliable, and reliance on them can, on occasion, lead to much bigger losses than might have been expected. To illustrate the point, if we take a reasonable period prior to any major exchange-rate crisis, any historically based estimate of the VaR or ETL of a relevant cross-currency portfolio would have indicated relatively little exchange-rate risk: the exchange rate would have been stable for a considerable time, so no historical approach would have had any reason to indicate major exchange-rate risk. The exchange rate then changes very abruptly and anyone on the wrong side of the market would have taken major losses, and yet this vulnerability could easily be picked up by a simple stress test. Volatility can also change suddenly in other markets as well, particularly in equity and commodities markets.

Similarly, we can also use stress tests to highlight dependence on correlation assumptions. Since the risk of a portfolio depends on the expected correlations of the various positions included in it, a major change in correlation could leave our portfolio much more exposed than we thought it was going to be. Historical correlations can themselves be very volatile, and the most drastic changes in correlations tend to occur in crises such as market crashes.[3] If we wish to survive such events, it is important that we not only examine our exposure to large market moves, but also examine what we stand to lose if 'normal' correlations break down and markets all move against us, and the only way to gauge this sort of exposure is to carry out scenario analyses.

Last, but not least, stress tests can be very useful for highlighting other weaknesses in our risk management set-up. The process of actually going through a stress testing exercise should force risk managers and senior managers to think through the ramifications of bad scenarios, as well as help them to pinpoint weaknesses that they might have underestimated or overlooked. If it is done well, it should not only give some indication of where the institution is vulnerable, but also show up flaws in contingency planning. In fact, what risk managers learn about these hidden weaknesses is often as valuable for risk management purposes as the loss figures that the exercise finally produces.[4]

10.1.2   Difficulties with Stress Tests

Stress testing is generally much less straightforward than it looks. Stress tests are based on large numbers of decisions about the choice of scenarios and/or risk factors to stress, how risk factors should be combined, the range of values to be considered, the choice of timeframe, and so forth.

Stress testing is also completely dependent on the chosen scenarios and, hence, on the judgement and experience of the people who carry out the stress tests. This is a serious drawback because, as we all know, the negative events that we want to guard against can often be hard to predict. Choosing the 'right' scenarios is therefore an important but sometimes very difficult task. There have been many cases in the last few years of large companies being severely embarrassed or bankrupted by events that their management did not see coming (and, in some cases, by events that they clearly *should* have seen coming). When portfolios are complex, it can also be very difficult to identify the risk factors to look at. The usefulness of stress testing therefore boils down to the skill, good sense and intuition of those who carry out the stress tests — and, in the final analysis, this is why good risk management is at least as much craft as science.

Another problem with stress testing is the sheer difficulty of working through scenarios in a consistent, sensible way, *without* being overwhelmed by a mass of different possibilities. There are three main issues here:

- We need to be able to follow through scenarios, and the consequences of some scenarios can be very complex: a trigger event occurs, and affects a number of variables; each of these affected variables then impacts on a number of others, and each other; these affect other variables; and so on. A trigger event can rapidly lead to a plethora of possibilities, and if we are not careful, the number of possibilities can become unmanageable and make the whole exercise meaningless.

---

[3]To illustrate the volatility of correlations, in the first quarter of 1993, the average correlation between the Nikkei 225 and the FT-SE 100 stock market indices varied from +0.9 to −0.9 (Jackson (1996, p. 181)). Similarly, over the first quarter of 1995, correlations between the Nikkei 225 and the US$/yen exchange rate varied from less than −0.4 to about +0.7 (Mori *et al.* (1996, chart 3)). The evidence also indicates that correlations can jump very suddenly, and not just when there is a major market crash.

[4]In order to make best use of stress tests, a good practice is to specify a threshold beyond which the loss would be regarded as a serious problem. This threshold would be set in terms of the institution's capital or in terms of the capital allocated to the business unit concerned. If a stress test threw up a loss that exceeded this threshold, the institution would respond with a formal review to examine the circumstances under which a very high loss could occur (Lawrence (1996, p. 176)). This process would look closely at the co-movements leading to the loss and assess how likely the outcome is. An informed decision can then be made as to whether and, if so, how to cover the risk.

- In working through scenarios, we will often (though not necessarily always) want to take account of the interactions of different risks. While it is sometimes useful to carry out scenario analyses in which all correlations are assumed to move in the most damaging ways, the fact is that we will not always want to make such assumptions and, on the contrary, will often want to take account of the interrelationships between different variables. Our stress test might indicate that the maximum loss could occur when one price rises and the other falls, and yet the prices of the two assets might be very strongly correlated. The stress test then ignores the likelihood that the two prices will move up or down together, and may produce a loss estimate much higher than any loss that could plausibly occur. In using stress tests, we must therefore decide when and, if so, how to allow for correlations.

- In designing our scenarios, we must also recognise that there are often situations where prices cannot move independently of each other because doing so would violate a zero-arbitrage condition. To carry out stress testing sensibly, we need to eliminate all co-movements that are inconsistent with zero arbitrage.

Stress tests can also run into various computational problems. (1) The first of these is the need to take account of the differing sensitivities of instrument prices to underlying risk factors. The point here is that pushing all prices by the same multiple of their standard deviation ignores the sensitivity of each position to the underlying risk factors: for example, an option that is deeply out-of-the-money is insensitive to a change in the underlying price, but an option that is in-the-money could be very sensitive to it. The probability of an option price change that is α times the option volatility is therefore much higher for a deeply in-the-money option than for a deeply out-of-the-money option. Consequently, it does not make much sense to push all prices by the same number of standard deviations, when the probability of such a change varies considerably from one position to another. The solution is not to push the individual prices by any particular multiple, but to push the underlying risk factors instead. (2) Stress tests can be computationally expensive, and computational considerations impose a limit on how frequently they can be carried out. This is often the case where options positions are fully revalued during stress tests using intensive procedures such as simulation methods. Many firms also face computational problems because of system incompatibilities of one sort or another. (3) There are serious difficulties in integrating market and credit risk factors in stress analysis, and a recent BIS survey of stress testing in financial institutions reported that none of the surveyed firms had systems that fully integrated market and credit risk in stress testing (Bank for International Settlements (2000, p. 15)). Much of the time, integration appears to have gone little further than taking account of the impact of credit-related changes in the prices of traded instruments.

There is also the issue of probability: since stress tests as such do not give any indication of likelihood, we always face the problem of judging the importance of stress test results. Suppose a stress test suggests that a particular event would drive our firm into insolvency. Does this matter? The answer is that we cannot say without more information. If the event concerned could occur with a significant probability, then clearly the stress test result is important and should be taken seriously. But if the probability of occurrence was negligible, there is no real point paying much attention to it: rational people don't waste time and resources dealing with dangers that are too improbable to worry about. As Berkowitz (2000a, p. 12) puts it, this absence of probabilities leaves 'stress testing in a statistical purgatory. We have some loss numbers, but who is to say whether we should be concerned about them?' In order to use stress tests meaningfully, we need to form some idea, even a very loose and informal one, of the likelihood of the events concerned.[5]

---

[5]Evaluating the plausibility (or, more formally, the probability) of stress scenarios is not difficult, at least in principle, and one straightforward way to do so is suggested by Breuer and Krenn (2000, p. 16). If we identify our stress scenario in terms of an n-dimensional vector of stress factors $\mathbf{r}_{\text{stress}}$, this vector and the factor variance–covariance matrix Σ define

---

Box 10.2   A Coherent Framework for Stress Testing

A risk manager typically faces two separate types of risk estimate — probabilistic estimates such as VaR or ETL, and the loss estimates produced by stress tests — with no obvious way of combining them. So how can we combine a probabilistic risk estimate with an estimate that such-and-such a loss will occur if such-and-such happens? The traditional answer is that we can't: we have to work with these estimates separately, and the best we can do is use one set of estimates to look for possible problems with the other.

Berkowitz (2000a) suggests a solution to this problem: he suggests that we integrate stress testing into formal risk modelling by assigning probabilities to stress test scenarios. The resulting risk estimates then incorporate both traditional market risk estimates and the outcomes of stress tests, as well as the probabilities of each, and so give risk managers a single, integrated set of risk estimates to work with. This suggests the following four-step risk modelling process:

- We go through our stress testing in the traditional way, and the outputs of this process will be a set of realised profits/losses associated with each scenario.
- Once we have gone through our scenarios and established their P/L outcomes, we go through a second, judgemental, process and assign probabilities to each of our scenarios.
- We then go through a formal risk modelling process of the traditional kind, and model our risks using appropriate risk measurement techniques. We can think of the outcome of this process as a set of P/L figures and their associated probabilities.
- We now have all the information we need, so we bring together our two sets of P/L figures and two sets of associated probabilities, and carry out an integrated risk estimation.

Naturally, these estimates are dependent on the judgemental factors that go into stress testing and into the evaluation of scenario probabilities, but there is a good argument that it is better to incorporate our judgements of stress test events into risk modelling than to ignore them completely. It is better to be approximate and probably right in our risk assessments, than to be precise and probably wrong.

10.2   SCENARIO ANALYSIS

We now turn to the first of our two main approaches to stress testing — scenario analysis.

10.2.1   Choosing Scenarios

The first step in scenario analysis is to choose the scenarios to be considered, and the scenarios can come in three main forms.

10.2.1.1   Stylised Scenarios

One type of scenario is a stylised scenario — a simulated movement in one or more major interest rates, exchange rates, stock prices or commodity prices. These scenarios can range from relatively moderate changes to quite extreme ones, and the movements considered can be expressed in terms of absolute changes, percentage changes or standard deviation units (i.e., the price change divided by

---

an n-dimensional ellipsoid of scenarios given by $(\mathbf{r} - \mathbf{r}_{\text{stress}})^{\text{T}} \Sigma^{-1} (\mathbf{r} - \mathbf{r}_{\text{stress}})$. If $\mathbf{r}$ is normally distributed, the mass of the normal distribution contained in this ellipsoid will give us the probability of the stress scenario $\mathbf{r}_{\text{stress}}$; but even if $\mathbf{r}$ is not normally distributed, we can often interpret the normal mass contained in this ellipsoid as an informal measure of plausibility.

the historical standard deviation of the relevant price). Some possible scenarios have been suggested by the Derivatives Policy Group (1995), and include parallel yield curve shifts of plus or minus 100 basis points, yield curve shifts of plus or minus 25 basis points, stock index changes of plus or minus 10%, currency changes of plus or minus 6%, and volatility changes of plus or minus 20%. If the institution is concerned about more extreme events, it might also want to consider such relatively rare events as 5- or 10-standard deviation changes in the relevant underlying price. We might also want to consider the impact of other factors too, such as changes in the slope or shape of the yield curve, a change in correlations, and a change in credit spreads (e.g., a jump or fall in the TED spread).

Stylised scenarios have been used for a long time in asset–liability management, where they are suited to handling portfolios that are exposed to a small number of risk factors. The usual idea is to imagine hypothetical changes in the value of each risk factor and then use pricing equations (e.g., simple linear equations for straightforward positions, duration or duration–convexity approximations for bonds, or delta or delta–gamma approximations for options) to determine the change in the portfolio value resulting from the market factor change. We might assume that the exchange rate rises by $x\%$, interest rates fall by $y\%$, and so on. Each particular combination of risk factor movements leads to a particular new portfolio value and hence a particular profit or loss. If we can combine the analysis with some assessment of the likelihood of the changes, even an informal one, these computations can give a good picture of the risks confronting our portfolio. However, the main limitation of this approach is that it easily becomes unmanageable when there is more than a small number of risk factors. If there are too many risk factors or too many different scenarios for each factor, then the risk manager can easily end up with thousands of loss figures, each for a different combination of risk factor movements. The information can be overwhelming, and the risk manager can have great difficulty in getting any overall sense of portfolio risk.

10.2.1.2 Actual Historical Events

We can also choose our scenarios from actual historical events. Historical scenarios can be based on relatively moderate market changes, which presumably have a reasonable chance of repeating themselves, or more extreme market changes, which are much less likely but more significant if they do, and they can also be based on bootstrap exercises from historical data. Historical scenarios have two advantages relative to other scenarios:

- The fact that historical scenarios have actually occurred reduces their arbitrariness and gives them a certain plausibility that other scenarios lack. It is also hard(er) to dismiss historical scenarios on the grounds that they couldn't happen.
- They are readily understood. A statement like 'the firm would lose $X million if there were a repeat tomorrow of the October 1987 stock market crash' is easy to understand, and this type of clarity is very useful in communicating risk information effectively.

Whilst the precise choice of historical scenario — the data period used, the prices or price indices considered, whether and how to bootstrap, etc. — is inevitably subjective, we can make the selection process a little more systematic by using a well-produced scenario catalogue, rather than just a handful of ad hoc scenarios pulled out of thin air.[6] Such a catalogue might include:

- Moderate market scenarios, such as bootstrapped recent market return scenarios, changes in market volatility, a bond market squeeze due to fiscal surpluses, changes in the euro, a widening or falling TED spread, and others from recent market experience.

---

[6]A good example of such a catalogue is provided by Algorithmics' Mark-to-Future system, which provides a wide selection of historical and other scenarios.

- More extreme market scenarios, such as repeats of major stock market crises (e.g., the 23% fall in the Dow-Jones on October 19, 1987, the 48% fall in the Nikkei over 1990, etc.) or exchange rate crises (e.g., the ERM devaluations in September 1992, the fall in the peso in December 1994, the East Asian devaluations in 1997, the 40% fall in the rouble in August 1998, etc.), a bond market crash (e.g., the near doubling of US interest rates in 1994), major country shocks (e.g., the Latin American crisis in 1995, the Asian crisis in 1997, Russia in August 1998, and Brazil in 1999), or the failure or near failure of a large institution (e.g., LTCM in 1998, Enron in 2001).

A good guide is to choose scenarios of much the same order of magnitude as the worst-case events in our historical (or bootstrapped historical) data sets. In doing so, we should obviously keep in mind that these events are notoriously difficult to predict in advance. We should also keep in mind that market experience suggests that maximum price falls vary enormously from one market to another and, within any given market, are often very much bigger than the next largest price fall.[7]

Box 10.3   Points to Watch for in Scenario Analysis

Many firms could improve their stress testing by looking out for the following points:[8]

- Where maximum losses are associated with large changes in risk factors, it is important to allow for large changes in risk factors: in other words, stress situations should be fairly stressful.
- We need to take proper account of the speed and duration of stress events.
- We should identify key assumptions, and gauge our vulnerability to them. Unless they are made explicit, important assumptions often remain hidden.
- We should take account of linkages between risk factors, particularly in crises: we must account for connections between market, credit and liquidity risks, and so forth.
- Stress tests should be done reasonably frequently, so that results are up-to-date and relevant to the firm's current situation.

Successful stress testing also requires that the firm avoid or at least mitigate a number of common pitfalls:[9]

- Senior management might not buy into the stress test exercise, and so ignore stress test results.
- Managers might fail to conduct adequate ad hoc tests because the results of standard historical and mechanical stress tests indicate that the portfolio is safe.
- Results might be evaluated by managers who lack the authority to take remedial action.
- Stress testers and managers might develop a 'what if?' mentality and rely too much on stress tests, or they might develop an excessively reactive mentality and rely too much on VaR or ETL.
- Stress tests can rely too much on historical scenarios, and not enough on plausible scenarios that are not reflected in the historical record.

---

[7]A potential drawback with historical scenarios is that a firm can easily become over-reliant on them, and such over-reliance can make it excessively backward-looking and oblivious to new dangers. The solution is to strike an appropriate balance between historical and other possible scenarios — which is of course easier said than done. A second drawback is that it is hard to apply historical scenarios to new products or new markets, or to risk factors that are known to have changed significantly in the recent past. However, we can deal with this drawback, to some extent at least, by using suitable proxies or scenarios from comparable markets.

[8]For more on these points, see Wee and Lee (1999, pp. 16–17).

[9]For more on these, see Blanco (1999b).

- Stress tests only capture a limited number of extreme scenarios, and stress testers and managers need to keep in mind that real extreme losses could be substantially higher.
- Stress testing can become politicised: stress tests can become a political weapon to be used or ignored by interested parties within the firm in the pursuit of other objectives, thus compromising the integrity and credibility of the stress testing process.

Institutions can try to avoid these pitfalls by ensuring that senior managers buy into stress testing exercises, that all interested parties are involved in selecting scenarios, that there is a balance between purely hypothetical and historical scenarios, and that results are reported to interested parties in appropriate detail.

10.2.1.3   Hypothetical One-off Events

Scenarios can also come from plausible hypothetical scenarios that have no direct historical precedents. These scenarios would not be replays of past historical events, as such, although they would have some similarity with past events. These scenarios might be natural (e.g., a major earthquake in California), political (e.g., the outbreak of a war or a sovereign default), legal (e.g., a ruling on the legality of a derivatives contract), economic or financial (e.g., the default of a major financial institution or a new financial crisis), credit-related (e.g., the downgrading of a major counterparty), or liquidity-related (e.g., a major hike in credit spreads). We can often — though not always — formulate such scenarios by looking at historical experience and asking what might have been.

We can also look to the historical record to give us an indication of what such an event might look like. A good example highlighted in the recent BIS report on stress testing is a 'flight to quality' (Bank for International Settlements (2000, p. 12)). Such scenarios involve shocks to credit spreads, such as a jump in the TED spread. However, the flight to quality experienced in late 1998 also involved close connections between credit spreads and liquidity factors, so the flight-to-quality scenarios now used by financial institutions have been refined further to take more account of liquidity considerations, with more emphasis on liquidity-related changes in spreads, such as changes in the spread between on- and off-the-run US Treasury instruments.[10]

10.2.2   Evaluating the Effects of Scenarios

Having specified each scenario as fully as we can, we need to consider the effect of each scenario on the prices of all instruments in our portfolio. The key task is to get an idea of the sensitivities of our various positions to the underlying risk factors whose hypothetical changes we are considering. This is very easy for some positions. Thus, a straight FX position changes one-for-one in value with changes in the exchange rate, and the value of a diversified stock portfolio changes (roughly) one-for-one with changes in the stock market index. Many other positions also change one-for-one (or thereabouts) with changes in the underlying market risk factor. Some other positions have less straightforward sensitivities, but we can usually handle them by using approximations. For example,

---

[10]Some authors also treat EVT or stressed VaR approaches as forms of stress test as well. An EVT approach gives us the VaR or ETL associated with an extreme event; this is very useful, but is perhaps best regarded as a form of parametric risk measurement rather than a stress test as such. However, this is a semantic issue and there is no denying that EVT is very useful for estimating extreme scenario risks. A stressed VaR exercise involves changing risk factors (e.g., volatilities or correlations) and seeing the impact on VaR. This is a stress test by anyone's definition — and a very useful one at that — but we should keep in mind that it gives us the change in VaR (or ETL) rather than a loss as such. Stressed VaR exercises are very useful tools for helping us manage our risks, but the results of these exercises are measures of the riskiness of our risk measures, rather than 'straight' risk measures as such. For more on stressed VaR, see Box 10.4.

we could obtain the approximate sensitivities of option prices to changes in underlying risk factors from estimates of their deltas, gammas, vegas and other risk parameters, all of which should be readily available; and where bonds are concerned, we might proxy their sensitivities to changes in market interest rates by taking duration or duration–convexity approximations.

Once we have determined the effect of each scenario on all relevant prices, we can infer the effect of each scenario on the portfolio value as a whole. The portfolio loss is then found by subtracting the portfolio's existing value from its post-scenario value.

In evaluating the effects of scenarios on our portfolio, we should also consider the impact of our hypothesised events on the markets in which we operate. In particular, it is very unwise to assume that markets will continue to function 'normally' when subjected to extreme stress. To illustrate, under normal stock market conditions we could expect to see sell orders executed within a matter of minutes; yet, on October 19, 1987, stock markets were so overwhelmed that it could take hours to get orders executed. Sell orders either expired because of time or price limits or else were executed at much lower prices than the sellers had expected. Market liquidity consequently dried up just when sellers were most dependent on it. Firms whose risk management strategies are based on dynamic hedging or an assumed ability to rebalance portfolios quickly should therefore pay considerable attention to the impact of extreme events on market liquidity. They should also watch out that volatility and correlation assumptions that may appear reasonable in 'normal' times do not break down when markets are stressed and leave them with much bigger exposures than they thought they might have.

Companies that use futures contracts to hedge illiquid positions should also take into account the funding implications of their hedge positions. Gains or losses in futures positions must be settled on a daily basis, while changes in other positions (e.g., forward ones) will not be settled until the position is finally closed out. Hence, even otherwise well-designed hedges can lead to mismatches between the timing of receipts and the timing of the payments that theoretically cover them. If the hedges are large, these interim funding requirements can also be large. Indeed, it was the failure to consider just this point that played a key factor in bringing the German industrial giant Metallgesellschaft to its knees in 1993–4.

Box 10.4   Stress Testing in a VaR Framework

A major problem with traditional stress testing is that it throws away valuable information, particularly about volatilities and correlations. To remedy this drawback, Kupiec (1999) proposes a new approach — a form of conditional stress testing or stress VaR approach — that seeks to make use of this information in stress testing. Suppose we have a set of risk factors that are, say, normally distributed. We partition these into two sets — a set of k factors, $\tilde{\mathbf{R}}_{1t}$, that are to be stressed to take values $\mathbf{R}_{1t}$, and those that are not, $\tilde{\mathbf{R}}_{2t}$. If the variance–covariance matrix Σ is unaltered in the stress test,[11] the unstressed factors $\tilde{\mathbf{R}}_{2t}$ are conditionally distributed as:

$$\tilde{\mathbf{R}}_{2t}\big|_{\tilde{\mathbf{R}}_{1t}=\mathbf{R}_{1t}} \sim N(\mu_c, \Sigma_c)$$

where $\mu_c = \Sigma_{21}\Sigma_{11}^{-1}\mathbf{R}_{1t}$, $\Sigma_c = \Sigma_{22} - (\Sigma_{21}\Sigma_{11}^{-1}\Sigma_{12})$, and the Σ_{11} and so forth are the partitioning sub-matrices of Σ, given the values $\mathbf{R}_{1t}$ of the stressed factors. Given this conditional density

---

[11]This assumption and the earlier assumption of normality are only made for convenience: they are not essential, and we can relax them if we are prepared to make the analysis a little more difficult.

function, the stress scenario change in portfolio value is a normally distributed random variable with mean $\mathbf{X}_{1t}\mathbf{R}_{1t} + \mathbf{X}_{2t}\mu_c$ and variance $\mathbf{X}_{2t}\Sigma_c\mathbf{X}_{2t}^{\mathsf{T}}$, where $\mathbf{X}_{1t}$ and $\mathbf{X}_{2t}$ are the position vectors corresponding to the two types of risk factors. Once the joint distribution of the risk factors is taken into account, our stress test thus produces a distribution of scenario loss values, not just a single loss value. If we wish, we can then focus on one of the percentile points of the scenario loss distribution, in which case our output can be interpreted as a stress VaR: the likely worst outcome at a chosen confidence level.

Alternatively, we can focus on the mean of the conditional loss distribution, in which case our stress loss is $\mathbf{X}_{1t}\mathbf{R}_{1t} + \mathbf{X}_{2t}\Sigma_{21}\Sigma_{11}^{-1}\mathbf{R}_{1t}$. This expected loss differs from the expected loss we get under traditional stress testing because it takes account of the correlations between different risk factors: under a traditional stress test, we would stress the stressed risk factors and take the other risk factors to be unaltered, and therefore get an expected loss of $\mathbf{X}_{1t}\mathbf{R}_{1t}$. The results reported by Kupiec (1999, p. 12) indicate that this traditional loss measure performs very poorly in backtesting exercises, and that his proposed new expected loss measure fares better.[12]

10.3   MECHANICAL STRESS TESTING

We turn now to mechanical stress tests. These procedures attempt to avoid the subjectivity of scenario analyses and put stress testing on a firmer methodological foundation: instead of choosing scenarios subjectively, we generate them from a set of mathematically or statistically defined possibilities. We then work through these to determine the most damaging combination of events and the loss it would produce. Mechanical approaches are therefore more thorough and more systematic than traditional scenario analysis, but can also be computationally more intensive. Some mechanical stress testing procedures also differ from scenario analysis in that they are able to give some indication of the likelihood of different outcomes, and this information can be useful when trying to decide how seriously to take them.

10.3.1   Factor Push Analysis

The simplest of these procedures is factor push analysis, in which we 'push' the price of each individual security or (preferably) the relevant underlying risk factor in the most disadvantageous direction and work out the combined effect of all such changes on the value of the portfolio.[13] We have already met this type of approach in the shape of Wilson's delta–gamma approach to VaR, which was discussed in the Appendix to Chapter 5. We start by specifying a level of confidence, which gives us a confidence level parameter α. We then consider each risk factor on its own, 'push' it by α times its standard deviation, and revalue the portfolio at the new risk factor value; we do the same for all risk factors, and select that set of risk factor movements that has the worst effect on the portfolio value. Collecting these worst price movements for each instrument in our portfolio gives

---

[12]Since it was first proposed, the Kupiec stress VaR approach has been refined further by Zangari (1998) and Cherubini and Della Lunga (1999): they suggest that we translate our prior views about risk factors into prior estimates of their mean and variance, and then feed these into a VaR calculation engine in much the same way that Kupiec does. These approaches are good for helping to evaluate the sensitivity of our risk measures to prior assumptions or intuitions about risk factors, and for evaluating the sensitivity of risk measures to individual scenarios.

[13]For more on this approach, see, e.g., Meegan (1995, pp. 25–26), Frain and Meegan (1996), Page and Costa (1996), Rouvinez (1997, pp. 60–62), Studer and Lüthi (1997) and Studer (1999).

us our worst-case scenario, and the maximum loss (ML) is equal to the current value of our portfolio minus the portfolio value under this worst-case scenario.[14]

Factor push analysis is relatively easy to program, at least for simple positions, and is good for showing up where and how we are most vulnerable. It does not require particularly restrictive assumptions and can be used in conjunction with a non-linear P/L function (e.g., such as a P/L function that is quadratic in underlying risk factors), and can be modified to accommodate whatever correlation assumptions we care to make (e.g., using a Choleski decomposition, as in Studer and Lüthi (1997)). Furthermore, in common with measures such as those generated by the SPAN risk measurement system or by worst-case scenario analysis, not to mention ETL, the ML risk measure also has the major theoretical attraction of being coherent.[15]

If we are prepared to make certain additional assumptions, factor push can also tell us something about the likelihood of the losses concerned.[16] If we have just one risk factor and make appropriate parametric assumptions (e.g., such as normality), α enables us to infer the tail probability, and the maximum loss on the boundary of the confidence region is our VaR. α can still tell us something about the probabilities when we have multiple risk factors and make appropriate parametric assumptions (e.g., multivariate normality, given a set of correlation assumptions), but the analysis is more complicated and we find that the ML on the boundary of the confidence region is a conservative estimate (i.e., an overestimate) of our VaR (see Studer (1999, p. 38)).[17] However, we can also adjust the α-value to make the ML equal to our VaR, and if we make this adjustment, we can interpret ML as a VaR and use the factor push approach as an alternative way of estimating VaR.[18]

However, FP rests on the not-always-appropriate assumption that the maximum loss occurs at extreme values of the underlying risk variables (i.e., it assumes that the maximum loss occurs when the underlying factor moves up or down by α times its standard deviation).[19] Yet this assumption is only appropriate for certain relatively simple types of portfolio (e.g., uncomplicated equity or FX positions) in which the position value is a monotonic function of a (typically, single) risk factor, and there are many other instruments for which this assumption does not hold. A good example is a long

---

[14] To do factor push analysis properly, we should also take account of relevant constraints, such as zero-arbitrage conditions, and we might also want to work with mapped positions, delta–gamma approximations, and so on. However, none of these modifications alters the basic nature of factor push analysis.

[15] For more on the SPAN and worst-case scenario analysis approaches, see Box 2.4.

[16] There are various ways we can get probability figures out of stress tests. Besides the Wilson–Studer–Lüthi–Rouvinez approach discussed in the text and the Berkowitz coherent stress test approach discussed in Box 10.2, we can also use the dominant factor method suggested by Bouchaud and Potters (2000). This approach is based on a dominant factor approximation that is ideally suited to handling non-normal risk factors, and the approximation can be fitted to any of a large number of fat-tailed distributions to estimate the probabilities concerned.

[17] This is the same problem raised by Britten-Jones and Schaefer (1999) in their critique of Wilson's QP approach (e.g., Wilson (1996)), discussed earlier in the Appendix to Chapter 5 — namely, that identifying outcomes as being inside or outside a confidence region does not tell us the probability of those outcomes, with the result that Wilson's ML (or capital-at-risk, to use his terminology) is an overestimate of VaR.

[18] An alternative method of obtaining VaR estimates from a factor push methodology is provided by Rouvinez (1997). Suppose we start by assuming that the changes in the risk factors are independent normal. The sum of the squares of these changes is then distributed as a chi-squared, and (assuming a zero mean) the VaR is equal to the relevant quantile of the chi-squared distribution, say β, times the portfolio standard deviation. Since β is generally bigger than the standard normal quantile α, this approach generally leads to bigger VaR estimates than, say, a delta–normal approach. For more on this method, see Rouvinez (1997, pp. 60–62).

[19] One other problem with mechanical stress tests is that the largest losses might come from conjunctions of events that will not in fact occur. For example, we might find that the maximum loss occurs when there is a large fall in the stock market associated with a large fall in stock market volatility. Since such combinations cannot plausibly occur, the losses associated with them are not really worth worrying about. In carrying out mechanical stress tests, we need to screen for such implausible combinations and remove them from consideration.

straddle — a combination of a long call and a long put written against the same underlying asset. The profit on a straddle depends on movements in the underlying variable, either up or down — the greater the movement, the bigger the profit — and the maximum loss on a straddle actually occurs when the underlying price does not move at all. A naïve factor push methodology applied to a straddle position would then give a misleading picture of maximum loss, since it would assume that the maximum loss occurred in exactly those circumstances where it would in fact make its maximum profit! There is also good reason to believe that this type of problem is quite serious in practice. To quote Tanya Beder:

> In our experience, portfolios do not necessarily produce their greatest losses during extreme market moves ... portfolios often possess Achilles' heels that require only small moves or changes between instruments or markets to produce significant losses. Stress testing extreme market moves will do little to reveal the greatest risk of loss for such portfolios. Furthermore, a review of a portfolio's expected behavior over time often reveals that the same stress test that indicates a small impact today indicates embedded land mines with a large impact during future periods. This trait is particularly true of options-based portfolios that change characteristics because of time rather than because of changes in the components of the portfolio.
>
> (Beder (1995a, p. 18))

When using factor push, we first need to satisfy ourselves that our portfolio suffers its maximum loss when the risk factors make their biggest moves.

10.3.2 Maximum Loss Optimisation

The solution to this latter problem is to search over the losses that occur for intermediate as well as extreme values of the risk variables. This procedure is known as maximum loss optimisation.[20] Maximum loss optimisation is essentially the same as factor push analysis, except for the fact that it also searches over intermediate as well as extreme values of the risk variables. There are therefore more computations involved, and MLO will take longer if there are many risk factors involved and a lot of intermediate values to search over. Consequently, the choice between FP and MLO depends on the payoff characteristics of our portfolio. If the portfolio is made up of straightforward positions, each of which takes its maximum loss at extreme values of the underlying risk factors, then FP and MLO will deliver exactly the same results and we may as well use the computationally simpler FP approach. However, if the portfolio has less straightforward payoff characteristics (e.g., as with some options positions), it may make sense to use MLO. MLO can also help pick up interactions between different risks that we might otherwise have overlooked, and this can be very useful for more complex portfolios whose risks might interact in unexpected ways. As a general rule, if the portfolio is complex or has significant non-linear derivatives positions, it is best to play safe and go for MLO.[21]

---

[20]For more on maximum loss optimisation, and on the difference between it and factor push analysis, see Frain and Meegan (1996, pp. 16–18).

[21]The actual calculations can be done using a variety of alternative approaches. The most obvious approach is a grid search, in which we discretise the possible movements in risk factors and search over the relevant n-dimensional grid to find that combination of risk factor changes that maximises our loss. However, we can also use simulation methods, or numerical methods such as a multidimensional simplex method, or hybrid methods such as simulated annealing, all of which are discussed further in Breuer and Krenn (2000, pp. 10–13). These methods are also capable of considerable refinement to increase accuracy and/or reduce computation time.

Box 10.5   CrashMetrics

CrashMetrics is a form of maximum loss optimisation that is designed to estimate worst-case losses (see Hua and Wilmott (1997) or Wilmott (2000, ch. 58)). If we have a long position in a single option, the option P/L can be approximated by a second-order Taylor approximation (see Equation (8.12)), and the maximum possible loss is $\delta^2/(2\gamma)$ and occurs when the change in underlying value is $-\delta/\gamma$. We can get comparable expressions for multi-option portfolios provided we can model the relationship — and more particularly, the variance–covariance matrix — between the underlying variables. Hua and Wilmott suggest that we do so by modelling how they move in a crash relative to a market benchmark, and they estimate the coefficients involved using data on extreme market moves. This approach can also be extended to deal with the other Greek factors, changes in bid–ask spreads, and so on.

10.4   CONCLUSIONS

Stress tests have three main attractions. First and foremost, they can give us a lot of information about what we stand to lose in bad states — and, indeed, stress testing is explicitly designed to give us information about losses in bad states. The information provided by stress testing is a natural complement to that provided by probabilistic risk measures, most particularly VaR. Second, stress test results can be very useful in risk management decision-making — in setting capital requirements and position limits, and so on. Finally, stress tests can highlight weaknesses in our risk management systems (such as awkward assumptions in risk measurement models or failures in contingency plans). If we do not engage in stress tests, it is only a matter of time before we become seriously unstuck by something or other: we will delta hedge, say, and take a big negative gamma hit when the underlying price crashes, or correlations will alter suddenly and leave us much more exposed than we thought we would be. Stress testing is essential for sound risk measurement and management.

However, we ought not to lose sight of the limitations of stress testing. In particular, scenario analysis gives rise to important subjectivity issues and, as Schachter nicely puts it:

> represent[s] only a limited number of scenarios, the likelihood of any one being impossible to estimate. As a result neither the completeness nor the reliability of the information provided can be scientifically assessed. In addition, hypothetical stress scenarios cannot be 'validated' based on actual market events. That is, even when the events specified in a hypothetical scenario actually occur, there is usually no way to apply what was 'right' and 'wrong' in the scenario to other hypothetical scenarios to improve them. These limitations are not shared by value-at-risk models, which are statistically based. In these, it is possible to construct statistical confidence intervals around the VaR estimate and to conduct meaningful 'backtests' of the VaR model's predictions.
>
> (Schachter (1998, p. 5F-8))

Scenario analysis is not very scientific, in other words, but for many risk management purposes it is still the only game in town.

10.5   RECOMMENDED READING

Bank for International Settlements (2000); Berkowitz (2000a); Blanco (1999b); Breuer and Krenn (1999, 2000); Cherubini and Della Lunga (1999); Fender and Gibson (2001); Kim and Finger (1999); Kupiec (1999); Mori *et al.* (1996); Rouvinez (1997); Schachter (1998, 2000); Shaw (1997); Studer (1999); Wee and Lee (1999); Zangari (1998).

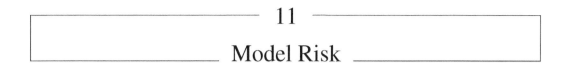

11

Model Risk

This chapter considers the subject of model risk — which is, loosely speaking, the risk of error in our risk estimates due to inadequacies in the risk measurement models we use. Model risk is an inescapable consequence of model use, but it is impossible to make good use of any model without understanding its limitations and appreciating what can go wrong when we use it.

We therefore begin by reviewing model methodology; we then consider what model risk entails, where it comes from and, finally, how to deal with it.

11.1 MODELS AND MODEL RISK

11.1.1 Models

Models are formal frameworks that enable us to determine the values of outputs (e.g., such as asset prices, hedge ratios, VaR, etc.) based on postulates about the factors that determine those outputs. There are three main types of models, and the most important are 'fundamental' models, which are formal systems tying outputs to inputs based on assumptions about dynamic processes, interrelationships between variables, and so on. Some examples are the Black–Scholes option pricing model, which links the option price to the underlying price, the strike price, etc., based on assumptions such as a lognormally distributed asset price, and parametric VaR models, which link VaR to assumptions about the distribution of P/L or returns. The second class of models are 'descriptive' models, which are more superficial, but often insightful and easier to work with, and which we can regard as short-cuts to fundamental models. An example is a bond price model based on assumptions about yield movements — a model that sidesteps the complexities of the term structure by focusing instead on simplified 'stories' about yields. Both fundamental and descriptive models attempt to explain cause and effect — for instance, to explain bond prices in terms of the term structure or bond yields. The third class of models are statistical models that attempt to capture the regression or statistical best-fit between variables, with the emphasis on the correlation between them rather than any causal connection.

A model is only a representation of something, and should never be mistaken for what it represents. In the eloquent words of Emanuel Derman:

> even the finest model is only a model of the phenomena, and not the real thing. A model is just a toy, though occasionally a very good one, in which case people call it a theory. A good scientific toy can't do everything, and shouldn't even try to be totally realistic. It should represent as naturally as possible the most essential variables of the system, and the relationships between them, and allow the investigation of cause and effect. A good toy doesn't reproduce every feature of the real object; instead, it illustrates for its intended audience the qualities of the original object most important to them. A child's toy train makes noises and flashes lights; an adult's might contain a working miniature steam engine. Similarly, good models should aim to do only a few important things well.
>
> (Derman (1997, p. 85))

The best way to understand how models can go wrong is to understand how they are constructed: after all, a model is only an engine, and the key to understanding any engine is to pull it to bits, get to know its components, then reassemble it and (hopefully) get it to work properly. To understand a financial model, we must therefore get to know the financial nuts and bolts. Derman suggests that we should:

- Understand the securities involved, and the markets in which they are traded.
- Isolate the most important variables, and separate out the causal variables (or exogenous variables, to use the jargon) from the caused (or endogenous) variables.
- Decide which exogenous variables are deterministic and which are stochastic or random, decide how the exogenous variables are to be modelled, and decide how the exogenous variables affect the endogenous ones.
- Decide which variables are measurable, and which are not; decide how the former are measured, and consider whether and how the non-measurable variables can be proxied or implicitly solved from other variables.
- Consider how the model can be solved, and look for the simplest possible solutions. We should also consider the possible benefits and drawbacks of using approximations instead of exact solutions.
- Program the model, taking account of programming considerations, computational time, and so on.
- Test and backtest the model.
- Implement the model, and evaluate its performance.

11.1.2 Model Risk

A model, by definition, is a highly simplified structure, and we should not expect it to give a perfect answer. Some degree of error is to be expected, and we can think of this risk of error as a form of model risk. However, the term 'model risk' is more subtle than it looks: we should keep in mind that not all output errors are due to model inadequacy (e.g., simulation methods generally produce errors due to sampling variation) and models that are theoretically flawed or inappropriate can sometimes give very good results (e.g., simple options pricing models often perform well even when some of the assumptions are known to be invalid).

The main outputs of financial models are prices (e.g., option prices for option pricing models, etc.), Greek hedge ratios (i.e., option deltas, gammas, etc.) or risk measures such as VaR or ETL. But whatever the output, model risk in financial models always boils down to pricing error. This is self-evident when the output is itself a price, but is equally true for the other outputs as well. If we are estimating hedge ratios, we have to estimate the instrument prices for differing parameter values, and take the hedge ratio from differences between these prices relative to differences in parameter values; and if we are estimating VaR or ETL, we have to estimate the value or price of the portfolio at the end of the holding period as an intermediate step. So whatever the output we are seeking, we still have to estimate the current or prospective future price of the instruments concerned: model risk always boils down to pricing risk.

Model risk is not a particularly big issue when we have simple instruments: for example, we can easily price a bond using present-value methods. However, model risk can be a much greater problem for complex positions because lack of transparency, unobserved variables (e.g., such as volatilities), interactions between risk factors, calibration issues, numerical approximations, and so on all make pricing more difficult. Calculating the price of a bond is one thing; calculating the price of a complicated exotic derivative is quite another.

Box 11.1   How Good are Banks' Risk Measurement Models?

Given the amounts invested in risk measurement models, one would hope that the models banks actually use would be fairly good ones — but, in fact, the evidence on this issue is not especially reassuring. A recent study by Berkowitz and O'Brien (2001) examines the VaR models used by six leading US financial institutions. Their results indicate that these models tend to be too conservative and in some cases highly inaccurate: banks sometimes experience high losses, very much larger than their models predicted, which suggests that these models are poor at dealing with fat tails or extreme risks. Their results also indicate that banks' models have difficulty dealing with changes in volatility.

In addition, a comparison of banks' models with a simple univariate GARCH model (of bank P/L) indicates that the latter gives roughly comparable coverage of high losses, but also tends to produce lower VaRs and is much better at dealing with volatility changes (e.g., such as those of August–September 1998). These results suggest that the banks' structural models embody so many approximations and other implementation compromises that they lose any edge over much simpler models such as GARCH ones. They could also be interpreted as suggesting that banks would be better off ditching their structural risk models in favour of much simpler GARCH models.[1]

These results suggest that the Basle regulations on the internal models approach to capital adequacy regulation might be counterproductive. Banks' models might be too conservative in part because regulations require sub-portfolio VaRs to be added for capital adequacy purposes: this would ignore any diversification benefits that arise when sub-portfolios are combined together, and so produce conservative (i.e., excessively high) VaR estimates. Banks' models might also have difficulty tracking changes in volatility, because Basle regulations require VaR estimates to reflect market volatility over a period of at least a year, and this prevents them from responding to large sudden changes in market volatility.

11.2   SOURCES OF MODEL RISK

11.2.1   Incorrect Model Specification

Model risk can arise from many different sources, and one of the most important is incorrect model specification.[2] This can manifest itself in many ways:

- *Stochastic processes might be misspecified.* We might assume that a stochastic process follows a geometric Brownian motion when it is in fact fat-tailed, we might mistake a lognormal P/L process for a normal one, and so forth. The solution is of course to use the right stochastic process — but identifying the right process might not be easy.
- *Missing risk factors.* We might ignore stochastic volatility or fail to consider enough points across the term structure of interest rates.

---

[1] Similar findings are also reported by Lucas (2000) and Lopez and Walter (2001, p. 25), who find that sophisticated risk models based on estimates of complete variance–covariance matrices fail to perform much better than simpler univariate VaR models that require only volatility estimates.

[2] However, we should also keep in mind that models that are theoretically overly simplistic often give adequate results in practice, particularly if we know their limitations. The obvious examples are the famous 'holes in Black–Scholes' that enable us to make good use of Black–Scholes provided we understand how to work with its biases.

- *Misspecified relationships*. We might misspecify relationships between variables — for instance, we might ignore correlations or get correlations wrong in VaR estimation.
- *Transactions costs and liquidity factors*. Many models ignore transactions costs and assume that markets are perfectly liquid. Such assumptions are very convenient for modelling purposes, but can lead to major errors where transactions costs are significant or market liquidity is limited.

There is evidence that model misspecification risk can be substantial. Hendricks (1996) investigated differences between alternative VaR estimation procedures applied to 1,000 randomly selected simple FX portfolios, and found that these differences were sometimes substantial. More alarmingly, Beder (1995a) examined eight common VaR methodologies used by a sample of commercial institutions and applied to three hypothetical portfolios. She found that alternative VaR estimates for the same portfolio could differ by a factor of up to 14 — a worrying magnitude by anyone's standards. VaR estimates are thus widely dependent upon the methodology and assumptions underlying the estimation: 'straight' model risk is clearly a major problem when estimating VaR or ETL.

There are many well-publicised examples where this sort of model risk led to major losses. For example, the need to take full account of the lower tail of returns was illustrated by the collapse of the Niederhoffer investment fund. Based on the view that the market would not fall by more than 5% on a single day, Niederhoffer sold out-of-the-money puts on stock index futures, and did well until the stock market fell by 7% on October 27, 1997 and wiped him out.

But arguably the most common problem is the failure to take account of illiquidity factors. Such failures were highlighted by the difficulties experienced by portfolio insurance strategies in the October 1987 crash — where strategies predicated on dynamic hedging were unhinged by the inability to unwind positions as the market fell. The failure to allow for illiquidity thus led to much larger losses than the models anticipated — a classic form of model risk. Another case in point was the collapse of Askin Capital Management during the bond market crash of 1994. Askin had invested heavily in leveraged collateralised mortgage obligations (CMOs) and bet the fund on continued low interest rates. When interest rates rose, almost all the value of his fund was wiped out. During this crash, market liquidity dried up — some dealers were quoted spreads on CMOs of 10% — and Askin resorted to valuing his positions by marking them to his own model. Marking to model disguised his losses for a while but did not impress the Securities and Exchange Commission later on.

Box 11.2   Quantifying Model Risk

We can quantify model risk if we are prepared to make suitable assumptions to specify what we are uncertain about. To start with, imagine we are certain that P/L is normal with mean 0 and standard deviation 1: in this case, we have assumed all model risk away and our 1-day VaR at the 95% confidence level is known to be (or, strictly speaking, implied to be) 1.645. Now suppose that we are still certain about the P/L distribution, but uncertain about the mean and variance. This means that we are uncertain about the VaR, but can still specify a range of possible VaRs depending on our parameter uncertainty. For example, if we believe that the mean can be either -0.1 or 0.1, and the standard deviation can be -0.9 or 1.1, then we can easily show (by algebra or search) that the VaR lies in the range $[1.380, 1.909]$. The uncertainty of our VaR is thus a direct reflection of our parameter uncertainty or model risk.

We can extend this approach to incorporate the effects of any source of model risk, provided only that we can specify the uncertainty in a sufficiently precise way. For instance, if we are certain about the parameters being 0 and 1, but uncertain whether the distribution is a normal or, say, a Student t with five degrees of freedom, then the VaR is either 1.645 (if P/L is normal) or 1.561 (if P/L is a t-5), so we might say it lies in the range [1.561,1.645]. And if we are uncertain about both the distribution and the parameters, with the latter having the same possible values as before, then our VaR would lie in the range [1.305,1.909].

We can also specify our uncertainty in the form of parameter pdfs (i.e., so the 'true' parameter is taken as a drawing from a parameter density function) and in terms of a mixture distribution (i.e., so the 'true' P/L distribution depends on a drawing from a binomial or multinomial distribution, with the VaR found by applying the chosen distribution).[3]

However, the price we pay for these estimates of model risk is that we must specify our uncertainty in sufficiently precise form — as Milton Friedman said, there ain't no such thing as a free lunch.

11.2.2 Incorrect Model Application

Model risk can also arise because a good model is incorrectly applied. To quote Derman again:

> There are always implicit assumptions behind a model and its solution method. But human beings have limited foresight and great imagination, so that, inevitably, a model will be used in ways its creator never intended. This is especially true in trading environments, where not enough time can be spent on making interfaces fail-safe, but it's also a matter of principle: you just cannot foresee everything. So, even a 'correct' model, 'correctly' solved, can lead to problems. The more complex the model, the greater this possibility.
>
> (Derman (1997, p. 86))

One can give many instances of this type of problem: we might use the wrong model (e.g., we might use a Black–Scholes model for pricing interest-rate options when we should have used a Heath–Jarrow–Morton model, etc.); we might have initially had the right model, but fallen behind best market practice and not kept the model up-to-date, or not replaced it when a superior model became available; we might run Monte Carlo simulations with an insufficient number of trials, and so on. 'The only practical defence', as Derman continued, 'is to have informed and patient users who clearly comprehend both the model and the method of solution, and, even more important, understand what can go wrong' (Derman (1997, p. 86)).

11.2.3 Implementation Risk

Model risk can also arise from the way in which models are implemented. A formal model does not and cannot provide a complete specification of model implementation in every conceivable circumstance, because of the very large number of possible instruments and markets, and their varying institutional and statistical properties. However complete the model, implementation decisions still need to be made: about valuation (e.g., mark to market vs. mark to model, whether to use the mean bid–ask spread, etc.), whether and how to clean the P/L series, how to map instruments, and so on. The extent of implementation risk can be appreciated from a study by Marshall and Siegel (1997). They sought to quantify implementation risk by looking at differences in how different commercial systems applied

---

[3]Dowd (2000a) has more on this subjective approach to VaR or VaR model risk, and Cairns (2000) has a discussion of similar issues in the context of insurance risk.

the RiskMetrics variance covariance approach to specified positions based on a common set of assumptions (i.e., a 1-day holding period, a 95% VaR confidence level, delta valuation of derivatives, RiskMetrics mapping systems, etc.). They found that any two sets of VaR estimates were always different, and that VaR estimates could vary by up to nearly 30% depending on the instrument class; they also found these variations were in general positively related to complexity: the more complex the instrument or portfolio, the greater the range of variation of reported VaRs (Marshall and Siegel (1997, pp. 105–106)). These results suggested that:

> a naive view of risk assessment systems as straightforward implementations of models is incorrect. Although software is deterministic (i.e., given a complete description of all the inputs to the system, it has well-defined outputs), as software and the embedded model become more complex, from the perspective of the only partially knowledgeable user, they behave stochastically. . . .
>
> Perhaps the most critical insight of our work is that as models and their implementations become more complex, treating them as entirely deterministic black boxes is unwise, and leads to real implementation and model risks.
>
> (Marshall and Siegel (1997, pp. 105–106))

11.2.4   Other Sources of Model Risk

11.2.4.1   Incorrect Calibration

Model risk can also arise from incorrect calibration of an otherwise good model. Parameters might be estimated with error, not kept up-to-date, estimated over inappropriate sample periods, and so forth. Incorrect calibration can lead to major losses if the models are then used to price traded instruments. A very good example is the £90m loss made by the NatWest Bank over 1995–7. Over this period, a trader had fed his own estimates of volatility into a model used to price long-dated OTC interest-rate options. These estimates were too high and led to fictitious profits, and the resulting trading losses were covered up by unauthorised transfers and only uncovered in 1997. Shortly after, BZW sustained a £15m loss on mispriced currency options, and the Bank of Tokyo-Mitsubishi announced a loss of $83m from faulty use of a one-factor Black–Derman–Toy model to trade swaptions. In the latter case, this model had initially been calibrated to the market prices of at-the-money swaptions, but was subsequently used to price out-of-the-money and Bermudan swaptions. Unfortunately, it wasn't designed for these options, and the mispricing didn't come to light for several years.

VaR models can also suffer from calibration problems, particularly with the estimation of volatility and correlation. When volatility rises unexpectedly, firms tend to experience higher losses than suggested by their risk models, because 'true' volatility is higher than previously estimated volatility. A highly publicised example was the experience of LTCM in the summer of 1998: LTCM's volatility estimates during that period were way too low, and any VaR figures based on these estimates would also have been far too low. Similar problems can arise when correlations unexpectedly polarise: in such cases, the portfolio loses much of its effective diversification, and 'true' risk is likely to be considerably greater than estimates based on earlier correlations would suggest.

11.2.4.2   Programming Problems

Model risk can also arise from poor programming. Programs might have errors or bugs in them, simulation methods might use poor random number generators or suffer from discretisation errors, approximation routines might be inaccurate or fail to converge to sensible solutions, rounding errors might add up, and so on. We can also get problems when programs are revised by people who did not originally write them, when programs are not compatible with user interfaces or other systems (e.g., datafeeds), when programs become complex or hard to read (e.g., when programs are rewritten to make them computationally more efficient but then become less easy to follow). We can also get simple counting problems, and Derman (1997, p. 87) reports the example of a convertible bond model that was good at pricing many of the options features embedded in convertible bonds, but sometimes miscounted the number of coupon payments left to maturity.

11.2.4.3   Data Problems

Finally, models can give incorrect answers because poor data are fed into them. The outputs of models are only as good as the inputs fed into them — 'garbage in, garbage out', as the old saying goes. Data problems can arise from the way P/L data are constructed (e.g., whether we mark to market or mark to model, whether we use actual trading data or end-of-day data, how we deal with bid–ask spreads, etc.), from the way time is handled (e.g., whether we use calendar time, trading time, how we deal with holidays, etc.), from data being non-synchronous, and from many other sources.

Box 11.3   Endogenous Model Risk

We can also get model risk arising from the way in which traders or asset managers respond to VaR limits or VaR incentives. Traders are likely to have a reasonable idea of the errors in the parameters — particularly volatility or correlation parameters — used to estimate VaR, and such knowledge will give the traders an idea of which positions have under- and overestimated risks. If traders face VaR limits, or face risk-adjusted remuneration with risks specified in VaR terms, they will have an incentive to seek out such positions and trade them. To the extent they do, they will take on more risk than suggested by going VaR estimates, and our VaR estimates will be biased downwards. VaR estimates are also likely to be biased even if traders do not have superior knowledge of underlying parameter values. The reason for this is that if a trader uses an estimated variance–covariance matrix to select trading positions, then he or she will tend to select positions with low estimated risks, and the resulting changes in position sizes mean that the initial variance–covariance matrix will tend to underestimate the resulting portfolio risk.

Some plausible estimates of the sizes of this bias are reported by Ju and Pearson (1999, p. 22). For instance, if a trader maximises expected returns subject to a risk constraint specified in terms of estimated VaR, their results suggest that this bias is large when K, the dimension of the variance–covariance matrix, is high (e.g., 50 or more) and the sample size is small or moderate. The bias is also high when an exponentially weighted moving average estimator is used, regardless of the size of K. These results suggest that firms should be very careful about using VaR estimates to control or remunerate trading — particularly when VaR is estimated using exponentially weighted moving average procedures. Put differently, they suggest that such VaR estimates are subject to considerable endogenous model risk.

11.3   COMBATING MODEL RISK

There can be no waterproof methods for eliminating model risk entirely, but there are many ways of reducing it. These methods fall under three main headings: those applicable by the individual risk measurement/management practitioners who build models and use them; those applicable by the managers the risk practitioners report to; and organisational methods, which involve the establishment of suitable institutional or procedural structures to detect and counteract model risk.

11.3.1   Combating Model Risk: Some Guidelines for Risk Practitioners

The first line of defence against model risk is for practitioners to be on their guard against it, and some useful guidelines are:

- *Be aware of model risk.* Practitioners should keep in mind that all models are subject to model risk, so users should always be aware of the limitations of the models they use. They should also be aware of the comparative strengths and weaknesses of different models, be knowledgeable of which models suit which instruments, and be on the lookout for models that are applied inappropriately.
- *Identify, evaluate and check key assumptions.* Users should explicitly set out the key assumptions on which the model is based, evaluate the extent to which the model's results depend on these assumptions, and check them (e.g., using standard statistical tests).
- *Test models against known problems.* It is always a good idea to check a model on simple problems to which one already knows the answer, and many instruments or problems can be distilled to simple special cases that have known answers. If the model fails to give the correct answer to a known problem, then we immediately know that there is something wrong with it.
- *Choose the simplest reasonable model.* Exposure to model risk is reduced if practitioners always choose the simplest reasonable model for the task at hand. Occam's razor applies just as much in model selection as in anything else: unnecessary complexity is never a virtue. If we choose a more complex model over a simpler one, we must have a clear reason for doing so.
- *Backtest and stress test the model.* Practitioners should evaluate model adequacy using standard backtest procedures (explained in Chapter 9) or stress tests (explained in Chapter 10).
- *Estimate model risk quantitatively.* Practitioners should estimate model risk quantitatively using simulation methods (e.g., as explained in Box T11.2), or using out-of-sample historical forecasts (i.e., forecasts on data not used to estimate the model itself).
- *Don't ignore small problems.* Practitioners should resist the temptation to explain away small discrepancies in results and sweep them under the rug. Small discrepancies are often good warning signals of larger problems that will manifest themselves later if they are not sorted out.
- *Plot results and use non-parametric statistics.* Graphical outputs can be extremely revealing, and simple histograms or plots often show up errors that might otherwise be hard to detect. For example, a plot might have the wrong slope or shape or have odd features such as kinks that flag up an underlying problem. Summary statistics and simple non-parametric tests can also be very useful in imparting a feel for data and results.
- *Re-evaluate models periodically.* Models should be re-calibrated and re-estimated on a regular basis, and the methods used should be kept up-to-date.

11.3.2   Combating Model Risk: Some Guidelines for Managers

Managers can combat model risk by ensuring that they are properly informed themselves: without being expert risk modellers, they should have some basic appreciation of the issues involved so they can understand what their risk people are talking about. They should avoid thinking of risk models as black boxes, and they should learn what questions to ask and how to judge the answers. Most of all, they should learn from the mistakes of others: derivatives mistakes are well publicised and many of these stem from model risk problems and the failure of managers to pay attention to warning signals or ensure that their risk control systems are working.

Managers can also combat model risk by listening to their risk managers and taking their concerns seriously. Managers should be on their guard against the temptation to put too much trust in traders, and disregard those who question what they are up to. All too often, 'star' traders have turned out to be making large losses rather than profits, and the managers they reported to have turned a blind eye because they were dazzled by the profits they appeared to be making. The tendency to believe what one wants to believe is a key factor in many major derivatives disasters, and featured highly in Orange County in 1994 (where the board of supervisors ignored warnings about the exposure of the County's investment portfolio to a rise in interest rates), in Barings in 1994–5 (where Barings senior management ignored repeated warnings about the activities of Nick Leeson), and in many other cases. Managers need to inculcate a culture that takes risk management seriously — and they need to resist the temptation to regard risk management as an obstacle to their next bonus.

To combat model risk, managers should also be on their guard for 'model creep'. This occurs where a model is initially designed for one type of instrument, and performs well on that instrument, but is gradually applied to more diverse instruments to which it is less suited or even not suited at all. A good model can then end up as a major liability not because there is anything wrong with it, but because users don't appreciate its limitations. Similarly, managers need to be aware of product cycles and the constraints of product development: when a new model is initially developed, its superior pricing properties will tend to make large profits for those who first trade it; these profits will encourage others to enter the market, and profits will rapidly fall. This is of course as it should be, but the initially high profits will tempt other firms to get into the market prematurely, before their own models are fully functional: firms that enter the market too quickly will be unable to compete effectively with more established operators, and will sometimes make large losses. This too is just as it should be (i.e., a fair reward for greed and incompetence). Managers need to be aware of this type of cycle and conscious of the dangers of pushing their subordinates into new markets too quickly.

Managers should also have a good appreciation of how risk estimates are affected by trading strategies (i.e., they should be aware of the endogenous model risk issue; see Box 11.3). As Shaw points out:

> many factor models fail to pick up the risks of *typical* trading strategies which can be the greatest risks run by an investment bank. According to naïve yield factor models, huge spread positions between on-the-run bonds and off-the-run bonds are riskless! According to naïve volatility factor models, hedging one year (or longer dated) implied volatility with three month implied volatility is riskless, provided it is done in the 'right' proportions — i.e., the proportions built into the factor model! It is the *rule*, not the exception, for traders to put on spread trades which defeat factor models *since they use factor type models to identify richness and cheapness!*
>
> (Shaw (1997, p. 215; his emphasis))

In other words, managers need to appreciate how the choice of model affects trading strategies, and how the latter in turn can then distort the model outputs.

Finally, managers need to be on their guard against the tricks that people play — how traders can hide losses and 'game' VaR models to their advantage (see, e.g., Box 11.3), and so on. It is also important that managers don't under-rate the abilities of those below them to play the system and get away with it: a 1997 survey by Cap Gemini found that although three-quarters of risk managers believed that their organisation was immune to a Barings-style scandal, almost the same proportion of traders believed the opposite, and 85% of traders believed they could hide trades from their managers.[4] These findings suggest that many firms are a lot less secure than their managers think. In combating these sorts of problems, managers also need to recognise that their model validators and risk managers must have the knowledge and skills to match traders, and this means that they must be remunerated in ways comparable to traders — otherwise, there is little incentive for those with the necessary skills to want to do anything but trade.

Managers can also reduce their vulnerability to model risk problems by encouraging a multi-disciplinary team approach to model building. They should not see models as incomprehensible formulas that quants or risk modellers hand over to programmers to make even more incomprehensible. Instead, they should see models as the product of an interdisciplinary team, involving inputs from mathematicians, statisticians, computer scientists, finance experts, accountants, traders, model users, and others. They should encourage people from these disparate groups to understand each other, and foster a climate of constructive criticism.

11.3.3 Institutional Methods to Combat Model Risk

Firms can also combat the dangers of model risk by establishing suitable procedures or institutional structures to deal with them.

11.3.3.1 Procedures to Vet, Check and Review Models

One very basic defence is a sound system to vet models before they are approved for use and then check and periodically review them. A good model-vetting procedure is proposed by Crouhy *et al.* (2001, pp. 607–608) and involves the following four steps:

- *Documentation.* First, the risk manager should ask for a complete specification of the model, including its mathematics, components, computer code, and implementation features (e.g., numerical methods and pricing algorithms used). The information should be in sufficient detail to enable the risk manager to reproduce the model from the information provided.
- *Soundness.* The risk manager should check that the model is a reasonable one for the instrument(s) or portfolio concerned.
- *Benchmark modelling.* The risk manager should develop a benchmark model and test it against well-understood approximation or simulation methods.
- *Check results and test the proposed model.* The final stage involves the risk manager using the benchmark model to check the performance of the proposed model. The model should also be checked for zero-arbitrage properties such as put–call parity, and should then be stress tested to help determine the range of parameter values for which it will give reasonable estimates.

All these stages should be carried out free of undue pressures from the front office: it goes without saying that traders should not be allowed to vet their own pricing models and then bet the firm's money on them. However, there is also a need to vet VaR and ETL models as well, and this raises a difficult problem: if we use risk managers to check the traders' models, then who checks the risk managers' models? Who guards the guardians? The best answer is to provide for some independent assessment of the risk models too, and this can only come from a separate risk measurement assessment unit (i.e., separate from the normal risk measurement unit) that reports to the senior risk officer or above.

---

[4]Paul-Choudhury (1997, p. 19).

It is important to keep good records, so each model should be fully documented in the middle (or risk) office. Risk managers should have full access to the model at all times, as well as access to real trading and other data that might be necessary to check models and validate results. The ideal should be to give the middle office enough information to be able to check any model or model results at any time, and do so using appropriate (i.e., up-to-date) data sets. This information set should also include a log of model performance with particular attention to any problems encountered and what (if anything) has been done about them. Finally, there should be a periodic review (as well as occasional spot checks) of the models in use, to ensure that model calibration is up-to-date and that models are upgraded in line with market best practice, and to ensure that obsolete models are identified as such and taken out of use.

11.3.3.2 Independent Risk Oversight

At a more fundamental level — and this is absolutely critical to sound risk management — the firm should also set up a suitable independent risk oversight (IRO) or middle office unit. This unit should encompass risk measurement as well as risk management, should be independent of line execution areas (e.g., such as treasury, trading, portfolio management, asset–liability management, etc.), and its head, the chief risk officer (CRO), should report to the CEO and, ideally, sit on the board or other governing body. The middle office should have a clear mandate from senior management, and its policies should reflect the corporate policies towards risk — the corporate risk appetite, and so on. To help avoid any temptation for the middle office to go along with excessive risk-taking elsewhere in the organization, the remuneration of the CRO and his or her staff should not be tied to the performance of other units (e.g., such as trading profits).

This unit should have authority to approve or block the use of any pricing or risk measurement models anywhere in the organization. It should have authority to analyse and monitor risk independently of other business units, and particularly the front office. It should seek to ensure a balance between an excessively prohibitionist stance on risk (i.e., everything not expressly allowed is forbidden) and an excessively lenient stance (i.e., everything not expressly forbidden is allowed), and also aim to ensure that all interested parties are fully involved in the firm's internal risk measurement/management dialogue. Naturally, the middle office should also be responsible for risk measurement, including stress testing, backtesting and (at least some) contingency planning, for ensuring that all models are adequate for the tasks to which they were being put (i.e., and so taking responsibility for vetting, checking and monitoring the models used), for reporting and disseminating risk information throughout the organization, and for protecting and maintaining the integrity of the firm's risk measurement and risk management systems.

Box 11.4   Other Institutional Methods of Dealing with Model Risk

Besides having good model vetting procedures and independent risk oversight, there are also other ways that firms can deal with model risk.

One sound practice is for firms to keep reserves against possible losses from model risk. The reserves attributed to a position should reflect some measure of the model risk involved, so that positions with higher model risk get higher reserve charges than positions with lower model risk. Such charges not only provide the firm with a cushion to absorb possible losses from model risk, but also help to ensure that the cost of model risk is accounted for and attributed to the positions concerned.

Firms can also help to limit their exposure to model risk by running stress tests or scenario analyses to test their degree of dependence on particular assumptions — that is, to run tests to determine prospective losses if these assumptions don't hold. This is especially recommended when trying to assess the potential model risk arising from incorrect volatility, correlation and liquidity assumptions.

Finally, firms can counteract model risk by taking account of it in setting position limits. If a position is known to have considerable model risk, a firm can limit its exposure to this source of model risk by imposing a tighter position limit.

Once we can measure model risk (or, indeed, any risk), the way is open to deal with it by setting reserves, charging for capital, and imposing position limits. But — as always in these matters — the quality of our results is entirely dependent on the quality of our risk measurement and risk management systems.

11.4   CONCLUSIONS

Model risk is one of the most important and least appreciated areas of market risk measurement: everything we do in market risk measurement presupposes that we already know the models, parameter values or other specifications we are using; and yet the embarrassing truth is that we actually *know* very little at all. The result is a yawning chasm between what we assume we know and what we actually know, and it is this gap that makes us vulnerable to model risk. Model risk therefore casts its shadow over everything we do in risk measurement, and prudence suggests that we should take it seriously — that we should keep asking ourselves what would happen if our assumptions fail to hold. Of course, this is much easier to say than to do, but the financial markets are littered with the corpses of those who have ignored model risk and thought they could get away with it, and these include some of the biggest names of their day. At the end of the day, model risk is like the ghost at the banquet — an unwelcome guest, but one that we would be wise not to ignore.

11.5   RECOMMENDED READING

Beder (1995a,b); Berkowitz and O'Brien (2001); Cairns (2000); Crouhy *et al.* (2001, ch. 15); Derman (1997); Dowd (2000a); Ju and Pearson (1999); Kato and Yoshiba (2000); LHabitant (2000); Marshall and Siegel (1997); Shaw (1997).

An Introduction to Market Risk
Measurement: Toolkit

Toolkit Contents

Tool No. 1
Estimating VaR and ETL Using
Order Statistics

The theory of order statistics is very useful for risk measurement because it gives us a practical and accurate means of estimating a VaR or ETL distribution function — and this is useful because it enables us to estimate VaR and ETL confidence intervals.

If we have a sample of n profit/loss observations, we can regard each observation as giving an estimate of VaR at an implied confidence level. For example, if $n = 100$, we can take the VaR at the 95% confidence level as the negative of the sixth smallest P/L observation,[1] the VaR at the 99% confidence level as the negative of the second smallest, and so on. We therefore take the VaR at a confidence level cl to be equal to the negative of the rth lowest observation, where r is equal to $100(1 - cl) + 1$. More generally, with n observations, the VaR is equal to the negative of rth lowest observation, where $r = n(1 - cl) + 1$.

The rth order statistic is the rth lowest (or highest) in a sample of n observations, and the theory of order statistics is well established in the statistical literature (see, e.g., Kendall and Stuart (1972, ch. 14) or Reiss (1989)). Suppose our observations $x_1, x_2, \ldots, x_n$ come from some known distribution (or cumulative density) function $F(x)$, with rth order statistic $x_{(r)}$. Hence, $x_{(1)} \leq x_{(2)} \leq \cdots \leq x_{(n)}$. The probability that j of our n observations do not exceed a fixed value x must then obey the following binomial distribution:

$$\Pr\{j \text{ observations} \leq x\} = \binom{n}{j} \{F(x)\}^j \{1 - F(x)\}^{n-j} \tag{T1.1}$$

It follows that the probability that at least r observations in the sample do not exceed x is also a binomial:

$$G_r(x) = \sum_{j=r}^{n} \binom{n}{j} \{F(x)\}^j \{1 - F(x)\}^{n-j} \tag{T1.2}$$

$G_r(x)$ is therefore the distribution function of our order statistic (Kendall and Stuart (1973, p. 348) or Reiss (1989, p. 20)). It follows, in turn, that $G_r(x)$ also gives the distribution function of our VaRs.

Given the VaR confidence level and holding period, this VaR distribution function provides us with estimates of our VaR *and* of its associated confidence intervals. The median (i.e., 50-percentile) of the estimated VaR distribution function gives us a natural estimate of our VaR, and estimates of the lower and upper percentiles of the VaR distribution function give us estimates of the bounds of our VaR confidence interval. This is useful, because the calculations are accurate and easy to carry out on a spreadsheet. Equation (T1.2) is also very general and gives us confidence intervals for *any* distribution function $F(x)$, parametric (normal, t, etc.) or empirical.

---

[1] There are two reasons why I take the VaR to be the negative of the sixth observation. The first is that a P/L series gives positive values for profitable outcomes and negative values for losses, so we have to negate the P/L series to find the VaR because the latter is the maximum likely *loss* (rather than profit) at the specified level of confidence. The sixth observation is then chosen because we want 5% of the probability mass to lie to the left of our VaR. Of course, we might equally well choose any point between the fifth and sixth observations (e.g., such as their mean), but I stick with the sixth observation here because it is simpler.

To use this approach, all we therefore need to do is specify $F(x)$ (as normal, t, etc.), set our parameter values, and use Equation (T1.2) to estimate our VaR distribution function.

T1.1   THE ORDER STATISTICS APPROACH APPLIED TO NORMAL VAR

Suppose we want to apply the order statistics (OS) approach to estimate the normal VaR distribution function. We assume that $F(x)$ is normal and use Equation (T1.2) to estimate three key parameters of the VaR distribution: the median or 50-percentile of the estimated VaR distribution, which can be interpreted as an OS estimate of normal VaR; and the 2.5- and 97.5-percentiles of the estimated VaR distribution, which can be interpreted as the OS estimates of the bounds of the 95% confidence interval for normal VaR.

Some illustrative estimates for the VaR at the 99% confidence level are given in Table T1.1. To facilitate comparison, the table also shows the estimates of normal VaR based on the 'standard' normal VaR formula:

$$Estimated\ VaR = -\alpha_{cl}s - m \qquad (T1.3)$$

where α_{cl} is the standard normal variate corresponding to the chosen VaR confidence level. The main results are:

- The confidence interval — the gap between the 2.5- and 97.5-percentiles — is quite wide for low values of n, but narrows as n gets larger.
- As n rises, the median of the estimated VaR distribution converges to the standard estimate of VaR given by Equation (T1.3).
- The confidence interval is (in this case, a little) wider for more extreme VaR confidence levels than it is for the more central ones.

Table T1.1   Order statistic estimates of normal VaRs and confidence intervals

	(a) As n varies				
No. of observations	100	500	1,000	5,000	10,000
Upper bound of confidence interval	2.82	2.62	2.54	2.43	2.40
Median of VaR distribution	2.13	2.28	2.30	2.32	2.32
Standard estimate of VaR	2.33	2.33	2.33	2.33	2.33
Lower bound of confidence interval	1.60	1.99	2.09	2.22	2.25
Width of interval/median	57%	28%	20%	9%	6%
	(b) As VaR confidence level varies				
VaR confidence level	**0.90**		**0.95**		**0.99**
Upper bound of confidence interval	1.43		1.82		2.62
Median of VaR distribution	1.27		1.63		2.28
Standard estimate of VaR	1.28		1.64		2.33
Lower bound of confidence interval	1.13		1.45		1.99
Width of interval/median	23%		23%		28%

Note: (a) Estimated with VaR confidence level 0.99, $m = 0$, and $s = 1$. (b) Estimated with $n = 500$, VaR confidence level = 0.99, $m = 0$, and $s = 1$. The confidence interval is specified at a 95% level of confidence, and the lower and upper bounds of the confidence interval are estimated as the 2.5- and 97.5-percentiles of the estimated VaR distribution (Equation (T1.2)).

T1.2   OTHER VaRs AND ETLs

The same approach can also be used to estimate the percentiles of other VaR distribution functions (or if we wish to estimate confidence intervals for non-normal VaRs). If we wish to estimate the percentiles of a non-normal parametric VaR, we replace the normal distribution function $F(x)$ by the non-normal equivalent — the t-distribution function, the Gumbel distribution function, and so on. We can also use the same approach to estimate the confidence intervals for an empirical distribution function (i.e., for historical simulation VaR), where $F(x)$ is some empirical distribution function.

We can also apply an OS approach to the estimation of ETL confidence levels. We can do so in one of two ways: we can derive an average tail loss series from the original P/L series and then apply an OS approach to the average tail loss series; or we can derive the percentile of the VaR distribution function and take the ETL percentile as the average of losses in excess of the VaR percentile.

T1.3   CONCLUSIONS

The OS approach to VaR and ETL provides an ideal method for estimating the confidence intervals for our VaRs and ETLs. In particular, the OS approach is:

- Completely general, in that it can be applied to any parametric or non-parametric VaR or ETL.
- Reasonable even for relatively small samples, because it is not based on asymptotic theory — although it is also the case that estimates based on small samples will also be less accurate, precisely because the samples are small.
- Easy to implement in practice.

In short, the OS approach is ideal for market risk practitioners worried about the accuracy of their VaR and ETL estimates. It also means that practitioners no longer have any excuse for reporting parametric VaR and ETL estimates without also giving some indication of their accuracy.

**Box T1.1   Applying the Order Statistics Approach to VaR and ETL
in the IMRM Toolbox**

We can easily implement the OS approach using the IMRM Toolbox. We can estimate specified (e.g., 2.5, 50 and 97.5) percentiles of a normal VaR distribution function using functions 'normalvardfperc', and the corresponding percentiles of t, Gumbel, Fréchet and empirical (or historical simulation) VaR distribution functions using the functions 'tvardfperc', 'gumbelvardfperc', 'frechetvardfperc' and 'hsvardfperc'. If we wish to estimate ETLs instead of VaRs, we can use the corresponding ETL functions: 'normaletldfperc', 'tetldfperc', 'gumbeletldfperc', 'frechetetldfperc' and 'hsetldfperc'.

T1.4   RECOMMENDED READING

Dowd (2001); Kendall and Stuart (1972, ch. 14); Reiss (1989, ch. 0 and 10).

Tool No. 2

The Cornish–Fisher Expansion

The Cornish–Fisher expansion is used to determine the percentiles of distributions that are near normal. The actual expansion provides an adjustment factor that can be used to adjust estimated percentiles (or variates) for non-normality, and the adjustment is reliable provided departures from normality are 'small'. We can therefore use the Cornish–Fisher expansion to estimate VaR and ETL when the P/L distribution has some (but not too much) non-normality.

Suppose that α_{cl} is a standard normal variate for a confidence level cl (i.e., so $\alpha_{0.95} = -1.645$, etc.). Then the Cornish–Fisher expansion is:

$$\alpha_{cl} + (1/6)(\alpha_{cl}^2 - 1)\rho_3 + (1/24)(\alpha_{cl}^3 - 3\alpha_{cl})\rho_4 - (1/36)(2\alpha_{cl}^3 - 5\alpha_{cl})\rho_3^2 + \text{higher order terms}$$
$$\text{(T2.1)}$$

where ρ_3 is the distribution's skewness coefficient and ρ_4 is its kurtosis (see Lee and Lin (1992, p. 234) and Zangari (1996a, p. 9)). If we treat the higher order terms as negligible — which is tantamount to assuming that departures from normality are 'small' — the expansion becomes:

$$\alpha_{cl} + (1/6)(\alpha_{cl}^2 - 1)\rho_3 + (1/24)(\alpha_{cl}^3 - 3\alpha_{cl})\rho_4 - (1/36)(2\alpha_{cl}^3 - 5\alpha_{cl})\rho_3^2 \qquad \text{(T2.2)}$$

To use the expansion, we simply replace α_{cl} by (T2.2) as our estimated percentile. This is equivalent to adjusting the normal variate α_{cl} for non-normal skewness and/or kurtosis.

For example, suppose we have a slightly non-normal distribution with mean 0, standard deviation 1, skewness 0.5 and kurtosis 4. (A normal has skewness and kurtosis equal to 0 and 3 respectively.) The values of the Cornish–Fisher expansion for cl values equal to 0.5, 0.90, 0.95 and 0.99 are reported in Table T2.1, along with values of the standard normal variate α_{cl} for each of these cl-values. These results show that the Cornish–Fisher expansion can make a notable difference to estimated percentiles, even for small departures from normality.[1]

Table T2.1 The Cornish–Fisher expansion

	$cl = 0.5$	$cl = 0.9$	$cl = 0.90$	$cl = 0.99$
Cornish–Fisher expansion	0.083	1.171	1.478	2.098
Normal variate	0	1.282	1.645	2.326
% error in normal variate	N/A	−9.5%	−11.3%	−10.9%

---

[1] The IMRM Toolbox has two Cornish–Fisher functions: we can use the function 'cornishfishervar' to estimate the Cornish–Fisher VaR and the function 'cornishfisheretl' to estimate the corresponding ETL. These take as their inputs the first four moments of the P/L distribution and the VaR confidence level.

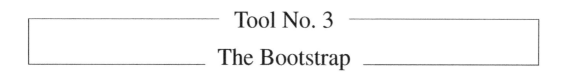

Tool No. 3

The Bootstrap

The bootstrap is a simple and useful method of assessing the accuracy of parameter estimates without having to resort to strong parametric assumptions or formula derivations. The roots of the bootstrap go back a couple of centuries, but the idea only took off in the last couple of decades after it was developed and popularised by the work of Bradley Efron (Efron (1979)). It was Efron, too, who first gave it its name. The name 'bootstrap' refers to the phrase 'to pull oneself up by one's bootstraps', and is believed to be based on the 18th century *Adventures of Baron Munchausen*. In one of these stories, the Baron had fallen to the bottom of a deep lake and was not able to free himself; but just when all seemed lost, he thought to pick himself up by his own bootstraps and so saved himself.

The main purpose of the bootstrap is to assess the accuracy of parameter estimates — and, in particular, the bootstrap enables us to assess the accuracy of parameter estimates without having to resort to potentially dangerous parametric assumptions (e.g., as in standard parametric density estimation approaches). The bootstrap is easy to use because it does not require the user to engage in any difficult mathematical or statistical analysis and, even where we have formulas for parameter accuracy (e.g., as under some parametric approaches), the bootstrap often gives us more accurate estimates of parameter accuracy than these formulas do.

T3.1   THE BOOTSTRAP PROCEDURE

Suppose we have a sample drawn from a population. The parameters of the population distribution are unknown — and, more likely than not, so too is the distribution itself. We estimate a parameter θ — such as a mean, median, standard deviation, or quantile (VaR) — and wish to assess the accuracy of our estimate $\hat{\theta}$. The bootstrap allows us to do this by giving us an estimate of the standard error of our parameter estimator $\hat{\theta}$ or an estimate of the confidence interval for our parameter θ. We can always use the bootstrap regardless of how complicated the derivation of $\hat{\theta}$ might be, and regardless of whether we have any formulas for the standard error of $\hat{\theta}$.

The basic bootstrap procedure is very simple. We start with a sample of size n. We now draw a new sample of the same size from this original sample, taking care to replace each chosen observation back in the sample pool after it has been drawn. In doing so, we would typically find that some observations get chosen more than once, and others don't get chosen at all: so the new sample would typically be different from the original one, even though every observation included in it was drawn from the original sample. Once we have our new sample, we obtain a new parameter estimate. We then repeat the process B times, say, and obtain a bootstrapped sample of B parameter estimates; and we use this sample to estimate a confidence interval.

The programs to compute bootstrap statistics are easy to write and, as Efron and Tibshirani write, 'With these programs in place, the data analyst is free to use any estimator, no matter how complicated, with the assurance that he or she will also have a reasonable idea of the estimator's accuracy' (Efron and Tibshirani (1993, p. 15)). The most obvious price of the bootstrap is increased computation,[1] but this is no longer a serious problem.[2]

T3.2   BOOTSTRAPPED CONFIDENCE INTERVALS

There are various ways we can use bootstrap methods to construct confidence intervals for a parameter of interest. For a start, we know that the distribution of $\hat{\theta}$ often approaches normality as the number of samples gets large. In such circumstances, we can estimate a confidence interval for θ assuming $\hat{\theta}$ to be approximately normal: if $\hat{\theta}$ is our estimate of θ and $\hat{\sigma}$ is our estimate of the standard error of $\hat{\theta}$, our 95% confidence level is:

$$[\hat{\theta} - 1.96\hat{\sigma}, \hat{\theta} + 1.96\hat{\sigma}] \tag{T3.1}$$

If the sample size is not so large, we can replace the normal confidence interval with a Student t confidence interval with $n - 1$ degrees of freedom (e.g., if $n = 30$, we replace 1.96 in (T3.1) with 2.045).

We can also estimate confidence intervals using percentiles of the sample distribution: the upper and lower bounds of the confidence interval would be given by the percentile points (or quantiles) of the sample distribution of parameter estimates. This percentile interval approach does not rely on parametric theory, asymptotic or otherwise.[3]

T3.3   DEALING WITH DATA DEPENDENCY

Perhaps the main limitation of the bootstrap is that standard bootstrap procedures presuppose that observations are independent, and they can be unreliable if this assumption does not hold. Fortunately, there are ways in which we can modify bootstraps to allow for dependence:

- If we are prepared to make parametric assumptions, we can model the dependence parametrically (e.g., using a GARCH procedure). We can then bootstrap from the residuals, which should be independent. However, the drawback of this solution is that it requires us to make parametric assumptions and of course presupposes that those assumptions are valid.
- An alternative is to use a block approach: we divide sample data into non-overlapping blocks of equal length, and select a block at random. However, this approach can be tricky to implement and can lead to problems because it tends to 'whiten' the data.
- A third solution is to modify the probabilities with which individual observations are chosen. Instead of assuming that each observation is chosen with the same probability, we can make the

---

[1] If we wish to, we can also reduce the number of computations needed and/or increase the accuracy of results by using variance reduction methods such as control variates or importance sampling. These methods are discussed further in Tool No. 6: Monte Carlo Simulation Methods.

[2] One other potential problem with the bootstrap is bias. A large bias can be a major problem, but in most applications the bias is — fortunately — small or zero. There are various ways we can estimate the bias and correct for it. However, the bias can have a (relatively) large standard error, and in such cases, correcting for the bias is not always a good idea, because the bias-corrected estimate can have a larger standard error than the unadjusted, biased, estimate.

[3] Nonetheless, this basic percentile interval approach is limited itself, and particularly if our parameter estimates are biased. It is therefore often better to use more refined percentile approaches, and perhaps the best of these is the bias-corrected and accelerated (or BC_a) approach, which generates a 'substantial improvement' in both theory and practice over the basic percentile interval approach (Efron and Tibshirani (1993, p. 178)). For more on this and other improvements, see Efron and Tibshirani (1993, ch. 14).

probabilities of selection dependent on the time indices of recently selected observations: so, for example, if the sample data are in chronological order and observation i has just been chosen, then observation $i + 1$ is more likely to be chosen next than most other observations.

Box T3.1   MATLAB Bootstrap Procedures

For those wishing to use MATLAB to carry out bootstrap operations, the basic MATLAB package has the 'bootstat' function which provides bootstrapped results for a number of specified statistics.

The IMRM Toolbox also has some bootstrap procedures tailor-made for risk measurement. These include: 'bootstrapvar', which estimates VaR using a basic bootstrap approach; 'bootstrapvarfigure', which plots a histogram of bootstrapped VaR estimates; and 'bootstrapvarconfinterval', which estimates the bounds of a bootstrapped VaR confidence interval outlined in the text. This Toolbox also has comparable ETL estimation procedures — 'bootstrapetl', etc.

T3.4   RECOMMENDED READING

Efron and Tibshirani (1993); Davison and Hinkley (1997).

Tool No. 4

Principal Components Analysis

Principal components analysis (PCA) is a method of gaining insight into the characteristics of a data set. It is helpful in risk management because it can provide a simpler representation of the processes that generate a data set. This is useful because it enables us to reduce the dimensionality of a data set and so reduce the number of variance–covariance parameters we need to estimate. Such methods are very useful — and sometimes even necessary — when we have large dimensionality problems (e.g., when measuring the risks of portfolios with hundreds of different assets). They can also be useful for other tasks, such as cleaning data and developing mapping systems.

T4.1 THEORY

Let Σ be a real, symmetric, positive semidefinite matrix of dimension $m \times m$. An eigenvector of Σ is an $m \times 1$ vector $\mathbf{v} \neq 0$ that exists if there is a real number λ, known as an eigenvalue, such that $\Sigma \mathbf{v} = \lambda \mathbf{v}$. If Σ has rank k, then Σ has k non-trivially distinct eigenvectors, $\mathbf{v}_i$, each of which has its own positive eigenvalue λ_i. However, any scalar multiple of an eigenvector is also an eigenvector, so a given eigenvector is unique only up to a linear transformation.

Now suppose that $\mathbf{x}$ is an $m \times 1$ random vector, with covariance matrix Σ, and let Λ be a diagonal matrix (i.e., a matrix whose off-diagonal terms are zero) of dimension $m \times m$, such that:

$$\Sigma = \mathbf{A}^T \Lambda \mathbf{A} \tag{T4.1}$$

where $\mathbf{A}$ is the matrix of eigenvectors of Σ, and the diagonal elements of Λ, namely, $\lambda_1, \lambda_2, \ldots, \lambda_m$, are the eigenvalues of Σ. For convenience, and without losing any generality, assume also that $\mathbf{A}\mathbf{A}^T = \mathbf{I}$. The principal components of $\mathbf{x}$ are the linear combinations of the individual $\mathbf{x}$-variables produced by premultiplying $\mathbf{x}$ by $\mathbf{A}$:

$$\mathbf{p} = \mathbf{A}\mathbf{x} \tag{T4.2}$$

The variance–covariance matrix of $\mathbf{p}$, $\mathbf{VC}(\mathbf{p})$, is then:

$$\mathbf{VC}(\mathbf{p}) = \mathbf{VC}(\mathbf{A}\mathbf{x}) = \mathbf{A}\Sigma\mathbf{A}^T = \mathbf{A}\mathbf{A}^T\Lambda\mathbf{A}\mathbf{A}^T = \Lambda \tag{T4.3}$$

(see, e.g., Thisted (1988, p. 121)). Since Λ is a diagonal matrix, Equation (T4.3) tells us that the different principal components are uncorrelated with each other. It also tells us that the variances of our principal components are given by the diagonal elements of Λ, the eigenvalues.

In addition, we can choose the order of our principal components so that the eigenvalues are in declining order, i.e:

$$\lambda_1 \geq \lambda_2 \geq \cdots \geq \lambda_n > 0 \tag{T4.4}$$

The first principal component therefore 'explains' more of the variability of our original data than the second principal component, the second 'explains' more than the third, and so on.[1]

---

[1] However, in using principal components analysis, the way we measure our data can significantly affect our results. It is therefore important to adopt a measurement/scaling system that makes sense for the data we have. We can do so using

In short, the principal components of our m original variables are m artificial variables constructed so that the first principal component 'explains' as much as it can of the variance of these variables; the second principal component 'explains' as much as it can of the remaining variance, but is uncorrelated with the first principal component; the third principal component explains as much as it can of the remaining variance, and is uncorrelated with the first two principal components; and so forth.

Since the principal components are constructed as linear combinations of the original variables, the complete set of m principal components will explain all (i.e., 100%) of the movement (or total variance) of our original variables. However, it will often be that the first few principal components will explain a very considerable proportion of the total variance of our original variables. The standard financial example is where the original variables might be different spot (or interest) rates across the maturity spectrum, and where the first three principal components are commonly reported to explain over 95% of spot rate behaviour (see, e.g., Golub and Tilman (1997, p. 73)). In this particular application of PCA, the first three principal components also have ready interpretations in terms of interest rate dynamics: the first can be interpreted as reflecting the level of the spot rate curve, the second can be interpreted as reflecting its steepness, and the third can be interpreted as reflecting its curvature.

PCA is particularly useful for reducing the dimensionality of a problem. If we have m variables with a variance–covariance matrix Σ, then Σ will have $m(m + 1)/2$ separate terms — reflecting m diagonal (or variance) and $m(m - 1)/2$ off-diagonal (or covariance) terms, but the eigenvalue matrix Λ has only m terms. PCA therefore reduces the number of variance–covariance terms we need to work with from $m(m + 1)/2$ to m — which is a very considerable reduction if m is large. Consider the following:

- If $m = 10$, Σ has 55 separate terms and Λ has 10, so PCA reduces the number of covariance terms by over 80%.
- If $m = 50$, Σ has 1,275 separate terms and Λ has 50, so PCA reduces the number of covariance terms by over 96%.
- If $m = 100$, Σ has 5,050 separate terms and Λ has 100, so PCA reduces the number of covariance terms by over 98%.

PCA can therefore lead to very substantial savings in the number of parameters we need to estimate, and the savings rise with the dimensionality of the problem or number of original variables.

We would usually expect to make even bigger savings in the number of variance–covariance parameters because we would rarely want to use all the principal components. In practice, we would often expect to use no more than the first three or four principal components. For example, if we had spot rate data, we might use the first three principal components and then have only three variance–covariance terms to estimate, namely, the variances of the first three principal components.[2]

T4.2 PRINCIPAL COMPONENTS ANALYSIS: AN ILLUSTRATION

To give an illustration, suppose we have a set of 1,000 observations of the returns on each of five assets. These returns are randomly drawn from a multivariate standard normal distribution, with

standardised data (i.e., using data measured relative to means and standard deviations) or by working with correlation rather than variance–covariance matrices. In finance, we might also want to make sure that all our data are measured as returns or as P/L measured in the same units.

[2]The basic PCA approach is of course open to modification. For example, we can adjust the variance–covariance matrix Σ for non-linear factors such as the gamma effects of derivatives (as in Brummelhuis *et al.* (2000)). This sensitivity-adjusted approach is particularly useful for derivatives positions.

Table T4.1   Principal components VaR and ETL estimates

VaR confidence level	Number of principal components				
	1	2	3	4	5
	(a) VaR				
0.90	0.791	0.783	0.820	0.821	0.818
0.95	1.063	1.044	1.017	1.020	1.017
	(b) ETL				
0.90	1.107	1.102	1.103	1.103	1.103
0.95	1.302	1.296	1.297	1.299	1.297

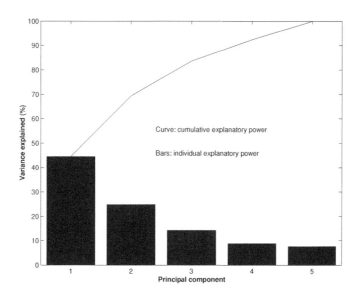

Figure T4.1   Explanatory power of the principal components.

the correlation between assets i and j equal to $0.5\sqrt{(i-j)^2}$, and we have \$0.20 invested in each asset. We begin with a preliminary analysis of the principal components of our returns, the results of which are presented in Figure T4.1.[3] These indicate that the first principal component explains about 45% of the movement in our data, the second about 25%, the third about 15%, and so forth.

We now estimate the VaRs and ETLs of our portfolio, for the 90% and 95% confidence levels.[4] These results are presented in Table T4.1, and show that the PCA estimates of VaRs are stable with 3 or more principal components, and the ETL estimates are stable with 2 or more principal components.

T4.3   USING PCA: FURTHER CONSIDERATIONS

When using PCA, it is important to keep in mind a couple of warnings made by Wilson (1994a). One of these is that estimates of principal components based on historical data can be quite unstable,

---

[3] These results are obtained using the 'pcaprelim' function.

[4] These results are obtained using the 'pcavar' and 'pcaetl' functions.

so forecasts based on PCA need to be used with care. However, his results also suggest that some simple rules of thumb — such as taking moving averages of our principal components — can help to mitigate this instability.

A second point is that we should be careful about using too many principal components. Whilst it is always true that adding more principal components will increase the fit of our PCA model to the historical data, we are more concerned in practice with the predictive ability of our model. This means that we only want to add principal components that represent stable relationships that are good for forecasting, and there will often come a point where additional principal components merely lead to the model tracking noise — and so undermine the forecasting ability of our model. Modellers should therefore be careful in the number of principal components they choose to work with.

T4.4   RECOMMENDED READING

Adelman (1990); Golub and Tilman (1997); Kennedy and Gentle (1980, ch. 12.3); Kloek (1990); Niffikeer *et al.* (2000); Phoa (2000); Singh (1997); Thisted (1988); Wilson (1994a).

Tool No. 5

Extreme Value VaR and ETL

There are many problems in risk management that deal with extreme events — events that are unlikely to occur, but can be very costly when they do. These include large market falls (e.g., as occurred on October 19, 1987), the failures of major institutions (Long-Term Capital Management, Enron, etc.) and the outbreak of financial crises. Consequently, risk management practitioners sometimes need to estimate risk measures for extreme events.

However, estimating VaR and ETL at extreme confidence levels forces us to confront a difficult problem: we have, by definition, relatively few extreme observations on which to base our estimates. Estimates of extreme VaR and ETL are very uncertain, and this uncertainty increases as our confidence level gets higher (or as our extremes become more extreme). This uncertainty is particularly serious if we are interested in extreme VaRs and ETLs not only *within* the range of observed data, but *well beyond* it — as might be the case if we were interested in the risks associated with events more extreme than any in our historical data set (e.g., an unprecedented stock market fall).

Practitioners must inevitably respond by relying on assumptions to make up for lack of data, but, unfortunately, the assumptions they make are often questionable. For example, in the risk management area, practitioners often assume that financial returns are normal, and this assumption is highly questionable because observed financial returns tend to have fatter than normal tails, and because assuming normality in such cases can lead to serious underestimates of the risks concerned. A more satisfactory response is to assume that returns follow a fat-tailed distribution, and a number of such distributions have been proposed. However, the chosen distribution is often selected arbitrarily and then fitted to the whole data set. This means that the fitted distribution will tend to accommodate the more central observations, because there are so many of them, rather than the extreme observations, which are rare by definition. This type of approach is good if we are interested in the central part of the distribution (e.g., such as the mean), but ill suited to handling extremes.

We therefore need an approach that comes to terms with the basic problem posed by extreme value estimation: that the estimation of the risks associated with low-frequency events with limited data is inevitably problematic, and that these difficulties increase as the events concerned become rarer. Inference about the extreme tail is always uncertain, because we have so few tail observations to go on, and our results can be very sensitive to the values of individual extreme observations.

Yet these problems are not unique to risk management, but also occur in other disciplines as well. The standard example is hydrology, where engineers have long struggled with the question of how high dikes, sea walls and similar barriers should be to contain the probabilities of floods within reasonable limits. They have had to do so with even less data than financial risk practitioners usually have, and their quantile estimates — the flood water levels they were contending with — were also typically well out of the range of their sample data. So hydrologists have had to grapple with comparable problems to those faced by insurers and risk managers, but in more difficult circumstances.

The good news is that they have made considerable progress with this type of problem, and researchers in these fields have developed a tailor-made approach — extreme value (EV) theory — that is ideally suited to these sorts of problems.[1] This EV approach focuses on the distinctiveness of extreme values and makes as much use as possible of what theory has to offer. The key to this approach is a theorem — the extreme value theorem — that tells us what the limiting distribution of extreme values should look like. This theorem and various associated results tell us what we should be estimating, and the EV literature also gives us some guidance on how to estimate the parameters involved. Furthermore, the EV approach not only enables us to estimate extreme VaRs and ETLs, but also enables us to gauge the precision of our risk estimates by constructing confidence intervals around them.

T5.1 GENERALISED EXTREME VALUE THEORY

T5.1.1 Theory

Suppose we have n observations of a loss/profit series X (i.e., positive for losses, negative for profits). We assume to begin with that X is independently and identically distributed (iid) from some unknown distribution $F(x) = \text{Prob}(X \leq x)$, and we wish to estimate the extreme risks, the extreme VaRs and ETLs, associated with the distribution of X. Clearly, this poses a problem because we don't know what $F(x)$ actually is.

This is where EVT comes to our rescue. Under these and other relatively innocuous assumptions, the celebrated Fisher–Tippett theorem (1928) tells us that as n gets large, the distribution of extreme values of X (interpreted as the maximum of our set of observations) converges to the following generalised extreme value (GEV) distribution:

$$H_{\xi,\mu,\sigma} = \begin{cases} \exp[-(1 + \xi(x - \mu)/\sigma)^{-1/\xi}] \\ \exp[-\exp(-(x - \mu)/\sigma)] \end{cases} \quad \text{if} \quad \begin{matrix} \xi \neq 0 \\ \xi = 0 \end{matrix} \tag{T5.1}$$

where x satisfies the condition $1 + \xi(x - \mu)/\sigma > 0$, and where the case $\xi = 0$ is the limit of the distribution function as $\xi \to 0$ (see, e.g., Embrechts *et al.* (1997, p. 316)). This distribution has three parameters. The first two are μ, the location parameter, which is a measure of central tendency, and σ, the scale parameter, which is a measure of dispersion. These are related to, but distinct from, the more familiar mean and standard deviation, and we will return to them presently. The third parameter, ξ, the tail index, gives an indication of the shape (or fatness) of the tail. The GEV (T5.1) has three special cases:

- If $\xi > 0$, the GEV becomes the Fréchet distribution, corresponding to $F(x)$ being fat-tailed. This case is particularly useful for financial returns because they are typically fat-tailed, and we often find that estimates of ξ for financial returns data are positive but less than 0.25 (McNeil (1998, p. 2)).
- If $\xi = 0$, the GEV becomes the Gumbel distribution, corresponding to the case where $F(x)$ has normal kurtosis.
- If $\xi < 0$, the GEV becomes the Weibull distribution, corresponding to the case where $F(x)$ has thinner than normal tails. However, the thin-tailed Weibull distribution is not particularly useful for modelling financial returns.

---

[1] There is a very extensive literature on EVT and its applications, including a considerable amount on its applications to financial risk problems. This literature includes a large number of articles and papers, including those cited later, and a number of books. Among the latter, I particularly recommend Embrechts *et al.* (1997), Reiss and Thomas (1997), and Kotz and Nadarajah (2000).

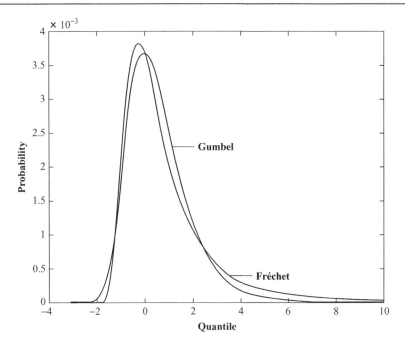

Figure T5.1   Gumbel and Fréchet probability density functions.

The standardised (i.e., $\mu = 0$, $\sigma = 1$) Fréchet and Gumbel probability density functions are illustrated in Figure T5.1. Both are skewed to the right, but the Fréchet is more skewed than the Gumbel and has a noticeably longer right-hand tail. This means that the Fréchet has considerably higher probabilities of producing very large X-values.

Note that most of the probability mass is located between x-values of -2 and $+6$. When dealing with non-standardised Gumbel and Fréchet distributions (i.e., those with $\mu \neq 0$ or $\sigma \neq 1$), we can then expect that most of the probability mass will lie between x-values of $\mu - 2\sigma$ and $\mu + 6\sigma$.

Reiss and Thomas (1997, pp. 15–18) show that the mean and variance are related to the location and scale parameters as follows:

$$Variance = \left[\frac{\Gamma(1 - 2\xi) - \Gamma^2(1 - \xi)}{\xi^2} \right] \sigma^2 \rightarrow \frac{\pi^2}{6}\sigma^2 \quad as \quad \xi \rightarrow 0 \qquad (T5.2a)$$

$$Mean = \mu + \left[\frac{\Gamma(1 - \xi) - 1}{\xi} \right] \sigma \rightarrow \mu + 0.577216\sigma \quad as \quad \xi \rightarrow 0 \qquad (T5.2b)$$

so we can easily obtain estimates of the mean and variance from μ and σ, and vice versa.[2]

To obtain the quantiles associated with the GEV distributions, we take logs of (T5.1) and rearrange to get:

$$\log(cl) = \begin{cases} -(1 + \xi(x^* - \mu)/\sigma)^{-1/\xi} \\ -\exp(-(x^* - \mu)/\sigma) \end{cases} \quad if \quad \begin{array}{l} \xi \neq 0 \\ \xi = 0 \end{array} \qquad (T5.3)$$

---

[2]Note, therefore, that the values of the location and scale parameters are rather different from those of the mean and standard deviation, and we should take care not to confuse them!

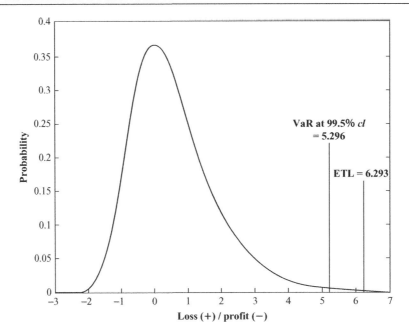

Figure T5.2   Gumbel VaR and ETL.

Note: Produced using the 'gumbeletlfigure' function for parameter values of $\mu = 0$ and $\sigma = 1$.

We then unravel the x^*-values to get the quantiles or VaRs associated with our chosen confidence level:[3]

$$VaR = \mu - \frac{\sigma}{\xi}[1 - (-\log(cl))^{-\xi}] \quad \text{(Fréchet VaR, } \xi > 0) \tag{T5.4a}$$

$$VaR = \mu - \sigma \log(\log(1/cl)) \quad \text{(Gumbel VaR, } \xi = 0) \tag{T5.4b}$$

Our ETLs can now be derived from these VaR estimates using our 'average tail VaR' algorithm explained in Chapter 3.

Figure T5.2 shows the standardised Gumbel VaR and ETL for a confidence level of 99.5%, a not unreasonable extreme level. As we can see, these are well out on the long right-hand tail: the VaR is 5.296 and the ETL, at 6.293, is even higher.

Some illustrative VaRs are given in Table T5.1, which shows the Gumbel VaRs for our standardised parameter values ($\mu = 0$ and $\sigma = 1$) and the corresponding Fréchet VaRs for the additional parameter values $\xi = 0.1$ and $\xi = 0.2$. Since the Gumbel can be regarded as the limiting case of the Fréchet as $\xi \to 0$, we can also regard these VaRs as the GEV VaRs for $\xi = 0$, $\xi = 0.1$ and $\xi = 0.2$. For the sake of comparison, the table also shows the normal VaRs — the VaRs based on the assumption that x is normally distributed — for our standardised parameter values. The VaRs shown are predicated on two extreme confidence levels — 99.5% and 99.9%.

---

[3]See, e.g., Embrechts *et al.* (1997, p. 324) and Evans *et al.* (2000, p. 86). We can obtain estimates of EV VaR over longer time periods by using appropriately scaled parameters, bearing in mind that the mean scales proportionately with the holding period *hp*, the standard deviation scales with the square root of *hp* and (subject to certain conditions) the tail index does not scale at all. In general, we find that the VaR scales with a parameter κ (i.e., so $VaR(hp) = VaR(1)(hp)^\kappa$, and empirical evidence reported by Hauksson *et al.* (2001, p. 93) suggests an average value for κ of about 0.45. The square root scaling rule (i.e., $\kappa = 0.5$) is therefore usually inappropriate for EV distributions.

Table T5.1   Gumbel, Fréchet and normal VaRs at extreme confidence levels

Confidence level	Gumbel, $\xi = 0$	Fréchet, $\xi = 0.1$	Fréchet, $\xi = 0.2$	Normal
99.5%	5.296	6.982	9.420	3.881
99.9%	6.907	9.952	14.903	4.541

Table T5.2   Gumbel, Fréchet and normal ETLs at extreme confidence levels

Confidence level	Gumbel, $\xi = 0$	Fréchet, $\xi = 0.1$	Fréchet, $\xi = 0.2$	Normal
99.5%	6.293	10.321	18.523	4.285
99.9%	7.903	14.154	28.269	4.894

The table shows that the VaRs rise with the confidence level (as we would expect) and with the value of ξ. For example, at the 99.9% confidence level, the GEV VaRs rise from 6.907 when the tail index is 0 to 14.903 when the tail index is 0.2. EV VaRs are thus quite sensitive to the value of the tail index.

The table also shows that the EV VaRs are considerably greater than the corresponding normal VaRs. For example, the median Fréchet VaRs (i.e., those occurring for a tail index of 0.1) are of the order of twice the corresponding normal VaRs. The application of EVT can therefore make a very considerable difference to our VaR estimates: put differently, assuming normality when estimating VaR at very high confidence levels can lead us to underestimate VaR by a very considerable extent.

Table T5.2 shows the corresponding ETL results. The ETLs are of course greater than the VaRs, but show similar properties: in particular, the ETL rises with the confidence level and is sensitive to the tail index, and the EV ETLs are much bigger than their normal equivalents. In fact, the ratios of EV ETL to normal ETL are even larger than the ratios of EV VaR to normal VaR.

T5.1.2   Estimation

To estimate EV risk measures, we need to estimate the relevant EV parameters — μ, σ and, in the case of the Fréchet, the tail index ξ, so we can insert their values into our quantile formulas (i.e., Equations (T5.4a and b)). We can obtain estimators using either maximum likelihood (ML) methods or semi-parametric methods.

ML methods derive the most probable parameter estimators given the data, and are obtained by maximizing the likelihood function using suitable (e.g., Lagrangian) methods and solving the first-order conditions. However, these first-order conditions lack closed-form solutions, so an ML approach requires the use of an appropriate numerical solution method, which requires suitable software, and there is also the danger that ML estimators might not be robust.

The semi-parametric methods do not require any specialised software, and can easily be implemented on a spreadsheet: we estimate the first two parameters, μ and σ, using conventional methods (e.g., standard spreadsheet formulas), and estimate the tail index — if we want it — using an appropriate formula. The most popular of these is the Hill estimator, $\hat{\xi}_{n,k}^{(H)}$:

$$\hat{\xi}_{n,k}^{(H)} = k^{-1} \sum_{j=1}^{k} \ln X_{j,n} - \ln X_{k+1,n} \qquad \text{(T5.5)}$$

where k, the tail threshold used to estimate the Hill estimator, has to be chosen in an appropriate way.[4] The Hill estimator is the average of the k most extreme (i.e., tail) observations, minus the $(k + 1)$th observation, or the one next to the tail. The Hill estimator is known to be consistent and asymptotically normally distributed, but its properties in finite samples are not well understood, and there are concerns in the literature about its small-sample properties and its sensitivity to the choice of threshold k. However, these (and other) reservations notwithstanding, many EVT practitioners regard the Hill estimator as being as good as any other.[5]

Perhaps the main problem in practice is the difficulty of choosing a cut-off value for k. We know that our tail-index estimates can be sensitive to the choice of k, but theory gives us little guidance on what the value of k should be. The choice of k is also complicated by a trade-off between bias and variance. If we increase k, we get more data and so move to the centre of distribution. This increases the precision of our estimator (and therefore reduces its variance), but also increases the bias of the tail estimator by placing relatively more weight on observations closer to the centre of our distribution. Alternatively, if we decrease k and move further out along we tail, we decrease the bias but have less data to work with and get a higher variance. The choice of k thus translates into how we address a trade-off between bias and variance.

There are essentially two approaches to handling this trade-off. The first is essentially judgemental and is strongly recommended by the Zürich researchers (i.e., Embrechts, McNeil and their co-workers). They suggest that we estimate Hill (or Pickands) estimators for a range of k-values, and go for k-values where the plot of estimators against k-values (hopefully) becomes more or less horizontal: if the plot stabilises and flattens out, then the plateau value should give a reasonable estimate of our tail index.[6] This suggestion has the attraction that it tries to extract the maximum possible information from all our data, albeit in an informal way.

Whilst everyone agrees on the need to exercise judgement on these issues, Danielsson, de Vries and their co-authors have suggested an ingenious (though rather involved) procedure to estimate an 'optimal' value of k. This value of k is chosen to minimise a mean squared error (MSE) loss function and reflects an optimal trade-off, in an MSE sense, between bias and variance. The idea is that we take a second-order approximation to the tail of the distribution function $F(x)$, and exploit the point that the tail size is optimal in an asymptotic MSE sense where bias and variance disappear at the same rate. This optimal size can be found by a sub-sample bootstrap procedure.[7] However, this approach requires a large sample size — at least 1,500 observations — and is therefore impractical with small sample sizes. In addition, any automatic procedure for selecting k tends to ignore other, softer, but nonetheless often very useful, information, and this leads some writers to be somewhat sceptical of such methods.

T5.1.3   Short-cut EV Methods

There are also several short-cut ways to estimate VaR (or ETL) using EV theory. These are based on the idea that if $\xi > 0$, the tail of an extreme loss distribution follows a power law times a slowly

---

[4]See, e.g., Bassi *et al.* (1998, p. 125).

[5]An alternative is the Pickands estimator (see, e.g., Bassi *et al.* (1998, p. 125) or Longin (1996, p. 389)). This estimator does not require a positive tail index (unlike the Hill estimator) and is asymptotically normal and weakly consistent under reasonable conditions, but is otherwise less efficient than the Hill estimator.

[6]See Bassi *et al.* (1998, p. 125). Unfortunately, the 'Hill plot' is not always well-behaved; however, we can sometimes improve its behaviour by inserting a constant intercept term in Equation (T5.5). I thank Jon Danielsson for this suggestion.

[7]For more details on this method, see Danielsson and de Vries (1997a,b) and de Vries and Caserta (2000).

varying function, i.e.:

$$F(x) = k(x)x^{-1/\xi} \tag{T5.6}$$

where $k(x)$ varies slowly with x. Equation (T5.6) gives us a couple of easy ways to estimate quantiles (or VaRs), including quantiles outside our sample range.

T5.1.3.1   A Quantile Projection Approach

The first of these is to project the tail using an existing in-sample quantile. To do so, we make the simplifying assumption that $k(x)$ is approximately constant, and Equation (T5.6) then becomes:

$$F(x) \approx kx^{-1/\xi} \tag{T5.7}$$

Following Danielsson and de Vries (1997b), we now consider two probabilities, a first, 'in-sample' probability $p_{in\text{-}sample}$, and a second, smaller and typically out-of-sample probability $p_{out\text{-}of\text{-}sample}$. Equation (T5.7) implies:

$$p_{in\text{-}sample} \approx kx_{in\text{-}sample}^{-1/\xi} \quad \text{and} \quad p_{out\text{-}of\text{-}sample} \approx kx_{out\text{-}of\text{-}sample}^{-1/\xi} \tag{T5.8}$$

which in turn implies:

$$p_{in\text{-}sample}/p_{out\text{-}of\text{-}sample} \approx (x_{in\text{-}sample}/x_{out\text{-}of\text{-}sample})^{-1/\xi}$$
$$\Rightarrow \quad x_{out\text{-}of\text{-}sample} \approx x_{in\text{-}sample}(p_{in\text{-}sample}/p_{out\text{-}of\text{-}sample})^{\xi} \tag{T5.9}$$

This allows us to estimate one quantile (denoted here as $x_{out\text{-}of\text{-}sample}$) based on a known in-sample quantile $x_{in\text{-}sample}$, a known out-of-sample probability $p_{out\text{-}of\text{-}sample}$ (which is known because it comes directly from our VaR confidence level), and an unknown in-sample probability $p_{in\text{-}sample}$. However, the latter can easily be proxied by its empirical counterpart, t/n, where n is the sample size and t the number of observations higher than $x_{in\text{-}sample}$. Using this proxy then gives us:

$$x_{out\text{-}of\text{-}sample} \approx x_{in\text{-}sample}(p_{out\text{-}of\text{-}sample}n/t)^{-\xi} \tag{T5.10}$$

which is easy to estimate using readily available information (e.g., Embrechts *et al.* (1997, p. 348)).

To use this approach, we take an arbitrarily chosen in-sample quantile, $x_{in\text{-}sample}$, and determine its counterpart empirical probability, t/n. We then determine our out-of-sample probability from our chosen confidence level, estimate our tail index using a suitable method, and our out-of-sample quantile estimator immediately follows from Equation (T5.10).

T5.1.3.2   A Regression Approach

The second short-cut approach is to use regression. If we take logs of and again assume that $k(x)$ is approximately constant, we get Equation (T5.6):

$$\log \Pr(X > x) = \log(k) - (1/\xi)\log(x) \tag{T5.11}$$

which is an easy-to-estimate relationship (see Diebold *et al.* (2000, pp. 31–32)). Estimating Equation (T5.11) would give us our parameter estimators, $\hat{k}$ and $\hat{\xi}$. We then substitute these into Equation (T5.6) and invert the latter to derive our quantile estimator:

$$\hat{x} = (\hat{k}/p)^{\hat{\xi}} \tag{T5.12}$$

This approach is easy to use and is capable of considerable refinement using recursive estimation methods to guide the selection of m, robust estimation methods to take account of the distributional considerations, and so forth (see Diebold *et al.* (2000, p. 32)).

However, we know very little about the properties of estimators obtained using this method, and the method itself is still relatively untried in practice. It can also be quite unreliable because there is no easy way to ensure that the regression procedure produces a 'sensible' estimate of the tail index.

T5.2   THE PEAKS OVER THRESHOLD APPROACH: THE GENERALISED PARETO DISTRIBUTION

T5.2.1   Theory

We turn now to the second strand of the EV literature, which deals with the application of EVT to the distribution of excess losses over a (high) threshold. This gives rise to the peaks over threshold (POT) or generalised Pareto approach, which (generally) requires fewer parameters than EV approaches based on the generalised extreme value theorem.

If X is a random loss with distribution function $F(x)$, and u is a threshold value of X, we can define the distribution of excess losses over our threshold u as:

$$F_u(y) = \Pr\{X - u \le y \mid X > u\} \tag{T5.13}$$

This gives the probability that a loss exceeds the threshold u by at most y, given that it does exceed the threshold. The distribution of X itself can be any of the commonly used distributions: normal, lognormal, t, etc., and will usually be unknown to us. However, as u gets large, the Gnedenko–Pickands–Balkema–deHaan (GPBdH) theorem states that the distribution $F_u(y)$ converges to a generalised Pareto distribution, given by:

$$G_{\xi,\beta}(x) = \begin{cases} 1 - (1 + \xi x/\beta)^{-1/\xi} \\ 1 - \exp(-x/\beta) \end{cases} \quad \text{if} \quad \begin{matrix} \xi \ne 0 \\ \xi = 0 \end{matrix} \tag{T5.14}$$

where $\beta > 0$ and $x \ge 0$.[8]

This distribution has only two parameters: a positive scale parameter, β, and a shape or tail-index parameter, ξ, that can be positive, zero or negative. The cases that usually interest us are the first two, and particularly the first (i.e., $\xi > 0$), as this corresponds to data being fat-tailed.

The GPBdH theorem is a very useful result, because it tells us that the distribution of excess losses always has the same form (in the limit, as the threshold gets high), pretty much regardless of the distribution of the losses themselves. Provided the threshold is high enough, we should therefore regard the GP distribution as *the* natural model for excess losses.

To apply the GP distribution, we need to choose a reasonable threshold u, which determines the number of observations, N_u, in excess of the threshold value. Choosing u involves a trade-off: we want a threshold u to be sufficiently high for the GPBdH theorem to apply reasonably closely; but if u is too high, we won't have enough excess threshold observations on which to make reliable estimates. We also need to estimate the parameters ξ and β. As with the GEV distributions, we can estimate these using maximum likelihood approaches or semi-parametric approaches.

Following McNeil (1999a, pp. 6–8), we now set $x = u + y$ and move from the distribution of beyond-threshold losses y (or $x - u$) to the parent distribution $F(x)$ defined over 'ordinary' losses:

$$F(x) = (1 - F(u))G_{\xi,\beta}(x - u) + F(u) \tag{T5.15}$$

---

[8] See, e.g., McNeil (1999a, p. 4). Note, furthermore, that if $\xi < 0$, then x is bounded above by $-\beta/\xi$.

Table T5.3   Extreme POT risk measures

Excess threshold probability	u(threshold)	POT VaR	POT ETL
5%	3.458	8.246	9.889
2.5%	4.443	8.240	9.773
1%	5.841	8.430	9.829

where $x > u$. To make use of this equation, we need an estimate of $F(u)$, the proportion of observations that do not exceed the threshold, and the most natural estimator is the observed proportion of below-threshold observations, $(n - N_u)/n$. We then substitute this for $F(u)$, and plug Equation (T5.14) into Equation (T5.15):

$$F(x) = 1 - \frac{N_u}{n}[1 + \xi(x - u)/\beta]^{-1/\xi} \tag{T5.16}$$

The estimated VaR is given by the x-value in Equation (T5.16), which can be recovered by inverting Equation (T5.16) and rearranging to get:

$$VaR = u + \frac{\beta}{\xi}\left\{\left[\frac{n}{N_u}(1 - cl)\right]^{-\xi} - 1\right\} \tag{T5.17}$$

where cl, naturally, is the VaR confidence level.

The ETL is equal to the VaR plus the mean excess loss over VaR. Provided $\xi < 1$, our ETL estimate is then:[9]

$$ETL = \frac{VaR}{(1 - \xi)} + \frac{(\beta - \xi u)}{(1 - \xi)} \tag{T5.18}$$

Some examples are shown in Table T5.3. This table shows the POT VaRs and POT ETLs for $\beta = 1$, an assumed tail index value of $\xi = 0.1$, and a VaR confidence level of 99.9%. The table shows the VaRs and ETLs for excess threshold probabilities (i.e., probabilities of a loss that exceeds the threshold) of 5%, 2.5% and 1%.[10] The VaRs are in the region 8.24 to 8.43, and the ETLs in the region 9.77 to 9.9. These values are fairly insensitive to the excess threshold probabilities (or, if one likes, to the threshold values u), and are of a similar order of magnitude to (although a little lower than) the values of the corresponding Fréchet risk measures reported in Tables T5.1 and T5.2.

T5.2.2   Estimation

To obtain estimates, we need to choose a reasonable threshold u, which then determines the number of excess threshold observations, N_u. (Alternatively, we can choose the probability of an excess threshold outcome, which we take to be N_u/n, and infer u from that.) However, choosing u involves a trade-off: we want the threshold u to be sufficiently high for the GPBdH theorem to apply reasonably closely; but if u is too high, we will not have enough excess threshold observations from which to obtain reliable estimates. We also need to estimate the parameters ξ and β and, as with the earlier GEV approaches, we can estimate these using maximum-likelihood or semi-parametric approaches.

---

[9] See also, e.g., McNeil (1999a, p. 8).

[10] Note that the thresholds, u, are assumed for convenience to be those generated by a corresponding Fréchet distribution with $\xi = 0.1$: this makes the thresholds and the excess threshold probabilities in the table consistent with each other.

T5.2.3 GEV vs. POT Approaches?

But which is best — the GEV or the POT approach? At a theoretical level, there is nothing much to choose between them, but at a practical level, the POT approach (usually) involves fewer parameters than the GEV approach. This makes the POT approach both easier to implement and more reliable, if only because results are (usually) dependent on one less parameter. McNeil and Saladin are therefore probably correct when they say that the 'POT method is to our knowledge the best parametric approach available for [the EV] estimation problem'.[11]

T5.3 REFINEMENTS TO EV APPROACHES

Having outlined the basics of EVT and its implementation, we now consider some refinements to it. These fall under four headings:

- Estimating EV confidence intervals.
- Conditional estimation.
- Dealing with dependent (or non-iid) data.
- Multivariate EVT.

T5.3.1 EV Confidence Intervals

We should always try to assess the precision of VaR and ETL estimates: after all, if our estimates are very imprecise, they are not really of much use. If we are to bet real money on our estimates, we should check whether they are precise enough to be worth using.

Assessing precision boils down to estimating confidence intervals, and there are at least two reasonable ways we can estimate confidence intervals for EV risk estimates:[12]

- The first of these is the profile likelihood method, outlined by McNeil (1998, appendix), which uses likelihood theory to derive a confidence interval for an EV VaR. However, this method is not very tractable, applies only to VaR (i.e., and not to ETL), and relies on asymptotic or limiting theory, which makes it potentially unreliable with small samples.
- The second approach is to apply the theory of order statistics. This approach is easier to implement, can be applied to ETL as well as VaR, and (provided the distributions chosen fit the data properly, admittedly a big 'if') provides estimates of confidence intervals that should be fairly accurate even for small samples. The OS approach is therefore probably the best one to use when estimating confidence intervals for EV risk measures.

We should also note that any reasonable approach to EV VaR should produce asymmetric confidence intervals. This asymmetry arises because we know less about the upper bound of our confidence interval than about the lower one, due to the fact that more extreme observations are scarcer than less extreme ones.

---

[11] See McNeil and Saladin (1997, p. 19).

[12] There is also one unreasonable way. We can estimate standard errors for quantile estimators (see, e.g., Kendall and Stuart (1972, pp. 251–252), and construct confidence intervals with these. However, this approach is not recommended for EV VaRs and ETLs because it produces symmetric confidence intervals, which are misleading for extremes.

T5.3.2   Conditional Estimation

The EVT procedures described above are all unconditional: they are applied directly (i.e., without any adjustment) to our data. Unconditional EVT is particularly useful when forecasting VaR or ETL over a long horizon period. However, it will often be the case that we wish to apply EVT to data adjusted for (i.e., conditional on) some dynamic structure. This conditional or dynamic EVT is most useful when we are dealing with a short horizon period, and where returns have a dynamic structure that we can model. A good example is where returns might be governed by a GARCH process. In such circumstances we might want to take account of the GARCH process and apply EVT not to raw returns, but to the random innovations that drive them.

One way to take account of this dynamic structure is to estimate the GARCH process and apply EVT to its residuals. This suggests the following two-step procedure, suggested by McNeil and Frey (2000):

- We estimate a GARCH-type process (e.g., a simple GARCH, a GARCH with stochastic volatility, etc.) by some appropriate econometric method and extract its residuals. These should turn out to be iid. The GARCH-type model can then be used to make one-step ahead predictions of next period's location and scale parameters, μ_{t+1} and σ_{t+1}.
- We apply EVT to these residuals, and then derive VaR estimates taking account of both the dynamic (i.e., GARCH) structure and the residual process.

T5.3.3   Dealing with Data Dependency

We have assumed so far that the stochastic process driving our data is iid, but most financial returns exhibit some form of time-dependency (or pattern over time). This time-dependency usually takes the form of clustering, where high/low observations are clustered together. Clustering matters for a number of reasons:

- It violates an important premise on which the earlier results depend, and the statistical implications of clustering are not well understood.
- The results of Kearns and Pagan (1997) suggest that data dependence can produce very poor estimator performance.
- Clustering alters the interpretation of our results. For example, we might say that there is a certain quantile or VaR value that we would expect to be exceeded, on average, only once every so often. But if data are clustered, we do not know how many times to expect this value to be breached in any given period: how frequently it is breached will depend on the tendency of the breaches to be clustered.[13] Clustering therefore has an important effect on the interpretation of our results.

There are two simple methods of dealing with time-dependency in our data. Perhaps the most common (and certainly the easiest) is just to apply GEV distributions to per-period maxima instead of raw returns. This is the simplest approach and has been used by Longin (1996), McNeil (1998), and many others. This approach exploits the point that maxima are usually less clustered than the underlying data from which they are drawn, and become even less clustered as the periods of time from which they are drawn get longer. We can therefore completely eliminate time dependence if the block periods are long enough.

---

[13] See McNeil (1998, p. 13).

This block maxima approach has the attraction of being very easy to use, if we have enough data. Nonetheless, the block maxima approach involves some efficiency loss, because we throw away extreme observations that are not block maxima. There is also the drawback that there is no clear guide about how long the block periods should be, and this leads to a new bandwidth problem comparable to the earlier problem of how to select k.

A second solution to the problem of clustering is to estimate the tail of the conditional distribution rather than the unconditional one: we would first estimate the conditional volatility model (e.g., via a GARCH procedure), and then estimate the tail index of conditional standardised data. The time-dependency in our data is then picked up by the deterministic part of our model, and we can treat the random process as independent.[14]

T5.3.4   Multivariate Extreme Value Theory

We have been dealing so far with univariate EVT, but there also exists multivariate extreme value theory (MEVT), which can be used to model the tails of multivariate distributions in a theoretically appropriate way. The key issue here is how to model the dependence structure of extreme events. To appreciate this issue, it is again important to recognise how EV theory differs from the more familiar central value theory. As we all know, when dealing with central values, we often rely on the central limit theorem to motivate a normal (or more broadly, elliptical) distribution. When we have such a distribution, the dependence structure can then be captured by the (linear) correlations between the different variables. Given our distributional assumptions, knowledge of variances and correlations (or, if we like, covariances) suffices to specify the multivariate distribution. This is why correlations are so important in central value theory.

However, this logic does not carry over to extremes. When we go beyond normal (or more generally, elliptical) distributions, knowledge of variances and correlations is not always sufficient to specify the multivariate distribution. Modelling multivariate extremes requires a different approach, and the answer is to be found in the theory of copulas. Copulas enable us to separate the marginal behavior of variables (i.e., the marginal density or distribution functions) from their dependence structure, and the copula can be considered that part of the multivariate distribution that describes this dependence. Knowledge of the marginal functions and of the copula will always suffice to describe the complete multivariate distribution. It follows, then, that the copula is the key to modelling multivariate returns.

MEVT tells us that the limiting distribution of multivariate extreme values will have one of a restricted family of EV copulas, and we can model multivariate EV dependence by assuming one of these EV copulas. In theory, our copulas can also have as many dimensions as we like, reflecting the number of variables to be considered. However, in practice, such methods are only viable if we keep dimensionality low. If univariate extreme events are rare, cases of multiple variables simultaneously taking extreme values are much rarer still. For example, if we have two independent variables and classify univariate extreme events as those that occur 1 time in a 100, then we should expect to see one multivariate extreme event (i.e., both variables taking extreme values) only 1 time in 100^2, or 1 time in 10,000 observations. As the dimensionality rises, more parameters need to be estimated and our multivariate EV events rapidly become rarer: with three independent variables, we should expect to see a multivariate extreme event 1 time in 100^3, or 1 time in 1,000,000 observations, and so on. This is the well-known curse of dimensionality, which gets its name for obvious reasons. Where we have a lot of variables to be considered, estimation with MEVT is not practically feasible.

---

[14]There is also a third, more advanced but also more difficult, solution. This is to estimate an extremal index — a measure of clustering — and use this index to adjust our quantiles for clustering. For more details on the extremal index and how to use it, see, e.g., Embrechts *et al.* (1997, ch. 8.1) or McNeil (1998, pp. 8–9).

T5.4   CONCLUSIONS

EVT provides a tailor-made approach to the estimation of extreme probabilities and quantiles (e.g., such as VaRs at very high confidence levels). It is intuitive and plausible; and it is relatively easy to apply, at least in its more basic forms. It also gives us considerable practical guidance on what we should estimate and how we should do it; and it has a good track record. It therefore provides *the* ideal, tailor-made, way to estimate extreme VaRs and ETLs.

EVT is also important in what it tells us *not* to do, and the most important point is not to use distributions justified by central limit theory — most particularly, the normal or Gaussian distribution — for extreme value estimation. If we wish to estimate extreme risks, we should do so using the distributions suggested by EVT, not arbitrary distributions (such as the normal) that go against what EVT tells us.

But we should not lose sight of the limitations of EV approaches, and certain limitations stand out:

- EV problems are intrinsically difficult, because by definition we always have relatively few extreme value observations to work with. This means that any EV estimates will necessarily be very uncertain, relative to any estimates we might make of more central quantiles or probabilities. EV estimates will therefore have relatively wide confidence intervals attached to them. Uncertainty is not a fault of EVT as such, but an inevitable consequence of our paucity of data.

- EV estimates are subject to considerable model risk. We have to make various assumptions in order to carry out extreme value estimations, and our results will often be very sensitive to the precise assumptions we make. At the same time, the veracity or otherwise of these assumptions can be difficult to verify in practice. Hence, our estimates are often critically dependent on assumptions that are effectively unverifiable. EVT also requires us to make ancillary decisions, most particularly about threshold values, and there are no easy ways to make those decisions either. In short, the application of EV methods involves a lot of 'judgement'.

- EV estimates can be highly affected by non-linearities, the peculiarities of individual data sets, and so on.

- Handling extreme correlations is subject to notorious difficulties associated with the curse of dimensionality.

In the final analysis, we need to make the best use of theory whilst acknowledging that the paucity of our data inevitably limits the reliability of our results. To quote McNeil again:

> We are working in the tail ... and we have only a limited amount of data which can help us. The uncertainty in our analyses is often high, as reflected by large confidence intervals . . . . However, if we wish to quantify rare events we are better off using the theoretically supported methods of EVT than other ad hoc approaches. EVT gives the best estimates of extreme events and represents the most honest approach to measuring the uncertainty inherent in the problem.
>
> (McNeil (1998, p. 18))

In sum, EVT has a very useful, albeit limited, role to play in risk measurement. As Diebold *et al.* nicely put it:

> EVT is here to stay, but we believe that best-practice applications of EVT to financial risk management will benefit from awareness of its limitations — as well as its strengths. When the smoke clears, the contribution of EVT remains basic and useful: It helps draw smooth curves through the extreme tails of empirical survival functions in a way that is guided by powerful theory. . . . [But] we shouldn't ask more of the theory than it can deliver.
>
> (Diebold *et al.* (2000, p. 34))

Box T5.1   Extreme Value Estimation Using the IMRM Toolbox

The IMRM Toolbox offers a variety of procedures that are useful for EV analysis.

We can estimate Gumbel VaR command 'gumbelvar' and percentage points of the Gumbel VaR distribution function using 'gumbelvardfperc'. We can produce a figure of the Gumbel VaR using 'gumbelvarfigure', we can produce 2D plots of Gumbel VaR against confidence level and holding period respectively using 'gumbelvarplot2D_cl' and 'gumbelvarplot2D_hp', and we can produce a 3D plot of Gumbel VaR against both confidence level and holding period using the function 'gumbelvar3Dplot'.

We can carry out similar procedures for Gumbel ETL by replacing 'gumbelvar' in each of these functions by 'gumbeletl': we can estimate Gumbel ETL by 'gumbeletl', we can estimate percentage points of the Gumbel ETL distribution function using 'gumbeletldfperc', and so on.

Each of these Gumbel procedures can be carried out on a Fréchet by replacing 'gumbel' with 'frechet' in the relevant function. Hence, we can estimate Fréchet VaR by 'frechetvar', Fréchet ETL by 'frechetetl', and so on.

We can estimate generalised Pareto VaR and ETL using the functions 'gparetovar' and 'gparetoetl'.

T5.5   RECOMMENDED READING

Bassi *et al.* (1998); Cotter (2001); Danielsson and de Vries (1997a,b); Diebold *et al.* (2000); Embrechts *et al.* (1997); Guermat *et al.* (1999); Kotz and Nadarajah (2000, ch. 1); Lauridsen (2000); Longin (1996, 1999); McNeil (1998, 1999a); McNeil and Frey (2000); McNeil and Saladin (1997); Neftci (2000); Reiss and Thomas (1997).

Tool No. 6

Monte Carlo Simulation Methods

Tool No. 6 deals with Monte Carlo simulation methods. These methods can be used to price derivatives, estimate their hedge ratios, and solve risk measurement problems of almost any degree of complexity. The idea is to simulate repeatedly the random processes governing the prices or returns of the financial instruments we are interested in. If we were interested in estimating VaR, say, each simulation might give us a possible value for our portfolio at the end of our holding period. If we take enough of these simulations, the simulated distribution of portfolio values will converge to the portfolio's unknown 'true' distribution, and we can use the simulated distribution of end-period portfolio values to infer the VaR.

This simulation process involves a number of specific steps. The first is to select a model for the stochastic variable(s) of interest. Having chosen our model, we estimate its parameters — volatilities, correlations, and so on — on the basis of whatever historical or market data are available. We then construct fictitious or simulated paths for the stochastic variables using 'random' numbers — or strictly speaking, pseudo-random numbers — produced by a 'random number generator' that produces deterministic numbers mimicking the properties of genuine random numbers. Each set of 'random' numbers then produces a set of hypothetical terminal price(s) for the instrument(s) in our portfolio. We then repeat these simulations enough times to be confident that the simulated distribution of portfolio values is sufficiently close to the 'true' (but unknown) distribution of actual portfolio values to be a reliable proxy for it. Once that is done, we can then read off the VaR from this proxy distribution.

MCS methods are very powerful tools and can handle many types of portfolio, including quite complex and exotic ones. What makes them particularly appealing is that they can solve these problems in the presence of complicating factors — such as path-dependency, fat tails, and non-linearity — that most other approaches have difficulty with. For example, whilst analytic approaches to derivatives pricing have difficulty with path-dependency features, simulation methods can easily handle them provided we take a large enough number of simulations. Similarly, simple parametric approaches to VaR estimation tend to have difficulty with optionality and non-linearity in risk factors, but simulation methods can handle these features with few difficulties.

Nonetheless, there is no point using simulation methods when simpler approaches will do: if simpler methods work, we should use them instead. If we are trying to price a Black–Scholes vanilla call option or estimate normal VaR, there would be no point using simulation methods because we can solve these problems very easily using established methods (i.e., the Black–Scholes pricing equation, or a formula for normal VaR). We would therefore use simulation methods only in more difficult situations where such direct approaches are unavailable, computationally too intensive, or insufficiently accurate for our purposes. Simulation approaches are particularly useful when dealing with multidimensional problems (i.e., where outcomes depend on more than one risk variable) and, as a rule, become relatively more attractive as the dimensionality of a problem increases.

However, we should also take account of the limitations of simulation methods: these methods are less easy to use than some alternatives; they are computer-intensive, and calculations can take time if they are to be sufficiently accurate; and they are not well suited for instruments with significant early-exercise features.

Box T6.1   Uses of Monte Carlo Methods to Manage Derivatives Positions

The use of MCS to price derivatives positions and manage derivatives risks was suggested by Boyle (1977) and is now common among financial institutions with major derivatives positions. It tends to be used for exotic derivatives for which alternative approaches such as lattice procedures are computationally too intensive (e.g., when handling certain types of interest-rate derivatives) or inaccurate (e.g., when handling options with discontinuous payoffs, such as barrier options).

MCS is used both to price derivatives and to estimate Greek hedging parameters, such as delta, gamma, vega, and so forth. Derivatives can be priced using simulations in a risk-neutral framework: we carry out lots of simulations, and the price is the expected discounted value of the risk-neutralised payoff. The Greeks can be estimated by pricing the derivative on the basis of one current value of the relevant underlying factor and then pricing the derivative again on the basis of one (or more) other value(s) close to the original one. The difference(s) between the two derivative prices enable(s) us to estimate our Greek parameters.

Institutions that already have the capability to carry out MCS for their derivatives positions should have little difficulty building up an MCS capability to estimate VaR. Indeed, they will almost certainly have to: the very fact that they already use MCS to handle their derivatives positions implies that those positions must be both large and complex, which implies that MCS is almost certainly an appropriate way for them to estimate their VaRs.

T6.1   MONTE CARLO SIMULATION WITH SINGLE RISK FACTORS

Suppose we wish to carry out a Monte Carlo analysis of a stock price. Our first task is to choose a model to describe the behaviour of the stock price over time. Assume that the stock price S follows a geometric Brownian motion process:

$$dS/S = \mu dt + \sigma dx \qquad (T6.1)$$

where μ is its expected (per unit time) rate of return and σ is the volatility of the stock price. dx is known as a Wiener process, and can be written as $dx = \phi(dt)^{1/2}$, where ϕ is a drawing from a standard normal distribution. If we substitute out dx, we get:

$$dS/S = \mu dt + \sigma \phi(dt)^{1/2} \qquad (T6.2)$$

This is the standard model used in quantitative finance, at least for stock prices,[1] and it holds that the (instantaneous) rate of increase of the stock price dS/S evolves according to its mean drift term μ and realizations from the random term ϕ.[2] In practice, we would often work with this model in

---

[1] The GBM model is widely used for equity prices because it is simple and it accommodates the main stylised features of equity prices, namely, that stock prices are non-negative, random, and tend to drift upwards (which we can accommodate by letting μ be positive).

[2] However, the GBM process is not a good description of the behaviour of some other random variables. Most obvious among these are spot interest rates, in part because the GBM process fails to account for the well-established tendency of interest/spot rates to revert towards their mean. If we are dealing with fixed income positions, we would therefore want a more appropriate process (e.g., a Cox–Ingersoll–Ross one). For more on interest-rate processes, see Broadie and Glasserman (1998, pp. 175–176), Hull (2000, ch. 21–22), James and Webber (2000), Rebonato (1998) or Wilmott (2000, ch. 40–41 and 45–47). The GBM process is also inappropriate where the underlying variable is subject to jumps, stochastic volatility, asymmetric barriers or policy targets (e.g., as exchange rates are in some exchange rate regimes), and similar features.

its discrete-form equivalent. If Δt is some small time increment, we can write:

$$\Delta S/S = \mu \Delta t + \sigma \phi \sqrt{\Delta t} \qquad (T6.3)$$

ΔS is the change in the stock price over the time inteval Δt, and $\Delta S/S$ is its (discretised) rate of change. Equation (T6.3) tells us that the rate of change of the stock price is normally distributed with mean $\mu \Delta t$ and standard deviation $\sigma \sqrt{\Delta t}$.

Now suppose that we wish to simulate the stock price over some period of length T. We would usually divide T into a large number N of small time increments Δt (i.e., we set $\Delta t = T/N$). The simplest way to simulate S is the Euler method: we take a starting value of S, say $S(0)$, and draw a random value of ϕ to update S using Equation (T6.3); this gives $S(\Delta t)$ from $S(0)$; we then derive $S(2\Delta t)$ from $S(\Delta t)$ in the same way; and carry on until we have a terminal value for S, $S(T)$. To spell out the process in more detail, we first rewrite Equation (T6.3) as:

$$\Delta S = S\mu \Delta t + S\sigma \phi \sqrt{\Delta t} \Rightarrow S(t + \Delta t) = S(t)\left(1 + \mu \Delta t + \sigma \phi \sqrt{\Delta t}\right) \qquad (T6.4)$$

Starting from $S(0)$, we take a drawing from ϕ — say $\phi(\Delta t)$, where the term in brackets refers to the time the drawing is taken—and so obtain a value for $S(\Delta t)$ using:

$$S(\Delta t) = S(0)\left(1 + \mu \Delta t + \sigma \phi(\Delta t)\sqrt{\Delta t}\right) \qquad (T6.5)$$

We now take another drawing from ϕ, $\phi(2\Delta t)$, and obtain a value for $S(2\Delta t)$ using:

$$\begin{aligned} S(2\Delta t) &= S(\Delta t)\left(1 + \mu \Delta t + \sigma \phi(2\Delta t)\sqrt{\Delta t}\right) \\ &= S(0)\left[1 + \mu \Delta t + \sigma \phi(\Delta t)\sqrt{\Delta t}\right]\left[1 + \mu \Delta t + \sigma \phi(2\Delta t)\sqrt{\Delta t}\right] \end{aligned} \qquad (T6.6)$$

The stock price after two time increments therefore depends on the initial stock price $S(0)$ and realisations from ϕ after time increments of Δt and $2\Delta t$. Carrying on in this way, we eventually find that:

$$\begin{aligned} S(T) &= S(T - \Delta t)\left(1 + \mu \Delta t + \sigma \phi(T)\sqrt{\Delta t}\right) \\ &= S(0) \prod_{i=1}^{N} \left[1 + \mu \Delta t + \sigma \phi(i \Delta t)\sqrt{\Delta t}\right] \end{aligned} \qquad (T6.7)$$

The simulated terminal stock price depends on the initial stock price, the parameters μ and σ, and each of N realisations of ϕ. To simulate the behaviour of the stock price, we now use a random number generator to produce a series of simulated values of $\phi(\Delta t), \phi(2\Delta t), \ldots, \phi(T)$, and substitute these into our Equation (T6.5), (T6.6) and so on, to produce a series of simulated stock prices $S(\Delta t)$, $S(2\Delta t), \ldots, S(T)$.

This Euler method provides a good illustration of the basic mechanics of Monte Carlo simulation. In general, it produces estimates with two sources of error. The first are discretisation errors: given that the Brownian motion process is a continuous one, taking a discrete approximation to it will produce errors proportional to the size of the discretisation (i.e., of order Δt).[3] This error therefore falls as Δt gets smaller, and goes to zero as Δt approaches zero. The second source of error comes from the number of simulation trials: each trial produces a single simulated path for the random variable, culminating in a single terminal value for that variable. If there are M independent simulation trials, and the terminal value has mean υ and standard deviation ω, the standard error of our estimate of υ is $\omega/\sqrt{M}$. The accuracy of our estimates therefore increases with the square root of the number of

---

[3] However, there also exist more refined methods that reduce the size of the error to something in the order of $(\Delta t)^2$ or even less (see Broadie and Glasserman (1998, p. 182)).

trials: if we wish to double the accuracy of our estimates, we must quadruple the number of trials, and so forth.[4]

However, it is often possible to cut down on the calculations involved and/or speed up the accuracy of our results. For instance, in the case of geometric Brownian motion, we can apply Ito's lemma to rewrite the stock price process as:

$$d \ln S = (\mu - \sigma^2/2)dt + \sigma dx \tag{T6.8}$$

We then take a discretisation of Equation (T6.8), set $t = 0$ and solve for $S(t + \Delta t)$:

$$\ln S(\Delta t) - \ln S(0) = (\mu - \sigma^2/2)\Delta t + \sigma \phi(\Delta t)\sqrt{\Delta t}$$
$$\Rightarrow S(\Delta t) = S(0) \exp\left[(\mu - \sigma^2/2)\Delta t + \sigma \phi(\Delta t)\sqrt{\Delta t}\right] \tag{T6.9}$$

Equation (T6.9) can be used repeatedly to simulate a path at times Δt, $2\Delta t$, and so on. Equation (T6.9) is also more useful than Equations (T6.5)–(T6.7) because it holds exactly, whereas the earlier equations are only true in the limit as Δt approaches zero. Consequently, if we are only interested in the terminal stock price (i.e., $S(T)$), we can jump from $S(0)$ to $S(T)$ in one giant step (i.e., we set $N = 1$ or $\Delta t = T$) using:

$$S(T) = S(0) \exp\left[(\mu - \sigma^2/2)T + \sigma \phi(T)\sqrt{T}\right] \tag{T6.10}$$

Provided we are only interested in the terminal stock value, this approach is both more accurate and less time-consuming than the Euler method.

T6.2   USES OF MONTE CARLO SIMULATION

We might use Monte Carlo for any of four different purposes. The first is to price a derivative. To do so, we run a sample path of S in a risk-neutral world (i.e., we run a sample path taking the mean expected return to be the risk-free return r instead of μ), and calculate the payoff from the derivative (e.g., so the payoff from a standard Black–Scholes call with strike price X would be max($S_T - X$, 0). We do this a large number (M) of times, calculate the sample mean payoff to our derivative, and discount this at the risk-free rate to obtain our derivative price. Where the derivative payoff depends only on the terminal stock price, we would use a terminal stock-price formula like (T6.10) and cut out any intermediate time increments. In this case, we need only ensure that M is large enough to give us the accuracy we want.

To give a practical illustration, suppose we apply this method to a standard (i.e., vanilla) Black–Scholes call option with $S_0 = X = 1$, $\mu = r = 0$, $\sigma = 0.25$ and a maturity of 1 year (or 360 days), but with M taking values up to 5,000. The results of this exercise are presented in Figure T6.1, and show that the simulated call price is initially unstable, but eventually settles down and converges to the 'true' Black–Scholes call price of 0.0995. However, the figure also makes it clear that we need a lot of trials (i.e., a large M value) to get accurate results.

Where the derivative payoff depends on the stock-price path, and not just the terminal stock price — as with barrier or Asian options, for instance — we would also have to ensure that the

---

[4]There is also a third possible source of error. In many applications, we do not have closed-form solutions for the derivative value (e.g., as with some American options). In such cases, we may have to resort to new simulations (or other methods, such as binomial or trinomial methods) to determine derivatives values, and our estimates are then subject to error from whatever simulation or other method is used to determine these values. For more on this issue, see Broadie and Glasserman (1998, p. 183).

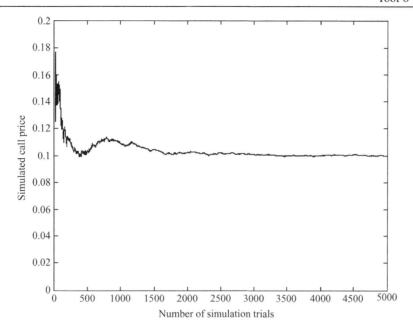

Figure T6.1   Monte Carlo simulation of a vanilla call price.

Note: Based on assumed parameter values $S = X = 1, r = \mu = 0, \sigma = 0.25$ and maturity $= 360$.

number of interim time steps, N, was large enough to give us accurate results, and this obviously involves more calculations.

A second use of MCS is to estimate the Greek parameters of option positions. The idea is to estimate the value of our derivatives position for two (or more, as relevant) slightly different values of the underlying value, and use the results to give us estimates of the Greek parameters. For example, the delta, δ, of a standard European call is approximately equal to the ratio of the change in option price to the corresponding (small) change in the underlying stock price, i.e.:

$$\delta \approx \Delta c / \Delta S = \frac{c(S+h) - c(S-h)}{2h} \qquad (\text{T6.11})$$

where the option price, c, say, is written as a function of the underlying variable, S, and the S-values are perturbed slightly each way so that their difference, ΔS, is equal to $2h$. When estimating these parameters, each of the two sets of underlying prices (i.e., $S + h$ and $S - h$) is subject to random 'sampling' error, but we can reduce their combined effect and the number of calculations needed by using the same set of simulated S-values to determine both sets of underlying prices: in short, run one set of simulations for S, perturb the S-values each way (i.e., up by h and down by h), determine two sets of option values, and thence obtain an estimate of the delta.[5] We can obtain estimates of the other Greek parameters in a similar way, using discrete approximations of their

[5]Obtaining our up and down paths from the same set of underlying simulations makes a very big difference to the precision of our delta estimates. If we run two separate sets of simulated underlying price paths, and estimate the delta by plugging these into Equation (T6.11), the variance of our delta estimator will be of order $1/h^2$, so the variance will get very large as h gets small (see Boyle *et al.* (1997, p. 1304)). Such estimates are clearly very unsatisfactory. On the other hand, if we use one set of simulated underlying price paths, the variance of our delta estimator will be of order 1, and will therefore get small as h gets small (Boyle *et al.* (1997, p. 1305)).

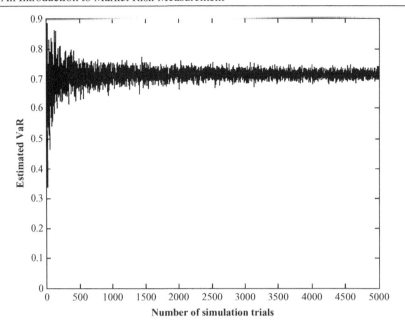

Figure T6.2   Monte Carlo simulation of a vanilla call VaR.

Note: Based on assumed parameter values $S = 1$, $X = 0.5$, $r = \mu = 0$, $\sigma = 0.25$, hp maturity $= 360$, and an investment of $1.

defining formulas (see, e.g., Boyle *et al.* (1997, pp. 1302–1309) or Clewlow and Strickland (1998, p. 105)).

A third use of MCS is, of course, to estimate VaR. If we wish to estimate the VaR of a vanilla call position, say, we run M simulations of the terminal stock value (e.g., using Equation (T6.10), because we are only interested in the terminal stock value, and not the rest of the stock-price path). However, in doing so we would use the 'real' stock-price process rather than the risk-neutralised one used to price derivatives and estimate their Greeks (i.e., we use the process with μ as the drift term rather than r). The value of T now corresponds to the end of our VaR holding period, and we revalue our option for each simulated terminal stock price (e.g., using the Black–Scholes pricing equation or, if the option expires at T, the option payoff function) and subtract from this value the current price of our option. This gives us M simulated P/L values for a portfolio consisting of one option, and we obtain the position P/L by multiplying these values by the number of options in our position. The result is a set of M simulated position P/L values, and we can read the VaR off from the histogram of simulated position P/L values or take the VaR as the relevant order statistic.

To illustrate MC simulation of VaR, suppose we invest $1 in a vanilla Black–Scholes call option with $S_0 = 1$, $X = 0.5$, $\mu = r = 0$, $\sigma = 0.25$ and a maturity of 1 year. We now assume a confidence level of 95% and a holding period of a year, and simulate the VaR of this position with M-values of up to 5,000. The results of this exercise are presented in Figure T6.2, and show that the simulated VaR is initially unstable, but slowly settles down and (very) gradually converges to its 'true' value of 0.715. However, the figure also makes it clear that we need a large number of trials to get accurate results, and suggests that the convergence is slower than it is for option pricing. The VaR estimate is less accurate because the VaR is a tail order statistic, rather than a measure of central tendency (e.g., such as the mean), and as we go further out into the tail, our results become dependent on fewer observations. A VaR estimate is therefore likely to be less accurate than a simulated derivatives price, and the relative inaccuracy of the VaR estimate will increase as the VaR confidence level becomes more extreme.

The fourth use of MCS is to estimate ETL. As we might expect, ETL estimation by MCS involves most of the same steps as VaR estimation. We estimate a set of simulated portfolio P/L values in exactly the same way, but use the P/L histogram to estimate the ETL instead of the VaR.

Box T6.2   Generating Random Numbers

Monte Carlo simulations depend on drawings from a random number generator. Strictly speaking, these 'random' numbers are not random at all. They are 'pseudo' random numbers generated from an algorithm using a deterministic rule (i.e., a rule that does not have any random elements). These rules take some initial value, a 'seed' number, and then generate a series of numbers that *appear* random and ought, if the number generator is well designed, to pass the standard tests for randomness (and, among these, especially the tests for independence). However, if a random number generator is poorly designed, the 'random' numbers it produces will not have the properties that we assume them to have (e.g., they may not be independent of each other) and our results could be compromised. It is therefore critical to use a good random number generator.

We should also keep in mind that a random number generator will always generate the same sequence of numbers from the same initial 'seed' number. Eventually, the seed number will recur and the sequence of 'random' numbers will repeat itself all over again. All random number generators therefore cycle after a certain number of drawings, and the only issue is how long they take to cycle: good ones will cycle after perhaps billions of draws, but bad ones will cycle after only a few thousand. If the cycle is too short relative to the number of drawings we want, the extra accuracy we think we are getting from taking so many drawings will be spurious and we may fool ourselves into thinking that our results are more accurate than they actually are. Consequently, it is important to use a random number generator with a long cycle.

T6.3   MONTE CARLO SIMULATION WITH MULTIPLE RISK FACTORS

MCS can easily handle problems with more than one random risk factor. If we have two risky stock prices, our discretised geometric Brownian motion process is:

$$\Delta S_1/S_1 = \mu_1 \Delta t + \sigma_1 \phi_1 \sqrt{\Delta t}$$
$$\Delta S_2/S_2 = \mu_2 \Delta t + \sigma_2 \phi_2 \sqrt{\Delta t} \qquad \text{(T6.12)}$$

$$\Rightarrow \quad S_1(t + \Delta t) = S_1(t) + S_1(t)\mu_1 \Delta t + S_1(t)\sigma_1 \phi_1 \sqrt{\Delta t}$$
$$S_2(t + \Delta t) = S_2(t) + S_2(t)\mu_2 \Delta t + S_2(t)\sigma_2 \phi_2 \sqrt{\Delta t}$$

$$\text{or} \quad \begin{bmatrix} S_1(t + \Delta t) \\ S_2(t + \Delta t) \end{bmatrix} = \begin{bmatrix} S_1(t)(1 + \mu_1 \Delta t) \\ S_2(t)(1 + \mu_2 \Delta t) \end{bmatrix} + \begin{bmatrix} \sigma_1 S_1(t) \phi_1 \sqrt{\Delta t} \\ \sigma_2 S_2(t) \phi_2 \sqrt{\Delta t} \end{bmatrix}$$

where we use the obvious notation. However, in this case we allow the random terms, ϕ_1 and ϕ_2, to be correlated, which means that their expectation, $E[\phi_1\phi_2]$, is equal to ρ, the correlation between S_1 and S_2.

We now want to generate these correlated random variables, ϕ_1 and ϕ_2, and the usual approach is by means of a Choleski decomposition.[6] Suppose we write the vector of ϕ_i terms as a 2×1 matrix $\boldsymbol{\varphi}$:

$$\boldsymbol{\varphi} = \begin{bmatrix} \phi_1 \\ \phi_2 \end{bmatrix} \tag{T6.13}$$

If $\boldsymbol{\varepsilon}$ is a 2×1 vector of uncorrelated standard normal variables, we can then write $\boldsymbol{\varphi}$ as:

$$\boldsymbol{\varphi} = \mathbf{A}\boldsymbol{\varepsilon} \tag{T6.14}$$

where $\mathbf{A}$ is an appropriate 2×2 matrix. If now post-multiply each side of Equation (T6.14) by its transpose, we get:

$$\boldsymbol{\varphi}\boldsymbol{\varphi}^{\mathrm{T}} = \mathbf{A}\boldsymbol{\varepsilon}\boldsymbol{\varepsilon}^{\mathrm{T}}\mathbf{A}^{\mathrm{T}} \tag{T6.15}$$

We then take expectations of each side, noting that the expectation of the left-hand side is also equal to the correlation matrix $\mathbf{C}$:

$$E[\boldsymbol{\varphi}\boldsymbol{\varphi}^{\mathrm{T}}] = \mathbf{C} = \mathbf{A}E[\boldsymbol{\varepsilon}\boldsymbol{\varepsilon}^{\mathrm{T}}]\mathbf{A}^{\mathrm{T}} = \mathbf{A}\mathbf{I}\mathbf{A}^{\mathrm{T}} = \mathbf{A}\mathbf{A}^{\mathrm{T}} \tag{T6.16}$$

i.e.:

$$\mathbf{C} = \mathbf{A}\mathbf{A}^{\mathrm{T}}$$

which tells us that $\mathbf{A}$, the matrix of $a_{i,j}$ terms, is the 'square root matrix' of the correlation matrix $\mathbf{C}$. One solution for $\mathbf{A}$ is the Choleski decomposition:

$$\mathbf{A} = \begin{bmatrix} 1 & 0 \\ \rho & (1 - \rho^2)^{1/2} \end{bmatrix} \tag{T6.17}$$

(The reader can easily verify this result by postmultiplying Equation (T6.17) by its transpose to give the correlation matrix $\mathbf{C}$).) Hence, once we have the correlation matrix $\mathbf{C}$, we take its Choleski decomposition, given by Equation (T6.17), and then use Equation (T6.14) to generate our correlated random variables $\boldsymbol{\varphi}$ from a set of uncorrelated variables $\boldsymbol{\varepsilon}$.

The Choleski decomposition approach also works with n random variables. Whatever the number of assets involved, the $\mathbf{A}$ matrix is still the $n \times n$ matrix square root of the $n \times n$ correlation matrix $\mathbf{C}$, as defined in Equation (T6.16).

All we then need is a means of taking the Choleski decomposition when n exceeds 2, and the best solution is to program it into a spreadsheet function.[7] If we have n correlated random variables ϕ_i, and the coefficient of correlation between variables i and j is $\rho_{i,j}$, we require that:

$$\phi_i = \sum_{k=1}^{i} a_{i,k}\varepsilon_k \quad , \quad \sum_{k=1}^{i} a_{i,k}^2 = 1 \tag{T6.18}$$

---

[6] The Choleski decomposition procedure is efficient when the covariance matrix Σ is positive definite, and more details on the approach are given in many places (e.g., Hull (2000, p. 409)). The main alternatives to Choleski decomposition are the eigenvalue decomposition and singular value decomposition approaches, but these are more computationally intensive. However, they have the advantage over the Choleski decomposition approach that they also work when the Σ matrix is positive semi-definite, while the Choleski decomposition procedure does not.

[7] The reader who wants the code can find it in Wilmott (2000, p. 935).

and, for all: $j < i$:

$$\sum_{k=1}^{j} a_{i,k}\, a_{j,k} = \rho_{i,j} \tag{T6.19}$$

(see Hull (2000, p. 409)). The Choleski decomposition has a nice recursive structure that makes it straightforward to program: ϕ_1 is set equal to ε_1; we then solve the relevant a-equations to determine ϕ_2 from ε_1 and ε_2; after that, we calculate ϕ_3 from ε_1, ε_2 and ε_3; and so forth.

Box T6.3   Full, Grid and Other MCS Procedures

There are a number of ways of applying MCS with multiple risk factors. The most elaborate and (usually) most demanding is full MC, which involves the exact valuation of (i.e., the computing of price paths for) every instrument in our portfolio.

However, there are approximation procedures that can cut down on the calculations required. One of these is grid MC, which is essentially MCS applied to a mapped position: we map our portfolio onto a grid of factor values and then carry out a full valuation of the mapped portfolio. However, the number of calculations grows geometrically with the number of primary factors, so if the number of factors is large, we would need to use some other method or simplify the grid procedure further. One possible way to do this — a modified grid MC approach — is suggested by Pritsker (1997). An alternative is to apply full valuation to an approximation of the actual portfolio, the typical case being a delta–gamma approximation. This is the delta–gamma MC approach.

Simulation results by Pritsker (1997) suggest that full MC generates the most accurate VaR estimates, but is also the most computer time-intensive procedure. He also found that the other two approaches were comparable in accuracy, but the delta–gamma MC approach was 8 times faster.

T6.4   SPEEDING UP MONTE CARLO SIMULATION

For most MCS procedures, the accuracy of our results will vary with the square root of the number of trials, M. MCS can therefore be very computer-intensive, particularly when we need a high level of accuracy. Naturally, the number of calculations required also depends on the number of random drawings we take in each trial. A simple linear position in n imperfectly correlated assets will typically depend on the realisations of n random variables, and non-linear or more complex positions will often depend on even more. Hence, the value of a position with n assets would generally require realisations of *at least* n random variables in any one trial. If we have to carry out, say, M trials to get results of acceptable accuracy, we would then have to take drawings of at least nM random variables. Moreover, where we need to take account of path-dependency, each trial path for each of our n random variables would require N drawings of its own. This means we would need at least nMN random drawings, and this can be a very large number. For example, if we have, say, $n = 50$, $M = 10{,}000$ and $N = 20$ — and these figures are by no means untypical — then we would need $50 \times 10{,}000 \times 20$ or 10 million random drawings. We can easily find ourselves having to run many millions of calculations.

However, it is possible to obtain great improvements in speed (or accuracy, for any given number of calculations) by using one or more of a number of refinements.

T6.4.1 Antithetic Variables

One of these is the use of antithetic variables, which are usually used for derivatives pricing. We begin in the usual way by generating a random number or random path ϕ, and use this number/path to produce a derivatives value, $f(+\phi)$ say. We now replace ϕ with its negative, $-\phi$, and obtain the corresponding derivatives value $f(-\phi)$. We then take our derivatives value as the average of $f(+\phi)$ and $f(-\phi)$ (i.e., $\bar{f} = [f(+\phi) + f(-\phi)]/2$), so producing one derivatives value $\bar{f}$ from one value/path ϕ. We repeat this process M times, and take our derivatives price as the average of our M values of $\bar{f}$.

Both the $f(+\phi)$'s and the $\bar{f}$'s give us estimates of the derivatives price, but the standard error of the latter is generally much lower. The reason for this can be appreciated by seeing $f(+\phi)$ as coming from an unhedged portfolio and $\bar{f}$ as coming from a hedged one. Both portfolios have the same expected payoff — and hence produce estimates of the value of our derivatives position — but our hedged portfolio has a lower standard deviation.[8] Hence, the use of antithetics enables us to estimate derivatives prices (and of course Greeks) with much greater accuracy. Antithetic routines are also easy to incorporate into MCS programs (see, e.g., Clewlow and Strickland (1998, pp. 89–91)).

T6.4.2 Control Variates

Another approach often used to price derivatives is to use a control variate. Suppose we wish to price a derivative A, and there exists some similar derivative B that also has a closed-form solution. (Obviously, A doesn't have an analytic solution, because otherwise we wouldn't need to use MCS in the first place.) The derivative A might be a call option with no analytic solution (e.g., a European call with stochastic volatility, as in Hull and White (1987)), and B might be a vanilla call or a delta hedge (as in Clewlow and Strickland (1998, pp. 96–105)). The idea behind the control variate method is that we revise our MCS estimate of the value of A by adjusting for the error in the MCS estimate of B. This works because the MCS errors for both derivatives are similar, and the MCS error for B is known. If f_A^{MCS} and f_B^{MCS} are the MCS estimates of the prices of A and B, and f_B is the true (i.e., analytic) value of B, then our control–variate estimate of f_A is:

$$f_A = f_A^{MCS} - f_B^{MCS} + f_B \tag{T6.20}$$

As with antithetics, we can also interpret the control variate technique in hedging terms: B, being similar to A, constitutes a hedge, and the control variate technique adds a zero-value hedge to A. The value of the 'hedged' portfolio is therefore the same as the value of the unhedged portfolio (i.e., A), but the standard deviation of the hedged portfolio is much less.

The effect of control variates on the error in the MCS of the value of A can also be illustrated in terms of standard statistical theory. If σ_A^2 and σ_B^2 are the variances of the MCS estimates of the values of A and B, then the variance of the control variate estimate of the value of A, $\sigma_{control}^2$, is:

$$\sigma_{control}^2 = \sigma_A^2 + \sigma_B^2 - 2\rho\sigma_A\sigma_B \tag{T6.21}$$

where ρ is the correlation between A and B. If we now make the convenient simplifying assumption that $\sigma_A^2 \approx \sigma_B^2$, then:

$$\sigma_{control}^2 \approx 2\sigma_A^2(1 - \rho) \tag{T6.22}$$

---

[8]This explanation is however rather loose, and the effectiveness of antithetic sampling can vary considerably on the particular application at hand. For more on the effect of antithetic sampling on variance reduction, see Boyle *et al.* (1997, p. 1273) and Broadie and Glasserman (1998, pp. 184–186).

This is very revealing, as it tells us that the effectiveness of the control variate methods depends to a large extent on the correlation coefficient ρ: the higher the correlation, the lower the variance of the control-variate error. Indeed, a very good control (i.e., one with $\rho \approx 1$) can bring the error variance down to negligible values — and a bad one (i.e., one with $\rho < 1/2$) can actually increase the variance of our error.[9]

The control variate technique can also be extended to incorporate gamma and other hedges; however, the effectiveness of Greek-based control variates — delta hedges and so on — can depend on the frequency with which the hedge is assumed to be rebalanced, so we need to take account of this frequency in our simulations (see Clewlow and Strickland (1998, p. 93)).[10]

The effectiveness of this technique depends to a large extent on using control variates that are good for the problem at hand: in particular, we want easily computed controls that are highly correlated with the object we are interested in. As Broadie and Glasserman (1998, p. 194) point out, the most effective controls are those that take advantage of special features, and a good example is where we might use an Asian option on a geometric mean, an option with a known closed-form solution, as a control for an Asian option on an arithmetic mean. They then present results showing that if we wish to price an arithmetic Asian option, then using the underlying variable as a control leads to a variance reduction of 66% and using a vanilla call leads to a reduction of 72%; however, using a geometric Asian leads to a reduction of 99%. These falls in the variance reflect the correlations of the controls with the option to be hedged, so the effectiveness of the control depends on the extent to which the control 'matches' the derivative we are interested in. When using control variates to estimate the VaR, we can use a related VaR as a control variate (e.g., a VaR for a similar instrument for which we have good analytical or algorithmic solutions). When dealing with non-linearity, we can also use delta–gamma approximations as control variates (e.g., as in Cárdenas et al. (1999) or Glasserman et al. (1999a)). However, the effectiveness of delta-gamma control variates will depend on the accuracy of the delta-gamma approximation, and Glasserman et al. (1999a) report that this accuracy falls as the VaR confidence level becomes more extreme.

What kind of improvements can we realistically expect with antithetic and control variate techniques? A good indication is provided by Clewlow and Strickland (1998, p. 123), who present some results for a European arithmetic Asian option obtained using simple MCS, and MCS as modified by antithetic and/or Greek-based control variate methods. It turns out that simple MCS has the quickest computation time, and the variance-reduction modifications increase computation time by up to 32%. However, these modifications reduce the standard error by a factor of about 37. If we were to achieve the same level of accuracy with simple MCS, we would therefore have to increase our number of trials by a factor of 37^2 or 1,369, and there would be a roughly comparable increase in computing time. Variance-reduction methods can thus lead to impressive increases in accuracy and/or falls in computational time.

---

[9]However, the method outlined in the text is not efficient and can be improved. If we replace Equation (T6.20) with a more general expression, $f_A = f_A^{MCS} + \beta(f_B - f_B^{MCS})$, where Equation (T6.20) is the special case of this expression with $\beta = 1$, then we can easily show that the variance-minimising value of β is $\beta^* = \text{cov}(f_A^{MCS}, f_B^{MCS})/\sigma_{f_B^{MCS}}^2$. β^* may or may not be close to 1 in any given instance, and where it is not close to 1, this refinement allows us to achieve notably greater variance reduction than we could achieve using the method in the text. Its estimator $\hat{\beta}^*$ also has the attraction of being a regression coefficient, which means that we can easily estimate it by standard regression.

[10]Where we have multiple controls, we can easily estimate the optimal (i.e., variance-minimising) coefficients β_1^*, β_2^*, etc. using an appropriate generalisation of the expression used in the last footnote. This is not only very easy to do, but also very helpful because we might not otherwise have much idea what values these coefficients might take (Boyle et al. (1997, p. 1276)).

T6.4.3   Importance Sampling

Another variance-reduction technique is importance sampling. Loosely speaking, importance sampling adjusts the probabilities to reflect the importance of the paths or events concerned for the purpose at hand. For example, if we wish to simulate the value of an out-of-the-money option, we know that most paths will lead to a zero payoff, and these paths are a waste of computational effort because they contribute little or nothing to help determine the option value.[11] To get around this problem, we can sample only from paths where the option ends up in the money: if F is the distribution function for the underlying, and p is the probability of the option ending up in the money, we might work with $G = F/p$, which is the distribution function for the underlying conditional on the option ending up in the money. The estimate of the option value is then the average discounted payoff multiplied by p.

The IS method works on the idea that an expectation under one probability measure can be expressed as an expectation under another through the use of an adjustment known as a likelihood ratio or Radon–Nikodyn derivative. The trick is to change the probability measure to produce a more efficient estimator.

To give a concrete example, suppose we wish to evaluate the Black–Scholes price of a call option. We know that we can estimate the value of such an option using a risk-neutralised stochastic process in which the drift term is taken as r, the risk-free rate, i.e., we generate a large number of terminal values S_T and take the option value to be:

$$E_r[\max(S_T - K, 0)] \qquad (T6.23)$$

discounted at the risk-free rate, where K is the strike price and E_r is the expectations operator with drift parameter r. However, we can also estimate the option value using any other drift term, because:

$$E_r[\max(S_T - K, 0)] = E_\mu[\max(S_T - K, 0)L] \qquad (T6.24)$$

where L is the ratio of the lognormal densities with drift parameters r and μ evaluated at S_T, and this is:

$$L = \left(\frac{S_T}{S_0}\right)^{(r-\mu)/\sigma^2} \exp\left(\frac{(\mu^2 - r^2)T}{2\sigma^2}\right) \qquad (T6.25)$$

(see Boyle *et al.* (1997, pp. 1283–1284)). In fact, we can sample S_T from any distribution we like, provided that the likelihood ratio L is well-defined. In using IS for variance reduction, we would choose an alternative distribution to minimise the variance of our option price, and in this particular case, we can obtain a zero-variance estimator by sampling S_T from:

$$f(x) = h^{-1} \max(x - K, 0)e^{-rT}g(x) \qquad (T6.26)$$

where g is the lognormal density of S_T and h is a normalising constant that makes f integrate to 1.

This example illustrates the potential variance-reduction gains from IS.[12] Unfortunately, this particular IS method also requires knowledge of the solution itself, because h, the normalising constant, turns out to be very closely related to the Black–Scholes value itself, and this begs the point

---

[11]This example is borrowed from Hull (2000, p. 412).

[12]Besides being used for variance reduction, IS can also be used to price bonds with no closed-form solution. If a bond has no closed-form solution, we can often change its drift so that it has a closed-form solution, and we can then apply IS methods to price it. For more on this application of IS, see Boyle *et al.* (1997, pp. 1284–1285).

at issue, because we wouldn't have to use IS (or any other simulation method) in the first place if we already knew the option value. However, the moral of the story is that we can still obtain substantial reductions in variance in cases where the solution is unknown (i.e., in all the cases in which we would use IS in practice), provided we can find a good approximation to h.

To estimate VaR using IS, we would first estimate a preliminary high loss value (or VaR), say L. We could base L on a quadratic or delta–gamma approximation, and many alternative quadratic approximations have been suggested (see Section A5.2.4). Having obtained L, we would then use an appropriate change of probability measure, and a good candidate would be an exponential change in measure, as this is known to be close to optimal if VaR is close to L (Glasserman *et al.* (1999b, p. 351)). This change in measure ensures that a loss in excess of L is no longer rare, and so gives us a much more accurate estimator of our VaR.

As we have just seen, IS is often used to make rare events less rare, and the efficiency gains from using IS will tend to rise as the 'original' rare event becomes rarer — that is, the benefits from IS increase as our tails become more extreme. These features of IS therefore make it very useful for pricing out-of-the-money options and for estimating VaR and ETL, particularly at high confidence levels:[13]

- In the options context, some simulation results for down-and-in calls reported by Boyle *et al.* (1997, p. 1287) indicate that IS can lead to very substantial variance reductions: they get variance reduction by factors ranging from a minimum of 7 to a maximum of over 1,100, and these efficiency gains are particularly impressive when the barriers are well below the current option price (i.e., when the rare event of the option paying off becomes even rarer).
- We can also get very impressive efficiency gains when using IS to estimate VaR. Thus, Glasserman *et al.* (1999b, p. 355) report results showing that simple IS applied to a set of stock option portfolios can reduce VaR variances by factors ranging from 6 to 54, and the higher the confidence level, the greater the variance reduction.

T6.4.4 Stratified Sampling

Another powerful variance-reduction technique is stratified sampling.[14] Suppose we wish to generate, say, 100 values, $Z_1, Z_2, \ldots, Z_{100}$, to approximate some chosen distribution. If we generate these values using a standard random number generator, then a random sample of independent draws will tend to leave gaps in the approximated distribution and possibly under-represent the tails. Stratified sampling enables us to avoid these problems. To apply it, we first set:

$$V_j = (j - 1) + U_j/100, \quad j = 1, \ldots, 100 \tag{T6.27}$$

where $U_1, U_2, \ldots, U_n$ are independently and identically distributed uniform numbers lying in the range [0,1[(see, e.g., Broadie and Glasserman (1998, p. 178)). This transformation ensures that each V_j is distributed between the $(j - 1)$ and jth percentiles (e.g., so V_1 lies in the range [0, 0.01[, V_2 lies in the range [0.01, 0.02[, etc.). Since these values can also be interpreted as cdf values for our chosen distribution, we can obtain a stratified sample from our chosen distribution by applying the appropriate inverse distribution function. For example, if our chosen distribution is a standard

---

[13] The only additional costs of applying IS are the costs of evaluating the likelihood ratio and estimating the quadratic terms. As these are not (usually) too high, IS does not require many more calculations than standard MCS, and we can approximately evaluate the efficiency of IS in terms of the reduction in variance.

[14] For further discussions of stratified sampling, see, e.g., Curran (1994), Boyle *et al.* (1997, pp. 1279–1281), Broadie and Glasserman (1998, pp. 178–179, 186–189), Glasserman *et al.* (1999b), and Hereford and Shuetrim (2000).

normal, we apply the inverse transform:

$$Z_j = \Phi^{-1}(V_j) \tag{T6.28}$$

where $\Phi(\ )$ is the standard normal distribution function. Our values $Z_1, Z_2, \ldots, Z_n$ are then a stratified sample from a standard normal distribution (i.e., we have a Z-value corresponding to each percentile of the normal distribution, so eliminating gaps and the possible under-representation of tail values).

Stratified sampling is guaranteed to reduce variance, because the variance from a random sample can be decomposed into within-strata variance and across-strata variance, and stratified sampling eliminates the second term (Broadie and Glasserman (1998, p. 186)).[15]

However, one drawback of stratified sampling is that it destroys the independence of our simulated Z-values, and this makes it more difficult to estimate confidence intervals: because our sample values are not independent, we can no longer obtain reliable estimates of confidence intervals by the usual method of estimating the sample standard deviation and then invoking the central limit theorem, which presupposes independence. Instead, we have little practical alternative but to resort to batching: if we have a computation budget of, say, M replications, we might run n independent stratified samples of size M/n, and then estimate the variance of our simulated output variable from the n sample outputs; since *these* are independent, we can apply the central limit theorem to them and thence estimate confidence intervals in the usual way. This batching procedure enables us to recover our confidence intervals, but at the price of some loss in variance reduction compared with 'regular' stratified sampling.

Stratified sampling is particularly suited to VaR estimation, because we can choose or target our strata to focus on the tail we are interested in (see, e.g., Hereford and Shuetrim (2000)). If we are estimating VaR, there is no point using equal percentile strata, because that would involve generating a lot of central mass values that would tell us relatively little about our VaR. It would make more sense to choose our strata so that we generate a lot of tail values and relatively few non-tail ones — or, put differently, we over-sample from the tail, and under-sample from the rest of the distribution. Since these simulations would tell us much more about VaR than equal-percentile stratified sampling, we could expect this approach to yield considerably more accurate VaR estimates. Naturally, the weights used would be chosen to ensure that our percentile estimates were still unbiased.

The only question then is how to allocate samples to our strata, and the answer to this question is not always obvious. However, one way to resolve this problem is to run a preliminary simulation exercise and use the results of this exercise to select our strata. We could also use IS to determine sample allocation, or use one or more of the heuristic rules (or rules of thumb) suggested by Glasserman *et al.* (1999b, pp. 353–354, 356), and their results suggest that these have the potential to capture a significant fraction of the potential variance reduction achievable using an optimal allocation of samples to strata. A final possibility is to use some 'learning rule' (e.g., such as a neural network approach) that starts with a given set of strata allocations, and periodically updates these as the simulations continue and interim VaR results come in, gradually 'fine-tuning' the strata allocations so they provide a better and better focus on points around the VaR.

The theory of stratified sampling also applies to higher dimensions. If we wish to generate a stratified sample from a d-dimensional hypercube with n strata, we can partition the unit hypercube into n^d equal-volume cubes with length $1/n$ along each dimension, these being the d-dimensional equivalents of our earlier partition of the unit interval $[0,1[$ into n sub-divisions. We then sample from within each hypercube to obtain a stratified sample from the hypercube $[0, 1[^d$, and transform them using the appropriate inverse function to obtain the stratified sample corresponding to our chosen

---

[15]For a more formal illustration of this point, see Cárdenas *et al.* (1999, p. 59).

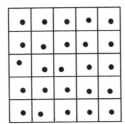 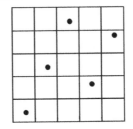

Figure T6.3   Stratified sampling vs. a Latin hypercube.

Note: The box on the left represents the data points generated using full stratified sampling, with $d = 2$ and $n = 5$, and that on the right represents the points generated with a Latin hypercube.

distribution function. To apply stratified sampling in d-dimensions, we would replace Equation (T6.27) by:

$$V_j = ((i_1, i_2, \ldots, i_d) + U_j)/n, \quad i_k = 1, \ldots, n-1, \ k = 1, \ldots, d \qquad (\text{T6.29})$$

which is just a straightforward d-dimensional generalisation of Equation (T6.27) (see, e.g., Boyle *et al.* (1997, p. 1280)).

Unfortunately, multidimensional stratified sampling rapidly becomes impractical as d gets large, because the number of data points we need to generate, n^d, grows rapidly with n. One solution to this problem is to keep down n, the number of strata, but this is often not particularly desirable because it can mean that we lose many of the benefits of stratification in the first place.

A more promising solution[16] to this problem is to use a Latin hypercube approach, the idea behind which is to select n stratified sample points and then project permutations of these points onto the n^d points in a d-dimensional hypercube.[17] The way this is done is illustrated in Figure T6.3 for $d = 2$. This figure shows two boxes each representing a two-dimensional hypercube, and each of which is divided into $n = 5$ rows and the same number of columns. Full stratification is illustrated in the box on the left-hand side, and requires $n^2 = 25$ random drawings, one for each little box. However, with a Latin hypercube, we choose n random points, subject to the constraint that each row and each column is represented exactly once. This is represented in the second box, where there are only $n = 5$ data points, and each row and each column has exactly one data point.

In both cases, the points within the boxes are selected according to a two-dimensional uniform distribution, and the difference between the two relates to the way in which the hypercubes are selected. To see how the LH approach does this, let U_j^i be identically and independently distributed over the interval [0,1], where $j = 1, \ldots, d$ and $i = 1, \ldots, n$. Now let $\pi_1, \pi_2, \ldots, \pi_d$ be independent random permutations of $\{1, \ldots, n\}$ sampled uniformly from the complete universe of $n!$ possible such permutations. We now set:

$$V_j^i = \frac{\pi_i(j) - 1 + U_j^i}{n} \qquad (\text{T6.30})$$

---

[16]It is, however, not the only alternative solution. We could also use a Brownian bridge method, which generates points in a smaller dimensional space and uses these to generate the most important points along a path. An example might be where we strip down the dimensionality of our problem using principal components analysis, and then apply stratified sampling to a space whose dimensionality is determined by the most important principal components. For more on the Brownian bridge approach, see Broadie and Glasserman (1998, pp. 187–188).

[17]Latin hypercubes are discussed in more detail in Boyle *et al.* (1997, pp. 1280–1281) and Broadie and Glasserman (1998, pp. 188–189).

The n points $V^1 = (V_1^1, \ldots, V_d^1), \ldots, V^n = (V_1^n, \ldots, V_d^n)$ make up a Latin hypercube sample of size n in dimension d (see, e.g., Broadie and Glasserman (1998, pp. 188–189)). Since the calculations involved are fairly easily programmed, the LH approach gives us a very practical means of applying stratified sampling to higher dimensional problems.[18]

T6.4.5 Moment Matching

A final variance-reduction method is moment matching, which was suggested by Barraquand (1995). The idea behind moment matching is to adjust the simulated data so that one or more of their sample moments matches (i.e., is equal to) the relevant moments from the assumed theoretical distribution. This adjusted sample then has the theoretically 'correct' sample moments, free of sample error, and this is very useful because it can ensure that the underlying is correctly priced. We can regard moment matching as attempting to exploit what we already know, in this case our (assumed) information about the 'true' moments of a distribution. Moment matching can also be regarded as a generalisation of the antithetic variate approach, since the antithetic approach ensures that the sample mean of our 'random' numbers is zero; however, unlike the antithetic approach, the moment-matching approach usually extends this treatment to the second and sometimes higher moments of our sample.

We can apply moment matching in various ways. For example, if our random sample values Z_i are drawn from a normal distribution with mean μ and standard deviation σ, but have sample mean m and sample standard deviation s, we can adjust our simulated values using:

$$\tilde{Z}_i = (Z_i - m)\sigma/s + \mu \tag{T6.31}$$

to ensure that the adjusted values $\tilde{Z}_i$ have (the first two) sample moments equal to their population moments. We would then feed the $\tilde{Z}_i$-values into our underlying stochastic process (e.g., Equation (T6.10)) instead of the original Z_i-values. Alternatively, we could match (say, the first two) moments of the sample distribution of the underlying, using something like:

$$\tilde{S}_i(T) = (S_i(T) - m_{S_T})\sigma_{S_T}/s_{S_T} + \mu_{S_T} \tag{T6.32}$$

where m_{S_T} and s_{S_T} are the sample mean and standard deviation, and μ_{S_T} and σ_{S_T} are the assumed 'true' mean and standard deviation. There is, therefore, some ambiguity with moment matching in terms of which variable should be chosen for matching and which features of its distribution should be matched.

Moment matching has both plus and minus points. On the plus side, it ensures that we make effective use of our assumptions about the moments of the variable(s) involved, and so rids us of at least some sample error. Moreover, as Broadie and Glasserman (1998, p. 192) point out, it produces exact prices for any instrument depending linearly and exclusively on the quantities with matched means. This implies, for example, that if zero-coupon bond prices have been matched, then we will get exact prices for coupon bonds and swaps. Obviously, this exactness breaks down with non-linearity, so matching the mean of the underlying does not ensure that options will be correctly priced, but we can still safely say that the more linear the payoff, the greater the likely error reduction. Finally, moment matching has the potential to reduce simulation errors by a respectable amount (e.g., Boyle *et al.* (1997, pp. 1278–1279) report results suggesting that matching the first two moments can reduce simulation errors by a factor ranging from 2 to 10).

On the negative side, all moment-matching methods produce biased estimates with non-linear payoffs, although the bias goes to zero as M gets large. This bias is likely to be small in most

---

[18]We can also combine stratified sampling with other variance-reduction methods, most obviously importance sampling. The combination of these methods is discussed further by Glasserman *et al.* (1999a) and Fuglsbjerg (2000).

financial problems, although there are extreme exceptions (see Boyle *et al.* (1997, pp. 1277–1278)), and we can sometimes, though not always, correct for it using standard bias adjustments (see Broadie and Glasserman (1998, p. 192)). The other drawback of these methods is one that they share with stratified sampling: because the adjustments are applied across all sample paths, they introduce dependence among the adjusted sample values when these would otherwise be independent. This dependence seriously complicates the problem of constructing confidence intervals and, as with stratified sampling, Boyle *et al.* (1997, p. 1277) suggest that the only practicable way to get confidence intervals is to apply moment matching to independent batches of runs and then estimate the standard error from the batch means — and this inevitably reduces the efficiency of the moment-matching approach.[19]

T6.5   ADVANTAGES AND DISADVANTAGES OF MONTE CARLO SIMULATION

T6.5.1   Advantages

MCS methods have a number of advantages and disadvantages. Their main advantages are:

- They are easy to use once the routines/programs have been set up, and there is plenty of good software available.
- They can easily accommodate more elaborate/sophisticated stochastic processes than GBM ones, unlike many closed-form or analytic approaches.
- They have no problems dealing with multiple risk factors, correlations and fat tails.
- They also have no problems dealing with the complexities of path-dependency, again unlike many analytic alternatives.
- They are easy to modify.
- They are capable of considerable refinement to increase accuracy and/or reduce calculation time.
- They give us indications of the accuracy of their results, and estimating confidence intervals is very easy.
- We can increase the accuracy of our results simply by running more trials.
- They are more powerful than finite difference methods when dealing with moderate or high dimension problems.
- We can easily extend them to deal with aspects of parameter risk and model risk. This is discussed further in Box T6.4.

T6.5.2   Disadvantages

The main disadvantages of MCS methods are:

- They can be slow because of the number of calculations involved, particularly when we have lots of risk factors.

---

[19] One other approach worth mentioning is conditional Monte Carlo simulation (CMCS). This is based on the idea that the conditional variance of a random variable X given some other random variable Y will usually be less, and never more, than the unconditional variance of X: in effect, replacing the unconditional variance by the conditional one reduces the variance because we are doing part of the integration analytically, so leaving less for MCS to do. This approach was used by Hull and White (1987) to price options in the presence of stochastic volatility, and Boyle *et al.* (1997, pp. 1288–1290) apply it to price other options. The results reported in the latter study suggest that these methods can produce substantial reductions in variance; however, they also take more calculation time because of the need to do more work analytically, so the optimal degree of conditioning reflects a trade-off between the time spent on simulation calculations and the time spent on analytical calculations.

- MCS approaches are less efficient than finite difference methods when we have very low dimensional problems.
- More importantly, MCS approaches have difficulty handling early-exercise features. The problem here is that because MCS methods work forward in time, they have no easy way of establishing whether instruments should be exercised early. In this respect, methods that work forward in time are inferior to methods that work backward in time, such as binomial trees or finite difference methods, and which (precisely because they work from the terminal date backwards) have no problem checking for possible early exercise. That said, MCS approaches can be tweaked to handle early exercise, but it is not easy.

Box T6.4   Using Simulation Methods to Deal with Parameter and Model Risk

One attractive feature of simulation methods is that we can also use them to estimate parameter and model risk. Parameter risk is the risk of error due to the use of incorrect parameter values (e.g., due to sampling error or inappropriate assumptions). We can assess parameter risk by obtaining estimates using ranges of alternative parameter assumptions or, more ambitiously, by replacing parameter values with drawings from pdfs. In many cases, we might not be sure of the value of a particular parameter, but we might be able to quantify our uncertainty about it in terms of a subjective (or Bayesian) pdf with particular parameter values of its own: for example, we might not know the value of a volatility parameter, but we might be able to describe our uncertainty about it in terms of a lognormal with a particular mean and standard deviation. We then replace the parameter concerned with a drawing from this distribution, and our results will reflect our parameter uncertainty as well as our other assumptions. In principle, we can apply much the same approach to any other parameters we are uncertain about.

Model risk is the risk of error due to inappropriate model assumptions (e.g., we might assume that a certain process is normal when it is really Student t). In principle, we can handle model risk in much the same way as we handle parameter risk: we specify our uncertainty about the model in terms of a subjective pdf, in this case, a binomial or multinomial pdf that selects the precise model to be used. We then replace the assumption of a given known model with a drawing from this pdf, and this drawing determines the model to be used in any given trial.

Naturally, the more parameters or stochastic processes we endogenise in this way, the more calculations are involved and the slower our simulation routines will be.[20]

T6.6   CONCLUSIONS

MCS approaches have a number of major attractions: they are easy to use once set up; they are very flexible and powerful; they can easily handle sophisticated stochastic processes, multiple risk factors and their correlations, and the complexities of path-dependency; and so forth. On the other hand, they can also be intensive, both in terms of computing time and in terms of the intellectual/human resources needed to run them; and they can have difficulty handling early-exercise features.[21]

---

[20]For more on this 'subjective' approach to VaR estimation and some specific examples, see Dowd (2000a).

[21]As mentioned elsewhere, the main issue here is computational time rather than intrinsic feasibility. If we wish to use simulation methods to price American options or estimate their VaR or ETL, we can do so using 'simulation (or tree pricing)

Despite these drawbacks, there are good reasons to expect simulation methods to become much more widely used in the future. Simulation methods depend largely on raw computing power, and IT costs have been falling at a rate of 25–30% or more a year for decades, and improvements in computing power have been even more rapid. We can expect these trends to continue into the foreseeable future, and they, in turn, will continue to make simulation methods increasingly fast and ever more user-friendly. Simulation methods will therefore become ever more attractive — and ever more popular — as times goes by.

T6.7   RECOMMENDED READING

Boyle *et al.* (1997); Broadie and Glasserman (1998); Brotherton-Ratcliffe (1994); Cárdenas *et al.* (1999); Clewlow and Caverhill (1994); Clewlow and Strickland (1998); Glasserman *et al.* (1999b, 2000a,b); Hull (2000, ch. 16); Press *et al.* (1992); Wilmott (2000, ch. 66).

---

within simulation' approaches stochastic meshes, least-squares simulation, etc. See p. 98, note 2. However, such methods are generally computationally intensive, and may or may not be practically feasible in any given context.

Tool No. 7
Forecasting Volatilities, Covariances
and Correlations

Tool No. 7 deals with the forecasting of volatilities, covariances and correlations.[1] This is one of the most important subjects in modern risk measurement, and is critical to derivatives pricing, hedging, and VaR and ETL estimation.[2]

The layout is as follows. Section T7.1 deals with the estimation of volatilities, and covers each of the four main approaches to volatility estimation: the equal-weighted moving average (or historical), exponentially weighted moving average (EWMA), GARCH, and implied approaches. The treatment of covariances and correlations in Section T7.2 parallels that of volatilities, and Section T7.3 deals with the estimation of variance–covariance and correlation matrices.

T7.1 FORECASTING VOLATILITIES

T7.1.1 Defining Volatility

We can define volatility as the standard deviation of returns. However, since returns increase with the time period over which they are measured, other things being equal, we need to standardise the period over which volatility is quoted, so we can make meaningful comparisons of volatilities across different horizon periods. The usual way of doing so is to quote volatility on an annualised percentage basis, i.e.:

$$\text{Volatility at time } t = (100\sigma_t)\% \tag{T7.1}$$

where σ_t is the annualised standard deviation of returns. If the volatility is constant, and the random variable follows a random walk, we can derive a straightforward rule to extrapolate the h-period variance from the 1-period variance: given these assumptions, the variance over h periods will be equal to h times the variance over one period, and it follows that:

$$\sigma|_{h\text{-period}} = \sqrt{h}\,\sigma|_{1\text{-period}} \tag{T7.2}$$

Hence, if $\sigma|_{1\text{-period}}$ is 1, the variance over two periods is $\sqrt{2}$, the variance over 10 periods is $\sqrt{10}$, and so on. This is the infamous 'square root of time' rule, which allows us to extrapolate a variance defined over one period to obtain a variance defined over another.

---

[1] In theory, we should be careful not to confuse forecasts and estimates. A forecast is what we expect the value of a certain parameter or other quantity to be, over a defined horizon period, so all forecasts are estimates but not all estimates are forecasts. However, in the present context, we can usually use the terms 'forecast' and 'estimate' as if they were interchangeable.

[2] There are a number of good discussions of this subject in the literature (e.g., Alexander and Leigh (1998), Giannopoulos (2000) and Alexander (1998)). For how these estimates are used (and misused) in derivatives pricing and risk management, see, e.g., Taleb (1997c).

T7.1.2 Historical Volatility Forecasts

We turn now to volatility forecasting. If we assume for the sake of argument that the 'true' volatility is constant, and if we ignore scaling factors for convenience, one obvious choice is the historical moving-average estimate:

$$\sigma_t^2 = \sum_{i=1}^{n} (x_{t-i} - \bar{x})^2/(n-1) \tag{T7.3}$$

which also provides an unbiased estimate of our volatility. However, if we are dealing with daily data the mean return will be very low, and we can dispense with the need to measure it by treating it as if it were zero. Setting the mean to zero often makes an insignificant difference to our estimates, and (usually) reduces their standard errors (Figlewski (1994)). With large samples, it is also common to work with n rather than $n-1$ in the denominator. These modifications lead to:

$$\sigma_t^2 = \sum_{i=1}^{n} x_{t-i}^2/n \tag{T7.4}$$

as our volatility equation. The important point to note about either of these equations — (T7.3) or (T7.4) — is that they give equal weight to all observations up to the last nth observation, and no weight to any other, more distant, observations.

There are several problems with the historical approach. One problem is that if we stick with the assumption that 'true' volatility is constant, then any differences in our volatility estimates must arise solely from sample error. A short-period (or low-n) estimate will then produce a more volatile volatility estimate than a long-period (or high-n) estimate, but any such differences can only be ascribed to sampling error, because we have assumed that the true volatility is constant. So if we wish to allow the true volatility to change over time, we need to make less restrictive assumptions about it.

A second problem arises because this model implies that more distant events in the sample period will have the same effect as more recent ones. If an unusual event occurs at date t, this weighting scheme implies that it will continue to influence our volatility estimate for the next n periods, even though the event has passed and markets have returned to normal conditions. The result is a ghost effect — our volatility estimates are artificially high (or low) for the next n periods after the event has taken place, and then suddenly return to normal after the event has dropped out of our sample period. This dropping off at the end of n periods has nothing to do with 'true' volatility, but is entirely a consequence of the way that volatility is estimated.

These effects are illustrated in Figure T7.1 for Equation (T7.3) estimated on hypothetical standard normal return data for values of n equal to 20 and 60. If n is large, the volatility estimate is more smooth over time and less responsive to individual observations. When our unusual event occurs — a big return observation that occurs at $t = 150$ — both estimates of volatility jump and remain high for a while. These high volatility estimates are ghost effects, and the high-volatility 'plateau' has a length n and a height inverse to n. The height and length of these 'plateaus' follow directly from the number of observations used to produce our volatility estimates: the smaller is n, the bigger the influence of any shock, but the shorter it lasts. We therefore face a trade-off in our ghost effects: if n is low, the 'plateau' is high but relatively short lasting; and if n is high, the 'plateau' is lower in height but lasts longer.

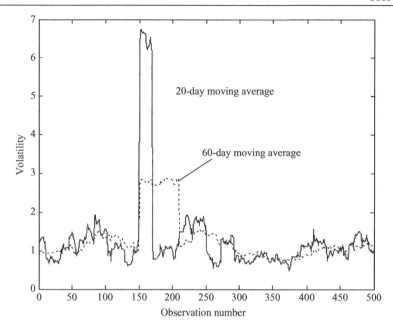

Figure T7.1 Historical volatilities.

T7.1.3 Exponentially Weighted Moving Average Volatility

One way to ameliorate the drawbacks of equal-weighed moving average schemes is to use a moving average scheme with declining weights, so we can give greater weight to more recent observations and less weight to more distant ones. This type of weighting scheme might (arguably) be justified by claiming that volatility tends to change over time in a stable way, which is certainly more reasonable than assuming it to be constant. Our volatility forecasting model then has the form:

$$\sigma_t^2 = \sum_{i=1}^{n} \alpha_i x_{t-i}^2 \tag{T7.5}$$

where the weights, the α_i terms, decline as i gets larger, and sum to 1. One of the simplest examples is the exponentially weighted moving average (EWMA) model, in which the weights decline exponentially over time: this means that $\alpha_{i+1}/\alpha_i = \lambda$, where λ is a constant between 0 and 1. The combination of $\alpha_{i+1}/\alpha_i = \lambda$ and the α_i terms summing to 1 leads to the following volatility forecasting equation:

$$\sigma_t^2 \approx (1 - \lambda) \sum_{i=1}^{n} \lambda^{i-1} x_{t-i}^2 \tag{T7.6}$$

The approximation is valid provided that n is sufficiently large. The EWMA scheme has the intuitively appealing property that the influence of any observation declines over time at a stable rate, and it is easy to apply because it relies on only one parameter, λ.[3]

---

[3] The EWMA approach can also be refined. For example, Guermat and Harris (2000) propose a modified EWMA estimator that is more robust to fat tails in return distributions, and they present evidence to suggest that this estimator produces superior results to the standard EWMA estimator.

The EWMA also leads to a very straightforward volatility-updating formula. If we lag Equation (T7.6) by one period, and multiply throughout by λ, we get:

$$\lambda\sigma_{t-1}^2 \approx \lambda(1-\lambda)\sum_{i=1}^{n}\lambda^{i-1}x_{t-i-1}^2 = (1-\lambda)\sum_{i=1}^{n}\lambda^i x_{t-i-1}^2 \qquad (T7.7)$$

We now subtract Equation (T7.7) from Equation (T7.6) and rearrange to get:

$$\sigma_t^2 = \lambda\sigma_{t-1}^2 + (1-\lambda)x_{t-1}^2 - (1-\lambda)\lambda^n x_{t-n-1}^2 \approx \lambda\sigma_{t-1}^2 + (1-\lambda)x_{t-1}^2 \qquad (T7.8)$$

This formula tells us that the estimate of volatility for day t, σ_t, made at the end of day $t-1$, is calculated from the previous day's volatility estimate, σ_{t-1}, and the previous day's return, x_{t-1}. The EWMA rule Equation (T7.8) can therefore be interpreted as a simple updating rule that allows us to update our daily volatility estimate each day based on the most recent daily return. A high λ means that the weight declines slowly, and a low λ means it declines quickly. Its value would need to be determined from the data at hand, but the *RiskMetrics Technical Document* suggests that we can often get away with taking λ to be about 0.94 for daily return data (*Technical Document* (1996, p. 97)).

Some EWMA volatility estimates are plotted in Figure T7.2 using the same data set as the last figure, with values of λ equal to 0.90 and 0.95. When the shock occurs at $t = 150$, both EWMA volatility estimates spike upwards, and then fall back down as time passes. The low-λ volatility rises the most, but declines more rapidly afterwards; the high-λ volatility rises less sharply, but also falls at a slower rate in later periods. It is clear from this figure that the EWMA tends to produce less prominent ghost effects than equal-weighted moving average schemes: instead of the n-period plateau that we get with equal-weighted schemes, the EWMA produces a continuous fall in volatility as the shock observation is assigned an ever-declining weight as the shock date recedes into the past.

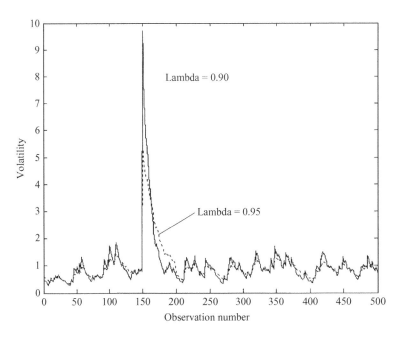

Figure T7.2   EWMA volatilities.

We can also use Equation (T7.8) to make forecasts of future volatility. We begin by leading Equation (T7.8) by one period:

$$\sigma_{t+1}^2 \approx \lambda\sigma_t^2 + (1 - \lambda)x_t^2 \tag{T7.9}$$

Taking expectations as of t, and noting that $E(x_t^2) = \sigma_t^2$, we get:

$$E\left(\sigma_{t+1}^2\right) \approx \lambda\sigma_t^2 + (1 - \lambda)\sigma_t^2 = \sigma_t^2 \tag{T7.10}$$

so the 1-period ahead forecast of our volatility is approximately equal to our current volatility estimate, σ_t^2. It is easy to show, by similar reasoning, that our k-period ahead volatility forecast is the same:

$$E\left(\sigma_{t+k}^2\right) = \sigma_t^2, \quad k = 1, 2, 3, \ldots \tag{T7.11}$$

The EWMA model therefore implies that our current volatility estimate also gives us our best forecast of volatility any period in the future. However, this 'flat' volatility forecast is not appealing, because it ignores any recent dynamics in our data: for example, even if volatility has been rising strongly in the recent past, the EWMA predicts — not too plausibly — that future volatility will immediately level off and remain at its current level.

T7.1.4   GARCH Models

A solution to this latter problem is provided by GARCH (generalised autoregressive conditional heteroscedasticity) models, which are a popular, and in some respects superior, set of alternatives to the EWMA model.[4] Two of the most important stylised facts with return data are that they show volatility clustering (i.e., they go through alternating periods of high and low volatility) and leptokurtosis (i.e., fatter than normal tails). GARCH models can accommodate both these stylised facts very easily. Indeed, they are tailor-made for volatility clustering, and this clustering produces returns with fatter than normal tails even if the innovations — the random shocks — are themselves normally distributed. The basic GARCH(p,q) model postulates that volatility depends on q past volatilities and p past returns:

$$\sigma_t^2 = \omega + a_1\varepsilon_{t-1}^2 + \ldots + a_p\varepsilon_{t-p}^2 + \beta_1\sigma_{t-1}^2 + \ldots + \beta_q\sigma_{t-q}^2$$
$$\omega > 0, \ \alpha_1, \ldots, \alpha_p, \beta_1, \ldots, \ \beta_q \geq 0 \tag{T7.12}$$

where the constraints on parameter values are necessary to ensure that the conditional variance is always positive. GARCH models thus postulate that current volatility depends on one or more past volatilities and past returns, but in a more general way than EWMA models do. GARCH models vary in the number of past terms used, and we should choose these terms according to the principle of parsimony (i.e., choose the minimum that fit the data acceptably). GARCH models also differ in the distribution governing the error term ε_t. This distribution will typically be conditionally normal, and conditional normality will produce leptokurtosis — greater than normal kurtosis — in our returns, consistent with the stylised fact that observed returns usually show excess kurtosis. We can also

---

[4]The basic ARCH model was first suggested by Engle (1982), and the GARCH generalisation was suggested by Bollerslev (1986). These subsequently led to a large family of GARCH-type models, including the AGARCH, EGARCH, IGARCH, MARCH, NARCH, QTARCH, SPARCH, STARCH, SWARCH and TARCH models, to name only the most pronounceable. Some of the more relevant ones for our purposes are discussed below.

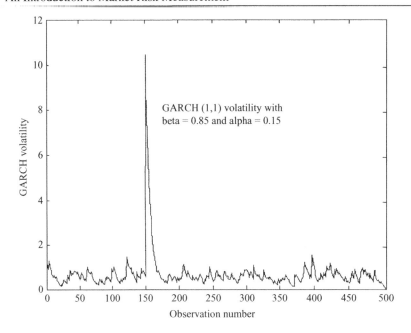

Figure T7.3   Plot of GARCH(1,1) volatility.

further fatten our tails if we replace the assumption of conditional normality by a conditional t or conditional mixture-of-normals distribution.[5]

T7.1.4.1   The GARCH(1,1) Model

The most popular GARCH model is the GARCH(1,1):

$$\sigma_t^2 = \omega + \alpha x_{t-1}^2 + \beta \sigma_{t-1}^2; \quad \omega > 0, \ \alpha, \beta \geq 0, \ \alpha + \beta \leq 1 \tag{T7.13}$$

This model is easy to apply, uses a small number of parameters, and often fits the data fairly well. A high value of β means that volatility is 'persistent' and takes a long time to change; and a high value of α means volatility is 'spiky' and quick to react to market movements. It is also common to get estimates of β of over 0.7, but α is usually less than 0.25 (Alexander (1998, p. 136)).

To give an indication of what a typical GARCH volatility looks like, Figure T7.3 gives a plot of a GARCH(1,1) process against our earlier hypothetical data set, estimated with $\beta = 0.85$ and $\alpha = 0.15$. As we can see, the GARCH volatility estimate is very responsive to the data, and the shock at $t = 150$ quickly dissipates from the volatility estimate. The GARCH process therefore suffers from relatively small ghost effects.

Note too that the GARCH(1,1) volatility depends on the same variables as the EWMA, but there are now three parameters instead of one, and we can regard the EWMA as a special case of the GARCH(1,1) process that occurs when $\omega = 0$, $\alpha = 1 - \lambda$ and $\beta = \lambda$.

---

[5]There are many pre-programmed procedures for carrying out GARCH estimation available in standard econometric and statistical packages, including MATLAB. The basic idea is to choose parameter estimates to maximise the likelihood under an assumed error density function. In applying GARCH models, we also have to choose the number of parameters, and there are a variety of standard tests to do so (e.g., the Box–Pierce and Ljung–Box tests). For more on these issues, see, e.g., Alexander (1998, pp. 141–145) or Giannopoulos (2000, pp. 53–55).

The GARCH(1,1) with positive intercept ω also has the attraction that it allows us to model the volatility as mean-reverting — so that if the volatility is relatively high, it will tend to fall over time; and if the volatility is relatively low, it will tend to rise over time. The long-run variance — the value to which the variance will tend to revert in the long run — is $\omega/(1 - \alpha - \beta)$.

GARCH models also give straightforward volatility forecasts. Following Hull (2000, p. 379), if we let $V = \omega/(1 - \alpha - \beta)$, then Equation (T7.13) implies:

$$\sigma_t^2 = (1 - \alpha - \beta)V + \alpha x_{t-1}^2 + \beta \sigma_{t-1}^2$$
$$\Rightarrow \sigma_t^2 - V = \alpha\left(x_{t-1}^2 - V\right) + \beta\left(\sigma_{t-1}^2 - V\right) \tag{T7.14}$$

We now lead Equation (T7.14) by k periods:

$$\sigma_{t+k}^2 - V = \alpha\left(x_{t+k-1}^2 - V\right) + \beta\left(\sigma_{t+k-1}^2 - V\right) \tag{T7.15}$$

Given that the expected value of $x_{t+k-1}^2 = \sigma_{n+k-1}^2$, it follows that:

$$E\left[\sigma_{t+k}^2 - V\right] = (\alpha + \beta)E\left(x_{t+k-1}^2 - V\right) \tag{T7.16}$$

and so our k-period ahead volatility forecast is:

$$E\left(\sigma_{t+k}^2\right) = V + (\alpha + \beta)^k\left(\sigma_t^2 - V\right) \tag{T7.17}$$

Since $\alpha + \beta < 1$, the second term in Equation (T7.17) falls as k gets larger, so the forecast variance converges to V as we look further into the future, which justifies the earlier claim that V can be interpreted as the long-run variance. If $\sigma_t^2 > V$, the expected k-period ahead variance is larger than V, and if $\sigma_t^2 < V$, the expected k-period ahead variance is smaller than V. The GARCH forecasts therefore tend to revert back to the long-run variance V.

These forecasts can then be used to derive estimates of the volatility term structure. Assuming that we are working with log returns, we know that the return at time t over the next n periods is:

$$r_{t,n} = \sum_{j=1}^{n} r_{t+j} \tag{T7.18}$$

This in turn implies that:

$$Var_t(r_{t,n}) = \sum_{i=1}^{n} Var_t(r_{t+i}) + \sum_{i=1}^{n}\sum_{j=1}^{n} Cor_t(r_{t+i}, r_{t+j}) \tag{T7.19}$$

We can therefore derive estimates of the volatility term structure from forecasts of future 1-period volatilities and covariances. However, in many cases the correlation terms in Equation (T7.19) will be small relative to the volatility terms, so we can often ignore them and treat the volatility of the n-period return as the sum of n 1-period volatilities:

$$Var_t(r_{t,n}) \approx \sum_{i=1}^{n} Var_t(r_{t+i}) \tag{T7.20}$$

So the basic GARCH model produces a volatility term structure that eventually converges on nV, because each of the $Var_t(r_{t+i})$ terms on the right-hand side of Equation (T7.20) eventually converges on V. This is reasonable enough for some purposes, but can sometimes be rather restrictive.[6]

T7.1.4.2 Integrated GARCH

Another popular GARCH model is the integrated GARCH or IGARCH model. This is applicable when our return series is not stationary — as is commonly the case — and so the long-term variance V does not exist. In the three-parameter case, we can think of $\alpha + \beta$ becoming 1, and the GARCH(1,1) model becoming:

$$\sigma_t^2 = \omega + \beta\sigma_{t-1}^2 + (1-\beta)x_{t-1}^2 \tag{T7.21}$$

This model is often used in currency markets and includes the EWMA as a special case when $\omega = 0$.

T7.1.4.3 Components GARCH

The standard GARCH model has the volatility converge to a long-term or baseline level that depends on the GARCH parameters, but is constant over time. This is somewhat restrictive, but can be relaxed using the components GARCH model. For example, if we are using a GARCH(1,1) model, we would replace the constant V by a baseline volatility equation:

$$V_t = \bar{\omega} + \rho(V_{t-1} - \bar{\omega}) + \phi\left(x_{t-1}^2 - \sigma_{t-1}^2\right) \tag{T7.22}$$

which allows the baseline volatility to vary in response to market conditions. Equations (T7.13) and (T7.22) together define the components GARCH(1,1) model.

T7.1.4.4 Factor GARCH

Another handy member of the GARCH family is the factor GARCH model (see, e.g., Engle and Mezrich (1996)).[7] This model allows a number of volatilities (and correlations) to be estimated from one (or more, if desired) volatility estimates. In the standard case, we wish to estimate a number of volatilities from a single market volatility index. For example, we might have n different assets, whose returns are linked to a market return by a CAPM-type equation:

$$r_{i,t} = \alpha_i + \beta_i M_t + \varepsilon_{i,t}; \quad i = 1, \dots, n \tag{T7.23}$$

The variance of asset $r_{i,t}$, $\sigma_{i,t}$, is then given by:

$$\sigma_{i,t}^2 = \beta_i^2 \sigma_{M,t}^2 + \sigma_{\varepsilon_{i,t}}^2 \tag{T7.24}$$

To apply the factor GARCH model, we estimate the set of equations (T7.23) and recover estimates of the β_i and $\sigma_{\varepsilon_{i,t}}^2$ terms. We then apply a standard univariate GARCH procedure to estimate the market volatility, $\sigma_{M,t}^2$, and input our parameter estimates into Equation (T7.24) to generate volatility estimates for our individual assets.

---

[6]There are also GARCH models that produce asymmetric effects, if we want them. The most prominent of these are the asymmetric GARCH (or AGARCH) and exponential GARCH (or EGARCH) models. For more on these, see, e.g., Giannopoulos (2000, pp. 52–53).

[7]The term factor GARCH is sometimes used in a rather different sense (e.g., by Christiansen (1998)), where GARCH is applied to the principal components or principal factors in a data sense. This second form of factor GARCH is discussed further below.

Box T7.1   Forecasting Volatility Over Longer Horizons

If we are interested in forecasting volatility over longer horizons, it is often suggested that we can do so by using a simple square root extrapolation rule. If $\sigma_{1,t}$ is our forecast at time t of volatility over the next 1-day period, then our forecast of volatility over the next h days is $\sqrt{h}\,\sigma_{1,t}$. This rule is valid if log returns r_t are independently and identically distributed (iid). In this case, the 1-period return $r_{1,t}$ has an iid error ε_t with zero mean and variance σ^2, the h-period return $r_{h,t}$ has a zero mean and variance $h\sigma^2$, and the square root rule immediately follows.

However, the square root rule depends on the iid assumption and can be very misleading when that assumption does not hold. For example, assume we have a GARCH(1,1) process similar to (13):

$$\sigma_{1,t}^2 = \omega + \alpha x_{1,t-1}^2 + \beta \sigma_{1,t-1}^2; \quad \omega > 0,\ \alpha,\ \beta \geq 0,\ \alpha + \beta < 1$$

that gives 1-day ahead forecasts. Drost and Nijman (1993) show that the corresponding h-day process is:

$$\sigma_{h,t}^2 = \omega_h + \alpha_h x_{h,t-1}^2 + \beta_h \sigma_{h,t-1}^2$$

where $\omega_h = h\omega[1-(\alpha+\beta)^h][1-(\alpha+\beta)]^{-1}$, $\alpha_h = (\alpha+\beta)^h - \beta_h$ and $|\beta_h| < 1$ is the solution to the quadratic equation:

$$\frac{\beta_h}{1+\beta_h^2} = \frac{a(\alpha+\beta)^h - b}{a[1+(\alpha+\beta)^{2h}] - 2b}$$

where:

$$a = h(1-\beta)^2 + 2h(h-1)\frac{(1-\alpha-\beta)^2(1-\beta^2-2\alpha\beta)}{(\kappa-1)[1-(\alpha+\beta)^2]}$$

$$+ 4\frac{[h-1-h(\alpha+\beta)+(\alpha+\beta)^h][\alpha-\alpha\beta(\alpha+\beta)]}{1-(\alpha+\beta)^2}$$

$$b = [\alpha - \alpha\beta(\alpha+\beta)]\frac{1-(\alpha+\beta)^{2h}}{1-(\alpha+\beta)^2}$$

where κ is the kurtosis of x_t (see also Diebold $et\ al.$ (1998, pp. 104–105)). It should be fairly obvious that this volatility forecast is very different from the volatility forecast we would get from a square root extrapolation rule: for example, the square root rule would have volatility forecasts rising with h, whereas the Drost–Nijman rule has them falling.

This suggests that we should not blindly apply the square root rule to volatility forecasting, unless returns are iid. It also suggests that if we have to forecast volatility over longer horizons, then we should use a correct volatility forecasting rule (i.e., one that correctly extrapolates the h-period volatility from parameters estimated over a 1-day period), or we should use an h-period model. Unfortunately, both routes are problematic: volatility forecasting rules can be difficult to derive, and often do not exist; and in working with h-period data frequencies, we lose a lot of data points and therefore have relatively few observations to work with. In any case, recent evidence by Christoffersen and Diebold (2000) suggests that volatility forecasts might not be much use anyway over horizons longer than 10 or 20 days.

T7.1.5 Implied Volatilities

A very different approach to the estimation of volatilities is to use implied volatilities from options prices. The idea is that where options exist on underlying assets and we know the values of the other variables involved, we can use established option pricing models to 'back out' the volatilities consistent with the known prices of these options. For example, suppose we have data on the prices of standard European Black–Scholes call options. Assuming the various Black–Scholes conditions hold (i.e., the underlying process follows a geometric Brownian motion, the underlying pays no dividend, etc.), the basic Black–Scholes theory tells us that the price of this option, c, should be:

$$c = SN(d_1) - Xe^{-rt} N(d_1 - \sigma \sqrt{t}) \tag{T7.25}$$

where S is the current stock price, X is the strike price, r is the risk-free rate of interest, t is the option's remaining term to maturity in years, σ is the volatility of the underlying asset, $d_1 = [\ln(S/X) + (r + \sigma^2/2)t]/(\sigma \sqrt{t})$ and $N(\cdot)$ is the cumulative value of the cumulative standard normal distribution. We know all of these variables except the volatility, so if the model is correct, we ought to be able to use Equation (T7.25) to derive the volatility it implies. These implied volatilities rarely have 'closed-form' solutions, but are very easy to derive numerically on a spreadsheet (e.g., using bisection or Newton–Raphson methods; see also Corrado and Miller (1996)). For instance, if we are given that $S = X = 1$, $r = 0.05$, $t = 1/2$ and $c = 0.0826$, then sigma must be 0.25, and this value can be verified by inserting it into Equation (T7.25) and checking that it produces the observed market price.

It is important to appreciate the implied volatility is not some backward-looking econometric volatility estimate, but a forward-looking forecast of volatility over the option's term to maturity. This gives implied volatilities two big advantages over other, historically-based, estimates of volatility: implied volatilities incorporate information that other approaches will ignore unless it is present in the historical data (e.g., expectations of the imminent devaluation of a hitherto stable currency), and they provide estimates of volatility on which experienced market operators have enough confidence to bet real money. The empirical evidence of Jorion (1995) also suggests that implied volatility forecasts are better than historically-based ones.

Unfortunately, the implied volatility method of estimating volatilities is contingent on the accuracy of the model used: if the model is biased or otherwise flawed, then it will produce biased or flawed estimates of implied volatility. This is a major problem, because standard option pricing models have well-known limitations. These include the failure of most of them to allow for transactions costs, bid–ask spreads, the effects of market illiquidity, and other 'imperfections'. They also include more fundamental problems with some of the key assumptions on which the models are based, including the famous 'holes in Black–Scholes' — the assumptions that the underlying follows a geometric Brownian motion, that the risk-free interest rate is constant, and so on. The failure of these assumptions to hold produces phenomena such as volatility smiles and skews that seriously complicate the derivation of implied volatilities: volatility smiles and skews mean that we get a number of different implied volatility estimates from options with different strike prices, and this leaves us with the problem of working out which of the implied volatilities on offer best corresponds to the one we are looking for. However, these sorts of problems are well known, and options practitioners have developed sophisticated ways of dealing with them (see, e.g., Taleb (1997c, ch. 7–16)).

Implied volatilities also suffer from one other limitation: they only exist for assets on which options have been written. This means that they are available only for a small subset of the assets for which we might seek volatility estimates. However, as time passes and options are written on more assets, we should expect more implied volatility estimates to become available. Nonetheless, these methods only go so far, and implied volatility estimates are always likely to be in short supply.

Box T7.2   Realised Volatility Estimators

One trend in the volatility literature is towards the use of ever higher frequency data, and a promising volatility estimator to emerge from this work is the so-called realised volatility estimator. The realised volatility is the average of intra-period high-frequency squared returns (e.g., the period might be a day, say, and the intra-period frequency every 5 minutes), and work by Anderson and Bollerslev (1998) shows that the realised volatility estimator is more or less error-free. Anderson *et al.* (2000, p. 107) point out that realised variances tend to be lognormally distributed, and that asset returns standardised by realised standard deviations tend to be normally distributed. Since realised returns are effectively observable, they can be handled directly by standard forecasting methods, and Anderson *et al.* suggest that we assume that the log-volatility process (which is normal) be estimated using Gaussian autoregressive moving average (ARMA) models. However, since realised volatility also has a long memory, we can allow for this by using a fractional order of integration in the ARMA process. This requires us to estimate the fractional order of integration — which is around 0.04, and then apply an ARMA model to the fractionally integrated series, $y_t = (1 - L)^{0.4} \log \sigma_t$. As these authors observe, 'The striking feature of this approach is that it builds directly on observed time series and utilises only standard linear Gaussian modelling and forecasting techniques. Hence, it is simple to assess in-sample performance and evaluate model forecasts through well-established out-of-sample procedures' (Anderson *et al.* (2000, p. 107)).

Moosa and Bollen (2001) use this realised volatility estimator to assess the bias in standard volatility estimators, and they find that this bias depends on both the methodology used and the length of the sample period. They also find that the best overall estimator — and also an unbiased one — is an exponentially weighted moving average with a large decay factor. This important finding suggests that the EWMA estimator might be best in practice after all, despite the theoretical superiority of GARCH.

T7.2   FORECASTING COVARIANCES AND CORRELATIONS

T7.2.1   Definitions of Covariances and Correlations

We turn now to covariance and correlation forecasting. The covariance between two series x and y is given by:

$$Cov(x, y) = E[xy] - E[x]E[y] \tag{T7.26}$$

and is approximately $E[xy]$ if x and y have negligible means. The correlation between x and y is then the covariance standardised by the square root of the product of the variances of x and y:

$$Corr(x, y) = \frac{Cov(x, y)}{\sqrt{\sigma_x^2 \sigma_y^2}} = \frac{Cov(x, y)}{\sigma_x \sigma_y} \tag{T7.27}$$

Equations (T7.26) and (T7.27) mean that we can obtain correlation estimates from covariance estimates, and vice versa.

Provided the variables concerned satisfy suitable (i.e., elliptical) distributions, the correlation coefficient gives a useful indication of the extent to which they move together. In such circumstances, the correlation will lie between −1 and +1, and take the value −1 if two series are perfectly negatively correlated, and +1 if they are perfectly positively correlated.

We should also keep in mind that the covariances and correlations of returns, like the volatilities of returns, are predicated on the period of time over which the return is measured, so each covariance or correlation refers to the returns of two assets over a specified period. For any pair of assets, there is a family of covariances and correlations, each member of which is predicated on returns measured over a different period.

However, when using correlations we must take care to ensure that x and y satisfy appropriate distributions. For correlation even to exist, it is necessary that x and y have finite variances and that they be jointly stationary: x and y must each be mean-reverting, and their joint distribution should satisfy standard stationarity properties.

Unfortunately, many empirical returns are not jointly stationary. In such cases, correlations often do not exist, and attempts to estimate them would be fundamentally misconceived. This leads to a clear practical danger: we might be dealing with a case where correlation is not defined, and yet we might not realise that the correlation does not exist and proceed to estimate the correlation coefficient anyway. Our results would then be meaningless and we would not know it. We must therefore take care to ensure that correlations actually exist before we attempt to estimate them, and where we do estimate them, we should be on the look out for instability in our estimates: unstable correlation estimates are a classic sign of non-joint stationarity in our returns.

T7.2.1   Equal-Weighted Moving Average Covariances and Correlations

The estimation of covariances and correlations directly parallels the estimation of volatilities. The most basic estimation method is therefore an equal-weighted moving average, which yields the following correlation estimator:

$$
Corr(x, y)_t = \frac{\sum\limits_{i=1}^{n} x_{t-i}\, y_{t-i}}{\sqrt{\sum\limits_{i=1}^{n} x_{t-i}^2 \sum\limits_{i=1}^{n} y_{t-i}^2}}
\tag{T7.28}
$$

which is a direct analogue of the earlier volatility estimator (T7.4). Traditionally, practitioners have sought to choose n so that it is large enough to produce reasonable correlation estimates, but small enough to be responsive to market 'news'. However, we need to keep in mind that estimated correlation coefficients will tend to become more stable as our sample period rises, regardless of whether our returns are jointly stationary or not. Consequently, we must be wary of the possibility that correlations might appear to be stable only because we use long sample periods to estimate them.

Some typical equal-weighted moving average correlations are shown in Figure T7.4. These are derived with rolling sample sizes of 20 and 40 respectively, and are estimated on simulated return data from a multivariate normal distribution with a 'true' correlation of 0.5. The fact that both correlations move around fairly wildly, despite the fact that the data are drawn from the most well-behaved distribution imaginable, is ample illustration of how unreliable these moving average correlation estimates can be. As we would expect, the most volatile estimate is the one based on the shorter sample period, but even the more stable estimate is itself fairly volatile: it varies between 0.025 at

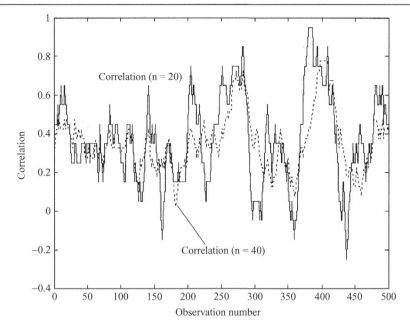

Figure T7.4   Equal-weight moving average correlation estimates.

one extreme, and 0.775 at the other, has a mean of 0.359 (which compares to the 'true' mean of 0.5), and has a standard deviation of 0.153. These correlations are very volatile indeed, and give relatively little indication of the 'true' correlation.

Our earlier discussion of volatilities also suggests that we should be on the look-out for ghost effects with our correlation estimates. To investigate these, I generated a new return data set from the same distribution used in the last example, and inserted a large shock to both x and y at $t = 150$. The resulting correlation plots are given in Figure T7.5. Our correlations are again very volatile, but we would never be able to tell from these plots that a very unusual event had taken place at $t = 150$: the ghost effects are drowned out by the general noise.[8] These results suggest that ghost effects might not be such a problem for correlation estimates, but 'noise' in our estimates certainly is.

However, even if ghost effects are not important for correlations, they *are* likely to be important for covariances. As Equation (T7.27) implies, a covariance can be considered as a correlation multiplied by the product of the standard deviations (or volatilities) of x and y:

$$Cov(x, y) = \sigma_x \sigma_y \, Corr(x, y) \tag{T7.29}$$

and we already know that volatilities can be subject to ghost effects. We should therefore expect our covariance estimates to exhibit ghost effects that reflect those in our volatility estimates: in effect, the ghost effects of our volatility estimates carry over to our covariance estimates.

---

[8]To check that our inability to find ghost effects was not due to our assuming that both x and y took unusual values at $t = 150$, I also produced comparable plots based on the assumption that only one variable was shocked but, once again, the resulting plots showed no easily detectable ghost effects.

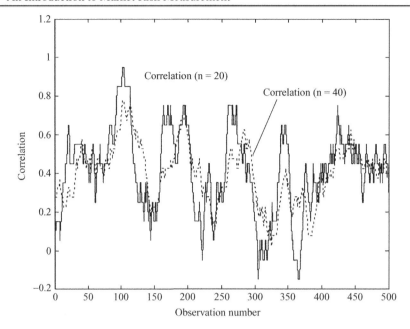

Figure T7.5   Do (correlation) ghosts exist?

T7.2.3   Exponentially-weighted Moving Average Covariances

As with our earlier volatility estimates, we would expect these ghost effects to be fairly severe if we estimate covariances with equal-weighted moving average schemes, and we could also expect to ameliorate them if we used exponential-weighted moving average estimates instead. The EWMA covariance model is:

$$Cov(x, y)_t = \lambda \, Cov(x, y)_{t-1} + (1 - \lambda)x_{t-1}y_{t-1} \qquad \text{(T7.30)}$$

This behaves in exactly the same way as the EWMA volatility model: the lower the value of λ, the more rapidly the weights on observations decline as time passes.

Some EWMA correlation estimates are presented in Figure T7.6 for n values of 20 and 40. These estimates are qualitatively much the same as the corresponding volatility estimates of Figure T7.2 — both estimates move around a lot, but the estimates based on a higher value of n are more stable.

It is also interesting to check our covariance estimates for ghost effects. To check for these, Figure T7.7 presents covariance estimates for random data drawn from the same distribution as before, but with the usual shock at $t = 150$. The figure shows that ghost effects are very similar to those we see in volatilities (see Figure T7.3) and can be very pronounced.[9]

---

[9]Of course, these particular ghost effects are as pronounced as they are because the unusual event in question affects both returns at the same time. If we had unusual events affecting one variable or the other, simulation results (not reported here) suggest that ghost effects will be less pronounced — exactly as we would expect.

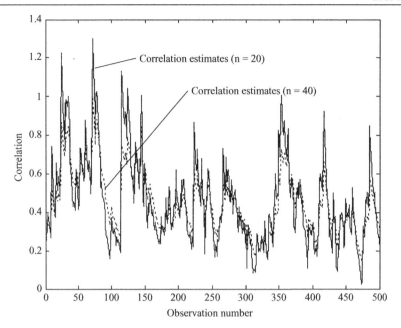

Figure T7.6   EWMA correlation estimates.

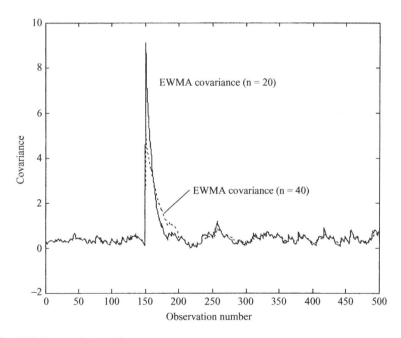

Figure T7.7   EWMA covariance estimates.

T7.2.4   GARCH Covariances

Besides exhibiting ghost effects, EWMA covariance estimates are also fairly restrictive. The natural solution to these problems is to estimate covariances with GARCH models. GARCH covariance models are directly analogous to GARCH volatility models. Thus, the GARCH(1,1) covariance model is:

$$Cov(x, y)_t = \omega_{x,y} + \alpha_{x,y} x_{t-1} y_{t-1} + \beta_{x,y} Cov(x, y)_{t-1} \tag{T7.31}$$

which corresponds to the GARCH(1,1) volatility model (T7.13):

$$\sigma_t^2 = \omega + \alpha x_{t-1}^2 + \beta \sigma_{t-1}^2$$

We can also estimate covariances (or correlations) with any of the other GARCH family models — IGARCH, components GARCH, factor GARCH, etc. — in an analogous way. For example, if we use the factor GARCH approach, the covariance of asset $r_{i,t}$ with asset $r_{j,t}$, $Cov(i, j)_t$, is:

$$Cov(i, j)_t = \beta_i \beta_j \sigma_{M,t}^2 + \sigma_{\varepsilon_{i,t}} \sigma_{\varepsilon_{j,t}} \tag{T7.32}$$

We then apply the factor GARCH model to covariance estimation in exactly the same way as we would apply it to volatility estimation (i.e., we estimate the parameters by regression, apply GARCH to the market return, and use Equation (T7.32) to estimate the covariance).

T7.2.5   Implied Covariances and Correlations

We can also estimate covariances and correlations by deriving implied covariances and correlations analogous to the implied volatilities discussed earlier. To understand how, first note that we can write out the variance of the difference between x and y as:

$$\sigma_{x-y}^2 = \sigma_x^2 + \sigma_y^2 - 2\rho\sigma_x\sigma_y \tag{T7.33}$$

where ρ is their coefficient of correlation. We then rearrange Equation (T7.33) to put the correlation on the left-hand side:

$$\rho = \left(\sigma_x^2 + \sigma_y^2 - 2\sigma_{x-y}^2\right)/(2\sigma_x\sigma_y) \tag{T7.34}$$

This tells us how we can derive a correlation estimate from estimates of the three volatilities σ_x^2, σ_y^2 and σ_{x-y}^2. However, we can only derive these implied correlations if the relevant options exist from which we can obtain the necessary implied volatilities. In this particular case, this means that we need options on x and on y, and also, more problematically, an option on the difference between x and y (e.g., a spread, quanto or diff option). These latter options are obviously fairly rare, so we will rarely have the opportunity to work with implied correlations. Even where we can derive them, we need to treat them carefully, as they have all the limitations and more of implied volatility estimates, and can also be very unstable (Alexander (1998, p. 151)).

T7.2.6   Some Pitfalls with Correlation Estimation

Finally, recent market experience suggests that when estimating correlations, practitioners should keep in mind some important reservations:

• Correlation estimates are often very volatile, so practitioners should interpret (and rely on) estimated correlations with great care.

- Precisely because of this volatility, it often takes a considerable number of observations to detect any substantial changes in correlations, and this means that changes in correlations can often be identified only after it is too late to do anything about them. Practitioners should be careful to protect themselves against the possibility that they might have estimated correlations incorrectly.
- Correlations can often appear to be fairly stable in 'normal' market conditions, and then jump to very high or very low values in stressful situations: in other words, correlations can break down just at the moment they are needed most. Correlation-based risk estimates should take this possibility into account, and should certainly not assume that markets will continue to behave 'normally' in a crisis.

T7.3   FORECASTING VARIANCE-COVARIANCE MATRICES

T7.3.1   Positive Definiteness

We now turn to the forecasting of variance–covariance (and correlation matrices). This is generally more difficult than the estimation of individual volatilities and covariances or correlations, because of the need to ensure that our estimated variance–covariance matrix (or estimated correlation matrix) is positive definite.[10] If Σ is an $n \times n$ variance–covariance matrix, $\mathbf{w}$ is an $n \times 1$ vector and $\mathbf{w}^T$ is its transpose, then Σ is positive definite if:

$$\mathbf{w}^T \Sigma \mathbf{w} > 0 \tag{T7.35}$$

for all possible $\mathbf{w}$ vectors. We can get an intuition for this condition if we think of $\mathbf{w}$ as a position vector for a portfolio, and we think of this condition as ensuring that our portfolio variance is always positive. We need to impose this condition to ensure that we get sensible (i.e., in this case, positive) estimates of portfolio variance.

The need to ensure positive definiteness imposes quite severe restrictions on what we can do in practice: we cannot estimate our volatilities and covariances/correlations independently of each other, and then expect that our variance–covariance matrix will be positive definite. We need systemic estimation approaches that estimate all our parameters simultaneously, but in a way that ensures that our estimated variance–covariance matrix will be positive definite.

The earlier discussion then suggests three possible ways to proceed: historical variance–covariance estimation, multivariate EWMA, and multivariate GARCH.

Box T7.3   Some Computational Problems with Variance–covariance Matrices

The estimation of covariance matrices often runs into computational problems (see, e.g., Davé and Stahl (1997)). One problem is that if the number of observations in our data set is not at least as large as the number of risk factors then the covariance matrix will have a rank defect and be singular, and any results we might get will be worthless. However, even if we have enough observations to avoid a blatant rank defect, we might get estimated

---

[10] Strictly speaking, we do not need our estimated matrix to be positive definite, and we can in theory make do with the weaker condition that Σ is positive semi-definite. The difference between the two is that positive semi-definiteness replaces the '$>$' inequality with the weaker requirement '$\geq$'. This means that the portfolio variance is now constrained to be non-negative instead of positive, which allows for the possibility of it being zero. However, for practical purposes it is often easier to work with a positive-definite variance–covariance matrix because important operations such as Choleski factorisation are not guaranteed to work on a positive semi-definite matrix.

covariance matrices that are nearly singular (e.g., because some risk factors might be closely correlated with each other), and near-singularity can produce pathological underestimates of risk. Indeed, even with a good model, we can get such underestimates of risk due simply to stochastic errors.

These problems can be aggravated if estimated covariance matrices are used to choose the portfolio (e.g., as in portfolio optimisation routines). Instead of pathological risk estimates being an occasional problem, we are then likely to find that portfolios are being selected precisely because of their low measured risk — so pathological underestimation of portfolio risks becomes the norm rather than the exception.

These are tricky problems, and there are no easy solutions. Part of the answer is to avoid singularity and near-singularity by keeping the number of risk factors down, and one way to do this is to map our assets onto a limited number of underlying risk factors. We should also choose risk factors that are not too closely correlated with each other, so as to reduce the danger that estimated covariance matrices will be singular or near-singular. We can also try to avoid pathologically low risk estimates by specifying what we believe the minimum reasonable risks should be. Any lower risk estimates are then identified as unreliable, and we can construct algorithms that ensure that our final risk estimates are plausible ones (e.g., as in Davé and Stahl (1997, pp. 40–42)).[11]

T7.3.2 Historical Variance–covariance Estimation

This is the most straightforward approach to the estimation of variance–covariance matrices: we choose our window size n and estimate our volatilities and covariances simultaneously. However, this approach has the same drawbacks as historical estimation applied to individual volatilities and correlations: it is strictly accurate only if the 'true' variance–covariance (or correlation) matrix is constant over time, which is a condition that will never be satisfied in practice, and it suffers from pronounced ghost effects.

T7.3.3 Multivariate EWMA

We can avoid these drawbacks by estimating our variance–covariance matrix using multivariate EWMA. This is more flexible (i.e., it accommodates changing volatilities and covariances over time) and has less pronounced ghost effects. However, in applying multivariate EWMA, we have to choose the number of separate λ (or decay) terms in our system, and this leads to a dilemma: ideally, we would want each volatility and covariance to have its own specific decay factor, so that we get the best fit for each of these estimates; but a large number of different λ values can be difficult to handle, and there is no guarantee that they will produce a positive definite estimate of our variance–covariance matrix. These considerations led RiskMetrics to choose a single decay factor — $\lambda = 0.94$ — when estimating the variance–covariance matrix of daily returns in their model.

---

[11]The estimation of variance–covariance matrices is more difficult than it looks at first sight, and the best approach to use depends on the context (e.g., large matrices are considerably more difficult to estimate than small ones, etc.). For more on these sorts of issues, and an idea of the current state of the art, see Alexander (2000) and Kreinin and Levin (2000).

T7.3.4 Multivariate GARCH

Since GARCH approaches are generally better than EWMA ones, theory suggests that we should, ideally, prefer to estimate our variance–covariance matrices using a multivariate GARCH approach.[12] However, this is easier said than done, as multivariate GARCH models need a lot of parameters, and the need to estimate these parameters restricts the size of the systems we can handle. Multivariate GARCH systems are also prone to convergence-in-estimation problems, making it difficult to obtain reliable estimates of all our parameters. As a result of these problems, unrestricted multivariate GARCH systems are only practically feasible if we have a relatively small number of different return series — say, no more than 10.

To give a flavour of the issues involved, consider one of the standard multivariate GARCH models — the BEKK model, named after its authors, Baba, Engle, Kraft and Kroner. This model takes the following matrix form:

$$\Sigma_t = \mathbf{A}^T\mathbf{A} + \mathbf{B}^T x_{t-1}^T x_{t-1}\mathbf{B} + \mathbf{C}^T\Sigma_{t-1}\mathbf{C} \tag{T7.36}$$

where there are n different returns, Σ_t is the $n(n+1)/2$ matrix of (distinct) conditional variance and covariance terms at t, x_t is the $1 \times n$ vector of returns, and $\mathbf{A}$, $\mathbf{B}$, and $\mathbf{C}$ are $n \times n$ matrices. This model imposes no (questionable) cross-equation restrictions, and ensures that our variance–covariance matrix will be positive definite.

However, the problem with this model is that it has a lot of parameters. For example, with only two different factors (i.e., $n = 2$), the BEKK model involves 11 different parameters, and the number of parameters rapidly rises as n gets larger. This model therefore requires far too many parameters to be used for large-dimensional problems. Of course, we can reduce the number of parameters by imposing restrictions on parameter values, but these only help us so much, and the restrictions can create problems of their own.

A potential solution to these problems is to use the orthogonal GARCH model suggested by Alexander and Chibumba (1997) (see also Alexander and Leigh (1998)): we divide our risk factors into groups of highly correlated risk categories and use principal components analysis to orthogonalise each sub-system of risk factors. We then apply univariate GARCH to each of the principal components of each risk category, and 'splice' the results together to produce the large covariance matrix we are really seeking. In principle, this method can be applied to any large-dimensional problem, but care needs to be taken with the initial calibration of the model (Alexander (1998, p. 147)).[13] A related solution is the factor GARCH model of Christiansen (1998), which is designed with fixed-income problems in mind: in this approach, we carry out GARCH analysis on the principal factors or principal components of our data set, and then use forecasts of these to estimate our VaR.

---

[12]But whether we would in practice is another matter. Leaving aside the difficulties of estimating variance–covariance matrices using GARCH methods, evidence also suggests that simple EWMA matrices are usually best when the matrices are used for VaR forecasting (see Lopez and Walter (2001, pp. 21–22)). Taken at face value, these results might suggest that it is pointless using sophisticated variance–covariance approaches for VaR purposes. However, this conclusion is controversial, and the next footnote gives at least one instance where GARCH models have led to better forecasts.

[13]Orthogonal GARCH models also appear to be more promising than traditional simple and weighted-average procedures in forecasting crisis volatilities: Byström (2000) presents evidence that orthogonal GARCH models performed much better than traditional models in dealing with the very high volatility of 1997–98.

Box T7.4   Estimating Volatilities, Covariances and Correlations with MATLAB

MATLAB has a variety of commands to help us estimate volatilities, covariances and correlations. The 'std' command produces an historic estimate of the standard deviation, and the 'var' command produces historic and more general weighted variance estimates. We can estimate individual covariances and variance–covariance matrices using the 'cov' command, and individual correlations and correlation matrices using the 'corrcoef' command.

In addition, the Financial Toolbox has the 'ugarch', 'ugarchpred' and 'ugarchsim' commands to estimate univariate GARCH parameters, make univariate GARCH predictions, and simulate returns using a univariate GARCH process. The Garch Toolbox has many different GARCH commands: 'garchfit' to estimate univariate GARCH models, 'garchpred' to make predictions, and so on.

T7.4   RECOMMENDED READING

Alexander (1998); Alexander and Leigh (1998); Brooks and Persand (2000); Christoffersen and Diebold (2000); Diebold *et al.* (1998); D'Vari and Sosa (2000); Engle and Mezrich (1996); Giannopoulos (2000); Hull (2000, ch. 15); Moosa and Bollen (2001).

Bibliography

Abken, P. A. (2000) 'An empirical evaluation of value at risk by scenario simulation.' *Journal of Derivatives* 7 (Summer): 12–29.

Acerbi, C. and D. Tasche (2001a) 'On the coherence of expected shortfall.' Mimeo. Abaxbank, Milan and Zentrum Mathematik, TU München.

Acerbi, C. and D. Tasche (2001b) 'Expected shortfall: a natural coherent alternative to Value at Risk.' Mimeo. Abaxbank, Milan and Zentrum Mathematik, TU München.

Adelman, I. (1990) 'Factor analysis.' Pp. 90–94 in J. Eatwell, M. Milgate and P. Newman (eds) *The New Palgrave Time Series and Statistics.* London and Basingstoke: Macmillan.

Albanese, C., K. Jackson and P. Wiberg (2001) 'Hedging with value-at-risk.' Mimeo. University of Toronto.

Alexander, C. (1998) 'Volatility and correlation: measurement, models and applications.' Pp. 125–171 in C. Alexander (ed.) *Risk Measurement and Analysis. Vol. 1: Measuring and Modelling Financial Risk.* Chichester and New York: John Wiley and Sons.

Alexander, C. (2000) 'Orthogonal methods for generating large positive semi-definite variance–covariance matrices.' University of Reading ISMA Centre *Discussion Paper in Finance* 2000–06.

Alexander, C. and A. Chibumba (1997) 'Orthogonal GARCH: an empirical validation in equities, foreign exchange and interest rates.' Mimeo. University of Sussex.

Alexander, C. and C. T. Leigh (1998) 'On the covariance matrices used in value at risk models.' *Journal of Derivatives* 4 (Spring): 50–62.

Almgren, R. and N. Chriss (1999) 'Value under liquidation.' *Risk* 12 (December): 61–63.

Almgren, R. and N. Chriss (2000) 'Optimal execution of portfolio transactions.' *Journal of Risk* 3 (Winter): 5–39.

Anderson, T. and T. Bollerslev (1998) 'Answering the skeptics: yes, standard volatility models do provide accurate forecasts.' *International Economic Review* 39: 885–905.

Anderson, T., T. Bollerslev, F. Diebold and P. Labys (2000) 'Great realisations.' *Risk* 13 (March): 105–108.

Aragonés, J. R., C. Blanco and J. Mascareñas (2001) 'Active management of equity investment portfolios.' *Journal of Portfolio Management* 27 (Spring): 1–8.

Artzner, P., F. Delbaen, J.-M. Eber and D. Heath (1997) 'Thinking coherently.' *Risk* 10 (November): 68–71.

Artzner, P., F. Delbaen, J.-M. Eber and D. Heath (1999) 'Coherent measures of risk.' *Mathematical Finance* 9 (November): 203–228.

Bahar, R., M. Gold, T. Kitto and C. Polizu (1997) 'Making the best of the worst.' *Risk* 10 (August): 100–103.

Bangia, A., F. Diebold, T. Schuermann and J. Stroughair (1999) 'Liquidity on the outside.' *Risk* 12 (June): 68–73.

Bank for International Settlements (2000) *Stress Testing by Large Financial Institutions: Current Practice and Aggregation Issues.* BIS Committee on the Global Financial System. Basel: Bank for International Settlements, April 2000.

Bank for International Settlements (2001) *Central Bank Survey of Foreign Exchange and Derivatives Market Activity in April 2001: Preliminary Global Data. Press Release.* October 9, 2001.

Barone-Adesi, G. and K. Giannopoulos (2000) 'Non-parametric VaR techniques. Myths and realities.' Mimeo. Universita della Svizzera Italiana, City University Business School and Westminster Business School. November 2000.

Barone-Adesi, G., F. Bourgoin and K. Giannopoulos (1998) 'Don't look back.' *Risk* 11 (August) 1998: 100–103.

Barone-Adesi, G., K. Giannopoulos and L. Vosper (1999) 'VaR without correlations for portfolios of derivatives securities.' *Journal of Futures Markets* 19: 583–602.

Barone-Adesi, G., K. Giannopoulos and L. Vosper (2000) 'Filtering historical simulation. Backtest analysis.' Mimeo. Universita della Svizzera Italiana, City University Business School, Westminster Business School and London Clearing House.

Barraquand, J. (1995) 'Numerical valuation of high dimensional multivariate European securities.' *Management Science* 41: 1882–1891.

Basak, S. and A. Shapiro (2001) 'Value-at-risk-based risk management: optimal policies and asset prices.' *Review of Financial Studies* 14: 371–405.

Basle Committee on Banking Supervision (1996) *Amendment to the Capital Accord to Incorporate Market Risks*. Basle: Bank for International Settlements.

Bassi, F., P. Embrechts and M. Kafetzaki (1998) 'Risk management and quantile estimation.' Pp. 111–130 in R. J. Adler, R. E. Feldman and M. S. Taqqu (eds) *A Practical Guide to Heavy Tails: Tails: Statistical Techniques and Applications*. Boston: Birkhaüser.

Bauer, C. (2000) 'Value at risk using hyperbolic distributions.' *Journal of Economics and Business* 52: 455–467.

Baumol, W. J. (1963) 'An expected gain confidence limit criterion for portfolio selection.' *Management Science* 10: 174–182.

Beder, T. (1995a) 'VaR: Seductive but dangerous.' *Financial Analysts Journal* 51 (September/October): 12–24.

Beder, T. (1995b) 'Ten common failures in independent risk oversight.' *Financial Derivatives and Risk Management* (December): 53–56.

Beder, T., M. Minnich, H. Shen and J. Stanton (1998) 'Vignettes on VaR.' *Journal of Financial Engineering* 7: 289–309.

Berkowitz, J. (2000a) 'A coherent framework for stress-testing.' *Journal of Risk* 2: 1–15.

Berkowitz, J. (2000b) 'Breaking the silence.' *Risk* 13 (October): 105–108.

Berkowitz, J. (2001) 'Testing density forecasts, with applications to risk management.' *Journal of Business and Economic Statistics* 19: 465–474.

Berkowitz, J. and J. O'Brien (2001) 'How accurate are value-at-risk models at commercial banks?' Mimeo. UC-Irvine and Division of Research and Statistics, Federal Reserve Board.

Billio, M. and L. Pelizzon (1997) 'A switching volatility approach to improve the estimation of value-at-risk.' Mimeo. University of Venice and London Business School.

Black, F. (1976) 'The pricing of commodity contracts.' *Journal of Financial Economics* 2: 167–179.

Black, F. and M. Scholes (1973) 'The pricing of options and corporate liabilities.' *Journal of Political Economy* 81: 637–654.

Blake, D. (2000) 'Does it matter what type of pension scheme you have?' *Economic Journal* 110 (February): F46–F81.

Blake, D. (2003) *Pension Schemes and Pension Funds in the United Kingdom*. Oxford: Oxford University Press. Forthcoming.

Blake, D., A. J. G. Cairns and K. Dowd (2001a) 'Pensionmetrics: stochastic pension plan design and value-at-risk during the accumulation phase.' *Insurance: Mathematics and Economics* 29 (October): 187–215.

Blake, D., A. J. G. Cairns and K. Dowd (2001b) 'Pensionmetrics: stochastic pension plan design during the distribution phase.' Mimeo. Birkbeck College, Heriot-Watt University and Nottingham University Business School.

Blake, D., A. J. G. Cairns and K. Dowd (2001c) 'The impact of gender and occupation on defined contribution pension plans: some simulation results.' Mimeo. Birkbeck College, Heriot-Watt University and Nottingham University Business School.

Blanco, C. (1999a) 'Component VaR, VaRdelta and VaRbeta in risk management.' Presentation to the Unicom Conference 'VaR and Beyond', London, October 1999.

Blanco, C. (1999b) 'Complementing VaR with 'stress testing' to account for abnormal market conditions.' Presentation to the Unicom Conference 'VaR and Beyond', London, October 1999.

Blanco, C. and G. Ihle (1998) 'How good is your VaR? Using backtesting to assess system performance.' *Financial Engineering News* (August): 1–2.

Bollserslev, T. (1986) 'Generalized autoregressive conditional heteroscedasticity.' *Journal of Econometrics* 31: 307–327.

Bouchaud, J. P. and M. Potters (1999) 'Theory of financial risk: basic notions in probability.' Mimeo. Science and Finance, 109–111 rue Victor Hugo, 92532 Levallois Cedex, France.

Bouchaud, J. P. and M. Potters (2000) 'Worse fluctuation method for fast value-at-risk estimates.' Mimeo. Science and Finance, 109–111 rue Victor Hugo, 92532 Levallois Cedex, France.

Boudoukh, J., M. Richardson and R. Whitelaw (1995) 'Expect the worst.' *Risk* 8 (September): 100–101.

Boudoukh, J., M. Richardson and R. Whitelaw (1998) 'The best of both worlds: a hybrid approach to calculating value at risk.' *Risk* 11 (May): 64–67.

Boyle, P. (1977) 'Options: A Monte Carlo approach.' *Journal of Financial Economics* 4: 323–338.

Boyle, P., M. Broadie and P. Glasserman (1997) 'Monte Carlo methods for security pricing.' *Journal of Economic Dynamics and Control* 21: 1267–1321.

Breckling, J., E. Eberlein and P. Kovic (2000) 'A tailored suit for risk management: Hyperbolic model.' Pp. 189–202 in J. Franke, W. Härdle and G. Stahl (eds) *Measuring Risk in Complex Stochastic Systems*. New York: Springer Verlag. Lecture Notes in Statistics Series No. 147.

Breuer, T. and G. Krenn (1999) *Guidelines on Market Risk. Volume 5. Stress Testing*. Vienna: Oesterreichische Nationalbank.

Breuer, T. and G. Krenn (2000) 'Identifying stress test scenarios.' Mimeo. Fachhochschule Voralberg, Dornbirn, Austria and Oesterreichische Nationalbank, Vienna.

Brier, G. W. (1950) 'Verification of forecasts expressed in terms of probability.' *Monthly Weather Review* 75: 1–3.

Britten-Jones, M. and S. M. Schaefer (1999) 'Non-linear value-at-risk.' *European Finance Review* 2: 161–187.

Broadie, M. and P. Glasserman (1996) 'Estimating security price derivatives using simulation.' *Management Science* 42: 269–285.

Broadie, M. and P. Glasserman (1997) 'Pricing American-style securities using simulation.' *Journal of Economic Dynamics and Control* 21: 1323–1352.

Broadie, M. and P. Glasserman (1998) 'Simulation for option pricing and risk management.' Pp. 173–207 in C. Alexander (ed.) *Risk Management and Analysis. Vol. 1: Measuring and Modelling Financial Risk*. Chichester and New York: John Wiley and Sons.

Brock, W. A., W. D. Dechert and J. Scheinkman (1987) 'A test for independence based on the correlation dimension.' University of Wisconsin-Madison *SSRI Workshop Paper* 8702.

Brooks, C. and G. Persand (2000) 'Value at risk and market crashes.' *Journal of Risk* 2 (Summer): 1–26.

Brotherton-Ratcliffe, R. (1994) 'Monte Carlo motoring.' *Risk* 7 (December): 53–57.

Brummelhuis, R., A. Córdoba, M. Quintanilla and L. Seco (2000) 'Principal component value-at-risk.' *International Journal of Theoretical and Applied Finance* 3: 541–545.

Butler, J. S. and B. Schachter (1998) 'Improving value at risk with a precision measure by combining kernel estimation with historical simulation.' *Review of Derivatives Research* 1: 371–390.

Byström, H. N. E. (2000) 'Orthogonal GARCH and covariance matrix forecasting in a stress scenario: The Nordic stock markets during the Asian financial crisis 1997–1998.' Mimeo. Lund University.

Caflisch, R. E., W. Morokoff and A. Owen (1997) 'Valuation of mortgage backed securities using Brownian bridges to reduce effective dimension.' *Journal of Computational Finance* 1: 27–46.

Cairns, A. J. G. (2000) 'A discussion of parameter and model uncertainty in insurance.' *Insurance: Mathematics and Economics* 27: 313–330.

Cárdenas, J., E. Fruchard, E. Koehler, C. Michel and I. Thomazeau (1997) 'VaR: one step beyond.' *Risk* 10 (October): 72–75.

Cárdenas, J., E. Fruchard, J.-F. Picron, C. Reyes, K. Walters and W. Yang (1999) 'Monte Carlo within a day.' *Risk* 12 (February): 55–59.

Chappell, D. and K. Dowd (1999) 'Confidence intervals for VaR.' *Financial Engineering News* March: 1–2.

Chernozhukov, V. and L. Umantsev (2001) 'Conditional value-at-risk: aspects of modelling and estimation.' *Empirical Economics* 26: 271–292.

Cherubini, U. and G. Della Lunga (1999) 'Stress testing techniques and value-at-risk measures: a unified approach.' Mimeo. Universities of Bologna and Siena.

Cherubini, U. and G. Della Lunga (2000) 'Fuzzy value-at-risk.' Mimeo. Polyhedron.

Cherubini, U. and E. Luciano (2000) 'Value at risk trade-off and capital allocation with copulas.' Mimeo. Universities of Bologna and Turin.

Chew, L. (1994) 'Shock treatment.' *Risk* 9 (September): 63–70.

Chew, L. (1996) *Managing Derivative Risks: The Uses and Abuses of Leverage.* Chichester: John Wiley and Sons.

Chriss, N. A. (1997) *Black–Scholes and Beyond: Option Pricing Models.* New York: McGraw-Hill.

Christoffersen, P. F. (1998) 'Evaluating interval forecasts.' *International Economic Review* 39: 841–862.

Christoffersen, P. F. and F. X. Diebold (2000) 'How relevant is volatility forecasting for financial risk management?' *Review of Economics and Statistics* 82: 12–22.

Christoffersen, P. F., J. Hahn and A. Inoue (2001) 'Testing and comparing value at risk measures.' *Journal of Empirical Finance* 8: 325–342.

Christiansen, C. (1998) 'Value at risk using the factor-ARCH model.' Mimeo. Aarhus School of Business.

Clewlow, L. and A. Carverhill (1994) 'Quicker on the curves.' *Risk* 7 (May): 63–65.

Clewlow, L. and C. Strickland (1998) *Implementing Derivatives Models.* Chichester and New York: John Wiley and Sons.

Corrado, C. and T. Miller (1996) 'Volatility without tears.' *Risk* 9 (July): 49–51.

Cosandey, D. (2001) 'Adjusting value-at-risk for market liquidity.' *Risk* 14 (October): 115–118.

Cotter, J. (2001) 'Margin exceedances for European stock index futures using extreme value theory.' *Journal of Banking and Finance* 25: 1475–1502.

Cox, J. C., J. E. Ingersoll and S. A. Ross (1985) 'A theory of the term structure of interest rates.' *Econometrica* 53: 385–407.

Crnkovic, C. and J. Drachman (1995) 'A universal tool to discriminate among risk measurement techniques.' Mimeo. Corporate Risk Management Group, JP Morgan.

Crnkovic, C. and J. Drachman (1996) 'Quality control.' *Risk* 9 (September): 139–143.

Crouhy, M., D. Galai and R. Mark (1998) "The new 1998 regulatory framework for capital adequacy: 'standardized approach' versus 'internal models'." Pp. 1–37 in C. Alexander (ed.) *Risk Management and Analysis. Vol. 1: Measuring and Modelling Financial Risk.* Chichester and New York: John Wiley and Sons.

Crouhy, M., D. Galai and R. Mark (2001) *Risk Management.* New York: McGraw-Hill.

Culp, C. and M. H. Miller (1995) 'Metallgesellschaft and the economics of synthetic storage.' *Journal of Applied Corporate Finance* 7 (Winter): 62–76.

Culp, C., M. H. Miller and A. M. P. Neves (1997) 'Value at risk: uses and abuses.' *Journal of Applied Corporate Finance* 10 (Winter): 26–38.

Curran, M. (1994) 'Recovering identity.' *Risk* 9 (May): 65.

Danielsson, J. (2001) 'The emperor has no clothes: limits to risk modelling.' Mimeo. London School of Economics.

Danielsson, J. and C. G. de Vries (1997a) 'Beyond the sample: Extreme quantile and probability estimation.' Mimeo. Tinbergen Institute, Rotterdam.

Danielsson, J. and C. G. de Vries (1997b) 'Tail index estimation with very high frequency data.' *Journal of Empirical Finance* 4: 241–257.

Danielsson, J. and J.-P. Zigrand (2001) 'What happens when you regulate risk? Evidence from a simple general equilibrium model.' Mimeo. London School of Economics Financial Markets Group.

Danielsson, J., P. Embrechts, C. Goodhart, C. Keating, F. Muennich, O. Renault and H. S. Shin (2001) 'An academic response to Basel II.' London School of Economics Financial Markets Group *Special Paper No. 130.*

Davé, R. D. and G. Stahl (1997) 'On the accuracy of VaR estimates based on the variance–covariance approach.' Mimeo. Olsen and Associates, Zürich and Federal Banking Supervision Office, Berlin.

Davison, A. C. and D. V. Hinkley (1997) *Bootstrap Methods and their Applications.* Cambridge: Cambridge University Press.

Deans, J. (2000) 'Backtesting.' Pp. 261–289 in M. Lore and L. Borodovsky (eds) *The Professional's Handbook of Financial Risk Management.* Oxford: Butterworth-Heinemann.

Denecker, K., S. Van Assche, J. Cromberz, R. Vander Vennet and I. Lemahieu (2001) 'Value-at-risk prediction using context modelling.' *European Physical Journal B* 20: 481–492.

Derivatives Policy Group (1995) *A Framework for Voluntary Oversight.* New York: Derivatives Policy Group.

Derman, E. (1997) 'Model risk.' Pp. 83–88 in S. Grayling (ed.) *VaR — Understanding and Applying Value-at-Risk.* London: Risk Publications.

de Vries, C. G. and S. Caserta (2000) 'Regular variation and extremes in finance and economics.' Mimeo.

Diebold, F. X., A. Hickman, A. Inoue and T. Schuermann (1998) 'Scale models.' *Risk* 11 (January): 104–107.

Diebold, F. X., T. Schuermann and J. D. Stroughair (2000) 'Pitfalls and opportunities in the use of extreme value theory in risk management.' *Journal of Risk Finance* 1: 30–35.

Dowd, K. (1998a) *Beyond Value at Risk: The New Science of Risk Management.* Chichester and New York: John Wiley and Sons.

Dowd, K. (1998b) 'VaR by increments.' *Risk (Enterprise-Wide Risk Management Special Report)* 11 (November): 31–33.

Dowd, K. (1999) 'A VaR approach to risk-return analysis.' *Journal of Portfolio Management* 25 (Summer): 60–67.

Dowd, K. (2000a) 'Estimating value-at-risk: a subjective approach.' *Journal of Risk Finance* 1 (Summer): 43–46.

Dowd, K. (2000b) 'Accounting for value at risk.' *Journal of Risk Finance* 2 (Fall): 51–58.

Dowd, K. (2001) 'Estimating VaR with order statistics.' *Journal of Derivatives* 8 (Spring): 23–30.

Dowd, K. (2002) *Measuring Market Risk.* Chichester and New York: John Wiley and Sons.

Dowd, K., D. Blake and A. G. J. Cairns (2001) 'Long-term value at risk.' Mimeo. University of Nottingham, Birkbeck College and Heriot-Watt University.

Drost, F. and T. Nijman (1993) 'Temporal aggregation of Garch processes.' *Econometrica* 61: 909–927.

Duffie, D. and J. Pan (1997) 'An overview of value at risk.' *Journal of Derivatives* 4 (Spring): 7–49.

Duffie, D. and J. Pan (1999) 'Analytical value-at-risk with jumps and credit risk.' Mimeo. Graduate School of Business, Stanford University.

D'Vari, R. and J. C. Sosa (2000) 'Value at risk estimates for Brady bond portfolios.' *Journal of Fixed Income* 10 (December): 7–23.

Eber, J.-M., P. Artzner, F. Delbaen and D. Heath (1999) 'Axiomatic structure of coherent measures of risk.' Presentation to the 6th ICBI Risk Management Conference, Geneva, November 30, 1999.

Eberlein, E. and K. Prause (2000) 'The generalized hyperbolic model: Financial derivatives and risk measures.' *FDM Preprint 56,* University of Freiburg.

Eberlein, E., U. Keller, and K. Prause (1998) 'New insights into smile, mispricing and value at risk: the hyperbolic model.' *Journal of Business* 71: 371–406.

Efron, B. (1979) 'Bootstrap methods: Another look at the jacknife.' *Annals of Statistics* 7: 1–26.

Efron, B. and R. J. Tibshirani (1993) *An Introduction to the Bootstrap.* New York and London: Chapman and Hall.

Elton, E. J. and M. J. Gruber (1995) *Modern Portfolio Theory and Investment Analysis.* Fifth edition. New York: John Wiley and Sons.

Embrechts, P., C. Klüppelberg and T. Mikosch (1997) *Modelling Extreme Events for Insurance and Finance.* Berlin: Springer-Verlag.

Engle, R. (1982) 'Autoregressive conditional heteroscedasticity with estimates of the variance of United Kingdom inflation.' *Econometrica* 50: 987–1007.

Engle, R. and S. Manganelli (1999) 'CAViaR: Conditional autoregressive value at risk by regression quantiles.' Mimeo. University of California, San Diego.

Engle, R. and J. Mezrich (1996) 'GARCH for groups.' *Risk* 9 (June): 36–40.

Estrella, A. (1996) 'Taylor, Black and Scholes: Series approximations and risk management pitfalls.' Pp. 359–379 in *Risk Measurement and Systemic Risk. Proceedings of a Joint Central Bank Research Conference.* Washington, DC: Board of Governors of the Federal Reserve System.

Estrella, A., D. Hendricks, J. Kambhu, S. Shin and S. Walter (1994) 'The price risk of options positions: Measurement and capital requirements.' Federal Reserve Bank of New York *Economic Policy Review* (Fall): 27–43.

Evans, M., N. Hastings and B. Peacock (2000) *Statistical Distributions.* Third edition. Chichester and New York: John Wiley and Sons.

Ewerhart, C. (2001) 'Market risks, internal models and optimal regulation: does backtesting induce banks to report their truer risks?' Mimeo. University of Mannheim.

Fabozzi, F. J. (1993) *Fixed Income Mathematics: Analytical and Statistical Techniques.* Revised edition. Chicago: Irwin.

Fabozzi, F. J. (2000) *Bond Markets, Analysis and Strategies.* Fourth edition. Upper Saddle River, NJ: Prentice Hall.

Fallon, W. (1996) 'Calculating value-at-risk.' Wharton School Financial Institutions Center *Working Paper* 96–49.

Fender, I. and M. Gibson (2001) 'The BIS census on stress tests.' *Risk* 14 (May): 50–52.

Feuerverger, A. and A. C. M. Wong (2000) 'Computation of value-at-risk for nonlinear portfolios.' *Journal of Risk* 3 (Fall): 37–55.

Fiedler, R. E. (2000) 'Liquidity risk.' Pp. 441–472 in M. Lore and L. Borodovsky (eds) *The Professional's Handbook of Financial Risk Management*. Oxford: Butterworth-Heinemann.

Figlewski, S. (1994) 'Forecasting volatility using historical data.' New York University *Working Paper* S-94-13.

Figlewski, S. and B. Gao (1999) 'The adaptive mesh model: a new approach to efficient option pricing.' *Journal of Financial Economics* 53: 313–351.

Finger, C. C. (1996) 'Accounting for 'pull to par' and 'roll down' for RiskMetrics™ cashflows.' *RiskMetrics™ Monitor*, Third Quarter 1996: 4–11.

Fishburn, P. C. (1977) 'Mean-risk analysis with risk associated with below-target returns.' *American Economic Review* 67: 116–126.

Frain, J. and C. Meegan (1996) 'Market risk: An introduction to the concept and analytics of value-at-risk.' Mimeo. Economic Analysis Research and Publications Department, Central Bank of Ireland.

Frankfurter, G. M. (1995) 'The rise and fall of the CAPM empire: a review on emerging capital markets.' *Financial Markets, Institutions and Instruments. Recent Developments in Financial Economics: Selected Surveys of the Literature* 5 (4): 104–127.

Frey, R. (2000) 'Market illiquidity as a source of model risk in dynamic hedging.' Mimeo. Swiss Banking Institute, University of Zürich.

Froot, K., P. O'Connell and M. Seasholes (2001) 'The portfolio flows of international investors.' *Journal of Financial Economics* 59: 151–193.

Frye, J. (1996) 'Principals of risk: Finding value-at-risk through factor-based interest rate scenarios.' Mimeo. NationsBank-CRT, Chicago.

Fuglsbjerg, B. (2000) 'Variance reduction techniques for Monte Carlo estimates of value at risk.' Mimeo. Finance Research Department, SimCorp A/S, Copenhagen. February 2000.

Fusai, G. and E. Luciano (1998) 'Measuring VaR under optimal and suboptimal portfolio policies.' Mimeo. Universities of Florence and Turin.

Garman, M. B. (1996a) 'Making VaR more flexible.' *Derivatives Strategy* (April): 52–53.

Garman, M. B. (1996b) 'Improving on VaR.' *Risk* 9 (May): 61–63.

Garman, M. B. (1996c) 'Making VaR proactive.' Berkeley, CA: Financial Engineering Associates. FEA.

Garman, M. B. (1997) 'Taking VaR to pieces.' *Risk* 10 (10): 70–71.

Giannopoulos, K. (2000) 'Measuring volatility.' Pp. 42–74 in M. Lore and L. Borodovsky (eds) *The Professional's Handbook of Financial Risk Management*. Oxford: Butterworth-Heinemann.

Gibson, M. S. (2001) 'Incorporating event risk into value-at-risk.' Mimeo. Federal Reserve Board.

Gilmour, I. (1997) 'Cash flow-at-risk — a corporate approach to VaR.' *The Treasurer* (July/August): 25–27.

Glasserman, P., P. Heidelberger and P. Shahabuddin (1999a) 'Importance sampling and stratification for value-at-risk.' Pp. 7–24 in Y. S. Abu-Mostafa, B. LeBaron, A. W. Lo and A. S. Weigend (eds) *Computational Finance 1999 (Proceedings of the Sixth International Conference on Computational Finance)*. Cambridge, MA: MIT Press.

Glasserman, P., P. Heidelberger and P. Shahabuddin (1999b) 'Stratification issues in estimating value-at-risk.' Pp. 351–358 in P. A. Farrington, H. B. Nembhard, D. T. Sturrock and G. W. Evans (eds) *Proceedings of the 1999 Winter Simulation Conference*. Piscataway, NJ: IEEE Computer Society Press.

Glasserman, P., P. Heidelberger and P. Shahabuddin (2000a) 'Portfolio value-at-risk with heavy-tailed risk factors.' Columbia Business School *Paine Webber Working Papers in Money, Economics and Finance* PW-00-06.

Glasserman, P., P. Heidelberger and P. Shahabuddin (2000b) 'Variance reduction techniques for estimating value-at-risk.' *Management Science* 46: 1349–1364.

Golub, B. W. and L. M. Tilman (1997) 'Measuring yield curve risk using principal components analysis, value at risk, and key rate durations.' *Journal of Portfolio Management* 23 (Summer): 72–84.

Gourieroux, G., J. P. Laurent and O. Scaillet (2000) 'Sensitivity analysis of value at risk.' *Journal of Empirical Finance* 7: 225–245.

Greenspan, A. (2000) 'Banking evolution.' Remarks to the 36th Annual Conference on Bank Structure and Competition of the Federal Reserve Bank of Chicago, May 4, 2000.

Group of Thirty (1993) *Derivatives: Practices and Principles*. New York: Group of Thirty.

Guermat, C. and R. D. F. Harris (2000) 'Robust conditional variance estimation and value-at-risk.' Mimeo. School of Business and Economics, University of Exeter, December 2000.

Guermat, C., R. D. F. Harris, C. C. Küçüközmen and F. Yilmaz (1999) 'Forecasting value-at-risk: Extreme events and volatility updating.' Mimeo. School of Business and Economics, University of Exeter.

Guldimann, T. (1996) 'Beyond the year 2000.' *Risk* 9 (June): 17–19.

Guldimann, T. (2000) 'The story of RiskMetrics.' *Risk* 13 (January): 56–58.

Gupta, F., E. Stubbs and Y. Thambiah (2000) 'U.S. corporate pension plans: a value at risk analysis.' *Journal of Portfolio Management* 26 (Summer): 65–72.

Haas, M. (2001) 'New methods in backtesting.' Mimeo. Financial Engineering Research Center Caesar, Friedensplatz, Bonn.

Hall, P. (1990) 'Using the bootstrap to estimate mean square error and select smoothing parameter in nonparametric problems.' *Journal of Multivariate Analysis* 32: 177–203.

Hallerbach, W. G. (1999) 'Decomposing portfolio value-at-risk: a general analysis.' Mimeo. Erasmus University.

Härdle, W. and G. Stahl (2000) 'Backtesting beyond VaR.' Pp. 119–130 in J. Franke, W. Härdle and G. Stahl (eds) *Measuring Risk in Complex Stochastic Systems.* New York: Springer-Verlag. Lecture Notes in Statistics Series No. 147.

Hauksson, H. A., M. Dacorogna, T. Domenig, U. Müller, and G. Samorodnitsky (2001) 'Multivariate extremes, aggregation and risk estimation.' *Quantitative Finance* 1: 79–95.

Heath, D., R. A. Jarrow and A. Morton (1990a) 'Bond pricing and the term structure of interest rates: A discrete time approximation.' *Journal of Financial and Quantitative Analysis* 25: 419–440.

Heath, D., R. A. Jarrow and A. Morton (1990b) 'Contingent claim valuation with a random evolution of interest rates.' *Review of Futures Markets* 9: 54–76.

Heath, D., R. A. Jarrow and A. Morton (1992) 'Bond pricing and the term structure of interest rates: A new methodology for contingent claims valuation.' *Econometrica* 60: 77–105.

Hendricks, D. (1996) 'Evaluation of value-at-risk models using historical data.' Federal Reserve Bank of New York *Economic Policy Review* 2 (April): 39–70.

Henrard, M. (2000) 'Comparison of cashflow maps for value-at-risk.' *Journal of Risk* 3 (Fall): 57–71.

Hereford, N. and G. Shuetrim (2000) 'Using stratified sampling methods to improve percentile estimates in the context of risk measurement.' Australian Prudential Regulation Authority *Working Paper 5*, June 2000.

Hill, B. M. (1975) 'A simple general approach to inference about the tail of a distribution.' *Annals of Statistics* 35: 1163–1173.

Ho, T. (1992) 'Key rate durations: Measures of interest rate risks.' *Journal of Fixed Income* 2: 29–44.

Ho, T., M. Chen and F. Eng (1996) 'VaR analytics: portfolio structure, key rate convexities and VaR betas.' *Journal of Portfolio Management* 23 (Fall): 89–98.

Holton, G. (1997) 'Subjective value at risk.' *Financial Engineering News* 1 (August): 1+.

Holton, G. (1998) 'Simulating value-at-risk.' *Risk* 11 (May): 60–63.

Holton, G. (1999) 'Simulating value-at-risk with weighted scenarios.' *Financial Engineering News* (January): 1, 7–8.

Holton, G. A. (2002) *Value-at-Risk: Theory and Practice.* San Diego: Academic Press.

Hoppe, R. (1998) 'VaR and the unreal world.' *Risk* 11 (July): 45–50.

Hoppe, R. (1999) 'Finance is not physics.' Mimeo. Kenyon College, Ohio.

Hua, P. and P. Wilmott (1997) 'Crash courses.' *Risk* 10 (June): 64–67.

Huisman, R., K. G. Koedjik and R. A. J. Pownall (1998) 'VaR-x: fat tails in financial risk management.' *Journal of Risk* 1: 47–61.

Hull, J. C. (2000) *Options, Futures and Other Derivatives.* Fourth edition. Upper Saddle River, NJ: Prentice-Hall.

Hull, J. and A. White (1987) 'The pricing of options on assets with stochastic volatilities.' *Journal of Finance* 42: 281–300.

Hull, J. and A. White (1998a) 'Value at risk when daily changes in market variables are not normally distributed.' *Journal of Derivatives* 5 (Spring): 9–19.

Hull, J. and A. White (1998b) 'Incorporating volatility updating into the historical simulation method for value-at-risk.' *Journal of Risk* 1 (Fall): 5–19.

Huschens, S. (1997) 'Confidence intervals for the value-at-risk.' Technische Universität Dresden Fakultät für Wirtschaftswissenschaften *Dresdner Beiträge zu Quantitativen Verfahren Nr. 9/97*.

Ingersoll, J. E., Jr. (1987) *Theory of Financial Decision Making.* Totowa, NJ: Rowman and Littlefield.

Jackson, P. (1996) 'Risk measurement and capital requirements for banks.' *Bank of England Quarterly Bulletin* (May): 177–184.

Jackson, P., D. J. Maude and W. Perraudin (1997) 'Bank capital and value-at-risk.' *Journal of Derivatives* 4 (Spring): 73–90.

Jahel, L. El, W. Perraudin and P. Sellin (1999) 'Value at risk for derivatives.' *Journal of Derivatives* 6: 7–26.

Jakobsen, S. (1996) 'Measuring value-at-risk for mortgage-backed securities.' Pp. 185–208 in F. Bruni, D. E. Fair and R. O'Brien (eds) *Risk Management in Volatile Financial Markets.* Dordrecht: Kluwer Academic Publishers.

James, J. and N. Webber (2000) *Interest Rate Modelling.* Chichester and New York: John Wiley and Sons.

Jamshidian, F. and Y. Zhu (1996) 'Scenario simulation model for risk management.' *Capital Market Strategies* 12 (December): 26–30.

Jamshidian, F. and Y. Zhu (1997) 'Scenario simulation: Theory and methodology.' *Finance and Stochastics* 1: 43–67.

Jarrow, R. A. and A. Subramanian (1997) 'Mopping up liquidity.' *Risk* 10 (December): 170–173.

Jarrow, R. A. and S. M. Turnbull (1995) 'Pricing options on derivative securities subject to credit risk.' *Journal of Finance* 50: 53–85.

Jarrow, R. A. and S. M. Turnbull (1998) 'The intersection of market and credit risks.' Working paper. Toronto: CIBC.

Jorion, P. (1995) 'Predicting volatility in the foreign exchange market.' *Journal of Finance* 50: 507–528.

Jorion, P. (1997) 'In defense of VaR.' *Derivatives Strategy* 2 (April): 20–23.

Jorion, P. (2001). 'How informative are value at risk disclosures?' Working paper, University of California, Irvine (March).

JP Morgan and Company (1996) *RiskMetrics* ™ — *Technical Document.* Fourth edition. New York: Morgan Guaranty Trust Company.

JP Morgan and Company (1997) *CreditMetrics* ™ — *Technical Document. The benchmark for understanding credit risk.* New York: JP Morgan and Company.

Ju, X. and N. D. Pearson (1999) 'Using value-at-risk to control risk taking: how wrong can you be?' *Journal of Risk* 1 (2): 5–36.

Kato, T. and T. Yoshiba (2000) 'Model risk and its control.' Bank of Japan Institute for Monetary and Economic Studies *Discussion Paper* No. 2000-E-15.

Kearns, P. and A. R. Pagan (1997) 'Estimating the density tail index for financial time series.' *Review of Economics and Statistics* 79: 171–175.

Këllezi, E. and M. Gilli (2000) 'Extreme value theory for tail-related risk measures.' Mimeo. Department of Econometrics, University of Geneva.

Kendall, M. and A. Stuart (1972) *The Advanced Theory of Statistics. Vol. 1: Distribution Theory*. Fourth edition. London: Charles Griffin and Co. Ltd.

Kendall, M. G. and A. Stuart (1973) *The Advanced Theory of Statistics. Vol. 2: Inference and Relationship*. Third edition. Griffin: London.

Kennedy, W. J., Jr. and J. E. Gentle (1980) *Statistical Computing*. New York and Basel: Marcel Dekker, Inc.

Kim, J. and C. C. Finger (1999) 'A stress test to incorporate correlation breakdown.' *RiskMetrics Journal* 1 (May): 61–76.

Kim, J., A. M. Malz and J. Mina (1999) *LongRun Technical Document: Long-Term Forecasting for Financial Markets*. New York: RiskMetrics Group.

Kloek, T. (1990) 'Principal components.' Pp. 204–207 in J. Eatwell, M. Milgate and P. Newman (eds) *The New Palgrave Time Series and Statistics*. London and Basingstoke: Macmillan.

Kotz, S. and S. Nadarajah (2000) *Extreme Value Distributions Theory and Applications*. London: Imperial College Press.

Krakovsky, A. (1999a) 'Gap risk in credit trading.' *Risk* 12 (March): 65–67.

Krakovsky, A. (1999b) 'Pricing liquidity into derivatives.' *Risk* 12 (December): 65–67.

Kreinin, A. and A. Levin (2000) 'Robust Monte Carlo simulation for approximate covariance matrices and VaR analyses.' Pp. 160–172 in S. Uryasev (ed.) *Probabilistic Constrained Optimization: Methodology and Applications*. Dordrecht: Kluwer Academic Publishers.

Kroll, Y. and G. Kaplansky (2001) 'VaR risk measures versus traditional risk measures: an analysis and survey.' Mimeo. Hebrew University.

Kupiec, P. (1995) 'Techniques for verifying the accuracy of risk management models.' *Journal of Derivatives* 3: 73–84.

Kupiec, P. H. (1999) 'Stress testing in a value at risk framework.' *Journal of Derivatives* 6: 7–24.

Kuruc, A. and B. Lee (1998) 'How to trim your hedge.' *Risk* 11 (December): 46–49.

Lagnado, R., G. Delianedis and S. Tikhonov (2000) 'Monte Carlo simulation of non-normal processes.' MKIRisk Discussion paper. MKIRisk, London.

Laubsch, A. (1996) 'Estimating index tracking error for equity portfolios.' *RiskMetrics ™ Monitor*, Second Quarter 1996: 34–41.

Lauridsen, S. (2000) 'Estimation of value at risk by extreme value methods.' *Extremes* 3: 107–144.

Lawrence, C. and G. Robinson (1995a) 'How safe is RiskMetrics?' *Risk* 8 (January): 26–29.

Lawrence, C. and G. Robinson (1995b) 'Liquid measures.' *Risk* 8 (July): 52–55.

Lawrence, C. and G. Robinson (1995c) 'Value at risk: addressing liquidity and volatility issues.' *Capital Market Strategies* 9 (November): 24–28.

Lawrence, D. (1996) *Measuring and Managing Derivative Market Risk*. London: International Thomson Business Press.

Leadbetter, M. R., G. Lindgren and H. Rootzén (1983) *Extremes and Related Properties of Random Sequences and Processes*. New York: Springer Verlag.

Lee, Y.-S. and T.-K. Lin (1992) 'Higher order Cornish–Fisher expansion.' *Applied Statistics* 41: 233–240.

Lekkos, I. (2001) 'Factor models and the correlation structure of interest rates: some evidence for USD, GBP, DEM and JPY.' *Journal of Banking and Finance* 25: 1427–1445.

LHabitant, F.-S. (2000) 'Coping with model risk.' Pp. 415–440 in M. Lore and L. Borodovsky (eds) *The Professional's Handbook of Financial Risk Management*. Oxford: Butterworth-Heinemann.

Lilliefors, H. W. (1967) 'The Kolmogorov-Smirnov test for normality with mean and variance unknown.' *Journal of the American Statistical Association* 46: 68–78.

Linsmeier, T. J. and N. D. Pearson (1996) 'Risk measurement: An introduction to value at risk.' Mimeo. University of Illinois at Urbana-Champaign.

Litterman, R. (1996) 'Hot spots™ and hedges.' *Journal of Portfolio Management Special Issue*: 52–75.

Litterman, R. (1997a) 'Hot spots and hedges (I).' *Risk* 10 (March): 42–45.

Litterman, R. (1997b) 'Hot spots and hedges (II).' *Risk* 10 (May): 38–42.

Longerstaey, J. (1995) 'Adjusting correlations for non-synchronous data.' *RiskMetrics ™ Monitor*, Third Quarter 1995: 4–13.

Longerstaey, J. and P. Zangari (1995) 'A transparent tool.' *Risk* 8 (January): 30–32.

Longin, F. (1996) 'The asymptotic distribution of extreme stock market returns.' *Journal of Business* 63: 383–408.

Longin, F. (1999) 'From value at risk to stress testing: the extreme value approach.' *Journal of Banking and Finance* 24: 1097–1130.

Longstaff, F. A. and E. S. Schwartz (2001) 'Valuing American options by simulation: A simple least-squares approach.' *Review of Financial Studies* 14: 113–14.

Lopez, J. A. (1998) 'Methods for evaluating value-at-risk estimates.' Federal Reserve Bank of New York *Economic Policy Review* (October): 119–124.

Lopez, J. A. (1999) 'Regulatory evaluation of value-at-risk models.' *Journal of Risk* 1: 37–64.

Lopez, J. A. and C. A. Walter (2001) 'Evaluating covariance matrix forecasts in a value-at-risk framework.' Mimeo. Federal Reserve Bank of San Fransisco and Credit Suisse Group, Zürich.

Lucas, A. (2000) 'A note on optimal estimation from a risk management perspective under possibly mis-specified tail behavior.' *Journal of Business and Economic Statistics* 18: 31–39.

Malevergne, Y. and D. Sornette (2001) 'General framework for a portfolio theory with non-Gaussian risks and non-linear correlations.' Mimeo. Laboratoire de Physique de la Matière Condensée, Université de Nice-Sophia Antipolis; Institute of Geophysics and Planetary Physics and Department of Earth and Space Science, UCLA. March 2001.

Markowitz, H. M. (1952) 'Portfolio selection.' *Journal of Finance* 7: 77–91.

Markowitz, H. M. (1959) *Portfolio Selection: Efficient Diversification of Investments.* New York: John Wiley and Sons.

Markowitz, H. M. (1992) 'Mean-variance analysis.' Pp. 683–685 in P. Newman, M. Milgate and J. Eatwell (eds) *The New Palgrave Dictionary of Money and Finance. Volume 2.* New York: Stockton Press.

Marshall, C. and M. Siegel (1997) 'Value at risk: Implementing a risk measurement standard.' *Journal of Derivatives* 4: 91–110.

Mausser, H. and D. Rosen (1998) 'Beyond VaR: From measuring risk to managing risk.' *Algo Research Quarterly* 1 (December): 5–20.

Mausser, H. and D. Rosen (2000) 'Managing risk with expected shortfall.' Pp. 198–219 in S. Uryasev (ed.) *Probabilistic Constrained Optimization: Methodology and Applications.* Dordrecht: Kluwer Academic Publishers.

McNeil, A. J. (1998) 'Calculating quantile risk measures for financial return series using extreme value theory.' Mimeo. ETHZ Zentrum, Zürich.

McNeil, A. J. (1999a) 'Extreme value theory for risk managers.' Mimeo. ETHZ Zentrum, Zürich.

McNeil, A. J. (1999b) 'New research in extreme value theory.' Presentation to the ICBI Risk Management Conference, Geneva, December 1999.

McNeil, A. J. and R. Frey (2000) 'Estimation of tail-related risk for heteroscedastic financial time series: an extreme value approach.' *Journal of Empirical Finance* 7: 271–300.

McNeil, A. J. and T. Saladin (1997) 'The peaks over thresholds model for estimating high quantiles of loss data.' Mimeo. ETHZ Zentrum, Zürich. April 1997.

McNew, L. (1996) 'So near, so VaR.' *Risk* 9 (October): 54–56.

Meegan, C. (1995) 'Market risk management: The concept of value-at-risk.' *Technical Paper* 3/RT/95. Central Bank of Ireland.

Milevsky, M. (1998) 'Optimal asset allocation towards the end of the life cycle: to annuitize or not to annuitize?' *Journal of Risk and Insurance* 65: 401–426.

Mina, J. (2001) 'Calculating VaR through quadratic approximations.' *Journal of Risk Finance* 2 (Winter): 49–55.

Moosa, I. A. and B. Bollen (2001) 'A benchmark for measuring bias in estimated daily value at risk.' Forthcoming, *International Review of Financial Analysis.*

Moosa, I. A. and J. J. Knight (2001) 'Firm characteristics and value at risk analysis: a survey of Australia's public shareholding companies.' Mimeo. La Trobe University.

Mori, A., M. Ohsawa and T. Shimizu (1996) 'A framework for more effective stress testing.' Bank of Japan Institute for Monetary and Economic Studies *Discussion Paper* 96-E-2.

Moro, B. (1995) 'The full Monte.' *Risk* 8 (February): 57–58.

Morokoff, W., L. Lagnado and A. Owen (1997) 'Tolerance for risk.' *Risk* 10 (June): 78–83.

Müller, U. A., M. M. Dacorogna and O. V. Pictet (1998) 'Heavy tails in high-frequency financial data.' Pp. 55–77 in R. J. Adler, R. E. Feldman and M. S. Taqqu (eds) *A Practical Guide to Heavy Tails: Statistical Techniques and Applications.* Boston: Birkhaüser.

Neftci, S. H. (2000) 'Value at risk calculations, extreme events, and tail estimation.' *Journal of Derivatives* 7 (Spring): 23–38.

Niffikeer, C. I., R. D. Hewins and R. B. Flavell (2000) 'A synthetic factor approach to the estimation of value-at-risk of a portfolio of interest rate swaps.' *Journal of Banking and Finance* 24: 1903–1932.

Ormoneit, D. and R. Neuneier (2001) 'Conditional value at risk.' Mimeo. Stanford University and Siemens AG, Munich.

Page, M. and D. Costa (1996) 'The value-at-risk of a portfolio of currency derivatives under worst-case distributional assumptions.' Mimeo. Susquehanna Investment Group and Department of Mathematics, University of Virginia.

Panning, W. H. (1999) 'The strategic uses of value at risk: long-term capital management for property/casualty insurers.' *North American Actuarial Journal* 3 (2): 84–105.

Pant, V. and W. Chang (2001) 'An empirical comparison of methods for incorporating fat tails into value-at-risk models.' *Journal of Risk* 3: 99–119.

Paul-Choudhury, S. (1997) 'This year's model.' *Risk* 10 (May): 18–23.

Persaud, A. (2000) 'The liquidity puzzle.' *Risk* 13 (June): 64–66.

Pflug, G. C. (2000) 'Some remarks on the value-at-risk and the conditional value-at-risk.' Pp. 272–281 in S. Uryasev (ed.) *Probabilistic Constrained Optimization: Methodology and Applications.* Dordrecht: Kluwer Academic Publishers.

Phelan, M. J. (1997) 'Probability and statistics applied to the practice of financial risk management: the case of J.P. Morgan's RiskMetrics™.' *Journal of Financial Services Research* 12 (2–3): 175–200.

Phoa, W. (2000) 'Yield curve risk factors: domestic and global contexts.' Pp. 155–184 in M. Lore and L. Borodovsky (eds) *The Professional's Handbook of Financial Risk Management.* Oxford: Butterworth-Heinemann.

Press, W. H., S. A. Teukolsky, W. T. Vetterling and B. P. Flannery (1992) *Numerical Recipes in C: The Art of Scientific Computing.* Second edition. Cambridge: Cambridge University Press.

Prinzler, R. (1999) 'Reliability of neural network based value-at-risk estimates.' Mimeo. Technical University of Dresden.

Pritsker, M. (1997) 'Evaluating value at risk methodologies: Accuracy versus computational time.' *Journal of Financial Services Research* 12: 201–242.

Pritsker, M. (2001) 'The hidden dangers of historical simulation.' Mimeo. Board of Governors of the Federal Reserve System. April, 2001.

Rachev, S. and S. Mittnik (2000) *Stable Paretian Models in Finance*. Chichester and New York: John Wiley and Sons.

Rebonato, R. (1998) *Interest-Rate Option Models*. Second edition. Chichester and New York: John Wiley and Sons.

Reiss, R.-D. (1989) *Approximate Distributions of Order Statistics with Applications to Nonparametric Statistics*. Berlin: Springer-Verlag.

Reiss, R.-D. and M. Thomas (1997) *Statistical Analysis of Extreme Values from Insurance, Finance, Hydrology and Other Fields*. Basel: Birkhäuser.

Ridder, T. (1997) 'Basics of statistical VaR-estimation.' Mimeo. SGZ-Bank AG, Frankfurt a. M./Karlsruhe. August 1997.

RiskMetrics Group (1999) *Corporate Metrics: The Benchmark for Corporate Risk Management. Technical Document.* New York: RiskMetrics Group.

Rockafellar, R. T. and S. Uryasev (2000) 'Optimization of conditional value-at-risk.' *Journal of Risk* 2 (3): 21–41.

Ross, S. A. (1976) 'The arbitrage theory of asset pricing.' *Journal of Economic Theory* 13: 341–360.

Rouvinez, C. (1997) 'Going Greek with VaR.' *Risk* 10 (February): 57–65.

Rubinstein, M. (2000) *Rubinstein on Derivatives*. London: Risk Books.

Saunders, A. (1999) *Credit Risk Measurement: New Approaches to Value at Risk and Other Paradigms*. New York: John Wiley and Sons.

Scaillet, O. (2000a) 'Nonparametric estimation of copulas for time series.' Mimeo. IRES, Catholic University of Louvain.

Scaillet, O. (2000b) 'Nonparametric estimation and sensitivity analysis of expected shortfall.' Mimeo. IRES, Catholic University of Louvain.

Scaillet, O. (2000c) 'Nonparametric estimation of conditional expected shortfall.' Mimeo. IRES, Catholic University of Louvain.

Schachter, B. (1995) 'Comments on 'Taylor, Black and Scholes: Series approximations and risk management pitfalls' by Arturo Estrella.' Mimeo. Office of the Comptroller of the Currency.

Schachter, B. (1997) 'The lay person's introduction to value at risk.' *Financial Engineering News* 1 (August): 2+.

Schachter, B. (1998) 'The value of stress testing in market risk management.' Pp. 5F.0-5F.11 in T. Haight (ed.) *Derivatives Risk Management Service*. Arlington, VA: A. S. Pratt & Sons.

Schachter, B. (2000) 'Stringent stress tests.' *Risk* 13 (No. 12, *Special Report on Enterprise-Wide Risk Management*): S22–S24.

Shaw, J. (1997) 'Beyond VaR and stress testing.' Pp. 221–224 in *VAR — Understanding and Applying Value at Risk*. London: KPMG/Risk Publications.

Shimko, D. (1996) 'VaR for corporates.' *Risk* 9 (June): 28–29.

Shimko, D., B. Humpheys and V. Pant (1998) 'Hysterical simulation.' *Risk* 11 (June): 47.

Singer, R. (1997) 'To VaR, a sister.' *Risk* 10 (August): 86–87.

Singh, M. K. (1997) 'Value at risk using principal components analysis.' *Journal of Portfolio Analysis* (Fall): 101–112.

Sinkey, J. F., Jr. (1992) *Commercial Bank Financial Management in the Financial-Services Industry*. Fourth edition. New York: Macmillan.

Studer, G. (1999) 'Market risk computation for nonlinear portfolios.' *Journal of Risk* 1 (4): 33–53.

Studer, G. and H.-J. Lüthi (1997) 'Analyzing nonlinear portfolios with quadratic maximum loss.' *Net Exposure* 1 (October). Available at http://www.netexposure.co.uk/regd/issues/1/studer/index.html.

Subramanian, A. and R. A. Jarrow (1998) 'The liquidity discount.' Mimeo. Cornell University.

Taleb, N. (1997a) 'The world according to Nassim Taleb.' *Derivatives Strategy* 2 (December/January): 37–40.

Taleb, N. (1997b) 'Against VaR.' *Derivatives Strategy* 2 (April): 21–26.

Taleb, N. (1997c) *Dynamic Hedging: Managing Vanilla and Exotic Options*. New York: John Wiley and Sons.

Taylor, J. W. (1999) 'A quantile regression approach to estimating the distribution of multi-period returns.' *Journal of Derivatives* 7 (Fall): 64–78.

Taylor, J. W. (2000) 'A quantile regression neural network approach to estimating the conditional density of multiperiod returns.' *Journal of Forecasting* 19: 299–311.

Thisted, R. A. (1988) *Elements of Statistical Computing: Numerical Computations*. New York and London: Chapman and Hall.

Tilman, L. M. and P. Brusilovskiy (2001) 'Measuring predictive accuracy of value-at-risk models: issues, paradigms, and directions.' *Journal of Risk Finance* 2 (3, Spring): 83–91.

Tuckman, B. (1995) *Fixed Income Securities: Tools for Today's Markets*. New York: John Wiley and Sons.

Turnbull, S. M. and L. M. Wakeman (1991) 'Quick algorithm for pricing European average rate options.' *Journal of Financial and Quantitative Analysis* 26: 377–389.

Turner, C. (1996) 'VaR as an industrial tool.' *Risk* 9 (March): 38–40.

Upper, C. (2000) 'How safe was the 'safe haven'? Financial market liquidity during the 1998 turbulences.' Deutsche Bundesbank Economic Research Group *Discussion Paper* 1/00.

Uryasev, S. (2000) 'Conditional value-at-risk: Optimization algorithms and applications.' *Financial Engineering News* 14 (February): 1–5.

Venkataraman, S. (1997) 'Value at risk for a mixture of normal distributions: The use of quasi-Bayesian estimation techniques.' Federal Reserve Bank of Chicago *Economic Perspectives* (March/April): 3–13.

Vlaar, P. J. G. (2000) 'Value at risk models for Dutch bond portfolios.' *Journal of Banking and Finance* 24: 1131–1154.

Wakeman, L. (1998) 'Credit enhancement.' Pp. 255–275 in C. Alexander (ed.) *Risk Analysis and Management. Vol. 1: Measuring and Modelling Financial Risk*. Chichester: John Wiley and Sons.

Wee, L.-S. and J. Lee (1999) 'Integrating stress testing with risk management.' *Bank Accounting and Finance* (Spring): 7–19.

Wilmott, P. (2000) *Paul Wilmott on Quantitative Finance. Volumes 1 and 2*. Chichester and New York: John Wiley and Sons.

Wilson, T. C. (1993) 'Infinite wisdom.' *Risk* 6 (June): 37–45.

Wilson, T. C. (1994a) 'Debunking the myths.' *Risk* 7 (April): 67–72.

Wilson, T. C. (1994b) 'Plugging the gap.' *Risk* 7 (October): 74–80.

Wilson, T. C. (1996) 'Calculating risk capital.' Pp. 193–232 in C. Alexander (ed.) *The Handbook of Risk Analysis and Management*. Chichester: John Wiley and Sons.

Yamai, Y. and T. Yoshiba (2001a) 'On the validity of value-at-risk: comparative analyses with expected shortfall.' Bank of Japan Institute of Monetary and Economic Studies *Discussion Paper* No. 2001-E-4.

Yamai, Y. and T. Yoshiba (2001b) 'Comparative analyses of expected shortfall and VaR: their estimation error, decomposition, and optimisation.' Bank of Japan Institute of Monetary and Economic Studies *Discussion Paper* No. 2001-E-12.

Yoshiba, T. and Y. Yamai (2001) 'Comparative analyses of expected shortfall and VaR (2): expected utility maximisation and tail risk.' Bank of Japan Institute of Monetary and Economic Studies *Discussion Paper* No. 2001-E-14.

Zangari, P. (1996a) 'A VaR methodology for portfolios that include options.' *RiskMetrics™ Monitor*, First Quarter: 4–12.

Zangari, P. (1996b) 'An improved methodology for measuring VaR.' *RiskMetrics™ Monitor*, Second Quarter: 7–25.

Zangari, P. (1996c) 'How accurate is the delta-gamma methodology?' *RiskMetrics™ Monitor*, Third Quarter: 12–29.

Zangari, P. (1996d) 'When is non-normality a problem? The case of 15 time series from emerging markets.' *RiskMetrics™ Monitor*, Fourth Quarter: 20–32.

Zangari, P. (1997) 'What risk managers should know about mean reversion and jumps in prices.' *RiskMetrics™ Monitor*, Fourth Quarter: 12–41.

Zangari, P. (1998) 'Exploratory stress-scenario analysis with applications to EMU.' *RiskMetrics Monitor Special Edition*: 30–53.

Author Index

Subject Index

Software Index

Printed and bound in the UK by
CPI Antony Rowe, Eastbourne

Printed and bound by CPI Group (UK) Ltd, Croydon, CR0 4YY

16/04/2025

14658512-0004